Implementing Augmented Reality Into Immersive Virtual Learning Environments

Donna Russell
Walden University, USA

IGI Global
PUBLISHER of TIMELY KNOWLEDGE

A volume in the Advances in Educational Technologies and Instructional Design (AETID) Book Series

Published in the United States of America by
IGI Global
Information Science Reference (an imprint of IGI Global)
701 E. Chocolate Avenue
Hershey PA, USA 17033
Tel: 717-533-8845
Fax: 717-533-8661
E-mail: cust@igi-global.com
Web site: http://www.igi-global.com

Library of Congress Cataloging-in-Publication Data

Names: Russell, Donna, 1955- editor.
Title: Implementing augmented reality into immersive virtual learning environments / Donna Russell, editor.
Description: Hershey : Information Science Reference, 2021. | Includes bibliographical references and index. | Summary: "This book provides a comprehensive review of educational programs that are integrating augmented reality into immersive virtual learning environments"-- Provided by publisher.
Identifiers: LCCN 2020038817 (print) | LCCN 2020038818 (ebook) | ISBN 9781799842224 (Hardcover) | ISBN 9781799842231 (eBook)
Subjects: LCSH: Virtual reality in education. | Augmented reality. | Computer-assisted instruction. | Internet in education. | Teaching--Computer network resources.
Classification: LCC LB1044.87 .I334 2021 (print) | LCC LB1044.87 (ebook) | DDC 371.33/44678--dc23
LC record available at https://lccn.loc.gov/2020038817
LC ebook record available at https://lccn.loc.gov/2020038818

This book is published in the IGI Global book series Advances in Educational Technologies and Instructional Design (AETID) (ISSN: 2326-8905; eISSN: 2326-8913)

British Cataloguing in Publication Data
A Cataloguing in Publication record for this book is available from the British Library.

All work contributed to this book is new, previously-unpublished material. The views expressed in this book are those of the authors, but not necessarily of the publisher.

For electronic access to this publication, please contact: eresources@igi-global.com.

Advances in Educational Technologies and Instructional Design (AETID) Book Series

Lawrence A. Tomei
Robert Morris University, USA

ISSN:2326-8905
EISSN:2326-8913

Mission

Education has undergone, and continues to undergo, immense changes in the way it is enacted and distributed to both child and adult learners. In modern education, the traditional classroom learning experience has evolved to include technological resources and to provide online classroom opportunities to students of all ages regardless of their geographical locations. From distance education, Massive-Open-Online-Courses (MOOCs), and electronic tablets in the classroom, technology is now an integral part of learning and is also affecting the way educators communicate information to students.

The **Advances in Educational Technologies & Instructional Design (AETID) Book Series** explores new research and theories for facilitating learning and improving educational performance utilizing technological processes and resources. The series examines technologies that can be integrated into K-12 classrooms to improve skills and learning abilities in all subjects including STEM education and language learning. Additionally, it studies the emergence of fully online classrooms for young and adult learners alike, and the communication and accountability challenges that can arise. Trending topics that are covered include adaptive learning, game-based learning, virtual school environments, and social media effects. School administrators, educators, academicians, researchers, and students will find this series to be an excellent resource for the effective design and implementation of learning technologies in their classes.

Coverage

- Digital Divide in Education
- Instructional Design
- Online Media in Classrooms
- Instructional Design Models
- E-Learning
- Classroom Response Systems
- Adaptive Learning
- Educational Telecommunications
- K-12 Educational Technologies
- Web 2.0 and Education

IGI Global is currently accepting manuscripts for publication within this series. To submit a proposal for a volume in this series, please contact our Acquisition Editors at Acquisitions@igi-global.com or visit: http://www.igi-global.com/publish/.

The Advances in Educational Technologies and Instructional Design (AETID) Book Series (ISSN 2326-8905) is published by IGI Global, 701 E. Chocolate Avenue, Hershey, PA 17033-1240, USA, www.igi-global.com. This series is composed of titles available for purchase individually; each title is edited to be contextually exclusive from any other title within the series. For pricing and ordering information please visit http://www.igi-global.com/book-series/advances-educational-technologies-instructional-design/73678. Postmaster: Send all address changes to above address.

Titles in this Series

For a list of additional titles in this series, please visit:
http://www.igi-global.com/book-series/advances-educational-technologies-instructional-design/73678

Advancing Online Course Design and Pedagogy for the 21st Century Learning Environment
Daniel Chatham (Middlebury Institute of International Studies at Monterey, USA)
Information Science Reference • © 2021 • 382pp • H/C (ISBN: 9781799855989) • US $195.00

Affordances and Constraints of Mobile Phone Use in English Language Arts Classrooms
Clarice M. Moran (Appalachian State University, USA)
Information Science Reference • © 2021 • 229pp • H/C (ISBN: 9781799858058) • US $175.00

Examining an Operational Approach to Teaching Probability
Alessio Drivet (Geogebra Institute of Turin, Italy)
Information Science Reference • © 2021 • 369pp • H/C (ISBN: 9781799838715) • US $195.00

4C-ID Model and Cognitive Approaches to Instructional Design and Technology Emerging Research and Opportunities
Guilhermina Maria Lobato Ferreira de Miranda (Instituto de Educação, Universidade de Lisboa, Portugal) Manuel Joaquim Henriques Rafael (Universidade de Lisboa, Portugal) Mário Marcelino Luis de Melo (UI, DEF, Instituto de Educação, Universidade de Lisboa, Portugal) Joana Martinho de Almeida Costa Pardal (ISTAR, Instituto Universitário de Lisboa (ISCTE-IUL), Lisboa, Portugal) and Thiago Bessa Pontes (Universidade Federal do Cariri, Brazil)
Information Science Reference • © 2021 • 243pp • H/C (ISBN: 9781799840961) • US $175.00

Handbook of Research on Innovations in Non-Traditional Educational Practices
Jared Keengwe (University of North Dakota, USA)
Information Science Reference • © 2021 • 462pp • H/C (ISBN: 9781799843603) • US $245.00

Handbook of Research on Using Educational Robotics to Facilitate Student Learning
Stamatios Papadakis (University of Crete, Greece) and Michail Kalogiannakis (University of Crete, Greece)
Information Science Reference • © 2021 • 651pp • H/C (ISBN: 9781799867173) • US $275.00

Teaching and Learning Practices That Promote Sustainable Development and Active Citizenship
Sandra Saúde (Polytechnic Institute of Beja, Portugal & CICS, NOVA University Lisbon, Portugal) Maria Albertina Raposo (Polytechnic Institute of Beja, Portugal & MARE, NOVA University Lisbon, Portugal) Nuno Pereira (Polytechnic Institute of Beja, Portugal) and Ana Isabel Rodrigues (Polytechnic Institute of Beja, Portugal)
Information Science Reference • © 2021 • 383pp • H/C (ISBN: 9781799844020) • US $185.00

IGI Global
PUBLISHER of TIMELY KNOWLEDGE

701 East Chocolate Avenue, Hershey, PA 17033, USA
Tel: 717-533-8845 x100 • Fax: 717-533-8661
E-Mail: cust@igi-global.com • www.igi-global.com

Table of Contents

Detailed Table of Contents

Preface

The global pandemic has radically changed education. It is a moment to look at the structures and procedures for teaching and learning. As educators struggle to reform because of the global pandemic, there are strategies, procedures, and protocols supported by research in the cognitive sciences that can be implemented into any educational program to support the development of the skills, knowledge and cognitive processes needed for the future knowledge workers of the 21st century.

This book is defined around the term immersive learning to make the case for the design, integration and evaluation of learning in immersive virtual learning environment that integrate augmented reality (AR). The chapters describe how learners can be immersed in their responses to augmented reality simulations, virtual worlds, educational games, and holographic mixed reality experiences. The book aims to provide both a conceptual and practical guide to integrating these immersive technologies into educational settings.

Immersive learning environments are by their nature constructivist. According to constructivist learning theories, the knowledge a learner constructs within social settings mediated by cultural tools involves not only the knowledge associated with the concepts embedded in the activity but also the knowledge associated with the context in which that activity occurred (Anderson et al., 1997; Brown, 1992; Jonassen & Rohrer-Murphy, 1999; Russell, 2005). In constructivist learning environments there is a need to consider the inter-related contextual impacts on the design and implementation of a constructivist-based learning environment. In these types of immersive learning environments, the learning is distributed by developmentally scaled responses of the learners within the context and with each other (Cole & Engestrom, 1993).

Constructivist immersive situated learning models require authentic contexts, activities, and assessment coupled with guidance from expert modeling, mentoring, and legitimate peripheral participation that asks learners to engage is a simulated real-world learning environment (Greeno, 1997; Lave & Wenger,1991). Learners construct knowledge within these social settings using cultural tools associated with the concepts embedded in the activity but also develop knowledge associated with the context in which that activity occurred.

Problem-based learning is a constructivist learning model that incorporates situated learning, distributed learning, inquiry-based learning and project-based learning. Problem-Based Learning (PBL) proposes that learning experiences build on the interdependent attributes of meaningful learning including authentic, intentional, active, constructive, and cooperative learning and involve meaningful application of knowledge and skills (Jonassen, 2000; Russell, 2009a; Russell, 2016a). In PBL environments a problem triggers cognitive engagement including the psychological processes of context for engagement, curiosity, inquiry and a quest to address a real-world issue . In productive problem-based learning environment learners consider themselves active members of their community of learners within the context of solving the problem (Russell, 2004; Russell, 2006). This type of design model for teaching and learning has shown to be effective at developing the advanced cognition, skills and functional knowledge required of students entering the 21st Century workforce (Russell, 2008).

IMMERSIVE VIRTUAL LEARNING ENVIRONMENTS

Immersive virtual learning environments (IVLE) can foster educational experiences that draw on situated learning. Immersive virtual learning simulations facilitates advanced critical thinking and problem-based learning processes that can address concepts about how people learn. IVLEs are learning situations that are constructed using a variety of techniques and software tools, including game-based learning, simulation-based learning and augmented reality. IVLEs are distinguished from other learning methods by their ability to simulate realistic scenarios and environments that give learners the opportunity to practice skills and interact with other learners. The learning which result from immersive virtual learning include

- real-world relevance,
- meaningful application that drives student engagement
- development of analytic skills (students can examine tasks from different perspectives using a variety of resources),
- collaboration,
- consequences of choice (reflection), and
- allowing a range of competing solutions with a diversity of outcomes. (Barab et al., 2005).

In IVLEs learners can immerse themselves in distributed, synthetic environments, becoming "avatars" who vicariously collaborate and learn-by-doing using virtual artifacts to construct knowledge (Russell, 2009b).This higher, more immediate level of engagement, telepresence, means that the learner can integrate more advanced knowledge and processes. Research by Warburton and Garcia (2009) identified the characteristics of a IVLE including:

- Immersion in virtual provides an augmented sense of co-presence through embodiment as an avatar impacting affective, empathic and motivational aspects of the learning experiences,
- Extended social interactions between individuals and communities, humans and objects and intelligent interaction between artifacts,
- Community presence promoting a sense of belonging and purpose that coalesces groups, subcultures and geographies,
- Exposure to authentic content and access to cultures that reflect diversity,
- Opportunities for individual and collective identity and role-play,
- Content production tools that provide opportunities for creation and ownership of object,
- Visualization and contextualization through the production and reproduction of normally inaccessible content including artifacts that may be historically lost, imaginary, futuristic, or impossible to see by the human eye,
- Simulations of existing real world contexts that may be too costly or dangerous in real-life (Warburton, & Garcia, 2009).

IVLEs have many benefits for educational organizations wanting to develop advanced learning processes and knowledge. The salient factors include:

- Learners have presence through their avatar. They engage in interactions in the environment and modify the environment through their character. This higher, more immediate level of engagement, telepresence, means that the learner can integrate more advanced knowledge and processes.
- The virtual environments provide multiple interactive, media-rich forums for the learner. This also means a higher level of engagement as the virtual worlds are designed to be visually rich and provide opportunities for the learner to interact with others in the environment through audio, text and visual media.
- The IVLE also provides a social context for the learner that increases engagement as they interact in the virtual worlds providing opportunities for training in simulated events that are live and collaborative such as a live simulation of an emergency room event for training medical and nursing students or the live simulation of a classroom activity for training teachers.
- The IVLEs environments are immersive learning experiences that engage students in proactive activities providing the students with the opportunity to problem-solve and collaborate. This type of ubiquitous learning empowers the students and motivates them to higher levels of cognitive response (Russell, 2016c).

DESIGN OF AN IMMERSIVE VIRTUAL LEARNING ENVIRONMENT

In the next section of this preface is a description of an immersive virtual learning environment that is designed based on the characteristics of a problem-based learning model. This model is called IDEA World. It is a virtual world that includes a learning management system (LMS), a learning analytic system (LAS), curriculum modules, the virtual world, and professional development guides for educators. The problems at the core of this PBL IVLE are based on the premise the development and assessment of (a) advanced cognitive processes such as critical thinking, evaluation, decision-making from multiple perspectives and collaborative abilities, (b) functional knowledge used to solve problems and (c) language, math, and other content area skills. Appendix A includes the curriculum design modules and the associated rubrics. This module can be modified for integration in k12 or higher education.

The Core Learning Goals are processes that are developed in each unit of study outside of the content. The Core Learning Goals for global citizenships include the below Strands that are integrated into each Unit of Study. Each Core IDEA Unit includes global issues relevant to developing a comprehensive understanding and response to the Core IDEA. Issues include a base in content knowledge. An example of an issues in Resource Management is Climate Change as an aspect of the Unit of Study, Resource Management. Climate Change is a STEM-based unit that focuses on the sciences inherent in understand the theme. The Core Learning Goals are cognitive processes that are developed in each unit of study outside of the content. The Core Learning Goals for global citizenships include the below Strands that are integrated into each unit of study and linked to the Core IDEAs. The Learning Strands for the protocols are:

1. Understanding Media

Media is a critical aspect for global citizens as it is endemic in the interactions of all citizens. The forums for media include more traditional forums such as books, tv, and radio. The new evolving media include social media, and the internet. Each Unit of Study develops relevant awareness of media throughout the interactions as students discuss, analyze and create media. New media awareness is assessed through their projects and their interactions formatively and summatively.

2. Human Computer Interface

HCI is an ongoing strand for students as they identify, analyze and create technology-based projects. Each Unit of Study will include a Strand on the critical aspects of technology inherent in the unit and the curriculum themes. Students will use technology and create projects using technology. Assessment will be integrated in the assessment of their projects and interactions.

3. Advanced Problem Solving Processes

Students will develop advanced problem solving processes throughout each unit. Examples of the cognitive processes integration and assessed in each unit include critical thinking, advanced decision-making, problem solving, analysis, evaluation, collaborative problem solving, and effective communication processes. All units will include holistic rubrics to assess the development of these advanced cognitive processes.

4. Social Awareness

Each unit will engage the students in discussions of social issues. The students will present their responses that include a social awareness component. The units will all include an assessment that identifies the social awareness component in the learners' activities and interactions.

5. Awareness of Areas of Expertise

Each unit will involve students in interactions with the community of private and public experts. Students will understand the areas of expertise involved each Core IDEA.

Core IDEA: Learning Strands – Curricular Themes

Themes are specific curriculum structures that provide an instructional space for content knowledge. Curricular Themes will be modular and designed on a problem-based learning educational setting (Russell, 2005). Themes all include a Core IDEA as a basis and the Learning Strands which are included in the ongoing formative and summative assessment model. Themes include assessment of the learner's responses to (a) content knowledge, (b) conceptual knowledge and (c) process skills will be assessed through holistic rubrics and tests. A Curricular Theme is a complete modular educational program that can be integrated into a traditional educational setting as a complete program or as isolated Units of Study.

The Theme is a curriculum structure with defined responses that engage students in developing advanced concepts, skills and knowledge based on the global theme. Each Theme has multiple Units of Study. These are individual modular curriculum that can be isolated and taught individually. For example, the Climate Change Theme in the Core IDEA Resource Management includes Water Management and Land Management. Water management will engage students in understand water globally, drought and climate change effects on water access. Students will develop new understandings of pollution, loss of marker species such as the coral reef, changes in global ocean patterns, coastal degradation and other patterns of change associated with Climate Change. Land Management will engage students in understanding issues related to land resources such as mining, carbon emissions, air pollution, health effects of pollution, greenhouse effect and clear cutting of forests.

Learning Management System

The online LMS includes a main login portal that is the link to all aspects of the online data management system. This unique Learning Management System includes a home page for learners and educators that provides them with

- access to all aspects of the learning environment
- access to resources outside the learning environment
- access to all learning activities descriptions and assessment of activities
- access to the learning assessments feedbacks
- access to the AR links
- access to the virtual simulations.

Learning Analytic System (LAS)

The LAS will include a continuous feedback model from the AR devices to the learners. This will be accomplished by a server array designed and aligned with the alignment with the evaluative research model. The learning analytics system (LAS) will include a coding and categorization process based on research on the nature of learning in immersive virtual learning environments (Russell, & Wallis, 2016). The LAS will be designed to align with the sequencing of assessment points throughout the learning environment including:

1. Tracking of activities in the virtual spaces
2. time and location of activity linked to medians
3. feedback model is a circular chart of progress
4. feedback near real time for learner/educators as a heads-up display
5. Assessment points that are programmed for structured feedback in near real-time
6. student response in electronic journals: coding of text based on dialogic analysis
7. student responses to learner activities while using the AR: coding of activity type and semantical analysis
8. feedback model is an emoticon-type logo scaling from very positive to negative to represent the dialogic analysis of the student writing or drawing
9. analysis based on interactive models based on semantic analysis (Russell, 2016b).
10. Assessment points that are structured around completed projects and holistic rubrics
11. student projects including

12. Summative assessments are rubrics designed using the Scheme of Knowledge taxonomy. (Bereiter, 2001; Bereiter & Scardamalia, 2002).
13. Feedback is given in a timely manner to learners.
14. Assessment is a scaled rubric integrated into the virtual space
15. Feedback model is an interactive rubric that includes links to additional info/websites/comments.

IDEA WORLD

The IDEA World is a virtual world that utilizes the LMS and LAS described previously that will develop advanced STEM knowledge and advanced cognitive processes through the development of

- an immersive virtual learning environment, virtual worlds, integrated into a
- Portal for entry and exit into the Course rooms simulations that includes access to the main home page for the learners and for the Course room
- a Learning Analytics System that will include a human computer interface including a graphic showing learner progress in relation to the core competencies, a reporting system identifying the learner's online interactions,
- a comprehensive Curriculum Guide for teachers that will be modular for ease of integration and includes a full lesson guide, assessments and
- a Technological Pedagogical Content Knowledge (TPCK) Teacher Professional Development protocol.

There are experimenter labs in the various locations that allow students to test theories or develop projects. Experimenter labs are virtual rooms setup with objects and interaction between objects that can be reset once they are used by students. These include chemistry labs, biology labs, experiments, and research labs. Experimenter labs are closed systems that can be reset over and over with one path to solution: procedural learning with levels 1-3 knowledge response on a Bereiter scale (Bereiter & Scardamalia, 2002).

Designer toolboxes are also designed to be in specific locations throughout IDEA world. They are sandboxes which allow students to modify and create new objects in response to the units. Students can build a solar car or develop a new object in the virtual world, or design an app using the coding structure in the virtual world. Each activity is linked to the curriculum learning goals and objectives and include associated learning assessment methods.

Explorer worlds are scenario worlds. These are the large worlds designed for live interactive events that are open-ended dilemma problem spaces. The students will go into these world to respond to a live event, build, design, or present through their avatar. In IDEA City they can design a solar grid working with a group including civic contact, e.g., citizen groups, civic engineers etc. Over time the students projects will build and redesign the city as part of the learning activities.

The media center is the main conference hall in IDEA world. It includes presentation forums for student projects including interactive museums, symposiums, high school ted talks, and interactive kiosks. Learners build their presentations in the online LMS or in their classroom but present in the main conference halls on a global stage with varying levels of live interactive presentations. The media in the media center gives tools for learners to build their electronic portfolios which is the main source of ongoing assessment for the students. Experiences

Innovation symposiums are scheduled for dialog on specific topics and the development of collaborative models and protocols. Innovation symposiums result in major publications and prototypes that incorporate the core themes from the student-generated research and projects. Science museums for the dissemination of presentations, models, and prototype. Each artifact are included in the development of comprehensive eportfolios for students. Ed-ted talks are live presentations chosen to demonstrate advanced knowledge on a specific innovative project or program. Students and groups will apply to present live in ted talks and for the dissemination of their talks in social media.

Community mentors will be linked to the units of study through a database of experts and companies who are partnering with the future of learning protocol. The curriculum guides for themes and units of study include public and private community mentors and organizations in fields related to the core idea such as medicine, engineering, genetics, mechanical engineering, aerospace, chemistry, biology and others. These mentors also provide a forum for students to be engaged in real-world authentic activities as a result of these interactions with these mentors. Mentors organizations will have an interactive presence in the world.

As the students progress, they will 'win' the simulations by completing the activities in each phase and responding to the formative assessments, such as checking into a kiosk and uploading their answers to the survey, posting an artifact that they have created in that Phase, dialoging with others in the game or with their mentors and presenting in the Sim World Media Center in a series of international interactive forums including:

- STEM Conferences for presentations and response to audiences where groups justify their research and development. Innovation Symposiums for dialog on specific topics and the development of collaborative models and protocols
- Innovation Symposiums result in major publications and prototype that incorporate the Big Ideas from the student-generated research and projects.
- Science Museums for the dissemination of presentations, models, and prototype
- TED Talks Live presentations chosen to demonstrate advanced knowledge on a specific innovative project or program. Students/groups will apply to present live in TED talks and for the dissemination of their Talks in social media.

The Media Center is the Sim World main entrance and includes

- Conference areas with large screens,
- Interactive forums that allow for texting and talking for Q and A
- Small group work areas where international groups can schedule meetings, post and share information and develop their projects resulting from the experiments, exploration and completion of the Scenarios.

Pedagogical agents are designed into all virtual worlds to automatize some of the interactions in virtual worlds. These programmed ai bots act as mentor bots, guide bots, and learner bots. The mentor bots provide feedback to learners in defined manners and locations in the virtual worlds. All pedagogical agents are linked to the LAS and used as both formative and summative assessments. These programmed ai bots act as mentor bots, guide bots, and learner bots.

- The mentor bots provide feedback to learners in defined manners and locations in the virtual worlds.
- The guide bots provide support to learners as they work on successfully completing the scenarios.
- The learner bots are linked to specific learner's progress and are used to track the learner's progress as a source of metacognitive feedback on learning activities and assessment.

Orientation to IDEA City

Students enter the simulation through a central location. In the IDEAL project they will come into a futuristic city that will be the catalyst for all the STEM-based scenarios they will respond to throughout the initial phase of development. They will get a brief orientation to the IDEA City from an avatar that will also direct them to several organizations and businesses that are resources to the city and later mentors for the students. Finally, this character, the mayor for instance, will provide them with a series of problems and issues plaguing this city that they can respond to in order to save the city and provide a safer, cleaner, more energy efficient place for the people. Below are brief overviews of units of study that take place in the virtual space of IDEA World. All units of study are linked to the LMS, the LAS that includes AI-supported interactions with the learners that are part of the assessment model.

UNIT 1: DESIGN A GREEN BUILDING

In the resource management/climate change/global warming unit of study students design a green building for IDEA City. They will be able to participate in a real-world competition using materials created in the scenario. They meet their guide, another character in the game, who will give them a set of guidelines including cost, environmental impact to build, and brief overview of city guidelines. They will then be able to go into an interactive workspace where they can work with other students, or individually, to design their building. They meet their AI guide, another character in the game, who will give them a set of guidelines including cost, environmental impact to build, and brief overview of city guidelines. They will then be able to go into an interactive workspace where they can work with other students, or individually, to design their building.

The students will then set up in international collaborative groups to develop a solar-powered program for their city or the rural farms associated with IDEA City. The will develop solar panels, do lab experiments, integrate solar panels in new areas and innovative ways. They will test their prototype for their solar project in the Media Center during the Alternative Energies Conference.

UNIT 2: SOLAR DESIGN: ENERGY FROM THE SUN

In IDEA World main area, students will be able to go into a local university, IDEA U and design a solar car. They will participate in a real-world competition in association with this scenario. They will go into the scenario and the guide character will describe the problem parameters including time lines, resources, and the how they will 'win' the solar race at the end. They can collaborate in the game; use resources from the real-world and virtual world and their mentors. Ultimately they will race the cars and redesign based on the differing environmental conditions and the physics of their design.

UNIT 3: WATER AS LIFE: PLANNING FOR WATER

In this unit of study, the students study water access worldwide. In the simulation, water is limited and drought is endemic. The students enter an island in the world and discover ways to conserve, clean and protect water. As a result of the scenario students will survive in a drought-ridden environment by conserving water and purifying water. Students will do experiments on how to purify ocean water, develop solar panels for cleaning water, plants that are drought resistant and other projects that conserve water. The core simulation includes weather patterns such as amount of rain for the region, soil conditions, anticipated plant growth for core species used in the region. Students will present their models in a Water Conference in the Media Lab After completion of the scenario, students will group in international groups and develop a project for an urban and rural water conservation model that involves reduction of ocean waste, purification models, and conservation effort globally.

UNIT 4: FEEDING THE WORLD

As a result of the Feeding the World scenario students develop projects in response to international agriculture and economic issues. Students receive core instruction on the nature of world hunger and then develop projects to reduce world hunger. The core simulation includes weather patterns such as amount of rain for the region, soil conditions, anticipated plant growth for core species used in the region. The simulation will introduce problems. The students will be able to go into the environment and 'plant' their new crop and monitor its growth. The standards include:

- Content Knowledge: biology, chemistry, math-graphing geometry, algebra
- Advanced Processes: communication, presentation, group work skills, social skills, writing, speech,
- Problem-Based Learning: scientific methods and business ethics
- Advanced Technologies; cloning, DNA mapping; smart medicine.
- Project: Develop an Innovative farming model that reduces waste, drought resistant, and can reduce global hunger
- Present on their international collaborative models in the Media Center Conference on Hunger.

UNIT 5: THE MISSION TO MARS

During the unit students respond to STEM content information by building a model of a Mars habitat that will support human life. The students receive core content information in biology, chemistry, physics and astronomy. The virtual Mars will include the needed resources for the students to build their habitat based on their knowledge of the core requirements for humans to live and work on Mars. The students' habitats can be 'tested' for their capacity to sustain human life. For instance, if the students design a hydroponics garden to provide oxygen for the astronauts the garden' oxygen output can be configured and the simulation can 'fail' if it is not sufficient. Students will design and test their Mars

UNIT 6: ADVANCED TECHNOLOGIES: ARTIFICIAL INTELLIGENCE, SOCIAL MEDIA, GAMING

In this simulation in IDEA World, the learners create a Collaborative International project to develop and 'sell' an Innovation HCI Prototype in a Media Center Entrepreneur Symposium scheduled with international innovators that creates a more efficient and effective interface between technology and humans for a beneficial purpose such as learning, smart homes, reducing waste in all areas, increasing productivity, smart homes. Their project is to present at a conference in a virtual version of a TED talk conference with students presenting and discussing their projects.

SUMMARY

The need for radical changes in the nature of education is becoming increasingly obvious. The needs of the increasingly diverse learners are not being met in a traditional model of teaching and learning. Direct instruction with itemized decontextualized content does not lead to the development of advanced knowledge. In response to a rapidly changing information age with a need for knowledge workers as economic drivers of our country, educators must adapt to stay relevant. Knowledge workers understand how to use information to solve problems, how to think critically, how to create, how to communicate their vision effectively and share their ideas in a variety of forums. The integration of immersive AR technologies into a problem-based learning environment matches the potentiality of AR technologies with a cogent design of the learning environment. This book provides a bridge to educators wanting to understand the conceptual basis and the practical procedures for integrating AR into their educational and training settings.

ORGANIZATION OF THE BOOK

This book is designed to bridge the gap between the potential of these immersive technologies with the practical application of them into classrooms at all levels of education. The chapters include philosophical, conceptual and practical ideas for integrating these technologies to support the development of advanced cognitive processes, content knowledge and skills that are needed to develop 21st century knowledge workers. The book is organized into fourteen chapters. A brief description of each of the chapters follows:

Chapter 1 discusses the immersive learning processes, the background information on AR design process, the benefits of AR immersive learning, and how to implement it in the classroom environment. The author also discusses how to evaluate the benefits of implementing AR.

Chapter 2 discusses the potential of augmented reality as a transformational tool. The chapter is a meta-analysis of 87 AR research studies situated in K-12 environments to determine what grade levels were involved, where was the research being done, what content areas were involved, what kinds of triggers were used, and what learning environments were created through the use of AR. This research found that the majority of studies were situated in elementary contexts in science and math. Diverse learning environments were found including Inquiry, Problem based learning, Visualization, and Gamification.

Chapter 3 takes philosophical orientation and debates the reality as the art of things which exist in our real life. Augmented reality is one of the technologies which cover a computer-generated image on a user's view of the real world by providing a composite view. Virtual Reality is a combination of technologies that are used to visualize and provide interaction with a virtual environment. In augmented reality part of the surrounding environment is actually 'real' with additional layers of virtual objects to the real environment. In this chapter, the author discusses the AR/VR applications in education.

Chapter 4 in This chapter introduces a framework for the virtual task design. The framework proposes that the process of designing language learning tasks for virtual immersive simulated environments also be immersive. The framework guides designers/teachers who are new to virtual worlds through 10 stages of the design process that incorporates designers/teachers' individual work and their collaboration with colleagues and learners. Developed for designing virtual language learning tasks, this framework also benefits other disciplines and informs the design of tasks implemented in other virtual environments.

Chapter 5 describes how immersive virtual reality simulations using virtual reality headsets and discuss the learning theories that lead to transferring skills from a virtual world to the real world. This chapter examines how creating virtual coaching and playing environments that mirror real in-game emotions, real in-game speed and pressure to make the correct split-second decision to train athletes.

Chapter 6 defines the procedures for integrating mobile tablets in their classrooms. The chapter also includes a set of resources educators can use to improve their lessons, a list of ways to improve their curriculum, and how to engage students via virtual reality when home learning is necessary.

Chapter 7 addresses how to integrative immersive virtual interventions for children with behavioral problems. This chapter reviews research on a new generation of tools using AR in learning environments. The goal is to examine how AR technologies can promote self-reflection, mindfulness, and meditation to support students who have experienced trauma.

Chapter 8 describes the design of a live emergency room simulation for emergency room nurse practitioners that integrates augmented reality . The authors describe the specific design and development procedures including the (a) the design of a learning analytic system for formative and summative assessment, (b) the design of the virtual space for the live event, (c) the development of a timed script for the emergency room event, and (d) the development of the virtual simulation.

Chapter 9 describes the potential of integrating AR technologies into Workshop Model remote learning environment. The chapter describes the utilization and integration of these immersive tools in Workshop Model remote learning environment would develop learners' 21st century skills to be decision makers, problem solvers, lifelong learners, creators, innovators, and to think critically in solving problems.

Chapter 10 presents the integration of digital technologies and simulations to meet the needs the young second language learners. The author describes gamified and simulated virtual technologies to facilitate the learning of Mandarin Chinese in an early childhood setting.

Chapter 11 identifies the integration of an AR simulation into a teacher education program at an online university. The authors examine the use of virtual to provide scaffolded learning experiences for pre-service teachers in an online learning environment.

Chapter 12 presents the integration of new information and communication technologies (NICTs), organizations' service structures and their processes have become increasingly flexible, interactive and virtual. The author describes the changes in the maintenance function between the classic strategy and the modern strategy, explaining the contribution of augmented reality to help solve problems in a remote maintenance or E-maintenance training protocol.

Chapter 13 presents the case for how spatial awareness contributes to learning in AR-based learning environments. The author discusses the Immersive learning process and the background information on how the AR use in educational industries.

Chapter 14 concludes with a definition of presence in AR settings. The author discusses a model that identifies the processes leading to the feeling of presence. According to our model, two unconscious phases of judgment condition the emergence of presence. The first judgment concerns the credibility of the environment, which depends on the satisfaction of the user's intellectual and perceptual expectations.

Donna Russell
Walden University, USA

REFERENCES

Anderson, J. R., Reder, L. M., & Simon, H. A. (1997). Situative versus cognitive perspectives: Form versus substance. *Educational Researcher*, *26*(1), 18–21. doi:10.3102/0013189X026001018

Barab, S., Thomas, M., Dodge, T., Carteaux, R., & Tuzun, H. (2005). Making learning fun: Quest Atlantis, a game without guns. *Educational Technology Research and Development*, *53*(1), 86–107. doi:10.1007/BF02504859

Bereiter, C. (2001). *Education and Mind in the knowledge age*. Lawrence Erlbaum Assoc.

Bereiter, C., & Scardamalia, M. (2002). *Beyond Bloom's taxonomy: Rethinking knowledge for the knowledge age: Developing higher-level approaches to knowledge*. http://unr.edu/homepage/luvisis/bereiter.html

Brown, A. L. (1992). Design experiments: Theoretical and methodological challenges in creating complex interventions in classroom settings. *Journal of the Learning Sciences*, *2*(2), 141–178. doi:10.120715327809jls0202_2

Cole, M., & Engestrom, Y. (1993). A cultural-historical approach to distributed cognition. In G. Salomon (Ed.), *Distributed cognition: Psychological and educational considerations*. Cambridge University Press.

Greeno, J. G. (1997). On claims that answer the wrong question. *Educational Researcher*, *26*(1), 5–17. doi:10.3102/0013189X026001005

Jonassen, D. H. (2000). Toward a design theory of problem solving. *Educational Technology Research and Development*, *48*(4), 63–85. doi:10.1007/BF02300500

Jonassen, D. H., & Rohrer-Murphy, L. (1999). Activity theory as a framework for designing constructivist learning environments. *Educational Technology Research and Development*, *47*(1), 61–79. doi:10.1007/BF02299477

Lave, J., & Wenger, E. (1991). *Situated learning: Legitimate peripheral participation*. Cambridge University Press. doi:10.1017/CBO9780511815355

Russell, D. (2004). Paradigm shift: A case study of innovation in an educational setting. *International Journal of Instructional Technology and Distance Learning, 1*(12), 17–22.

Russell, D. (2005). Transformation in an urban school: Using systemic analysis to understand an innovative urban teacher's implementation of an online problem-based unit. *International Journal of Instructional Technology and Distance Learning, 2*(2), 18–25.

Russell, D. (2006). Inquiry into mediated action: The implementation of an innovative online problem-based unit. In S. Barab, K. Hay, & D. Hickey (Eds.), *7th International Conference of the Learning Sciences* (pp. 648-655). Lawrence Erlbaum Associates.

Russell, D. (2008). The mediated action of educational reform: An inquiry into collaborative online professional development. In C. Ramesh, C. Sharma, & S. Mishra (Eds.), *Cases on Global E-Learning Practices: Successes and Pitfalls* (pp. 108–122). IDEA Group, Inc.

Russell, D. (Ed.). (2009a). *Cases on Collaboration in Virtual Learning Environments: Processes and Interactions*. IGI Global.

Russell, D. (2009b). Group collaboration in an online problem-based university course. In O. Tan (Ed.), *Problem-Based Learning and Creativity* (pp. 173–192). Cengage Learning.

Russell, D. (2016a). Flipping the Paradigm of Education: Developing a Comprehensive Educational Program Integrating Virtual Immersive Learning Environments. In D. Russell & J. Laffey (Eds.), *Handbook of Research on Gaming Trends in P-12 Education* (pp. 253–293). Information Science Reference., doi:10.4018/978-1-4666-9629

Russell, D. (2016b). *Simulations as an Educational Resource for Knowledge Workers*. Retrieved 17 Nov. 2015 from https://www.igi-global.com/gateway/video.aspx?titleid=137769&lid=139730

Russell, D. (2016c). The Design of Immersive Virtual Learning Environments Utilizing Problem-Based Learning Templates. In D. Russell & J. Laffey (Eds.), *Handbook of Research on Gaming Trends in P-12 Education* (pp. 105–123). Information Science Reference. doi:10.4018/978-1-4666-9629-7.ch005

Russell, D., & Wallis, S. E. (2016). Designing a Learning Analytic System for Assessing Immersive Virtual Learning Environments. In D. Russell & J. Laffey (Eds.), *Handbook of Research on Gaming Trends in P-12 Education* (pp. 502–526). Information Science Reference. doi:10.4018/978-1-4666-9629-7.ch024

Warburton, S. (2009). Second Life in higher education: Assessing the potential for and the barriers to deploying virtual worlds in learning and teaching. *British Journal of Educational Technology, 40*(3), 414–426. doi:10.1111/j.1467-8535.2009.00952.x

Section 1
Conceptual Topics

These chapters are focused on the overarching conceptual topics for integrating augmented reality (AR) into educational programs.

Chapter 1
Finding a Path Forward for Integrating Augmented Reality Into K-12 Classrooms:
A Literature Review

Marybeth Green
Texas A&M University – Kingsville, USA

Linda Challoo
Texas A&M University – Kingsville, USA

Mehrube Mehrubeoglu
Texas A&M University – Corpus Christi, USA

ABSTRACT

The potential of augmented reality (AR) as a transformational tool has long been touted in academic circles. However, in order for AR to attain this goal, we must seriously examine previous research to determine if we are on the right path. This study examined 87 AR research studies situated in K-12 environments to determine what grade levels were involved, where the research being done was what content areas were involved, what kinds of triggers were used, and what learning environments were created through the use of AR. This research found that the majority of studies were situated in elementary contexts in science and math. Diverse learning environments were found including inquiry, problem-based learning, visualization, and gamification. Based on these findings, suggestions were made for future research including more research on students creating AR experiences, broadening the grade levels and content areas that are involved, and aiming future AR projects at the transformational level of the SAMR model.

DOI: 10.4018/978-1-7998-4222-4.ch001

INTRODUCTION

"Simply put, we believe augmented reality is going to change the way we use technology forever." (Cook, 2019 as cited in Chmielewski, 2017)

The potential for augmented reality (AR) as a learning tool has been touted for decades. One of the earliest uses of AR in education was the heads-up display used in training the United States Air Force pilots in the 1990s. Reports from this project indicated that AR data overlays amplified human performance in real-world tasks (Rosenberg, 1992). Later studies also determined numerous benefits stemming from AR in education, including increasing student engagement in learning (O'Shea et al., 2009), developing the ability to see complex spatial relationships (Dünser et al., 2012), visualizing environments that are impractical in real life (Shelton & Hedley, 2002), safely recreating dangerous experiments (Wojciechowski & Cellary, 2013), and amplifying story development in narrative books (Billinghurst et al., 2001).

Teachers have been intrigued by the possibilities of AR in education. Noting how AR provided opportunities in real estate, sales, and healthcare, teachers have been persuaded to explore potentials in overlaying real objects with virtual objects in the classroom (Prodromou, 2019). As constructivism is increasingly embraced in learning environments, teachers find that AR applications support the student-centered focus and experiential learning, both core tenets of constructivism.

Wang et al. (2017) asserted that AR technologies "allow learners the freedom to actively experience digital content and integrate new information into their existing knowledge base on an individualized path of discovery" (p. 1393). Further, over the last few years, the devices needed for AR technologies have become more affordable and ubiquitous, enabling more schools to provide one-on-one programs for their students (Carreon et al., 2019). Similarly, AR apps have also become more available. In some cases, specially designed books or soft foam cubes are the only AR targets needed (Green et al., 2019; Ntuli, 2019). However, AR has not fulfilled the promise of becoming a transformative technology in education (Cook, 2019). This may be due to teachers' unfamiliarity with the technology or failure to see its utility in a sea of curricular demands.

Charting a path for AR in K-12 learning environments means understanding our past. As tools have improved and we have gained an understanding of AR in the classroom, researchers have reviewed historical AR literature and explored ways for AR to become a valuable educational tool (see Table 1).

There were many commonalities among the reviews in Table 1. Although they sampled literature from different sources, their findings were similar. Akçayır and Akçayır (2017) examined literature from a single source, the Social Sciences Citation Index, using the Web of Science as an entry point. Bacca-Acosta et al. (2014) searched for articles using the Google Scholar H5-index for the category "educational technology." Hennel et al. (2015) and Yuliono et al., (2018) chose a traditional approach, using library databases like ScienceDirect, IEEE Xplore, and ProQuest.

In the four reviews, all authors eliminated theoretical discussions of AR or applications of AR that fell outside the study. The only articles included in all four reviews were studies that demonstrated a solid research design and implemented AR tools in education. The studies' results intersected. Regardless of the construct named advantages, benefits, or promising roles, they all found that AR supported student achievement through motivation, engagement, and increased knowledge, and understanding of content. Additionally, all four found that AR promoted a student-centered learning environment.

The context of education was broadly defined in these reviews, including studies from both industry and higher education. While the reviews focused on learner outcomes, there was no clear understanding of the content areas supported with AR. K-12 education was defined as an area of interest in the studies;

however, there was no grade-level analysis either broadly (elementary, middle school, or high school) or specifically, such as first grade, beyond noting the inclusion of a few articles.

The purpose of this review is to investigate studies in PK-12 classroom settings between the years 2016-2020 to determine the following (a) targeted content areas; (b) targeted grade levels; and (c) how AR supports learning within these content areas. Further, this study proposes to examine teacher perspectives and expectations for AR. Thus, the following research questions guided this review:

1. What school levels and grades are targeted in the AR studies?
2. What content areas are included in the AR studies?
3. Where does the research take place?
4. What types of triggers are used?
5. What types of learning environments are invoked by the AR apps?

Based on these results, the authors expect to create a research agenda that will enable future researchers to broaden the scope and inform the practice of AR, as well as develop opportunities for AR in the classroom.

BACKGROUND

A systematic literature review method was chosen for the investigation of the research to review "existing research using explicit, accountable, rigorous research methods" (Gough et al., 2017, p. 4). In comparison with a traditional literature review, systematic reviews answer questions and test hypotheses (Petticrew & Roberts, 2006). Systematic literature reviews are also appropriate for answering a variety of questions like refining a theory in a field (Gough et al., 2017), examining impacts and effectiveness (Zawacki-Richter et al., 2020), and mapping areas of uncertainty in which new studies are needed (Petticrew & Roberts, 2006). It is the latter purpose that this review proposes to address.

For this review, the authors adapted the process proposed by Petticrew and Roberts (2006).

1. **Stage 1: Planning the Review**
    - Generating a search strategy
    - Developing an inclusion/exclusion strategy
2. **Stage 2: Conducting the Review**
    - Selecting primary studies
    - Studying quality assessment
    - Expert review
    - Extracting and monitoring data
    - Data synthesis
3. **Stage 3: Reporting the Review**
    - Analyzing results

Figure 1. The search strategy.

Planning the Review

In June 2020, data was collected via a tri-part strategy (see Table 1). The collection took place using international online databases like IEEE Xplore, ScienceDirect, Sage Group, SpringerLink, John Wiley & Sons, and Taylor & Francis. Also, data were collected from the Education Resources Information Center (ERIC), which is supported and maintained by the U.S. Department of Education. Finally, all included journal articles were reviewed by an expert in AR to determine if any important papers were missed by the researchers. Searches were limited to high-quality peer-reviewed journals with articles published between 2016 and 2020.

Table 2 illustrates the researchers' inclusion/exclusion guidelines to identify publications for inclusion.

Table 1. Search strategy

Researchers	Year Published	Research Interest	Years	Levels
Akçayır & Akçayır	2017	Advantages and/or disadvantages of AR in educational settings	2007 – 2015	K-University
Bacca-Acosta et al.	2014	AR trends in education: A systematic review of research and applications	2003 – 2013	Not specified
Hennel et al.	2015	Benefits of AR	2003 – 2014	K-University
Yuliono et al.	2018	Promising roles of AR	2009 – 1/26/18	K-University

Table 2. Inclusion/exclusion criteria

Inclusion	Exclusion
Research articles published in peer-reviewed journals or books	Theoretical and conceptual articles, essays, and tool demonstration
Full-length articles published in international conferences or workshops proceedings	Short papers or abstracts published in international conferences or workshops proceedings
Based on an empirical study and grounded in the literature	Based on weak or non-empirical research
Studies in a PK-12 school environment	Studies in an informal learning or undiscernible environment
Focus on AR in the school environment	AR is ancillary to the purposes of the study
Dates from 2016-2020	Dates before 2016

Conducting the Review

Research articles for the review were sourced through databases using keywords in a sequence (see Table 3).

In some databases, the authors were able to specify "Research." As articles were sourced, each researcher reviewed the title, abstract, and article as to its fit in the review specifications. Researchers evaluated the articles independently. Then, the researchers met to reach a consensus on the article list. An article was not included if it was found to be a technical report or theoretical discussion and/or had a weak research design. To code the data, each researcher read the selected articles. The researchers then met to discuss the coding categories and reach a consensus on coded data. Table 4 illustrates the coded data spreadsheet.

Table 3. Keywords in the search process

Main Keyword	Additional Keywords
"Augmented Reality"	"Elementary School"
	"Primary School"
	"Middle School"
	"High School"

Table 4. Research articles: Coding strategy A

Author		
Title		
School-level	Preschool, Elementary (1-6), Secondary (7-12)	
Curricular Content Domain	Math, Science, History, English Language Learning, Art, etc.	
Country of Origin	Any	
Curricular Content Area	Geometry, Biology, World History, Vocabulary, Art History, etc.	
Type of Marker	Triggered	1a Marker-based paper 1b Marker-based object 2 Location-based 3 Dynamic augmentation
		4 Indirect augmentation 5 Nonspecific digital augmentation*
Type of Experience	3D object, Video, Information Overlay, AR Game, Combination	
Type of Learning Environment	Visualization, Problem-Based Learning, Inquiry, Audiolingual, Gamification, Other	
Citation	Authors, Title, Publication, Year	

After the articles were evaluated, a list of potential articles was sent to the AR expert for review, including instructions to inspect the list for potential articles the researchers may have missed. Dr. David Hicks from Texas A&M University-Kingsville was selected based on his expertise evidenced by his extensive research and presentations on AR. Dr. Hicks was satisfied with the list; he suggested that the researchers apply the search strategies to the ACM Special Interest Group on Computer-Human Interaction (SIGHCI). The search strategies were applied to this database, resulting in one additional article that met the inclusion/exclusion criteria. The researchers then compiled the data to answer the research questions.

DESIGN and IMPLEMENTATION

The researchers completed a manual search of the databases, applied the exclusion criteria, and reviewed the critique of the AR expert. In doing so, they identified articles for their study. Numerous AR studies are being conducted on educational levels in schools. Of the 87 AR studies reviewed, 53% were at the elementary level, 41% were at the secondary level, and 6% were at the preschool level (see Figure 2). Figure 3 illustrates the number of AR studies by content domain and school level. Forty-six percent of the AR studies were in the science content domain, which was conducted equally in elementary and secondary levels.

The content areas ranged in content domains. Many of the reviewed AR studies were in the following content areas: science, math, and English language learning (ELL). Forty-six percent of the AR studies were in the area of science, 20% were math, and 9% were ELL. As shown in Figure 4, one study was observed in the following content domains: writing, music, language learning Chinese, language arts, history, familiarize students with school, and computer science and careers.

AR studies have been conducted across the globe, particularly in Asia. As shown in Table 5, 79% of the studies were conducted in Asia and 3% were in North America. Figure 5 displays the number of AR studies by location, which indicates that most studies took place in Taiwan.

Figure 2. Levels included in AR studies

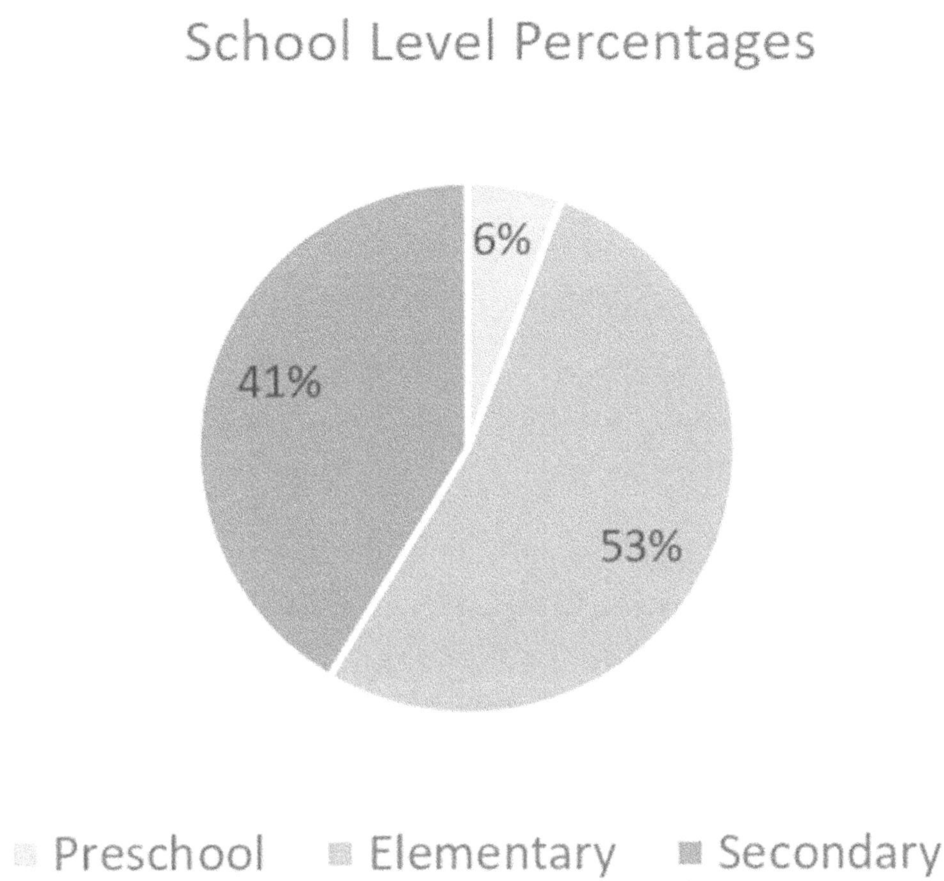

The technologies underlying AR have changed considerably over the last five years. To gain a perspective of available AR technologies, the researchers examined each article for triggers and markers and the experiences they generated. In some cases, the researchers contacted the corresponding author for more information. Edwards-Stewart et al., (2016) divided AR into a triggered-based and view-based category. The triggered-based category is subdivided into four types of triggers:

1. **Markers (paper and object):** Marker-based AR uses a marker to trigger the AR content. It works through object recognition. Paper-based markers use images or quick response (QR) codes as triggers. Object-based AR uses a physical object to trigger the AR content. Once the image or object is scanned by the camera, it produces the AR content.
2. **Geolocation:** This type of AR does not need a physical marker for a trigger. Instead, geolocation uses physical locations to trigger real-time data. Most smartphones have location-detection capabilities. AR programs featuring geolocation use a combination of global positioning systems (GPS), embedded compasses, and accelerometers to generate the AR content.

Figure 3. AR studies: Content domain by school level

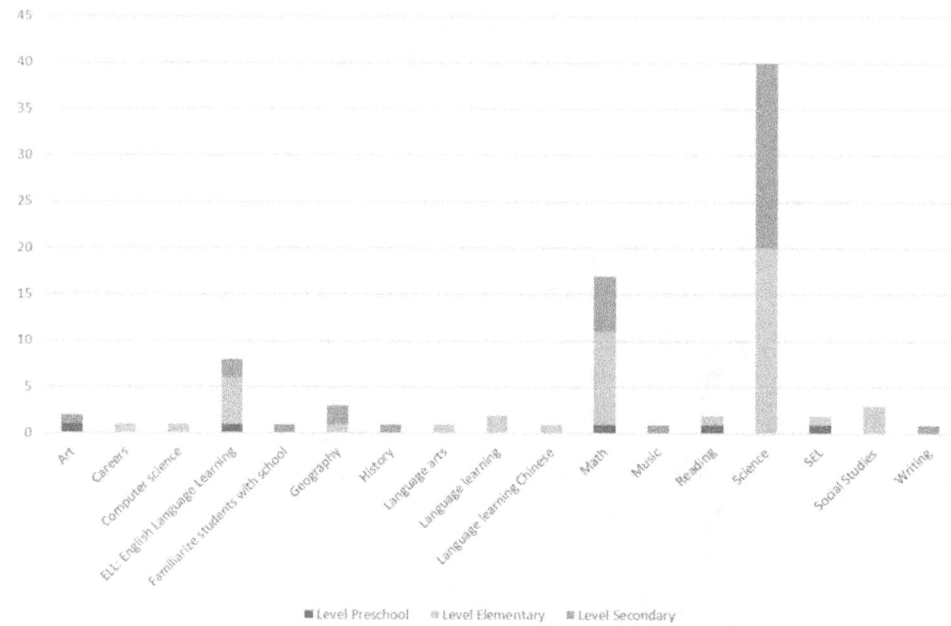

Figure 4. AR studies by content domain

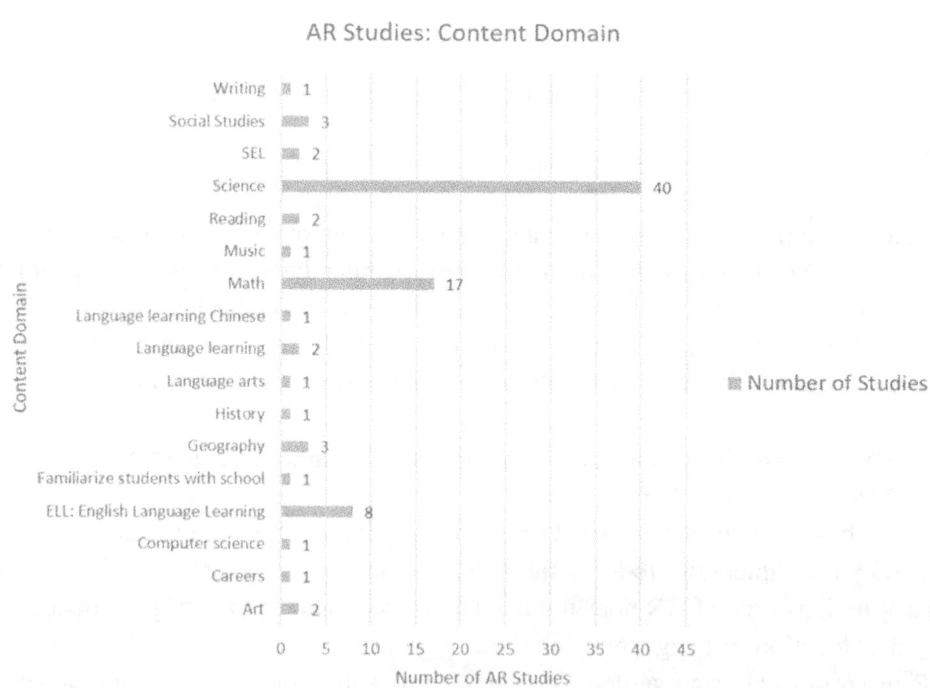

Table 5. AR studies by continent

Continent	Number of AR Studies	Percentage of AR Studies
Asia	69	79%
Europe	10	11%
North America	3	3%
South America	4	5%
Zealandia	1	1%

3. **Dynamic Augmentation:** In dynamic augmentation, the program leverages the motion-detection capabilities of the AR program to detect an object in its field. Then, it enhances the object with AR content.
4. **Complex Augmentation:** This type of augmentation combines marker, location, and dynamic augmentation. Complex augmentation is exemplified by Google Glass, which overlays a scene with relevant information about the user's surroundings.

The view-based category is subdivided into indirect augmentation and nonspecific augmentation categories.

1. **Indirect Augmentation:** In this category, a real-world image is augmented intelligently. For example, a wall color paint app can superimpose a new color on the wall.
2. **Nonspecific Augmentation:** This category augments the camera view regardless of location. For example, a bubbles app will superimpose bubbles in front of the viewer.

Most studies in this review (80%) were triggered using markers via paper, QR codes, or 3D objects. Another 8% used the geolocation trigger; 8% used Kinect or another device to create a dynamic AR

Figure 5. AR studies by location

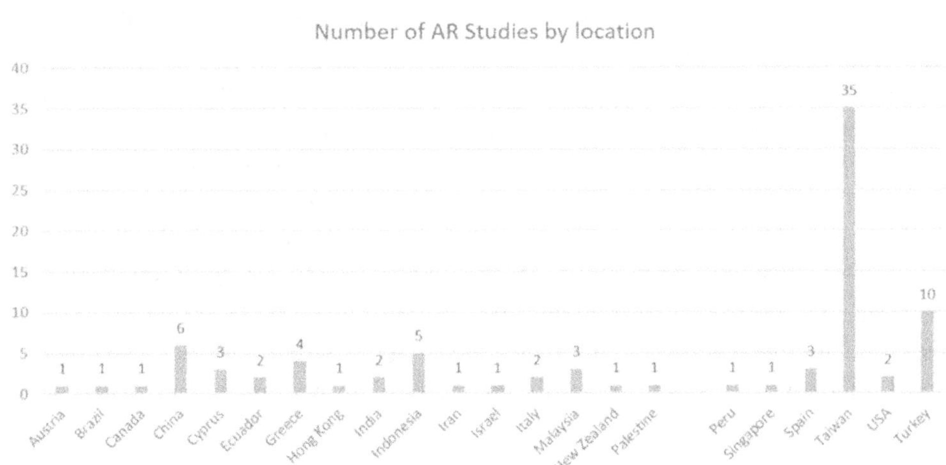

Figure 6. Triggered AR classes in the research

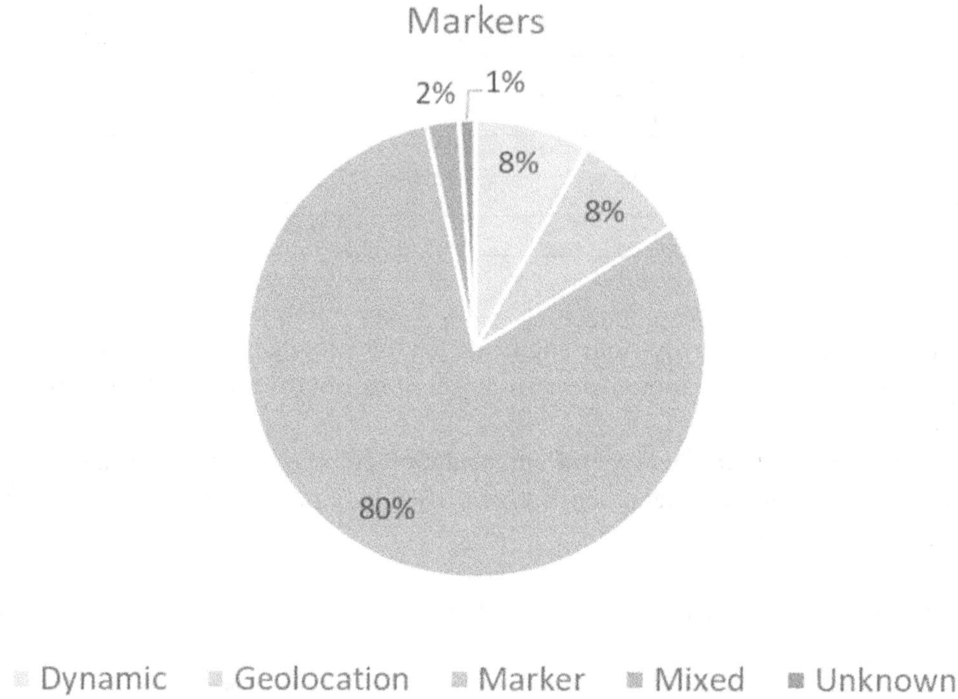

environment. Some studies (2%) used a mixture of methods. Finally, 1% was unknown. In this review, no studies used view-based triggers. The pie chart in Figure 6 summarizes these findings.

AR has a chameleon-like character as it adapts to learning environments. AR technologies, which have grown, can enable a more complex, dynamic student learning experience. The researchers explored the studies to identify learning environments through the authors' descriptions. The researchers identified six learning environments: (1) visualization; (2) problem-based learning; (3) gamification; (4) inquiry; (5) collaboration; and (6) other. The distribution of learning environments can be seen in Figure 7. As illustrated in Figure 7, many of the studies favored an inquiry-based learning format (30%). This was followed by visualization (29%), gamification (17%), problem-based learning (13%), and other (11%). The following sections address the learning environments' use of AR.

In early childhood, children investigate their environment and ask questions. Inquiry learning captures that curiosity through learning designs focused on understanding through asking questions. Inquiry learning is defined as an instructional approach "that encourages students to learn through their exploration, experience, and inquiry" (O'Brien & Collins, 2011, p. 143). Questioning is a central component of inquiry learning as the student develops questions, makes observations, and gathers data to guide and expand their exploration of ideas and concepts. Inquiry learning is rooted in constructivist learning principles, which assert that students take ownership of their learning through activities that enable students to use personal experiences and perspectives to construct rather than passively absorb knowledge.

Teachers operating within this philosophy facilitate learning by crafting learning activities founded on essential questions to pique students' interests and stimulate their natural curiosity. Researchers have found that inquiry-based learning environments provide many benefits to learners, including motiva-

Figure 7. Distribution of learning environments

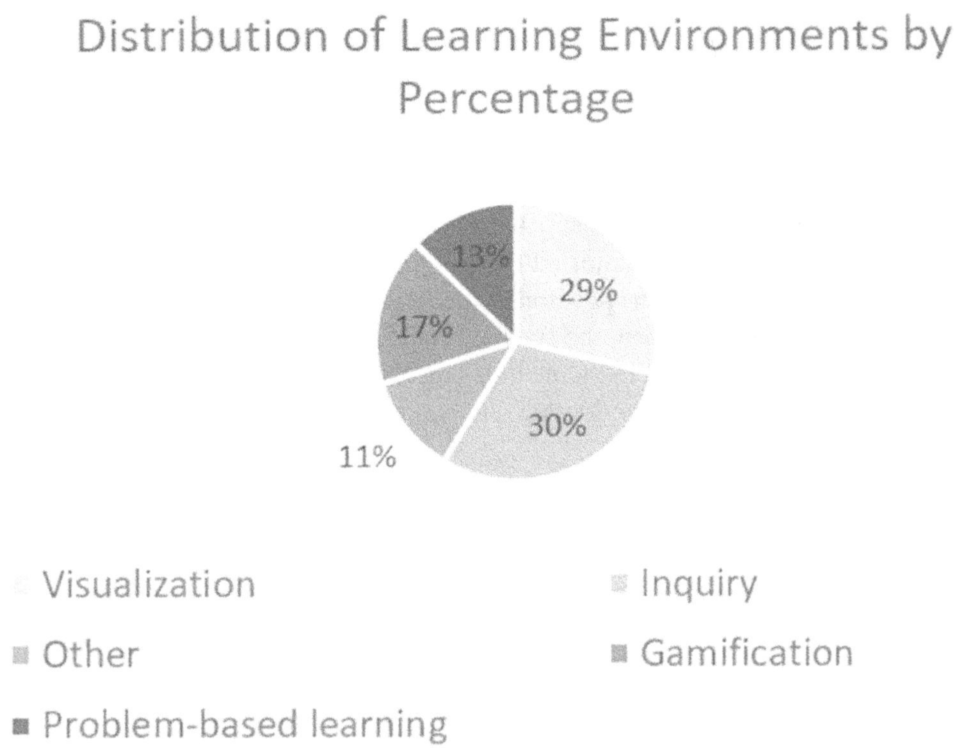

tion, engagement, and increased learning. AR technologies provide a robust platform for inquiry-based learning projects. Pedaste et al. (2015) identified five phases in the inquiry process: (1) orientation; (2) conceptualization; (3) investigation; (4) conclusion; and (5) discussion. According to this framework, students begin their work in the orientation phase, where they are introduced to a topic, gain background understanding, and/or make observations. In the conceptualization phase, students develop questions and make predictions. The investigation phase is divided into the following three phases:

1. **Exploration:** Students develop an action plan, designing an experiment or planning an observation.
2. **Experimentation:** Students experiment or observe and collect data.
3. **Data Interpretation:** Students analyze their data in light of their original questions, using the information to determine the best way to represent their data.

During the conclusion phase, students share their results and reflect on their process. Pedaste et al., (2020) concluded that AR is best suited to the first three phases of the inquiry process. In the first phase, orientation, for example, the affordances of AR enable the learner to gain awareness of a situation or explore a new concept or object. Also, affordances of AR during the conceptualization phase enable the learner to develop questions about an AR object or through AR objects superimposed on the real world. Finally, Pedaste et al. (2020) suggested the possibility of interacting with objects, collecting data, or running simple experiments.

Several of the AR platforms in this review either directly or indirectly supported inquiry-based learning and the processes described by Pedaste et al. (2020). Ewais and Troyer (2019), for example, used AR models of atoms with seventh-grade girls in Palestine. The girls could use mobile devices to view the AR atoms and their properties. Then, the girls could investigate the combinations of the atoms by placing markers together. The resulting molecule would appear with information about its properties. Thus, through AR, students gained familiarity with the atoms, planned a combination of atoms, and experimented by placing two markers together.

Similarly, Niu et al. (2019) developed an app that allowed sixth-grade students in China to investigate the physics behind a seesaw. Students adjusted the weight and position of objects on an AR seesaw, adjusting the arm length by dragging the position of the weight and changing the mass of the weight by pressing the corresponding button. Then, the students could see in real-time whether their seesaw was balanced. Niu's students also engaged in the inquiry process as they gained familiarity with the physics of a seesaw, using the opportunity to develop a hypothesis about the placement of the weights and observe the effects of their hypothesis.

Finally, Tomara and Gouscos's (2019) Greek high school students used an AR to experiment with electrical forces in Coulomb's law, testing forces between augmented charges in terms of charge size and charge type. After varying the numerical value of the charge, students could see changes in the size of the augmented charges. They observed subsequent changes in the forces' magnitude, as well as varied the charge type to identify changes in the direction of force. AR, therefore, can play a significant role in deepening students' understanding of concepts and phenomena through inquiry-based learning.

Issues, Controversies, Problems

This chapter examined previous research on AR studies in school contexts to determine the direction of the research and chart a path to better fulfill Cook's vision that AR will change the interaction of education and technology. The following sections discuss gaps identified by the researchers as they reviewed the previous articles from a variety of perspectives.

Only one study involved students creating with AR. In Gardeli and Vosinakis (2019), students designed a pirate adventure game for their student peers using AR components included in the research to develop their computational thinking. AR technologies like Merge Cubes, CoSpaces, and Metaverse are becoming more available and easier to program. Therefore, it is conceivable that students can create their own AR experiences. Creating AR repositions students from passive consumers of AR experiences to active learners. Further, authoring AR programs provides an interdisciplinary learning environment in which students create AR through science, technology, humanities, and art. Most importantly, when students build and code their AR experiences, they engage in Papert's (1980) theory of constructionism. This theory asserts that learning is more effective when students build knowledge by producing a tangible, meaningful artifact. Within this theory, the teacher acts as both a facilitator and coach (Gerstein, 2019). Future research could examine variables related to students' AR learning constructions through motivation, satisfaction, flow, and perseverance.

The current study's analysis of age groups found that most studies (57%) targeted elementary students. Other targets included secondary students (40%) and preschool (6%). Similar reviews found comparable results. Weerasinghe et al. (2019), in their review of studies on AR games, found that 56% were situated in elementary grades, 20% were in secondary education, and 6% were in undergraduate education.

Likewise, Pellas et al. (2019) found that 66% of their studies focused on primary education and 33% on secondary education.

After reviewing these results, the researchers pondered why so little attention has been given to secondary education. Sirakaya and Çakmak (2018) argued that secondary students move from Piaget's concrete phase to the abstract phase. A significant amount of AR supports younger students' abilities to visualize and achieve a concrete understanding of concepts. However, AR at the secondary level could help secondary students visualize abstract concepts. Further, some studies at the secondary level in this review demonstrated how students could use AR to engage in complex problem solving through problem-based learning and gamification. Students at the secondary level are ready for increased autonomy and challenging problems, which enable them to develop and practice a repertoire of problem-solving skills. AR offers a rich platform to support learning experiences through geolocation, encouraging students to interact with and explore diverse landscapes, pop-up characters, and just-in-time information.

Similarly, this review found limited activity at the preschool level, which is consistent with the findings of Akçayır and Akçayır (2017) and Sırakaya et al. (2018). An increasing number of children have access to smart devices at earlier ages. These children have become adept at navigating and manipulating programs. AR brings a multisensory edutainment environment with images, sounds, and haptic objects to engage preschoolers (Cascales et al., 2013). In the current review, the researchers engaged preschool students with AR flashcards, illustrated and animated books, and learning about shapes. The researchers reported that the students could use the AR tools and found them motivating and enjoyable.

Future research should broaden the scope of participation to include both preschoolers and secondary students. In school contexts, the focus will remain on learning; however, multiple areas are open for research with these underserved populations. Each of these populations has unique characteristics that would benefit from AR research.

Lessons Learned

Rooted in constructivism, problem-based learning is a pedagogy in which students learn by solving ill-structured real-world or open-ended problems. This type of learning is defined by Dabbagh et al. (2008) as "the learning that results from the process of working toward the understanding or resolution of a problem" (p. 60). Students in problem-based learning environments exercise critical thinking skills by analyzing problems rather than memorizing discrete facts (Brush & Saye, 2006). Small groups of students collaborate to determine the information needed to solve a problem, synthesize what they have learned, and articulate a solution (Klopfer & Squire, 2008).

Jonassen (2010) argued that problem-based learning is the most authentic learning environment, allowing students to better comprehend and retain information. Most teachers are comfortable with the role of the information provider; however, in a problem-based environment, the teacher serves as a facilitator who pushes students to think deeply, scaffolds knowledge construction, moves the discourse forward, and maintains group dynamics (Hmelo-Silver et al., 2019; Puntambekar, 2015). Pepper (2009) found that problem-based learning environments offer multiple benefits for students, including:

- Students determine the information and skills needed to investigate the issues. Then, they build on their current knowledge to synthesize and integrate the new information.
- Students take responsibility for the learning within their group. The instructors monitor and facilitate students' learning.

- Students are more engaged with the learning experience.

AR provides a rich learning environment to employ problem-based learning activities. In addition to the usual affordances of AR, including motivation and engagement, AR technologies support text, video, 2D and 3D graphics, animation, and sound, which can be triggered through physical markers, geolocation, and indirect augmentation technologies like Kinect. A key essential of problem-based learning is direct access to the required resources (Luis et al., 2013). AR bridges reality with virtual information that overlaps the real world. Therefore, AR can support the problem-solving process. For some learners, the ability to see an object in 3D may provide critical insight into an aspect of the problem. In other cases, AR through geolocation may provide just-in-time information in the context in which it is needed, creating additional meaning and significance for the learner. Providing information in a multisensory format may also enable students to learn through personal strengths (Akçayır & Akçayır, 2017). Students who may not have a sophisticated understanding of the problem may be able to form a more complex model through AR information (Ifenthaler & Eseryel, 2013). Finally, some learners may lack confidence in their ability to solve problems. However, Karagozlu (2018) found that AR increased students' confidence in their problem-solving skills.

A few of the authors of the reviewed research studies used a problem-based learning design in their AR research. Chang, Hsu, and Wu (2016) created a scenario for students in Taiwan based on the Fukushima Daiichi nuclear disaster. Upon noting that there was a school down the road from the Fukushima Daiichi nuclear plant, the researchers created a scenario where students in Taiwan faced a similar problem. In their study, the students worked with an AR app to gather simulated radiation readings from the soil around the school. After gathering the readings, they met via GPS with pop-up characters who proposed solutions for the irradiated soil. Students weighed decisions like growing plants (environmentally friendly) or removing soil (economically efficient).

Efstathiou et al. (2018) AR problem-based learning design had third-grade students in South Cyprus investigate conditions for a successful settlement in the Neolithic period. Students studied the history of their locale as part of their social studies curriculum. After an initial study on Choirokoitia, the students took a field trip to the Neolithic park. Each student received a tablet loaded with an AR app. This provided GPS-triggered information at various sites throughout the park, an interactive map to show their location in the park, a notepad, a tool to capture screenshots, a concept map tool, and a chat app so students could communicate with their peer groups. The researchers in this study investigated the ability of the app to create empathy with past civilizations. Also, the researchers theorized that the information to students as they worked to resolve the problem was akin to Moreno and Mayer's (1999) spatial contiguity principle, which asserts that pictures and explanatory text should be adjacent to each other.

SOLUTIONS AND RECOMMENDATIONS

A key affordance of AR is its ability to overlay the real world with 3D objects. AR enables students to visualize objects in 3D if they are too small to be seen without a microscope (for example, a cell) or impossible to see (for example, a molecule). AR also enables users to view objects that are too dangerous or far away as the bottom of the ocean (Wu et al., 2013). Students can rotate AR objects, zoom in, or walk around the AR object. Further, enabling students to visualize in 3D allows them to see the information that may not be apparent from a 2D picture. Finally, Dunleavy et al. (2009) argued that students navigate 3D experiences in virtual worlds outside of school, which reshapes students' learning styles, strengths, and preferences.

3D AR also allows students to develop their spatial visualization abilities. Spatial visualization is defined as "the ability to mentally manipulate, rotate, twist, or invert a pictorially presented stimuli" McGee (1979, p. 893). Kaufmann et al. (2000) asserted that students who work in a 3D space find it easier to comprehend and retain spatial relationships. Also, Kaufmann et al. (2000) maintained that 3D images "enhance, enrich, and compliment" the mental models held in students' minds. Barrett and Hegarty (2016) found that students with lower spatial ability skills demonstrated improved performance when 2D images were spatially enriched with 3D displays. While once thought of as an innate biological trait, researchers have now demonstrated that spatial thinking can be honed with experience (Newcombe, 2016). Improving spatial visualization skills in students is critical to their future success in fields like engineering, science, and medicine (Gagnier & Fisher, 2016).

Sweller et al.'s (1988) theory of cognitive load has also been used to explain the relationships between visualization and learning. According to this theory, working memory holds two to seven pieces of information at one time. Working memory can combine, contrast, or manipulate two to four elements at one time and without rehearsal. Also, nearly all the contents of working memory are lost within 20 seconds (Sweller et al., 1998). If high demands are placed on the learner due to the complexity of information (intrinsic cognitive load) or unorganized and/or unnecessary information (extraneous cognitive load), working memory can be overwhelmed. Leveraging carefully designed AR in learning environments, however, can decrease cognitive load, fostering an understanding of abstract concepts or knowledge (Cheng, 2017; Thees et al., 2020).

Several papers in this review used AR to create a 3D visualization of a concept. These visualizations spanned a variety of content domains, including science, math, and language arts. El Kouzi, Mao, and Zambrano (2019) created an AR app that modeled a human skeleton. Canadian fifth-grade students were able to view the skeleton and touch a specific bone to show its name. Similarly, Fokides and Mastrokoukou (2018) used AR in a biology classroom with sixth-grade Greek students. The study used a commercial app, ARLOON's *The Human Body Anatomy*. The app was not available in Greek. Therefore, the researchers translated the content into Greek with the permission of the app developers. In the study, students viewed, rotated, and explored the organs in the circulatory system and respiratory system as they completed the exercises.

Amir et al. (2020) created an app that enabled Indonesian fourth-grade students to view 3D geometric shapes through the following five lenses modeled after the components of the spatial ability scale (1a) representation; (b) visualization; (c) rotation; (d) reconstruction; and (e) constructive space. Amir et al. (2020) examined the perceptions of elementary school students after using 3Dmetric to learn geometric shapes. Finally, Yılmaz et al. (2017) created an app that enabled preschool students in Turkey to view 3D animations of scenes and characters in Turkish picture books for children. Students scanned with a marker to make animations appear on a page. The researchers of the study hoped the 3D animations would enhance the child's enjoyment and story comprehension.

In a slightly different vein, two researchers used AR to create visualizations that helped students picture and organize knowledge in their learning environment. Using AR visualizations in this manner is consistent with Sweller's cognitive load theory, which theorizes that working memory is limited in capacity, and information organization is key to maximizing mental resources. Chen et al. (2019) employed AR to create 3D concept maps to allow students to learn about the food web. Using a preset concept map, students followed nodes and links to learn about animals' predator-prey relationships. Wu, Hwang et al. (2018) took a slightly different approach, using AR to enable students to complete a repertory grid about butterflies. According to their study, a repertory grid enables “concept construction using a matrix whose rows show construct labels and whose columns present element labels” (Wu et al., 2018, p. 224). Concept maps and repertory grids, thus, are forms of knowledge visualization that enable students to interact with large, complex amounts of information while reducing the cognitive load (Ware, 2005).

In their survey of global consumers, Limelight Networks found that the world spends more time gaming today than ever before (Limelight Networks, 2020). Mobile devices have become ubiquitous in society. In 2017, children (ages 0 to 8) spent an average of 48 minutes per day gaming outside of school, which tripled from 15 minutes per day in 2013 (Rideout, 2017). Videogaming is more pervasive among teenagers, with 97% of teen boys and 83% of teen girls playing video games on some device (Perrin, 2020). Increasingly, teachers bring gaming into the classroom as a strategy to engage learners and gamify their curriculum. Kapp (2012) defined gamification as the “careful and considered application of game thinking to solve problems and encouraging learning using all of the elements of games that are appropriate” (p. 15).

Researchers and theorists are finding that games serve purposes beyond student engagement. Hu et al. (2018) found that games provide benefits in three areas (a) active engagement; (b) learning effects; and (c) personal experience. In active engagement, the researchers found that the story, dynamics, and mechanics of games contribute to student enjoyment and engagement as they participate. They further maintain that gamified learning helps students learn more deeply and for a longer period. Finally, they emphasize that students’ personal experiences are self-created as they complete missions and obtain rewards like points, badges, or levels.

On the other hand, Heinzen et al. (2015) described the effects of flow on the gamer, a concept first described by Csikszentmihalyi (1975). This theory proposes that a person’s experiences flow when they are fully immersed, energized, and enjoying a task. These authors argued that game developers strive for a flow zone that balances boredom and anxiety. Finally, Furdu et al. (2017) found that games combine fun with learning, which creates active, personalized learning experiences.

Many of the affordances of AR have been leveraged to provide an educational gaming platform. Using geolocation capabilities, for example, AR can move gameplay from an onscreen experience to one which incorporates real-world features and distributes activities across a physical landscape (Stewart et al., 2020). Further, AR platforms adapt to a variety of game genres, such as adventure, role play, treasure hunts, puzzles, or simulation (Weerasinghe et al., 2019).

Finally, with the exception of Kinect AR, AR technologies are flexible enough for games to be played on all manner of tablets and smartphone devices. Unlike gaming platforms that restrict students to one device, this flexibility enables students to engage in games through multiple devices. The games created by the researchers in this review drew from a variety of content areas. Science was the most popular content area (33%). This was followed by math games (23%), English language learning games (12%), social-emotional learning (SEL) games (12%), and other content like language arts games (8%) and computer science games (8%).

Games were drawn from multiple game genres. Some games were simple word games focused on English language learning. In Hsu (2019), Taiwanese students raced the clock to identify and spell school objects like pens, books, or pencil. In Lu et al.’s (2020) puzzle game, students matched dinosaur puzzle pieces from various geologic eras. Each geologic era had six dinosaurs; students had to match a dinosaur shadow, fossil, and name. When the dinosaur shadow was scanned, a 3D model of the dinosaur appeared on the mobile device. When the dinosaur shadow matched the dinosaur fossil, a trophy was awarded. In

López-Faican and Jaen's (2020) adventure game, students were tasked with finding emojis with specific emotions and attempting to make the emoji feel better. In Mathmon, a math adventure game by Cheng et al. (2019), students tried to rid the school of monsters by solving prime numbers problems. As teams of students solved the problems, a clue was given to locating the next monsters.

As with previous reviews (Yilmaz, 2018), most studies in this review focused on science education. Science provides a fertile environment for AR as students need assistance in visualizing concepts. Visuals like 2D charts and pictures provide some information. However, AR's dynamic environment allows students to view and interact with more complex subjects (Arvanitis et al., 2009), addresses misconceptions (Sotiriou & Bogner, 2008), and enables the representation of invisible or difficult-to-visualize events (Wu et al., 2013).

Several topics within science were addressed in the review (see Table 6).

Table 6. Science topics addressed in the AR research studies

Topic	%
Anatomy	3
Astronomy	15
Biology	33
Chemistry	10
Dinosaurs	3
Ecology	10
Geology	3
Physics	21
Weather	3
Thermodynamics	1

Many of the studies in this review visualized content or permitted students to interact with content. Some employed an inquiry-based approach and few permitted students to engage in the scientific method. Technologies have advanced over the last five years and should continue to progress. Future research could more formally introduce the scientific method into student interactions with content as a means of extending student understanding into the fundamental basis of science.

Math was a prominent subject (20%) in this study. Bujak et al. (2013) asserted that physical manipulatives have supported math instruction since the Babylonians by providing a concrete representation of math concepts like number operations and composition and/or decomposition of numbers and fractions. Bujak et al. (2013) contended that AR can further this understanding by providing a quick calculation of a math representation or views that cannot be seen in the physical world, such as a cross-sectional slice of a 3D object.

Most of the math topics addressed in this study, however, focus on a narrow range of possibilities for AR in math (see Table 7).

Fifty-six percent of the studies in this review focused on geometry. There is great potential for studies from other areas in math. For example, Cai et al. (2019) demonstrated the possibilities of teaching Chi-

Table 7. Math topics addressed in the AR research studies

Topic	%
Geometry	56
Algebra	6
Enumeration	6
Number Sense	6
Prime Numbers	6
Probability	6
Problem Solving	6
Volume	6

nese students the concept of probability by using a clever combination of virtual coins, cards, and dice. Similarly, Stylianidou et al. (2020) developed a problem-solving game where Greek Cypriot students helped a boy, Nemo, escape from an ancient tower in their village. By solving a series of problems and showing the correct sequence of number cards to the camera, virtual doors unlocked, freeing Nemo from the tower. Future research in math AR should move beyond visualizing math concepts and embrace other capacities of AR to address a broader scope of the math curriculum.

The remainder of the content topics in this review spanned art, English language learning, Chinese language learning, music, reading, and social studies. These areas also represent an opportunity for expansion. AR in art education, for example, has been a topic of conversation in museums for many years due to the potential for AR to create multisensory experiences with sound, images, animation, video, stories, and haptic inputs related to viewing art (Kang & Yang, 2020). Just-in-time scaffolds could be implemented in the classroom for duplicates of famous artwork, enabling students to find deeper meaning in each piece.

This review also found a new area of content that has not been discussed in previous reviews of AR. SEL is becoming a critical component of education as schools recognize the importance of social-emotional competencies to student success. SEL is defined as the:

the process through which children and adults acquire and effectively apply the knowledge, attitudes, and skills necessary to understand and manage emotions, set and achieve positive goals, feel and show empathy for others, establish and maintain positive relationships, and make responsible decisions. (CASEL, nd., para 1)

A notable example of SEL in AR is López-Faican and Jaen's (2020) EmoFinder. In this game, characters with emotions (i.e., anger, sadness, joy) are geolocated in the school environment. Upon locating the character and identifying its emotion, the students can launch a variety of emoticons at the character to improve its emotional state. If the students improve the character's emotional state, then the student can capture the character (like in Pokémon Go). Future research should consider broadening included curricular topics. There is an emphasis on science and math by way of the science, technology, engineering, and math (STEM) movement. Still, there is room to engage students in AR through other subject areas.

FUTURE TRENDS

AR has always been viewed as a transformative technology tool in education. How we achieve that transformative goal, however, has been open to debate. One perspective provides guidance through the substitution, augmentation, modification, redefinition (SAMR) model. Developed by Puentedura (2009), the SAMR model is hierarchical, with four levels of technology integration (two at the enhancement level and two at the transformation level). See Figure 8.

Figure 8. SAMR model

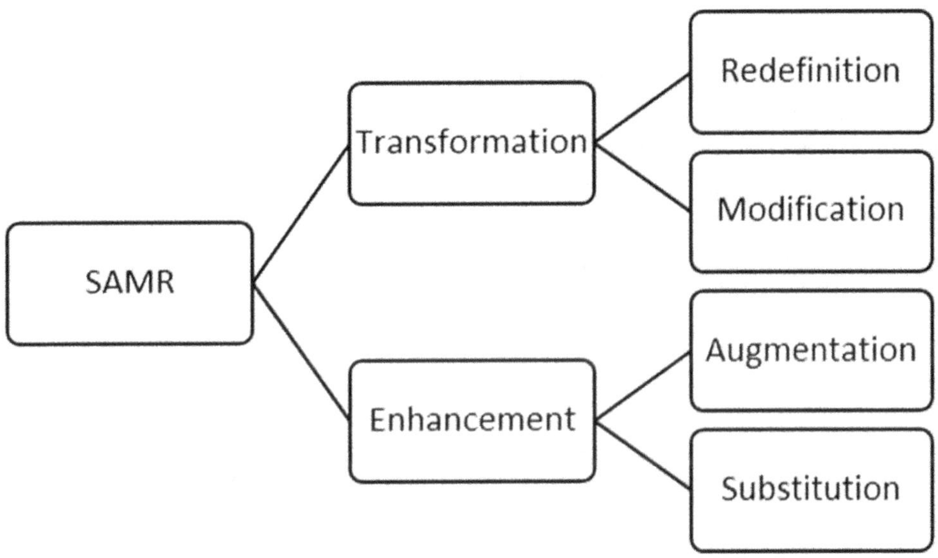

The purpose of the SAMR framework is to enable teachers to determine the level of technology integration and whether technology enhances or transforms knowledge and learning (Dreamson, 2019). At the substitution level, the technology acts as a direct substitute for the existing tool with no functional change. At the augmentation level, the technology acts as a direct substitute for functional improvement. At the modification level, the technology offers significant task redesign and changes the way that learning may have taken place. Finally, at the redefinition level, technology allows for the creation of tasks that were inconceivable. Cochrane et al. (2014) asserted that:

the SAMR framework argues that technology adoption in education can move beyond the substitution of existing activities and assessment practices to create new experiences previously impossible or difficult with prior technology. (p. 5)

AR has the potential to move education to the transformative level. Several of the studies in this review demonstrated that potential, particularly those that situated learning within the inquiry, gamification, or problem-based learning environments. A notable example from the transformative level is the study by Chang et al. (2017), which enabled students to virtually celebrate the Chinese Lantern Festival. Using

Kinect, students took part in activities associated with the festival like making virtual tangyuan (sticky rice dumplings) and launching a virtual lantern controlled by the children's stepping motions.

The intent of the SAMR model was to encourage teachers to reflect on their use of technology in the classroom and urge them to make small changes in their technology-driven experiences to reach the next level (Hashim, 2018). Moving learning forward to the transformative level fosters more meaningful learning experiences and enables students to be more engaged in their learning. In the future, AR researchers should consider the SAMR level of their project, determining whether it merely enhances a learning task or transforms the way that learning is accomplished.

CONCLUSION

The purpose of this article was to examine AR research between 2016 and 2020 in PK-12 school contexts to determine what was being done and what paths can be charted for the future. This research examined 1,166 articles to identify the final 86 for the research. The authors examined the articles to determine the grade levels involved, location of the research, content areas, triggers, and learning environments created through AR. The research discussed findings within each category. Then, the findings were examined for potential gaps for AR researchers. Finally, recommendations were made for future research.

REFERENCES

Akçayır, M., & Akçayır, G. (2017). Advantages and challenges associated with augmented reality for education: A systematic review of the literature. *Educational Research Review*, *20*, 1–11. doi:10.1016/j.edurev.2016.11.002

Amir, M. F., Fediyanto, N., Rudyanto, H. E., Afifah, D. S. N., & Tortop, H. S. (2020). Elementary students' perceptions of 3Dmetric: A cross-sectional study. *Heliyon*, *6*(6), e04052. doi:10.1016/j.heliyon.2020.e04052 PMID:32577547

Arvanitis, T. N., Petrou, A., Knight, J. F., Savas, S., Sotiriou, S., Gargalakos, M., & Gialouri, E. (2009). Human factors and qualitative pedagogical evaluation of a mobile augmented reality system for science education used by learners with physical disabilities. *Personal and Ubiquitous Computing*, *13*(3), 243–250. doi:10.100700779-007-0187-7

Bacca-Acosta, J. L., Baldiris, S. M., Fabregat, R., & Graf, S., & Kinshuk. (2014). Augmented reality trends in education: A systematic review of research and applications. *Journal of Educational Technology & Society*, *17*(4), 133–149.

Barrett, T. J., & Hegarty, M. (2016). Effects of interface and spatial ability on manipulation of virtual models in a STEM domain. *Computers in Human Behavior*, *65*, 220–231. doi:10.1016/j.chb.2016.06.026

Billinghurst, M., Kato, H., & Poupyrev, I. (2001). The MagicBook: A transitional AR interface. *Computers & Graphics*, *25*(5), 745–753. doi:10.1016/S0097-8493(01)00117-0

Brush, T., & Saye, J. (2006, April). *Scaffolding critical reasoning in history and social studies: Tools to support problem-based historical inquiry*. Presented as part of the Symposium, Scaffolding Disciplined Inquiry in Science and Social Studies: A Comparison to the Instructional Technology SIG.

Bujak, K. R., Radu, I., Catrambone, R., MacIntyre, B., Zheng, R., & Golubski, G. (2013). A psychological perspective on augmented reality in the mathematics classroom. *Computers & Education*, *68*, 536–544. doi:10.1016/j.compedu.2013.02.017

Cai, S., Liu, E., Yang, Y., & Liang, J. C. (2019). Tablet-based AR technology: Impacts on students' conceptions and approaches to learning mathematics according to their self-efficacy. *British Journal of Educational Technology*, *50*(1), 248–263. doi:10.1111/bjet.12718

Carreon, A., Smith, S. J., & Rowland, A. (2019). Augmented reality: Creating and implementing digital classroom supports. *Journal of Special Education Technology*, *35*(2), 109–115. doi:10.1177/0162643419882423

Cascales, A., Laguna, I., Pérez-López, D., Perona, P., & Contero, M. (2013, July). An experience on natural sciences augmented reality contents for preschoolers. In R. Shumaker (Ed.), *International Conference on Virtual, Augmented and Mixed Reality* (pp. 103-112). Berlin: Springer. 10.1007/978-3-642-39420-1_12

CASEL. (n.d.). *What is SEL.* https://casel.org/what-is-SEL/

Chang, H. Y., Hsu, Y. S., & Wu, H. K. (2016). A comparison study of augmented reality versus interactive simulation technology to support student learning of a socio-scientific issue. *Interactive Learning Environments*, *24*(6), 1148–1161. doi:10.1080/10494820.2014.961486

Chang, H. Y., Lin, Y. K., Fang, R. J., & Lu, Y. T. (2017). Errata: A situated cultural festival learning system based on motion sensing. *Eurasia Journal of Mathematics, Science and Technology Education*, *13*(5), 1411–1411. doi:10.12973/eurasia.2017.00677a

Chen, C., Huang, C., & Chou, Y. (2019). Effects of augmented reality-based multidimensional concept maps on students' learning achievement, motivation and c. *Universal Access in the Information Society*, *18*(2), 257–268. doi:10.100710209-017-0595-z

Cheng, K. H. (2017). Reading an augmented reality book: An exploration of learners' cognitive load, motivation, and attitudes. *Australasian Journal of Educational Technology*, *33*(4).

Cheng, Y. W., Wang, Y., Cheng, I. L., & Chen, N. S. (2019). An in-depth analysis of the interaction transitions in a collaborative augmented reality-based mathematic game. *Interactive Learning Environments*, *27*(5-6), 782–796. doi:10.1080/10494820.2019.1610448

Chmielewski, D. C. (2017, November 3). *Apple's Tim Cook says augmented reality will "change everything"*. https://deadline.com/2017/11/apple-tim-cook-augmented-reality-fourth-quarter-2017-earnings-1202200710/

Cochrane, T., Antonczak, L., Keegan, H., & Narayan, V. (2014). Riding the Wave of BYOD: Developing a Framework for Creative Pedagogies. *Research in Learning Technology*, *22*(1). Advance online publication. doi:10.3402/rlt.v22.24637

Cook, M. J. (2019). Augmented reality: Examining its value in a music technology classroom. Practice and potential. *Waikato Journal of Education*, *24*(2), 23–38. doi:10.15663/wje.v24i2.687

Csikszentmihalyi, M. (1975). *Beyond boredom and anxiety*. Jossey-Bass.

Dabbagh, N. H., Jonassen, D. H., Yueh, H.-P., & Samouilova, M. (2008). Assessing a problem-based learning approach to an introductory instructional design course: A case study. *Performance Improvement Quarterly, 13*(3), 60–83. doi:10.1111/j.1937-8327.2000.tb00176.x

Dreamson, N. (2019). *Critical understandings of digital technology in education: Meta-connective pedagogy*. Taylor & Francis. doi:10.4324/9780429277528

Dunleavy, M., Dede, C., & Mitchell, R. (2009). Affordances and limitations of immersive participatory augmented reality simulations for teaching and learning. *Journal of Science Education and Technology, 18*(1), 7–22. doi:10.100710956-008-9119-1

Dünser, A., Walker, L., Horner, H., & Bentall, D. (2012). Creating interactive physics education books with augmented reality. In V. Farrell (Ed.), *Proceedings of the 24th Australian Computer-Human Interaction Conference* (pp. 107-114). Melbourne, Australia: ACM. 10.1145/2414536.2414554

Edwards-Stewart, A., Hoyt, T., & Reger, G. (2016). Classifying different types of augmented reality technology. *Annual Review of Cybertherapy and Telemedicine, 14*, 199–202.

Efstathiou, I., Kyza, E. A., & Georgiou, Y. (2018). An inquiry-based augmented reality mobile learning approach to fostering primary school students' historical reasoning in non-formal settings. *Interactive Learning Environments, 26*(1), 22–41. doi:10.1080/10494820.2016.1276076

El Kouzi, M., Mao, A., & Zambrano, D. (2019, March). An educational augmented reality application for elementary school students focusing on the human skeletal system. In *2019 IEEE Conference on Virtual Reality and 3D User Interfaces (VR)* (pp. 1594-1599). IEEE. 10.1109/VR.2019.8798058

Ewais, A., & Troyer, O. D. (2019). A usability and acceptance evaluation of the use of augmented reality for learning atoms and molecules reaction by primary school female students in Palestine. *Journal of Educational Computing Research, 57*(7), 1643–1670. doi:10.1177/0735633119855609

Fokides, E., & Mastrokoukou, A. (2018). Results from a study for teaching human body systems to primary school students using tablets. *Contemporary Educational Technology, 9*(2), 154–170. doi:10.30935/cet.414808

Furdu, I., Tomozei, C., & Köse, U. (2017). Pros and cons gamification and gaming in classroom. *Broad Research in Artificial Intelligence and Neuroscience, 8*(2), 56–62.

Gagnier, K., & Fisher, K. (2016). *Spatial thinking: A missing building block in STEM education*. John Hopkins Institute for Educational Policy.

Gardeli, A., & Vosinakis, S. (2019, September). ARQuest: A tangible augmented reality approach to developing computational thinking skills. In *11th International Conference on Virtual Worlds and Games for Serious Applications (VS-Games)* (pp. 1-8). IEEE. 10.1109/VS-Games.2019.8864603

Gerstein, J. S. (2019). *Learning in the making: How to plan, execute, and assess powerful makerspace lessons*. ASCD.

Gough, D., Oliver, S., & Thomas, J. (2017). *An introduction to systematic reviews*. SAGE.

Green, M., McNair, L., Pierce, C., & Harvey, C. (2019). An investigation of augmented reality picture books: Meaningful experiences or missed opportunities? *Journal of Educational Multimedia and Hypermedia, 28*(4), 357–380.

Hashim, H. (2018). Application of technology in the digital era education. *International Journal of Research in Counseling and Education, 2*(1), 1–5. doi:10.24036/002za0002

Heinzen, T. E., Gordon, M. S., Landrum, R. E., Gurung, R. A. R., Dunn, D. S., & Richman, S. (2015). A parallel universes psychological science in the language of game design. In T. Reiners & L. C. Wood (Eds.), *Gamification in education and business* (pp. 133–151). Springer. doi:10.1007/978-3-319-10208-5_7

Hennel, P., Schmidt-Kraepelin, M., van den Eynden, S., & Basten, D. (2015). Benefits of augmented reality in educational environments – A systematic literature review. *Benefits, 3*(6), 1542–1556.

Hmelo-Silver, C. E., Bridges, S. M., & McKeown, J. M. (2019). Facilitating problem-based learning. In M. Moalem, W. Hung, & N. Daggagh (Eds.), *The Wiley handbook of problem-based learning* (pp. 297–319). Wiley. doi:10.1002/9781119173243.ch13

Hsu, T. C. (2019). Effects of gender and different augmented reality learning systems on English vocabulary learning of elementary school students. *Universal Access in the Information Society, 18*(2), 315–325. doi:10.100710209-017-0593-1

Hu, J., Kim, J., Song, K., Lockee, B., & Burton, J. (2018). *Gamification in learning and education: Enjoy learning like gaming*. Springer.

Ifenthaler, D., & Eseryel, D. (2013). Facilitating complex learning by mobile augmented reality learning environments. In R. H. Kinshuk, J. M. Spector, & Kinshuk (Eds.), Reshaping learning: Frontiers of learning technology in a global context (pp. 415-438). New York, NY: Springer. doi:10.1007/978-3-642-32301-0_18

Jonassen, D. H. (2010, September). Research issues in problem solving. In *11th International Conference on Education Research.* New Educational Paradigm for Learning and Instruction. https://www.aect.org/publications/whitepapers/2010/JonassenICER.pdf

Kang, Y., & Yang, K. C. (2020). Employing digital reality technologies in art exhibitions and museums: A global survey of best practices and implications. In *Virtual and augmented reality in education, art, and museums* (pp. 139–161). IGI Global. doi:10.4018/978-1-7998-1796-3.ch008

Kapp, K. M. (2012). *The gamification of learning and instruction: Game-based methods and strategies for training and education*. Pfeiffer.

Karagozlu, D. (2018). Determination of the impact of augmented reality application on the success and problem-solving skills of students. *Quality & Quantity, 52*(5), 2393–2402. doi:10.100711135-017-0674-5

Kaufmann, H., Schmalstieg, D., & Wagner, M. (2000). Construct3D: A virtual reality application for mathematics and geometry education. *Education and Information Technologies, 5*(4), 263–276. doi:10.1023/A:1012049406877

Klopfer, E., & Squire, K. (2008). Environmental detectives—The development of an augmented reality platform for environmental simulations. *Educational Technology Research and Development, 56*(2), 203–228. doi:10.100711423-007-9037-6

Limelight Networks. (2020). *The state of online gaming 2020.* https://www.limelight.com/resources/white-paper/state-of-online-gaming-2020/

López-Faican, L., & Jaen, J. (2020). Emofindar: Evaluation of a mobile multiplayer augmented reality game for primary school children. *Computers & Education, 149*, 103814. doi:10.1016/j.compedu.2020.103814

Lu, S. J., Liu, Y. C., Chen, P. J., & Hsieh, M. R. (2020). Evaluation of AR embedded physical puzzle game on students' learning achievement and motivation on elementary natural science. *Interactive Learning Environments, 28*(4), 451–463. doi:10.1080/10494820.2018.1541908

Luis, C. E. M., Mellado, R. C., & Díaz, B. A. (2013, January). PBL methodologies with embedded augmented reality in higher maritime education: Augmented project definitions for chemistry practices. In J. Martin-Gutierrez & E. Ginters (Eds.), *VARE* (pp. 402–405). Elsevier. doi:10.1016/j.procs.2013.11.050

McGee, M. G. (1979). Human spatial abilities: Psychometric studies and environmental, genetic, hormonal, and neurological influences. *Psychological Bulletin, 86*(5), 889–918. doi:10.1037/0033-2909.86.5.889 PMID:386403

Moreno, R., & Mayer, R. E. (1999). Cognitive principles of multimedia learning: The role of modality and contiguity. *Journal of Educational Psychology, 91*(2), 358–368. doi:10.1037/0022-0663.91.2.358

Newcombe, N. S. (2016). Thinking spatially in the science classroom. *Current Opinion in Behavioral Sciences, 10*, 1–6. doi:10.1016/j.cobeha.2016.04.010

Niu, B., Liu, C., Liu, J., Deng, Y., Wan, Q., & Ma, N. (2019, October). Impacts of Different Types of Scaffolding on Academic Performance, Cognitive Load and Satisfaction in Scientific Inquiry Activities Based on Augmented Reality. In *2019 Eighth International Conference on Educational Innovation through Technology (EITT)* (pp. 239-244). IEEE. 10.1109/EITT.2019.00053

Ntuli, E. (2019). Augmented reality in early learning: Experiences of K-3 teachers with merge cubes. In S. Carliner (Ed.), *Proceedings of e-learn: World conference on e-learning in corporate, government, healthcare, and higher education* (pp. 557-560). New Orleans, LA: Association for the Advancement of Computing in Education (AACE).

O'Brien, N. P., & Collins, J. W. (2011). *The Greenwood dictionary of education* (2nd ed.). ABC-CLIO.

O'Shea, P., Mitchell, R., Johnston, C., & Dede, C. (2009). Lessons learned about designing augmented realities. *International Journal of Gaming and Computer-Mediated Simulations, 1*(1).

Papert, S. A. (1980). *MINDSTORMS: Children, computers, and powerful ideas.* BASIC Books.

Pedaste, M., Mäeots, M., Siiman, L. A., de Jong, T., van Riesen, S. A., Kamp, E. T., Manoli, C. C., Zacharia, Z. C., & Tsourlidaki, E. (2015). Phases of inquiry-based learning: Definitions and the inquiry cycle. *Educational Research Review, 14*, 47–61. doi:10.1016/j.edurev.2015.02.003

Pedaste, M., Mitt, G., & Jürivete, T. (2020). What is the effect of using mobile augmented reality in K12 inquiry-based learning? *Education Sciences*, *10*(4), 94. doi:10.3390/educsci10040094

Pellas, N., Fotaris, P., Kazanidis, I., & Wells, D. (2019). Augmenting the learning experience in primary and secondary school education: A systematic review of recent trends in augmented reality game-based learning. *Virtual Reality (Waltham Cross)*, *23*(4), 329–346. doi:10.100710055-018-0347-2

Pepper, C. (2009). Problem based learning in science. *Issues in Educational Research*, *19*(2), 128.

Perrin, A. (2020, May 30). *5 facts about Americans and video games.* https://www.pewresearch.org/fact-tank/2018/09/17/5-facts-about-americans-and-video-games/

Petticrew, M., & Roberts, H. (2006). *Systematic reviews in the social sciences: A practical guide.* Blackwell. doi:10.1002/9780470754887

Prodromou, T. (2019). Introduction. In T. Promodoru (Ed.), *Augmented reality in educational settings.* Brill.

Puentedura, R. (2009). *Transformation, technology, and education* [blog post]. http://hippasus.com/resources/tte/

Puntambekar, S. (2015). Distributing scaffolding across multiple levels: Individuals, small groups, or a class of students. In A. Walker, H. Leary, C. E. Hmelo-Silver, & P. Ertmer (Eds.), *Essential readings in problem-based learning* (pp. 207–223). Purdue University Press. doi:10.2307/j.ctt6wq6fh.19

Rideout, V. (2017). *The common sense census: Media use by kids age zero to eight.* Common Sense Media.

Rosenberg, L. B. (1992). *The use of virtual fixtures as perceptual overlays to enhance operator performance in remote environments.* Technical Report AL-TR-0089, USAF Armstrong Laboratory, Wright-Patterson AFB OH.

Shelton, B. E., & Hedley, N. R. (2002). Using augmented reality for teaching earth-sun relationship to undergraduate geography students. *The First IEEE International Augmented Reality Toolkit Workshop* (pp. 1-8). Darmstadt, Germany: IEEE. 10.1109/ART.2002.1106948

Sotiriou, S., & Bogner, F. X. (2008). Visualizing the invisible: Augmented reality as an innovative science education scheme. *Advanced Science Letters*, *1*(1), 114–122. doi:10.1166/asl.2008.012

Stewart, M. K., Hagood, D. E., & Ching, C. C. (2020). Using multi-modal data to examine equity in activity-monitor gaming within real-world communities. In M. Farber (Ed.), *Global perspectives on gameful and playful teaching and learning* (pp. 118–142). IGI Global. doi:10.4018/978-1-7998-2015-4.ch006

Stylianidou, N., Sofianidis, A., Manoli, E., & Meletiou-Mavrotheris, M. (2020). "Helping Nemo!"—Using augmented reality and alternate reality games in the context of universal design for learning. *Education Sciences*, *10*(4), 95. doi:10.3390/educsci10040095

Sweller, J. (1988). Cognitive load during problem solving: Effects on learning. *Cognitive Science*, *12*(2), 257–285. doi:10.120715516709cog1202_4

Sweller, J., van Merrienboer, J., & Paas, F. (1998). Cognitive architecture and instructional design. *Educational Psychology Review*, *10*(3), 251–296. doi:10.1023/A:1022193728205

Thees, M., Kapp, S., Strzys, M. P., Beil, F., Lukowicz, P., & Kuhn, J. (2020). Effects of augmented reality on learning and cognitive load in university physics laboratory courses. *Computers in Human Behavior, 108*, 106316. doi:10.1016/j.chb.2020.106316

Tomara, M., & Gouscos, D. (2019). A Case Study: Visualizing Coulomb Forces With the Aid of Augmented Reality. *Journal of Educational Computing Research, 57*(7), 1626–1642. doi:10.1177/0735633119854023

Wang, M., Callaghan, V., Bernhardt, J., White, K., & Peña-Rios, A. (2017). Augmented reality in education and training: Pedagogical approaches and illustrative case studies. *Journal of Ambient Intelligence and Humanized Computing, 9*(5), 1391–1402. doi:10.100712652-017-0547-8

Ware, C. (2005). Visual queries: The foundation of visual thinking. In *Knowledge and information visualization* (pp. 27–35). Springer. doi:10.1007/11510154_2

Weerasinghe, M., Quigley, A., Ducasse, J., Pucihar, K. Č., & Kljun, M. (2019). Educational augmented reality games. In V. Geroimenko (Ed.), *Augmented reality games II* (pp. 3–32). Springer. doi:10.1007/978-3-030-15620-6_1

Wojciechowski, R., & Cellary, W. (2013). Evaluation of learners' attitude toward learning in ARIES augmented reality environments. *Computers & Education, 68*, 570–585. doi:10.1016/j.compedu.2013.02.014

Wu, H. K., Lee, S. W. Y., Chang, H. Y., & Liang, J. C. (2013). Current status, opportunities and challenges of augmented reality in education. *Computers & Education, 62*, 41–49. doi:10.1016/j.compedu.2012.10.024

Wu, P. H., Hwang, G. J., Yang, M. L., & Chen, C. H. (2018). Impacts of integrating the repertory grid into an augmented reality-based learning design on students' learning achievements, cognitive load and degree of satisfaction. *Interactive Learning Environments, 26*(2), 221–234. doi:10.1080/10494820.2017.1294608

Yuliono, T., Sarwanto, & Rintayati, P. (2018). The promising roles of augmented reality in educational setting: A review of the literature. *International Journal of Educational Methodology, 4*(3), 125–132.

Zawacki-Richter, O., Kerres, M., Bedenlier, S., Bond, M., & Buntins, K. (2020). *Systematic reviews in educational research: Methodology, perspectives and application.* Springer. doi:10.1007/978-3-658-27602-7

ADDITIONAL READING

Amir, M. F., Fediyanto, N., Rudyanto, H. E., Afifah, D. S. N., & Tortop, H. S. (2020). Elementary students' perceptions of 3Dmetric: A cross-sectional study. *Heliyon, 6*(6), e04052. doi:10.1016/j.heliyon.2020.e04052 PMID:32577547

Baran, B., Yecan, E., Kaptan, B., & Paşayiğit, O. (2019). Using augmented reality to teach fifth grade students about electrical circuits. *Education and Information Technologies*, 1–15.

Bhagat, K. K., Liou, W. K., Michael Spector, J., & Chang, C. Y. (2019). To use augmented reality or not in formative assessment: A comparative study. *Interactive Learning Environments, 27*(5-6), 830–840. doi:10.1080/10494820.2018.1489857

Bratitsis, T., Bardanika, P., & Ioannou, M. (2017, July). Science education and augmented reality content: the case of the water circle. In *IEEE 17th International Conference on Advanced Learning Technologies (ICALT)* (pp. 485-489). IEEE. 10.1109/ICALT.2017.64

Bressler, D. M., Bodzin, A. M., & Tutwiler, M. S. (2019). Engaging secondary students in scientific practice with a collaborative mobile game. *Journal of Computer Assisted Learning, 35*(2), 197–207. doi:10.1111/jcal.12321

Buchner, J., & Zumbach, J. (2018). *Promoting intrinsic motivation with a mobile augmented reality learning environment.* International Association for Development of the Information Society.

Bursali, H., & Yilmaz, R. M. (2019). Effect of augmented reality applications on secondary school students' reading comprehension and learning permanency. *Computers in Human Behavior, 95*, 126–135. doi:10.1016/j.chb.2019.01.035

Cai, S., Chiang, F. K., Sun, Y., Lin, C., & Lee, J. J. (2017). Applications of augmented reality-based natural interactive learning in magnetic field instruction. *Interactive Learning Environments, 25*(6), 778–791. doi:10.1080/10494820.2016.1181094

Cai, S., Liu, E., Yang, Y., & Liang, J. C. (2019). Tablet-based AR technology: Impacts on students' conceptions and approaches to learning mathematics according to their self-efficacy. *British Journal of Educational Technology, 50*(1), 248–263. doi:10.1111/bjet.12718

Chang, H. Y., Hsu, Y. S., & Wu, H. K. (2016). A comparison study of augmented reality versus interactive simulation technology to support student learning of a socio-scientific issue. *Interactive Learning Environments, 24*(6), 1148–1161. doi:10.1080/10494820.2014.961486

Chang, H.-Y., Hsu, Y.-S., Wu, H.-K., & Tsai, C.-C. (2018). Students' development of socio-scientific reasoning in a mobile augmented reality learning environment. *International Journal of Science Education, 40*(12), 1410–1431. doi:10.1080/09500693.2018.1480075

Chang, H. Y., Liang, J. C., & Tsai, C. C. (2020). Students' context-specific epistemic justifications, prior knowledge, engagement, and socioscientific reasoning in a mobile augmented reality learning environment. *Journal of Science Education and Technology, 29*(3), 399–408. doi:10.100710956-020-09825-9

Chang, H. Y., Lin, Y. K., Fang, R. J., & Lu, Y. T. (2017). Errata: A situated cultural festival learning system based on motion sensing. *Eurasia Journal of Mathematics, Science and Technology Education, 13*(5), 1411–1411. doi:10.12973/eurasia.2017.00677a

Chang, R.-C., Chung, L.-Y., & Huang, Y.-M. (2016). Developing an interactive augmented reality system as a complement to plant education and comparing its effectiveness with video learning. *Interactive Learning Environments, 24*(6), 1245–1264. doi:10.1080/10494820.2014.982131

Chang, S. C., & Hwang, G. J. (2018). Impacts of an augmented reality-based flipped learning guiding approach on students' scientific project performance and perceptions. *Computers & Education*, *125*, 226–239. doi:10.1016/j.compedu.2018.06.007

Chen, C., Huang, C., & Chou, Y. (2019). Effects of augmented reality-based multidimensional concept maps on students' learning achievement, motivation and acceptance. *Universal Access in the Information Society*, *18*(2), 257–268. doi:10.100710209-017-0595-z

Chen, C. H. (2020). AR videos as scaffolding to foster students' learning achievements and motivation in EFL learning. *British Journal of Educational Technology*, *51*(3), 657–672. doi:10.1111/bjet.12902

Chen, C.-H., Chou, Y.-Y., & Huang, C.-Y. (2016). An augmented-reality-based concept map to support mobile learning for science. *The Asia-Pacific Education Researcher*, *25*(4), 567–578. doi:10.100740299-016-0284-3

Chen, M. B., Wang, S. G., Chen, Y. N., Chen, X. F., & Lin, Y. Z. (2020). A preliminary study of the influence of game types on the learning interests of primary school students in digital games. *Education Sciences*, *10*(4), 96. doi:10.3390/educsci10040096

Chen, M. P., Wang, L. C., Lin, S. Y., Zou, D., Xie, H., & Tsai, C. C. (2019, July). Enhancing contextualized learning via AR. In *8th International Congress on Advanced Applied Informatics (IIAI-AAI)* (pp. 286-289). IEEE. 10.1109/IIAI-AAI.2019.00064

Chen, R. W., & Chan, K. K. (2019). Using augmented reality flashcards to learn vocabulary in early childhood education. *Journal of Educational Computing Research*, *57*(7), 1812–1831. doi:10.1177/0735633119854028

Chen, S. Y., & Liu, S. Y. (2020). Using augmented reality to experiment with elements in a chemistry course. *Computers in Human Behavior*, *111*, 106418. doi:10.1016/j.chb.2020.106418

Chen, Y. C. (2019). Effect of mobile augmented reality on learning performance, motivation, and math anxiety in a math course. *Journal of Educational Computing Research*, *57*(7), 1695–1722. doi:10.1177/0735633119854036

Cheng, Y. W., Wang, Y., Cheng, I. L., & Chen, N. S. (2019). An in-depth analysis of the interaction transitions in a collaborative augmented reality-based mathematic game. *Interactive Learning Environments*, *27*(5-6), 782–796. doi:10.1080/10494820.2019.1610448

Chu, H. C., & Sung, Y. H. (2016, July). A context-aware progressive inquiry-based augmented reality system to improving students' investigation learning abilities for high school geography courses. In *5th IIAI International Congress on Advanced Applied Informatics (IIAI-AAI)* (pp. 353-356). IEEE. 10.1109/IIAI-AAI.2016.112

Cook, M. J. (2019). Augmented reality: Examining its value in a music technology classroom. Practice and potential. *Waikato Journal of Education*, *24*(2), 23–38. doi:10.15663/wje.v24i2.687

Dalim, C. S. C., Sunar, M. S., Dey, A., & Billinghurst, M. (2020). Using augmented reality with speech input for non-native children's language learning. *International Journal of Human-Computer Studies*, *134*, 44–64. doi:10.1016/j.ijhcs.2019.10.002

Dehghani, M., Mohammadhasani, N., Hoseinzade Ghalevandi, M., & Azimi, E. (2020). Applying AR-based infographics to enhance learning of the heart and cardiac cycle in biology class. *Interactive Learning Environments*, 1–16. doi:10.1080/10494820.2020.1765394

Demitriadou, E., Stavroulia, K. E., & Lanitis, A. (2020). Comparative evaluation of virtual and augmented reality for teaching mathematics in primary education. *Education and Information Technologies*, *25*(1), 381–401. doi:10.100710639-019-09973-5

Efstathiou, I., Kyza, E. A., & Georgiou, Y. (2018). An inquiry-based augmented reality mobile learning approach to fostering primary school students' historical reasoning in non-formal settings. *Interactive Learning Environments*, *26*(1), 22–41. doi:10.1080/10494820.2016.1276076

El Kouzi, M., Mao, A., & Zambrano, D. (2019, March). An educational augmented reality application for elementary school students focusing on the human skeletal system. In *2019 IEEE Conference on Virtual Reality and 3D User Interfaces (VR)* (pp. 1594-1599). IEEE. 10.1109/VR.2019.8798058

Erbas, C., & Demirer, V. (2019). The effects of augmented reality on students' academic achievement and motivation in a biology course. *Journal of Computer Assisted Learning*, *35*(3), 450–458. doi:10.1111/jcal.12350

Ewais, A., & Troyer, O. D. (2019). A usability and acceptance evaluation of the use of augmented reality for learning atoms and molecules reaction by primary school female students in Palestine. *Journal of Educational Computing Research*, *57*(7), 1643–1670. doi:10.1177/0735633119855609

Fidan, M., & Tuncel, M. (2019). Integrating augmented reality into problem-based learning: The effects on learning achievement and attitude in physics education. *Computers & Education*, *142*, 103635. doi:10.1016/j.compedu.2019.103635

Fokides, E., & Mastrokoukou, A. (2018). Results from a study for teaching human body systems to primary school students using tablets. *Contemporary Educational Technology*, *9*(2), 154–170. doi:10.30935/cet.414808

Gardeli, A., & Vosinakis, S. (2019, September). ARQuest: A tangible augmented reality approach to developing computational thinking skills. In *11th International Conference on Virtual Worlds and Games for Serious Applications (VS-Games)* (pp. 1-8). IEEE. 10.1109/VS-Games.2019.8864603

Gecu-Parmaksiz, Z., & Delialioglu, O. (2019). Augmented reality-based virtual manipulatives versus physical manipulatives for teaching geometric shapes to preschool children. *British Journal of Educational Technology*, *50*(6), 3376–3390. doi:10.1111/bjet.12740

Herpich, F., Nunes, F. B., De Lima, J. V., & Tarouco, L. M. R. (2018, December). Augmented reality game in geography: An orientation activity to elementary education. In *International Conference on Computational Science and Computational Intelligence (CSCI)* (pp. 601-606). IEEE. 10.1109/CSCI46756.2018.00121

Hod, Y., & Twersky, D. (2020). Distributed spatial sensemaking on the augmented reality sandbox. *International Journal of Computer-Supported Collaborative Learning*, *15*(1), 115–141. doi:10.100711412-020-09315-5

Hou, H. T., & Lin, Y. C. (2017, July). The development and evaluation of an educational game integrated with augmented reality and virtual laboratory for chemistry experiment learning. In *6th IIAI International Congress on Advanced Applied Informatics (IIAI-AAI)* (pp. 1005-1006). IEEE. 10.1109/IIAI-AAI.2017.14

Hsu, T. C. (2017). Learning English with augmented reality: Do learning styles matter? *Computers & Education, 106*, 137–149. doi:10.1016/j.compedu.2016.12.007

Hsu, T. C., & Hwang, G. J. (2016). The application of augmented reality in English vocabulary learning for elementary school students. In M. Spector, B. Lockee, & M. Childress (Eds.), *Learning, design, and technology*. Springer. doi:10.1007/978-3-319-17727-4_28-1

Hsu, Y. S., Lin, Y. H., & Yang, B. (2017). Impact of augmented reality lessons on students' STEM interest. *Research and Practice in Technology Enhanced Learning, 12*(1), 2. doi:10.118641039-016-0039-z PMID:30613251

Huang, T. C., Chen, M. Y., & Hsu, W. P. (2019). Do learning styles matter? Motivating learners in an augmented geopark. *Journal of Educational Technology & Society, 22*(1), 70–81.

Huang, Y., Li, H., & Fong, R. (2016). Using augmented reality in early art education: A case study in Hong Kong kindergarten. *Early Child Development and Care, 186*(6), 879–894. doi:10.1080/03004430.2015.1067888

Hung, Y.-H., Chen, C.-H., & Huang, S.-W. (2017). Applying augmented reality to enhance learning: A study of different teaching materials. *Journal of Computer Assisted Learning, 33*(3), 252–266. doi:10.1111/jcal.12173

Hwang, G. J., Wu, P. H., Chen, C. C., & Tu, N. T. (2016). Effects of an augmented reality-based educational game on students' learning achievements and attitudes in real-world observations. *Interactive Learning Environments, 24*(8), 1895–1906. doi:10.1080/10494820.2015.1057747

Hwang, W. Y., Zhao, L., Shadiev, R., Lin, L. K., Shih, T. K., & Chen, H. R. (2019). Exploring the effects of ubiquitous geometry learning in real situations. *Educational Technology Research and Development*, 1–27.

İbili, E., & Billinghurst, M. (2019). Assessing the relationship between cognitive load and the usability of a mobile augmented reality tutorial system: A study of gender effects. *International Journal of Assessment Tools in Education, 6*(3), 378–395. doi:10.21449/ijate.594749

İbili, E., Çat, M., Resnyansky, D., Şahin, S., & Billinghurst, M. (2020). An assessment of geometry teaching supported with augmented reality teaching materials to enhance students' 3D geometry thinking skills. *International Journal of Mathematical Education in Science and Technology, 51*(2), 224–246. doi:10.1080/0020739X.2019.1583382

Jiang, S., Huang, X., Xie, C., Sung, S., & Yalcinkaya, R. (2020, June). Augmented scientific investigation: Support the exploration of invisible "fine details" in science via augmented reality. In *Proceedings of the Interaction Design and Children Conference* (pp. 349-354). 10.1145/3392063.3394406

Lin, P. H., Huang, Y. M., & Chen, C. C. (2018). Exploring imaginative capability and learning motivation difference through picture e-book. *IEEE Access: Practical Innovations, Open Solutions, 6*, 63416–63425. doi:10.1109/ACCESS.2018.2875675

Liou, H. H., Yang, S. J., Chen, S. Y., & Tarng, W. (2017). The influences of the 2D image-based augmented reality and virtual reality on student learning. *Journal of Educational Technology & Society, 20*(3), 110–121.

Liu, E., Liu, C., Yang, Y., Guo, S., & Cai, S. (2018, December). Design and implementation of an augmented reality application with an English Learning Lesson. In *2018 IEEE International Conference on Teaching, Assessment, and Learning for Engineering (TALE)* (pp. 494-499). IEEE. 10.1109/TALE.2018.8615384

Liu, Q., Xu, S., Yu, S., Yang, Y., Wu, L., & Ba, S. (2019, July). Design and implementation of an AR-based inquiry courseware—Magnetic field. In *2019 International Symposium on Educational Technology (ISET)* (pp. 134-138). IEEE. 10.1109/ISET.2019.00036

López-Faican, L., & Jaen, J. (2020). Emofindar: Evaluation of a mobile multiplayer augmented reality game for primary school children. *Computers & Education, 149*, 103814. doi:10.1016/j.compedu.2020.103814

Lorusso, M. L., Giorgetti, M., Travellini, S., Greci, L., Zangiacomi, A., Mondellini, M., Sacco, M., & Reni, G. (2018). Giok the alien: An AR-based integrated system for the empowerment of problem-solving, pragmatic, and social skills in pre-school children. *Sensors (Basel), 18*(7), 2368. doi:10.339018072368 PMID:30037067

Lozada-Yánez, R., La-Serna-Palomino, N., & Molina-Granja, F. (2019). Augmented reality and MS-Kinect in the learning of basic mathematics: KARMLS Case. *International Education Studies, 12*(9), 54–69. doi:10.5539/ies.v12n9p54

Lu, S.-J., Liu, Y.-C., Chen, P.-J., & Hsieh, M.-R. (2020). Evaluation of AR embedded physical puzzle game on students' learning achievement and motivation on elementary natural science. *Interactive Learning Environments, 28*(4), 451–463. doi:10.1080/10494820.2018.1541908

Montellanos, C., Luis, J., Vásquez, M., Alberto, C., & Salazar, H. (2019, November). Augmented reality mobile application and its influence in Quechua language learning. In *2019 IEEE Sciences and Humanities International Research Conference (SHIRCON)* (pp. 1-4). IEEE. 10.1109/SHIRCON48091.2019.9024860

Niu, B., Liu, C., Liu, J., Deng, Y., Wan, Q., & Ma, N. (2019, October). Impacts of different types of scaffolding on academic performance, cognitive load and satisfaction in scientific inquiry activities based on augmented reality. In *2019 Eighth International Conference on Educational Innovation through Technology (EITT)* (pp. 239-244). IEEE. 10.1109/EITT.2019.00053

Ponners, P. J., & Piller, Y. (2019). Investigating the impact of augmented reality on elementary students' mental model of scientists. *TechTrends, 63*(1), 33–40. doi:10.100711528-018-0366-6

Rossano, V., Lanzilotti, R., Cazzolla, A., & Roselli, T. (2020). Augmented reality to support geometry learning. *IEEE Access: Practical Innovations, Open Solutions, 8*, 107772–107780. doi:10.1109/ACCESS.2020.3000990

Sáez-López, J. M. S. L., Sevillano-García, M. L. S. G., Pascual-Sevillano, M. Á. P. S., Sáez-López, J. M., Sevillano-García-García, M. L., & de los Ángeles Pascual-Sevillano, M. (2019). Application of the ubiquitous game with augmented reality in Primary Education. *Media Education Research Journal, 27*(2).

Sahin, D., & Yilmaz, R. M. (2020). The effect of augmented reality technology on secondary students' achievements and attitudes towards science education. *Computers & Education*, *144*, 103710. doi:10.1016/j.compedu.2019.103710

Sarkar, P., Kadam, K., & Pillai, J. S. (2020). Learners' approaches, motivation and patterns of problem-solving on lines and angles in geometry using augmented reality. *Smart Learn. Environ.*, *7*(1), 17. doi:10.118640561-020-00124-9

Say, S., & Pan, V. (2017). The effect of instruction with augmented reality astronomy cards on 7th grade students' attitudes towards astronomy and academic achievement. *The Turkish Online Journal of Educational Technology*.

Sirakaya, M., & Kiliç Çakmak, E. (2018). Investigating student attitudes toward augmented reality. *Malaysian Online Journal of Educational Technology*, *6*(1), 30–44.

Stylianidou, N., Sofianidis, A., Manoli, E., & Meletiou-Mavrotheris, M. (2020). "Helping Nemo!"—Using augmented reality and alternate reality games in the context of universal design for learning. *Education Sciences*, *10*(4), 95. doi:10.3390/educsci10040095

Sun, K. T., & Chen, M. H. (2019). Utilizing free augmented reality app for learning geometry at elementary school in Taiwan: Take volumetric measurement of compound body for example. *International Journal of Distance Education Technologies*, *17*(4), 36–53. doi:10.4018/IJDET.2019100103

Tobar-Muñoz, H., Baldiris, S., & Fabregat, R. (2017). Augmented reality game-based learning: Enriching students' experience during reading comprehension activities. *Journal of Educational Computing Research*, *55*(7), 901–936. doi:10.1177/0735633116689789

Toledo-Morales, P., & Sanchez-Garcia, J. M. (2018). Use of augmented reality in social sciences as educational research. *Turkish Online Journal of Distance Education*, *19*(3), 38–52. doi:10.17718/tojde.444635

Tomara, M., & Gouscos, D. (2019). A case study: Visualizing Coulomb forces with the aid of augmented reality. *Journal of Educational Computing Research*, *57*(7), 1626–1642. doi:10.1177/0735633119854023

Tuli, N., & Mantri, A. (2020). Experience Fleming's rule in electromagnetism using augmented reality: Analyzing impact on students learning. *Procedia Computer Science*, *172*, 660–668. doi:10.1016/j.procs.2020.05.086

Vedadi, S., Abdullah, Z. B., & Cheok, A. D. (2019, April). The effects of multi-sensory augmented reality on students' motivation in English language learning. In *2019 IEEE Global Engineering Education Conference (EDUCON)* (pp. 1079-1086). IEEE. 10.1109/EDUCON.2019.8725096

Wan, A. T., San, L. Y., & Omar, M. S. (2018). Augmented reality technology for year 10 chemistry class: Can the students learn better? *International Journal of Computer-Assisted Language Learning and Teaching*, *8*(4), 45–64. doi:10.4018/IJCALLT.2018100104

Wang, W. Y., & Huang, Y. M. (2017). Interactive syllable-based English vocabulary learning in a context-aware environment. *Journal of Educational Computing Research*, *55*(2), 219–239. doi:10.1177/0735633116663212

Wang, Y. (2020). Exploring the effects of designing a role-playing game with single and peer mode for campus learning. *Educational Technology Research and Development*, *68*(3), 1275–1299. doi:10.100711423-019-09726-8

Wang, Y. H. (2017). Exploring the effectiveness of integrating augmented reality-based materials to support writing activities. *Computers & Education*, *113*, 162–176. doi:10.1016/j.compedu.2017.04.013

Wen, Y. (2018). Chinese character composition game with the augment paper. *Journal of Educational Technology & Society*, *21*(3), 132–145.

Weng, C., Otanga, S., Christianto, S. M., & Chu, R. J. C. (2020). Enhancing students' biology learning by using augmented reality as a learning supplement. *Journal of Educational Computing Research*, *58*(4), 747–770. doi:10.1177/0735633119884213

Winarni, E. W., & Purwandari, E. P. (2019). The effectiveness of Turtle mobile learning application for scientific literacy in elementary school. *Journal of Education and e-Learning Research, 6*(4), 156-161.

Wu, P. H., Hwang, G. J., Yang, M. L., & Chen, C. H. (2018). Impacts of integrating the repertory grid into an augmented reality-based learning design on students' learning achievements, cognitive load and degree of satisfaction. *Interactive Learning Environments*, *26*(2), 221–234. doi:10.1080/10494820.2017.1294608

Yilmaz, R. M., Kucuk, S., & Goktas, Y. (2017). Are augmented reality picture books magic or real for preschool children aged five to six? *British Journal of Educational Technology*, *48*(3), 824–841. doi:10.1111/bjet.12452

Yu, C. H., Liao, Y. T., & Wu, C. C. (2016, December). Using augmented reality to learn the enumeration strategies of cubes. In *2016 IEEE International Conference on Teaching, Assessment, and Learning for Engineering (TALE)* (pp. 412-418). IEEE. 10.1109/TALE.2016.7851832

Zhang, J., Ogan, A., Liu, T. C., Sung, Y. T., & Chang, K. E. (2016, September). The influence of using augmented reality on textbook support for learners of different learning styles. In *2016 IEEE International Symposium on Mixed and Augmented Reality (ISMAR)* (pp. 107-114). IEEE. 10.1109/ISMAR.2016.26

Chapter 2
Framework for 3D Task Design: An Immersive Approach

Iryna Kozlova
University of Pennsylvania, USA

ABSTRACT

This chapter introduces a framework for the 3D task design. The framework proposes that the process of designing language learning tasks for 3D immersive simulated environments also be immersive. The framework guides designers/teachers who are new to 3D worlds through 10 stages of the design process that incorporates designers/teachers' individual work and their collaboration with colleagues and learners. Following Breen's advice, collaboration with colleagues and learners allows for taking into account some possible interpretations of the tasks to help learners interpret the task as closely as possible to its original plan; it also improves task functionality. Developed for designing 3D language learning tasks, this framework also benefits other disciplines and informs the design of tasks implemented in other virtual environments.

INTRODUCTION

This chapter proposes a process-based conceptual framework for the design of 3D language-learning tasks implemented in 3D virtual environments, also known as virtual worlds, e.g., Second Life, AvayaLive™ Engage, VirBELA. The 3D worlds are multimodal collaborative environments that provide participants with simulated real-life experiences by embodying participants in graphical avatars situated in contexts resembling real-life geographical locations (Cooke-Plagwitz, 2008; Gerhard et al., 2004; Peterson, 2011). Since participants can interact through several communication channels and explore the world around them with others, they can be engaged in "experiential problem solving and complex and spatially distributed forms of collaboration" (Cornille et al., 2012, p. 245).

Task-based learning and teaching (TBLT) has been widely explored both in face-to-face (f2f) and online contexts with an abundance of studies addressing task design (see Breen, 2009; Collentine, 2011; Ellis, 2003, 2009; Ellis et al., 2020; Gánem-Gutiérrez, 2014; González-Lloret & Ortega, 2014; Hartwick & Savaskan Nowlan, 2018; Kozlova, 2018a, 2018b; Kozlova & Priven, 2015; Lan et al., 2016;

DOI: 10.4018/978-1-7998-4222-4.ch002

Lin et al., 2014; Nunan, 2004; Pica et al., 1993; Willis & Willis, 2007 among others). The literature on technology-mediated TBLT acknowledges the fact that technology affects the design of online tasks (e.g., Collentine, 2011; Gánem-Gutiérrez, 2014; González-Lloret & Ortega, 2014; Kozlova, 2018a, 2018b; Lan et al., 2016), but so far, a step-by-step process of task design has only been addressed in Kozlova and Priven (2015).

Kozlova and Priven (2015) show that 3D task design is rather complex because task designers must understand task-based pedagogy and the second language development processes that occur in learners, as well as the following: (1) the purpose and affordances of the 3D environment; (2) the purpose and use of tools embedded in the environment (e.g., voice- and text-based chat, collaboration boards); (3) how 3D technology can be integrated into the task design to facilitate language learning; (4) pedagogical practices appropriate for teaching in this environment; (5) how the geography and space of the immersive environment contribute to the task design; and (6) how learner interaction with the space facilitates learners' language development.

Kozlova and Priven (2015) also demonstrate that it is near impossible to use tasks designed for f2f classrooms in 3D contexts because 3D virtual environments "create learning spaces conceptually different from the face-to-face classroom and web-conferencing environments" (p. 83) by taking learners outside the classroom context and immersing them in a simulated real-life-like world. Since 3D environments are immersive and provide learners and teachers with immersive experiences, *the process of designing tasks should also be immersive.* Teachers who start working with 3D environments may be familiar with the TBLT approach but may *not* be familiar with the immersive approach to 3D task design, which can make for a challenging experience. This chapter provides a background of concepts for (technology-mediated) tasks and task design and introduces a framework for the process-based immersive model of 3D task design. Although this model is based on research on task-based learning in 3D environments, it can be extended and applied to designing tasks for other virtual contexts.

BACKGROUND

By definition (see Breen, 2009; Ellis, 2003, 2009; Ellis et al., 2020; González-Lloret & Ortega, 2014; Nunan, 2004; Pica et al., 1993; Willis & Willis, 2007 among others), tasks are goal-oriented activities with a clear task outcome (e.g., making a shopping list). Although the primary focus is on meaning, learners are to use their linguistic resources and pay attention to form to express meaning. The target forms required by the task may not be explicitly stated, but tasks can be designed to coerce learners to employ them, for example, by requiring learners to use prepositions to describe a room or use the simple past to describe a recent trip. Tasks include some kind of an information gap or a problem, which pushes learners to produce authentic and spontaneous language while attempting to recover the missing information or solve a problem. As learners interact with linguistic input, negotiate meaning and/or form, perform interactional modifications, and scaffold each other, they engage in second language acquisition (SLA) processes that facilitate language learning.

Components of Task Design

While task design has been widely addressed in the literature for both f2f and virtual contexts (e.g., Ellis, 2003; Ellis et al., 2020; González-Lloret & Orgega, 2014; Hampel, 2006, 2010; Nunan, 2004; Robinson,

2009; Rosell-Aguilar, 2005; Skehan, 2018; Willis & Willis, 2007), what task design encompasses can only be inferred. Most of the time, task design frameworks include a set of components that constitute a task. Some of the components have to do with second language learning processes (e.g., students having the opportunity to negotiate the meaning or form), and some are pedagogical in nature (e.g., the sequence of the activities or the roles of teacher and students). Nunan's (2004) framework, for example, includes components such as a task goal, input, sequence of activities to achieve the task goal, teacher and learner role in the task, and task settings, e.g., group work in a f2f classroom. Ellis's (2003) framework similarly incorporates a task goal, input, and settings, which he calls procedures. He also adds components such as the task outcome, linguistic and cognitive processes occurring in learners, and conditions or "the ways information is presented" (p. 21).

The task design frameworks developed by Willis and Willis (2007), Skehan (2018), and Robinson (2009) differ from Ellis's (2003) and Nunan's (2004) frameworks in that they emphasize a pedagogical sequence within a task. Willis and Willis (2007) regard a task as a cycle, which opens with pre-task activities preparing learners for the target task(s) and concludes with post-tasks in which learners share what they have accomplished in the task and practice the target language.

Skehan's (2018) task sequence also starts with pre-task activities that focus on the target forms. These activities facilitate learner integration of new linguistic features and help restructure existing knowledge. Knowledge restructuring reduces learner cognitive load and allows learners to pay more attention to expressing the meaning rather than how to use the form. The goal of the second stage, during the task performance, is balancing accuracy and fluency. This can be achieved by manipulating factors such as time required for the task completion, its modality (spoken or written), number of participants, the importance of doing the task correctly, and learner influence on the implementation of the task. Post-task activities constitute the next two stages. The first post-stage—repeating the task performance in front of peers, task analysis, or post-task tests—can direct learners' attention to accuracy. The second post-stage engages learners in tasks similar to the one they have completed and requires learners to analyze the tasks and synthesize their goals. Skehan argues that it is important for learners to explore and re-examine the task sequences because these post-task activities "driv[e] forward instruction" (p. 31). Robinson (2009) suggests that task sequence should take into consideration the complexity of the task features (e.g., description vs. reasoning) that can be maneuvered to make the task more or less cognitively demanding, participation features, and learner individual abilities (e.g., motivation, proficiency level, intelligence).

Components of the Technology-Mediated Task Design

Scholars agree that technology-mediated TBLT should take into consideration the affordances of virtual environments as well as the variety of communication channels and other features inherent to specific virtual environments. Some task design frameworks for technology-mediated tasks, however, do not seem to incorporate technology components into the task design or explain how technology should mediate communication and collaboration or be used for co-construction of the task products. Chapelle's (2003) framework, for instance, draws on frameworks by Pica et al. (1993) and Skehan (Skehan, 1996; Skehan & Foster, 2001) and adds some components from research on language learning with technology. These components, i.e., computer knowledge and learner ability to search for information, are not elements of the task design; however, they are skills that learners need to have to participate in online learning.

Hampel (2010) combines Ellis's (2003) and Oxford's (2006) task design features – a goal, task types, importance of the task, input, conditions, linguistic and cognitive complexity, task procedures, predicted outcomes, and roles of teacher and learner. Similar to Chapelle (2003), Hampel (2010) does not explain how all these components can be integrated with a technology-mediated task. Inspired by the research on task-based learning, González-Lloret and Ortega (2014) identify five key task features "in the context of technology-and-task integration" (p. 5), but these features—focus on meaning, goal orientation, learner-centeredness, holism, and reflective learning—apply to the task design in any environment, virtual or f2f. Although technology-related components are missing from the technology-mediated task framework, incorporating technology components in the task design is extremely important because tasks designed for one virtual environment may not be transferable to another virtual context since the affordances available in each environment may not be the same.

Researchers working with 3D immersive environments report that some technology-related components can affect how tasks are carried out. These components include (1) virtual geographical locations and landmarks (e.g., Deutschmann et al., 2009; Gánem-Gutiérrez, 2014; Hartwick & Savaskan Nowlan, 2018; Kozlova & Priven, 2015; Panichi & Deutschmann, 2012); (2) communication channels available in the environment (e.g., Kozlova, 2018a, 2018b; Kozlova & Priven, 2015; Peterson, 2006); (3) collaboration tools embedded in the environment (e.g., Kozlova, 2018a, 2018b; Kozlova & Priven, 2015; Peterson, 2006); and (4) learner interaction with space (e.g., Collentine, 2011; Hartwick & Savaskan Nowlan, 2018; Kozlova, 2018a, 2018b; Kozlova & Priven, 2015; Lan et al., 2016).

Incorporation of affordances in the task design is extremely important. Matching the task topic with a geographical location, for example, provides learners with cultural experiences (Collentine, 2011), decreases their reliance on imagination, and inspires learners to discuss what they observe (Kozlova, 2018a; Lan et al., 2016). Using different communication channels, such as voice- or text-based chat, allows for the practice of different language skills and attention to form, especially, if text-based channels are used (Kozlova, 2018b; Peterson, 2006). Having learners take notes on collaboration boards draws their attention to form. When learners work together to express ideas, they negotiate meaning and form and exercise various interactional patterns such as sharing information, giving feedback, requesting help, and supporting and negotiating their ideas (Kozlova, 2018b). Learner interaction with space occurs as learners explore the environment, which facilitates not only learner autonomy (Collentine, 2011; Kozlova, 2018a) but also the development of second language (L2) critical thinking skills as learners use the target language to identify the problem and come up with a solution. Since learner interaction with the linguistic input, other participants, and the space is mediated by the technology, the design of technology-mediated tasks, then, should also incorporate the technology-related components; otherwise, task functionality will be compromised.

Moving Towards the 3D Task Design: Characteristics of 3D Tasks

Since virtual environments differ in their purposes and affordances, it is essential to identify specific characteristics of the 3D tasks. While geographical landscape, landmarks, and the space that allows participants to travel in the environment make a 3D world very realistic, for instructional purposes, these features cannot be considered as the only ones that influence the 3D task design.

One of the most important features of a 3D world is communication channels, which determine how users interact. Figure 1 illustrates the immersive platform VirBELA, which allows for audio- and text-based communication. Users can mute/unmute themselves by clicking on the microphone button in the bottom left-hand corner or use the chatbox on the right of the microphone button to send public or private messages to nearby users or globally. Since 3D environments simulate real-life experiences,

Figure 1. Communication channels and collaboration boards in VirBELA.

users' avatars need to be close enough to each other to hear others speak unless they take advantage of the public volume areas, e.g., a stage in an auditorium.

3D environments are designed for collaboration, so the availability of collaboration spaces with collaboration tools is another feature that affects 3D task design. Figure 1 features collaboration boards located on the wall of a building in the downtown area. Both boards can be used as computer screens; learners can access the Internet from each of the boards and access Google Docs to take notes. In addition to being used as collaboration boards, they can also be used to post text, audio, or video input.

Non-player avatars can also be employed as tools for posting input. A woman avatar shown in Figure 2 has three buttons on the right. Learners can use the audio button to access pre-recorded audio files, the text button to read information, or the help button with an image of a light bulb to get different kinds of support, e.g., the definition of an unfamiliar word. Sticky notes, such as the one posted on the left of the non-player avatar in the picture, can be placed anywhere in the environment and used as an input source.

Navigation of the environment is also critical for the 3D task. If a 3D world has a vast territory, it may take much time to travel to some locations. Availability of shortcuts or teleporting stations can save users' travel time. Figure 3 shows that users can choose an intended location from the menu in the top left-hand corner or go through the wall of the teleporting station.

3D worlds simulate a real-world where users can experiment with different identities by changing the appearance and clothing of their avatars and express an array of emotions. Users can choose emotions from the menu in the top left-hand corner or use shortcuts on the computer keyboard. An avatar in Figure 4, for example, shows that she is thinking.

These are only some of the features available in a 3D world such as VirBELA, but they show that 3D environments are very complex systems and their features can influence the task design in the following ways: how learners communicate, collaborate, or move in the environment; what kind of linguistic and visual input is made available and how learners can access them; and how learners can incorporate the

Figure 2. Non-player avatar and a sticky note in VirBELA

features of the environment into their work. Since 3D worlds are so different from other virtual contexts, 3D tasks have some characteristics that do not apply to tasks designed for other virtual environments.

Figure 3. Traveling in VirBELA.

Figure 4. Expressing emotions in VirBELA.

1. 3D tasks are environment-specific. Tasks designed for the environment showcased in Figures 1-4 may not be functional in an environment where multiple communication channels, non-player avatars, sticky notes, collaboration boards or other affordances are not available.
2. 3D tasks require the designer to understand the purpose of the environment and its tools. This is illustrated by the Kozlova's (2018b) study in which one of the task components was learner use of collaboration boards embedded in the 3D world. The collaboration boards were meant to function as computers to access web-resources and a real-time web-based editor MoPad directly from within the environment. Although the functionality of web-resources and MoPad was tested before the task implementation, it was taken for granted that if the boards could be used as computers, then opening several tabs – one to search the Internet and another one to use MoPad—would be possible. However, students were not able to do so. Although the teacher trainees solved this problem by preparing additional collaboration boards in another virtual room, it was impractical and unproductive for students to go back and forth between the rooms. Although the theoretical framework and pedagogy were well incorporated in the task design, poor integration of the tools did not allow seamless functioning of the task.
3. An environment exploration component incorporated in the 3D task facilitates learner language development. The main difference between the 3D context and other virtual contexts is that 3D contexts provide rich visual input. This allows learners to experience the world, make observations, and use their observations to solve problems similar to how the process of solving problems occurs in real life. Environment exploration helps learners to think critically and come up with various solutions together. When sharing their thoughts and experiences, learners produce modified input (Lan et al., 2016) and negotiate meaning, form, and ideas (Kozlova, 2018a, 2018b), which facilitate language development.

4. The simple design of the 3D tasks helps to avoid learner information overload. 3D environments are complex systems that require intensive multitasking, including navigating the environment (e.g., to mute/unmute the microphone, use the computer keyboard to navigate the avatar, type on the collaboration board or in the chatbox, access web-resources), remembering task-related information such as instructions and information from multimodal task input, and employing critical thinking skills. If the task sequence contains many steps, learners may experience information overload that can interfere with their productivity, especially if the instructions are not well chunked or posted on the board (Kozlova & Priven, 2015).
5. 3D tasks' functionality depends on learner familiarity with technology and the activity itself. Although Breen (2009) argues that learners' interpretation of the task depends on their needs, linguistic knowledge, familiarity with the learning context, social settings, and their learning styles, Kozlova's (2018b) and Kozlova and Priven's (2015) studies highlight that learners' interpretation of the task also depends on their familiarity with the technology and the activity in which they participate. The participants in these studies understood the task instructions; however, they did not know how to proceed with the task as they did not know what collaboration involves. Instead of negotiating which information to include in their reports, they each typed a piece of information they found individually.
6. 3D tasks have the potential for the development of learner autonomy. 3D worlds offer opportunities for autonomous learning (Dalton & Devitt, 2016; Deutschmann et al., 2009; Lan et al., 2016; Schwienhorst, 1998) as learners make choices regarding which tools to use, which player- or non-player avatars to interact with, or which information to request or incorporate in their products (Collentine, 2011; Kozlova, 2018a). Although 3D environments can facilitate learner autonomy, Kozlova (2018a) found that not all of the learners use the opportunity to make their own choices. She concludes that to help learners develop this skill, successful completion of a 3D task should be measured not only by learner ability to achieve the task outcome but also by learners' autonomous actions while working towards the task outcome. The task should also clearly communicate the task expectations; if students are to explore the environment, then they need to know what exactly needs to be observed (e.g., oxygen sources in the buildings), and how their observations should be incorporated into the task outcome (e.g., calculation of the oxygen level in each of the buildings).

If these technology-related 3D task characteristics are not taken into consideration, they may unfavorably affect the task design in terms of the task functionality. Therefore, along with theoretical and pedagogical components, integration of technology-related components into the task design is critical as they mediate learning, interaction, and environment navigation.

Towards the Definition of the Task Design

While the task design frameworks discussed in the previous sections identify task components, they do not provide a clear definition of what task design is. Samuda (2015) argues that "although we are gradually accumulating evidence relating to features of the design that impact performance in different ways, we still know very little about what is involved in designing tasks" (p. 279). The frameworks seem to imply that task design refers to the task plan and the components included in the plan. However, task design goes beyond that. Design is defined as "a preliminary sketch or outline showing the main features of something to be executed," "an underlying scheme that governs functioning, developing, or unfolding," or "a plan or protocol for carrying out or accomplishing something" (Merriam-Webster, n.d., Definition 4, 5a, 5b). Based on these definitions, task design can be viewed as a plan showing how various components of the task are combined to function in a particular (virtual) environment (e.g., a 3D world) or "considerations of who does what, when, how well, and in what ways" (Johnson, 2003; Samuda, 2005, as cited in Samuda, 2015, p. 279).

Although tasks are created by material designers or teachers, they are unique in that learners also make contributions to the task design (Breen, 2009). Breen argues that learner re-interpretation of the task objectives, content, procedures, and learning context could occur per the following: (a) learners' own needs; (b) knowledge of the learning content (word meaning, use of language in social settings); (c) knowledge of grammar in the linguistic sense; (d) learner abilities to work with the task information and preferred ways of learning; and (e) their understanding of the learning context. According to Breen, to minimize the range of the learners' interpretation of the task plan and to help them interpret the task as closely as possible to the task work plan, task design should follow the following four principles:

1. Task objectives should match learning needs that are apparent to the learner as closely as possible.
2. Task content should be treated as "*only potential content for learning*" (p. 340). Since individual learners identify the portions of the content that are familiar to them, learner work, then, is organized around the unfamiliar content, which has to be integrated into the familiar content in the process of their task-based learning.
3. Task design could urge learners to analyze what aspects they identified as problematic and what they did to achieve their learning goal. Individual learners approach learning and achieve their learning goals using different procedures, which may help them uncover the most efficient ways of learning.
4. Task design could allow learners to decide how the social and physical context of the language classroom helps accomplish the task goals.

If learners' interpretation of the task impacts the task design, the task design should be viewed as a collaboration between the task designers/instructors and learners. Like learners, teachers may also re-interpret the tasks in the process of implementation. Samuda (2015) observed two instructors teaching the same task and discovered that each of the teachers re-shaped the original plan. One teacher removed the task outcome, thus converting the task into an exercise that "could be stopped at any point without affecting its design or impact" (p. 288). The other teacher made changes to the task content and procedures, thus "intentionally *re-tasking* elements of the original work plan" (p. 288). Kozlova and Priven (2015) also found that teacher trainees make changes to the ongoing task as they learn how to teach in the 3D worlds. When they could not interrupt students' discussion to give oral feedback, they changed the way they provided feedback. Instead of providing input orally, they used text-based chat.

Task design can also undergo revisions retrospectively in response to the challenges encountered during the task. When teacher trainees from Kozlova and Priven's (2015) study noticed that something did not work as planned in one task, they addressed these problems in the task to be taught in the next class session. Although the six tasks designed for the six-week project had different content, they had the same structure and used the same tools for collaboration and interaction. Making such changes helped the teacher trainees improve the functionality of future tasks.

Since task design can be re-interpreted at different stages of its development and implementation, Samuda (2015) recommends the task to be treated as "a *succession* of work plans that come into play in different ways at different points across a lesson or teaching cycle" (p. 281). Her multidimensional model of task design includes four versions of a work plan as it evolves chronologically. The designer's original work plan can be used as a teacher's lesson plan or it can be incorporated into a lesson plan. When the teacher implements the task in the classroom and incorporates changes to the plan in the process of its implementation, then, it becomes a dynamic work plan. The work plan changes into a retrospective plan when changes are made to re-shape the task for future use. Kozlova and Priven's (2015) study also suggests that the task design process is multi-level and spiral with some revisions made at the pre-teaching stage, some in the process of teaching in response to both teacher and student re-interpretation of the task, and some retrospectively to improve future task functionality. Thus, task design "involves considerably more than the constellation of features that make up the initial work plan of a task" (Samuda, 2015, p. 282) and is both a process and a result of a multilevel collaboration of task designers/teachers and learners.

Task Design Process

Although much is known about tasks and task components, there is not much research on how to start developing tasks, especially 3D tasks that require coordination of so many components. Nunan (2004) proposes that task design should start with identifying the goals and objectives of the task, followed by selecting linguistic input, especially, in regards to determining the degree of its authenticity. Nunan argues that the target grammar and vocabulary should not be pre-selected by the teacher but should come from the input so that students can observe how the target forms are used in context and then practice them in the task. The final step in the task design is developing activities. This is when teachers are to decide whether the activities have pedagogical and/or real-life goals, what learners' and teacher roles are, and how learners are grouped.

Willis and Willis (2007) suggest that the task design should start with "plan[ning] a task sequence" (p. 23). First, task designers need to identify the topic and then choose the *target* task(s). The next step is developing so-called "*facilitating* tasks" that are used at the pre-task stage to introduce vocabulary, content, and the task sequence, and at the preparatory stage to engage learners with the "topic and language." While Nunan (2004) and Willis and Willis (2007) offer some general steps in the task design processes, they focus on designing tasks for f2f contexts. The design of the 3D tasks, however, involves a lot of technology-related work (Kozlova & Priven, 2015) and the coordination of various components to make the task functional. The next section introduces the framework for the 3D task design and the process of its development.

DESIGN AND IMPLEMENTATION

Drawing on Kozlova's (2018a, 2018b) and Kozlova and Priven's (2015) research on training teachers to design 3D tasks and use TBLT to teach in the 3D world, an *immersive approach* to the 3D task design is proposed here. This framework is based on the "bottom-up" (Samuda et al., 2018, p. 5) or "*descriptive*" approach to the classroom "researched pedagogy" (Van den Branden, 2016, p. 177). The "descriptive" approach to the study of TBLT focuses on "pedagogical actions and decisions that are taken by teachers and students in authentic classrooms while they are working with tasks" (Van den Branden, 2016, p. 177). Since the studies by Kozlova (2018a, 2018b) and Kozlova and Priven (2015) are "grounded in what happens in the classroom" (Samuda et al., 2018, p. 5) as they explore teacher trainees' "pedagogical actions and decisions" when learning how to design and implement 3D tasks in instructional settings with real students, it is fair to say that the teacher trainees who participated in that pedagogically-oriented project pioneered the way 3D tasks are constructed, and their work can inform classroom research as well as teachers new to this pedagogical context.

As defined earlier, task design is a plan explicating how various components of the task are combined in a pedagogical sequence to function in a particular (virtual) space, and it is both a process and a result of a multilevel collaboration of task designers/teachers and learners. Since 3D tasks are designed for immersive environments, the framework for the 3D task design proposes that *the process of designing 3D tasks is also immersive.* Kozlova and Priven (2015) reveal that most of the 3D task designer's work occurs in the environment because coordination and fine-tuning of all of the task components as well as testing the task functionality is near the impossible outside of the 3D world. Designers may not remember numerous details of the virtual world and may need to often check whether and how learners can use communication and collaboration tools, how they can move from one location to another one, whether they can open and use a real-time editor, and how all these components function in harmony. The *immersive task design process* also helps task designers understand learner experiences with the task, observe how learners interpret the task in the process of its completion and make necessary changes to decrease the divergence between the intended and learner interpretation of the task (Breen, 2009).

Although the present framework is primarily based on the findings of previous research on teacher training in 3D worlds (Kozlova, 2018a, 2018b, Kozlova & Priven, 2015), it also relies on the data collected for the three studies—the six-week project detailed above. The data used here is teacher trainees' wikis in which they collaboratively planned the 3D tasks. Six teacher trainees participating in the project were enrolled in a teacher certification program preparing second/foreign language teachers at a Canadian college. The six tasks that they developed were used over a period of six weeks to help English-as-a-foreign-language learners from Turkey improve speaking skills (see Kozlova & Priven, 2015). The three environments used for this teacher-training project—a college campus, a downtown of a city, and an island—were built on a cloud-based platform AvayaLive™ Engage. All of the environments allowed for both audio- and text-based communication and collaboration on the boards that were used as presentation and collaboration boards and also as computer screens. Player avatars controlled by the participants could walk, run, and express emotions; non-player avatars were not available in the three environments.

As immersive 3D environments are designed for learner collaboration and provide space and tools for collaborative activities, 3D worlds are compatible with the sociocultural approach to language learning and development. According to sociocultural theory, collaboration is central to sociocultural learning because knowledge is socially owned and collaborative practice provides a social context to support individual (L2) development (Donato, 2004; Lantolf, 2000). As learners participate in a *collaborative activity*, they engage in "a synergetic process that can facilitate and indeed promote, the emergence of zones of proximal development among participants" (Gánem-Gutiérrez, 2018, p. 392).

Collaboration organized around collaboration boards is especially valuable as taking notes on collaboration boards keeps learners focused on the problem they solve and draws their attention to both the intended meaning and the form that supports this meaning (Kozlova, 2018b). When taking notes on collaboration boards, learners produce both oral and written input, which, according to Blake (2009), mobilizes the same cognitive processes. This allows for dual language processing, first, when sharing the meaning orally with a group, and then, when expressing the same meaning in a written form on the collaboration board (Kozlova, 2018b). Collaboration also facilitates learners' use and development of various interactional patterns, such as when they share their knowledge, support their position, make requests for information or clarification, and comment on the collaboration process (Kozlova, 2018b), to name just a few. Collaboration, therefore, is an essential component of the 3D task design.

The 3D task design process proposed in this chapter consists of 10 stages. At each of the stages, designers make several design-related decisions. As task design is an ongoing process, task-developers go back and forth between the stages since making changes to one task component may lead to changes to other components addressed at different stages.

Stage 1. Framing the Task

Framing the task, according to Kozlova and Priven (2015), is the first step towards designing a 3D task. Task designers make several decisions at this stage, including choosing a task topic, matching the topic with a geographical location or a feature in the 3D environment that simulates the real world to make the task more realistic, identifying a problem to solve or an information gap to fill in, coming up with a sequence of micro-tasks that will help learners achieve the task goal, determining learner roles in the task, as well as choosing the technology that would mediate communication and collaboration. At first glance, these decisions may create the impression that the entire task design process is completed in the first stage. However, this stage is about creating a general frame for the task and setting a tentative task scenario, which can be revisited and changed throughout the design process as more details are added or changed. Table 1 includes three Stage 1 task scenarios developed by three teacher trainees—Gerri, Joan, and Lynn—participating in the teacher training project. Each of the scenarios incorporates the following components: task topic, task geographical location, anticipated learner roles, environment exploration, task goal, learner collaboration, and outcome.

At this stage, designers also come up with a tentative sequence of the task. The participants of the teacher training project came up with the following sequence (Kozlova & Priven, 2015):

1. Brainstorming engages learners with the task topic and also activates vocabulary on the topic.
2. Research/exploration when learners interact with the input and collect information to solve the problem/fill in an information gap.
3. Preparation for presentation when learners collaborate on the outcome of the tasks, e.g., preparing plans.
4. Presentation stage when learners share their plans with others.

In this task sequence, brainstorming corresponds to the preparatory stage during which learners engage with the topic of the task and activate the vocabulary, whereas the next three stages are parts of the target task as described in Willis and Willis (2007).

Stage 2. Providing Input

In the task, learners interact with linguistic input; they also process information required to solve the task problem or fill in the information gap. In Stage 2, designers decide how the information learners need to achieve the task is presented to learners. For example, in the Canadian Art Exhibition task by Gerri, learners had to collect interesting facts about the selected painting using the Internet. In the Natural Disaster task by Joan, learners were required to interact with the oral input. AvayaLive™ Engage, the environment used for the teacher training project, did not have non-player avatars or sticky notes that

Table 1. Examples of task scenarios

Task components	Canadian Art Exhibition (Gerri)	Natural Disaster (Joan)	Disadvantaged Children (Lynn)
Topic	A special Canadian Art exhibition will take place at the famous Istanbul Museum of Modern Art.	There has been a nuclear accident at the power reactor on the mainland.	Twenty 12-year-old disadvantaged children who had difficult lives (some were sick, others abandoned) are learning how to hope for a better life.
Location	One of the paintings from the collection located in this building should be selected for display in the Istanbul Museum of Modern Art.	People are being evacuated to Tipontia island for safety.	They are coming to Tipontia island for a holiday.
Roles	You are curators selected by a Canadian culture committee to choose art for the collection.	You are an evacuation team.	You are a team that plans activities for these children.
Exploration	As a group, explore the paintings included in this collection and choose one that you would recommend for the Istanbul Exhibition.	As a team, explore the island and make observations of the island and its resources.	As a team, explore the environment and think about how it can be used for the children's vacation.
Goal	Your goal is to choose one painting and convince the committee that it should be included in the exhibition.	Your goal is to determine how the island resources can be used to help people survive on the island.	Your goal is to come up with a plan of how to use the island to help children become healthy, learn to trust others, and gain self-confidence.
Collaboration	Use collaboration boards to prepare a plan of how to convince the committee to select the painting of your choice.	Use collaboration boards to come up with a plan.	Use collaboration boards to come up with your plan.
Outcome	Reasons for the selection of the painting. Speech to convince the committee.	Plan of how to use the island resources. Presentation of the plan.	Plan of the activities. Giving an individual tour of an island to a teacher and explain your plan.

could be posted in the environment. So, Joan used player avatars, by recruiting her colleagues to play the role of park workers, to supply learners with the information about the waterfall, lake, treehouses, etc., upon learners' request.

Lynn, who developed the Disadvantaged Children task, chose learner-generated input. She hoped that learners would generate input for other learners as they came up with creative ideas while exploring the environment. Since some environments, like VirBELA, offer many possibilities for presenting the input, e.g., non-player avatars, collaboration boards, sticky notes, objects, or other player avatars, it could be very difficult to decide which sources of input to choose. Therefore, the designer's choice should be the input source that realistically matches the topic of the task as well as the task goal.

Stage 3. Environment Exploration

3D worlds provide learners with visual and "culturally authentic experience … (e.g., a garden centrally located in a home)" (Collentine, 2011, p. 63). Immersive environments also offer learners the opportunity to experience the environment and engage in "experiential problem solving and complex and spatially distributed forms of collaboration" (Cornille et al., 2012, p. 245). Experiential problem-solving is coming up with solutions using cues from the environment, the same way people do in the real world. For example, in the Natural Disasters task, learners had to find sources of fresh water and food on the island, decide where the evacuees would sleep, and talk about how to use landmarks such as the lighthouse or campfire. When designing the environment exploration component of the task, it is important to understand what exactly students need to observe, how their observations can contribute to the task outcome, what learners could talk about, and what language they will use.

Another decision that task designers make at this stage is how learners will participate in this activity. For example, learners can walk together as a group and discuss what they immediately see, or they can each explore a specific place and share their observations with their group members. Planning this stage outside the environment is practically impossible because designers first need to explore the environment themselves and decide which features of the environment are most relevant to the task.

Stage 4: Collaboration

This stage focuses on how learners will work together, in groups or pairs, and on what communication and collaboration tools learners will use for collaboration. Leaners can use audio- or text-based chat, or both, to interact with their group members depending on which skills (speaking, listening, reading, or writing) are the focus of the task. Some decisions that designers make at this stage include which real-time editor to use, e.g., Google Docs, and which of the collaboration boards to use. Since the territories of some environments are quite vast, it is more practical to choose boards located close to the location where the task is implemented, which reduces travel time and allows students to quickly go back to double-check the environment or make additional observations. Other factors to consider are whether learners know how to use collaboration boards, what collaboration involves, and whether they have prior experience with such an activity. If students are not familiar with this type of activity, then they need to be taught how to collaborate; otherwise, they will not be able to complete the task (see Kozlova, 2018b).

Stage 5: Autonomy

Although this stage had not emerged in the design process of the six teacher trainees, learner autonomy emerged later in the process of task implementation (see Kozlova, 2018a). After adding most of the components of the 3D task, Stage 5 is the time to double-check if the task design inspires learners to take control of their learning. Kozlova (2018a) argues that "[l]earner autonomy can take various shapes depending on the affordances available in a 3D environment" (p. 69). Therefore, it is important to identify what kind of learner actions would be considered as autonomous, e.g., searching for additional information on the Internet or paying attention to various details in the environment.

Some learners require training on how to become autonomous (Nunan, 1997), so it would be helpful to have the expectations explicitly stated. If learners are to explore the environment, then they need to know what exactly to pay attention to; if they are expected to learn new vocabulary, then they need to be instructed to negotiate the meaning of the new vocabulary and to include it in their final report. Most importantly, "reaching the task outcome (e.g., solving a problem) and students taking control of their learning as operationalized in the task (e.g., generating and controlling topics) should be considered as a successful task outcome" (Kozlova, 2018a, p. 69).

Stage 6: Teacher Role

Deciding on the teacher's role is another important decision to make. When learners work toward the completion of the task in a 3D world, most of the time they do not remain in the same location as other learners or the teacher. Even when they collaborate on the collaboration boards, groups may be located in different virtual rooms or places. Because the teacher cannot be at all of the locations at the same time, it is important to think ahead of time about how to stay connected with students, e.g., sending them text-messages to check how they are doing or teleporting to their location. Another challenge for the teacher is providing feedback to students. Since 3D worlds simulate real-life experiences, learners communicate like they do in real life. To maintain the authenticity of learners' real-life experiences, teachers need to consider feedback techniques that occur naturally in real life and do not interrupt the flow of interaction, such as clarification requests or recasting.

Stage 7. Preparing Instructions

Giving instructions for tasks in 3D worlds is almost an art. Because tasks consist of mini-tasks or activities sequenced in a way that helps learners achieve the task outcome, they involve a series of instructions telling learners what to do at each of the stages. If a task requires learners to process L2 input and task requirements simultaneously, remembering all of the information may be cognitively demanding no matter whether the instructions are provided orally or posted on a collaboration board (Kozlova & Priven, 2015). Even if students can revisit the posted instructions at their leisure, it would be impractical and time consuming for students to travel long distances or constantly back and forth within the 3D environment to do so. Some environments may not have enough boards to keep the instructions posted throughout the task.

Often, instructions are taken down so boards can be repurposed after the instructor introduces the task to learners. To help learners remember instructions and avoid information overload, teachers can provide instructions in chunks, before each part of the task. To illustrate, when teacher trainees from Kozlova and Priven's (2015) study divided instructions into several chunks and gave instructions before each part of the task, students remembered the instructions better. Kozlova and Priven (2015) also show that it is equally difficult for teachers to give instructions as it is for students to remember them. To make the practice of giving instructions easier and keep the instructions concise, teacher trainees wrote scripts for their instructions because "it was very difficult for teacher trainees to control avatars, explain the task, give directions in the environment, and manage the classroom" (p. 94).

Stage 8: Testing the Task

Testing the task is critical to the task design process. Because 3D tasks are very complex, it is easy to overlook details. Also, according to Breen (2009), those who engage in the tasks can interpret them in their own ways. Asking colleagues to test the task as if they were learners is very helpful as task-testing may reveal if the task will be interpreted the way it is expected. Testing the task can also generate a lot of helpful suggestions for improvement, but the most important feedback is related to the task functionality because it will be difficult for learners to complete the task if components are not well-coordinated, instructions are not clear, or the task is too complicated.

Stage 9: Teaching Stage

The teaching stage may bring some unexpected challenges that the testing stage may not reveal, so teachers need to be ready to solve problems that may emerge during the task (see Kozlova, 2018a, 2018b; Kozlova & Priven, 2015). Students may not understand instructions or what they are expected to do, or they may have problems with technology, e.g., the real-time editor will not open. Since task design is an ongoing process, the problems students encounter should be documented to be addressed later.

Stage 10: Reflection and Changes

Reflection on and analysis of the task that learners have just completed is very important. This helps teachers review learners' experiences with the task and make all necessary changes to it or to other tasks of similar structure so that the task can be implemented more smoothly in the future. As shown in Kozlova and Priven (2015), teacher trainees reflected on their teaching experience and the challenges they faced during the task. Since their tasks had similar structures, they made changes to the tasks that they taught in the following weeks, which improved not only the design of their tasks but also task functionality and students' participation in the task.

Issues, Controversies, Problems

The immersive framework of 3D task design presented in this chapter draws on the experiences of novice teachers learning how to develop 3D tasks and teach in 3D worlds. While this framework takes into consideration the fact that both learners and teachers may re-interpret the task in the process of its completion or implementation (Breen, 2009; Mori, 2002; Samuda, 2015), this framework does not address the issue of when and how to pre-teach the target structure and vocabulary that learners are expected to use in the task, or the issue of post-task activities used to improve accuracy (Skehan, 2018). The reason for that is that the teacher trainees, whose task development experiences were used for this framework, did not develop the curriculum themselves but were instead provided with the topics as well as with the grammar and vocabulary associated with each of the topics that were included in the course syllabus.

Another issue that needs to be addressed is that the teacher trainees were new to both 3D technology and TBLT, and it is possible that teachers more experienced with TBLT or 3D teaching could approach 3D task design differently. At the same time, even teachers who have experience using technology spend some time to explore, understand, and experiment with a new environment "in the situated contexts" (Haines, 2015, p. 176). This suggests that even though the framework was created using data from the experiences of novice teachers, it could still be a valuable resource for anyone new to working with 3D environments.

The immersive approach to task design brings some controversy over the practicality of the non-immersive approach to the design of computer-mediated tasks. Although the non-immersive frameworks developed by Chapelle (2003), González-Lloret and Ortega (2014), and Hampel (2010) incorporate key components of task design such as the focus on meaning, goal orientation, task outcome, and learner-centeredness, without careful consideration of the affordances of the environment, these frameworks do not guarantee the functionality of a computer-mediated task. As reported in the study of Kozlova and Priven (2015), one of the participants Jack developed a task outside of the 3D environment. Instead of exploring the space and its tools, he took a task originally developed for a f2f context and chose to slightly adjust it for an online context. Although his task was meaning-oriented and learner-centered, and had a goal and task outcome, Jack's colleagues found his task undoable. The tools and the space were not used effectively, and the scenario could not be realistically implemented in the geographical location he had chosen. To be more specific, Jack missed out on an important step of the proposed framework—teacher collaboration and task-testing at the pre-teaching stage of the designing process. This step is extremely important as it reveals task functionality.

However, testing the task in some teaching contexts could be problematic if no one is familiar with the environment. Although online teaching has become mainstream due to global pandemic, not all online environments are equally explored or used. While it would not be difficult to find someone to test tasks developed for the web-conferencing platform Zoom because of its popularity among educators, there are not many educators who use 3D worlds on an everyday basis.

Lessons Learned

The most valuable lesson learned from the teacher training in 3D virtual worlds (Kozlova & Priven, 2015) is that 3D task design is an immersive experience. Because 3D worlds resemble geographical locations and their landmarks feature many details, it is impossible to design a task without exploring the environment, e.g., visiting a room in a building, checking the availability of computers in the rooms, or food in the fridge. Being in the environment while designing a task and exploring the function of available tools is also critical because learner participation fully depends on the functionality of communication and collaboration tools. If a link to a document or an Internet resource does not work, learners will not be able to complete the task. Since 3D task design so heavily relies on the environment and its various features, for 3D designers, an immersive experience seems to be imperative.

SOLUTIONS AND RECOMMENDATIONS

Although 3D pedagogy attracts attention from many scholars and practitioners, our knowledge about how to use these environments for language instruction and, specifically for task-based learning and teaching, remains rather limited. To continue building the knowledge base for 3D task-based instruction including 3D task design, further exploration of these spaces is urgently needed.

One of the areas that is missing from 3D literature is how to use 3D worlds to pre-teach new vocabulary or grammatical structures that students would use in the task. Creating vocabulary games such as a scavenger hunt or problem-solving activities would help learners associate the new word with the objects or activities in the environment. If associations are created during the pre-task stage, it would be easier for learners to retrieve the words during the task when they see these objects or talk about the activities. Teaching and practicing grammar in the environment are also possible. When learning verb tenses, learners can talk about their experiences and observations using the simple past, e.g., I visited a coffee shop downtown and talked to a nurse in the hospital. Since language is learned for communication in the real world, using the simulated world for teaching vocabulary and grammar will help learners practice the target language in authentic contexts.

FUTURE TRENDS

The 3D task design framework presented in this chapter is informed by the research on teaching and learning languages in 3D worlds. Task-based teaching and learning, however, is not exclusive to language pedagogy; other disciplines may benefit from this framework as well. The stages of this task design framework encompass general practices, such as how to frame the task, how to organize learner collaboration, and how to address learner autonomy in the task design. Collaborative learning, which is at the center of the theoretical approach to the immersive 3D task design, is also used in other disciplines and is part of the social constructivist theory of learning. Therefore, this framework is highly applicable to other educational fields. The framework is also viable for use in other virtual environments. Technology-mediated tasks are highly reliant on the features of the specific environments; therefore, designing tasks while being in the environment is important and sometimes almost necessary. This chapter opens the discussion about how the task design can be approached and what path it can take, but more insights from researchers and practitioners are needed to continue this discussion.

CONCLUSION

To conclude, this chapter proposes a framework for 3D task design and shows that the process of designing tasks for immersive environments should also be immersive. 3D environments are sophisticated systems with various communication and collaboration tools for the participants to use in the environment as they travel through the virtual space and work together on a task. With so many technological features and tools available to users, it is easy to overlook important details, which will make the task difficult to complete.

The ten-step framework clearly shows that the affordances of specific environments should be integrated in the task design to ensure task functionality. The steps of the immersive task design are chronologically organized and guide task developers through the entire design process consisting of pre-teaching, teaching, and post-teaching stages. Starting with creating a general frame for the task and setting a tentative task scenario at the pre-teaching stage, designers make decisions on how learners will interact with the linguistic input and with virtual space, how they will collaborate and exercise learner autonomy, and how they will receive instructions and instructor feedback. The teacher role is also to be defined and explained. Testing the task at the end of the pre-teaching stage gives the opportunity to see what needs to be revised. Since learners bring their perspectives to the task design, the teaching stage can illuminate new problems, which can be addressed retrospectively.

Unlike other frameworks for task design, this immersive model takes into account the collaborative nature of task design and shows that task designers, who are typically the teachers implementing the task, and learners contribute to task design by re-interpreting and re-shaping the task both in the process of the task implementation and retrospectively. This framework is developed based on the research on teaching second/foreign languages in 3D immersive environments, but it can be applied in other virtual environments and inform other disciplines interested in task-based pedagogy.

REFERENCES

Blake, C. (2009). Potential of text-based Internet chats for improving oral fluency in a second language. *Modern Language Journal, 93*(2), 227–240. doi:10.1111/j.1540-4781.2009.00858.x

Breen, M. P. (2009). Learner contributions to the task design. In K. Van den Branden, M. Bygate, & J. M. Norris (Eds.), *Task-based language teaching: A reader* (pp. 333–356). John Benjamins.

Chapelle, C. A. (2003). *English language learning and technology: Lectures on applied linguistics in the age of information and communication technology*. John Benjamins. doi:10.1075/lllt.7

Collentine, K. (2011). Learner autonomy in a task-based 3D world and production. *Language Learning & Technology, 15*(3), 50–67.

Cooke-Plagwitz, J. (2008). New directions in CALL: An objective introduction to Second Life. *CALICO Journal, 25*(3), 547–557. doi:10.1558/cj.v25i3.547-557

Cornille, F., Thorne, S. L., & Desmet, P. (2012). Digital games for language learning: From hype to insight? *ReCALL Journal, 24*(3), 243–356. doi:10.1017/S0958344012000134

Dalton, G., & Devitt, A. (2016). Irish in a 3D world: Engaging primary school children. *Language Learning & Technology, 20*(1), 21–33.

Deutschmann, M., Panichi, L., & Molka-Danielsen, J. (2009). Designing oral participation in Second Life: A comparative study of two language proficiency courses. *ReCALL Journal, 21*(2), 206–226. doi:10.1017/S0958344009000196

Donato, R. (2004). Aspects of collaboration in pedagogical discourse. *Annual Review of Applied Linguistics, 24*, 284–302. doi:10.1017/S026719050400011X

Ellis, R. (2003). *Task-based Language Learning and Teaching*. Oxford University Press.

Ellis, R. (2009). Task-based research and language pedagogy. In K. Van den Branden, M. Bygate, & J. M. Norris (Eds.), *Task-based language teaching: A reader* (pp. 109–129). John Benjamins.

Ellis, R., Skehan, P., Li, S., Shintani, N., & Lambert, C. (2020). *Task-based language teaching: Theory and practice*. Cambridge University Press.

Gánem-Gutiérrez, G. A. (2014). The third dimension: A sociocultural theory approach to the design and evaluation of 3D virtual worlds tasks. In M. Gonzalez-Lloret & L. Ortega (Eds.), *Technology-mediated TBLT: Researching technology and tasks* (pp. 213–237). John Benjamins. doi:10.1075/tblt.6.08gan

Gánem-Gutiérrez, G. A. (2018). Collaborative activity in the digital world. In J. P. Lantolf, M. E. Poehner, & M. Swain (Eds.), *The Routledge handbook of sociocultural theory and second language development* (pp. 391–408). Routledge. doi:10.4324/9781315624747-25

Gerhard, M., Moore, D., & Hobbs, D. (2004). Embodiment and copresence in collaborative interfaces. *Human-Computer Studies, 61*(4), 453–480. doi:10.1016/j.ijhcs.2003.12.014

Gonzalez-Lloret, M., & Ortega, L. (2014). *Towards technology-mediated TBLT: An introduction. Technology-mediated TBLT: Researching technology and tasks*. John Benjamins. doi:10.1075/tblt.6

Haines, K. J. (2015). Learning to identify and actualize affordances in a new tool. *Language Learning & Technology*, *19*(1), 165–180.

Hampel, R. (2006). Rethinking task design for the digital age: A framework for language teaching and learning in a synchronous online environment. *ReCALL Journal*, *18*(1), 101–121. doi:10.1017/S0958344006000711

Hampel, R. (2010). Task design for a virtual learning environment in a distance language course. In M. Thomas & H. Reinders (Eds.), *Task-Based language learning and teaching with technology* (pp. 131–153). Continuum.

Hartwick, P., & Savaskan Nowlan, N. (2018). Integrating virtual spaces: Connecting affordances of 3D virtual learning environments to design for twenty-first century learning. In Y. Qian (Ed.), *Integrating multi-user virtual environments in modern classrooms* (pp. 111–136). IGI Global. doi:10.4018/978-1-5225-3719-9.ch006

Johnson, K. (2003). *Designing Language Teaching Tasks*. Palgrave Macmillian. doi:10.1057/9780230596672

Kozlova, I. (2018a). Factors affecting learner collaboration in 3D virtual worlds. In M. Kruk (Ed.), *Assessing the effectiveness of virtual technologies in foreign and second language instruction* (pp. 26–60). IGI Global.

Kozlova, I. (2018b). Task-based language learning and learner autonomy in 3D virtual worlds. In Y. Qian (Ed.), *Integrating multi-user virtual environments in modern classrooms* (pp. 50–73). IGI Global. doi:10.4018/978-1-5225-3719-9.ch003

Kozlova, I., & Priven, D. (2015). ESL teacher training in 3D virtual worlds. *Language Learning & Technology*, *19*(1), 83–101.

Lan, Y. J., Kan, Y. H., Sung, Y. T., & Chung, K. E. (2016). Oral performance language tasks for CSL beginners in Second Life. *Language Learning & Technology*, *20*(3), 60–79.

Lantolf, J. P. (2000). Introducing sociocultural theory. In J. P. Lantolf (Ed.), *Sociocultural theory and second language learning* (pp. 1–26). Oxford University Press.

Lin, T., Wang, S., Grant, S., Chien, C., & Lan, Y. (2014). Task-based teaching approaches of Chinese as a foreign language in Second Life through teachers' perspectives. *Procedia Technology*, *13*, 16–22. doi:10.1016/j.protcy.2014.02.004

Merriam-Webster. (n.d.). Design. In *Merriam-Webster.com dictionary*. Retrieved September 28, 2020 from https://www.merriam-webster.com/dictionary/design

Mori, J. (2002). Task design, plan, and development of talk-in-interaction: An analysis of a small group activity in a Japanese language classroom. *Applied Linguistics*, *23*(3), 323–347. doi:10.1093/applin/23.3.323

Nunan, D. (1997). Designing and adapting materials to encourage learner autonomy. In P. Benson & P. Voller (Eds.), *Autonomy and independence in language learning* (pp. 192–203). Longman.

Nunan, D. (2004). *Task-based language teaching*. Cambridge University Press. doi:10.1017/CBO9780511667336

Oxford, R. (2006). Task-based language teaching and learning: An overview. *Asian EFL Journal, 8*(3), 94–121.

Panichi, L., & Deutschmann, M. (2012). Language learning in virtual worlds: Research issues and methods. In M. Dooly & R. O'Dowd (Eds.), *Researching online foreign language interaction and exchange: Theories, methods and challenges* (pp. 205–231). Peter Lang.

Peterson, M. (2006). Learner interaction management in an avatar and chat-based virtual world. *Computer Assisted Language Learning, 19*(1), 79–103. doi:10.1080/09588220600804087

Peterson, M. (2011). Towards a research agenda for the use of three-dimensional virtual worlds in language learning. *CALICO Journal, 29*(1), 67–80. doi:10.11139/cj.29.1.67-80

Pica, T., Kanagy, R., & Falodun, J. (1993). Choosing and using communication tasks for second language instruction and research. In C. G. Crookes & S. M. Gass (Eds.), *Tasks and language learning: Integrating theory and practice* (pp. 9–34). Multilingual Matters.

Robinson, P. (2009). Task complexity, cognitive resources, and syllabus design: A triadic framework for examining task influences on SLA. In K. Van den Branden, M. Bygate, & J. M. Norris (Eds.), *Task-based language teaching: A reader* (pp. 193–226). John Benjamins.

Rosell-Aguilar, F. (2005). Task design for audiographic conferencing: Promoting beginner oral interaction in distance language learning. *Computer Assisted Language Learning, 18*(5), 417–442. doi:10.1080/09588220500442772

Samuda, V. (2005). Expertise in second language pedagogic task design. In K. Johnson (Ed.), *Expertise in language teaching* (pp. 230–254). Palgrave Macmillian. doi:10.1057/9780230523470_12

Samuda, V. (2015). Tasks, design, and architecture of pedagogical spaces. In M. Bygate (Ed.), *Domains and directions in the development of TBLT: A decade of plenaries from the international conference* (pp. 271–301). John Benjamins. doi:10.1075/tblt.8.10sam

Samuda, V., Bygate, M., & Van den Branden, K. (2018). Introduction. In V. Samuda, M. Bygate, & K. Van den Branden (Eds.), *TBLT as a researched pedagogy* (pp. 1–22). John Benjamins. doi:10.1075/tblt.12.01sam

Schwienhorst, K. (1998). The "third place": Virtual reality applications for second language learning. *ReCALL Journal, 10*(1), 118–126. doi:10.1017/S095834400000433X

Skehan, P. (1996). A framework for implementation of task-based instruction. *Applied Linguistics, 17*(1), 38–62. doi:10.1093/applin/17.1.38

Skehan, P. (2018). *Second language task-based performance: Theory, research assessment*. Routledge. doi:10.4324/9781315629766

Skehan, P., & Foster, P. (2001). Cognition and tasks. In P. Robinson (Ed.), *Cognition and second language instruction* (pp. 3–32). Cambridge University Press. doi:10.1017/CBO9781139524780.009

Van den Branden, K. (2016). The role of teachers in task-based language education. *Annual Review of Applied Linguistics, 36*, 164–181. doi:10.1017/S0267190515000070

Willis, D., & Willis, J. (2007). *Doing task-based teaching*. Oxford University Press.

KEY TERMS AND DEFINITIONS

3D Task: A task designed to be used in a 3D immersive virtual environment.

Immersive Task Design Process: Planning and developing a task while immersed in a 3D world.

Non-Player Avatar: A digital image of a character that cannot be controlled by a player.

Player Avatar: A digital image of a character controlled by a player, or a user of a 3D environment.

Task Design: A plan explicating how various components of a task are combined to function in a particular (virtual) environment. It is both a process and a result of a multilevel collaboration of task designers/teachers and learners.

Technology-Mediated Task: A task that integrates technology in the task design.

Chapter 3
What's So Special About Spatial?
A Review Study Joining Virtual Reality and Spatial Ability

Cigdem Uz Bilgin
https://orcid.org/0000-0001-6997-344X
Massachusetts Institute of Technology, USA

Melat R. Anteneh
Massachusetts Institute of Technology, USA

Meredith Thompson
Massachusetts Institute of Technology, USA

ABSTRACT

Virtual reality (VR) technology has been steadily used for research purposes over the past few decades and is now gaining attraction in educational settings. Spatial understanding of learners is one of these research topics. Although there are plenty of studies focusing on VR and spatial abilities separately, there has not been a comprehensive review of papers that focus specifically on both VR and spatial ability. To address this question, an electronic search of articles from 2015 to 2019 was conducted that found 923 articles, 26 of which met the criteria of specifically discussing 'spatial abilities' and 'VR environments'. Eleven out of 26 articles reported the reason for using VR as a spatial assessment tool. The most frequently-mentioned spatial ability that was studied was mental rotation ability. This review revealed a special link between spatial ability and VR. VR can be both diagnostic and therapeutic for spatial skills; VR is an excellent tool for examining spatial ability in individuals and also individuals can enhance their spatial abilities through using virtual reality.

DOI: 10.4018/978-1-7998-4222-4.ch003

INTRODUCTION

Virtual reality (VR) has steadily increased in popularity over the years as the technology develops and becomes more readily accessible to the general public. VR is an interactive, simulated environment that creates a sense of presence by providing regular feedback to at least one of the senses (Onyesolu & Eze, 2011; Steur, 1992; Woolgar, 2002). Spatial presence, the feeling of being in a real or artificial space, is an important component of high-quality VR experiences (Riva & Waterworth, 2014; Witmer & Singer, 1998). This sense of presence is dependent on the ability of the individual to concentrate selectively on stimuli from the simulation over that of the physical environment (Witmer & Singer, 1998). Immersion, the physical equivalent of presence, is a function of how one interacts with the virtual environment (Slater & Sanchez-Vives, 2016). Immersion is a result of the technological hardware; the more natural the user feels the hardware is to use, the greater the immersion in the VR experience (Atienza, Blonna, Saludares, Casimiro, & Fuentes, 2016; Seibert & Shafer, 2017).

Generally, VR setups involve some type of headset that provides visual, and oftentimes auditory, inputs to the user. This can be supplemented with equipment that provides additional feedback such as haptic stimulation or devices such as hand-held controllers that allow for more seamless interaction with the environment (Sherman & Craig, 2018). Although headsets can cost hundreds of dollars, cheaper alternatives like Google Cardboard, a low budget option that transforms smartphones into VR headsets, have emerged (Brown & Green, 2016). The increased portability and reduced cost have allowed VR to be applied to a wide variety of fields including medicine (Larsen et al., 2009; Laver et al., 2017), the military (McLay et al., 2011; Reger et al., 2011), education (Hwang & Hu, 2013), and cognitive psychology (de la Torre-Luque, Valero-Aguayo, & de la Rubia-Cuestas, 2017).

Spatial ability refers to the wide range of cognitive skills that one uses to interact with the environment and perceive how objects are related within that space (Yılmaz, 2017). Types of spatial abilities include mental rotation, the ability to manipulate objects in one's mind to view them from a different perspective; spatial orientation, the ability to maintain one's heading in space; object location, the ability to recall the position of an object in space; and spatial navigation, the ability to maintain and implement a mental representation of a route that can be used to travel between two points. Some of the most commonly used tests for assessing spatial ability include the Mental Rotation Test (MRT) (Jang, et al., 2017), the Boxes Room Task (Tascón et al., 2017), and the Walking Corsi Test (Wal-CT) (Parsons et al., 2004). Although the majority of spatial ability tests were administered as either paper-and-pencil or website-based assessments in the past, VR versions of several spatial measures have been developed and tested (Nori et al., 2015; Tascón et al., 2017).

Since VR assessments can provide a more valid representation of the real world than paper-and-pencil tests, researchers have begun studying spatial ability of individuals while in VR (Leó et al., 2018; Negut, et al., 2016; Meade et al., 2019). Many studies have focused on the educational aspects of this topic. High spatial ability has been found to correlate with increased learning and academic performance (Cheng & Mix, 2014; Wai et al., 2009), and research suggests that VR environments can be used to help develop spatial ability for students with a lower spatial ability (Lee & Wong, 2014; Merchant et al., 2013).

Several reviews have looked at how VR has been used to identify and treat patients with various spatial disorders, including those suffering from navigational problems (Cogné et al., 2017) and unilateral spatial neglect (Tsirlin et al.,2009). Spatial neglect, the inability to recognize, interact with, and/or orient in respect to stimuli located in a certain half of a person's visible space, results from some type of trauma to the brain such as a stroke (Tsirlin et al., 2009). Although many reviews have compiled and detailed articles relating to some aspect of spatial ability in VR, there has not been a comprehensive review of papers that focus specifically on both VR and spatial ability. The purpose of this article is to fill this gap in knowledge by systematically reviewing articles that have been published on both VR and spatial ability. Specifically, the present study poses the following three research questions:

Research Questions:

Q1. What were the reasons for using VR and what type of VR environments were used in the reviewed studies?
Q2. What types of spatial abilities were mentioned in the reviewed studies?
Q3. What were the characteristics, research purposes, and results of the reviewed studies?

Method

In this narrative literature review, articles that met the inclusion criteria of specifically discussing 'spatial abilities' and 'virtual reality environments' and conclusions were drawn into a holistic interpretation. Four well-known research databases ScienceDirect, ERIC, SpringerLink, and EBSCO, were searched for relevant literature sources. An electronic search of articles from 2015 to 2019 was performed using the query string: "virtual reality" AND ("spatial ability" OR "spatial navigation" OR "spatial orientation" OR "spatial rotation" OR "spatial visualization" OR "spatial presence"). The inclusion criteria were: (1) research articles with a focus on virtual reality and spatial ability (2) were written in English (3) and are journal articles (4) published from 2015 to 2019.

Clarifying the definition of VR was crucial before selecting articles. Virtual reality is "the simulation of a real or imagined environment that can be experienced visually in the three dimensions of width, height, and depth and that may additionally provide an interactive experience visually in full real-time motion with sound and possibly with tactile and other forms of feedback" (Onyesolu & Eze, 2011, p. 53). The search produced 923 articles. After conference papers, duplicates, review articles, editorials, discussions, examinations, and book chapters were removed, the search query led to 182 publications (see Fig 1).

In the second step, titles, abstracts, and main bodies of the articles were reviewed to ensure they met the inclusion criteria and the remaining 26 articles were selected for the present study. Virtual reality relies upon technological tools to simulate rich, interactive environments that engage users' visual, auditory, and tactile senses. Spatial presence, which is the user's perception of the 3D environment as actual, is crucial in VR. One of the factors in spatial presence is immersion, which relates to the technical capabilities of the system (Slater & Sanchez-Vives, 2016). In this respect, articles that described the creation or function of technology were excluded, while articles that focused on how participants learned or were affected by the technology were included. Articles that did not meet or violate the inclusion requirements were further evaluated by both researchers until they came to a 100% agreement about whether to include or exclude the article in the review.

Results

The reviewed studies used VR in three ways:

1. as an assessment tool,

Figure 1. A representation of the literature search

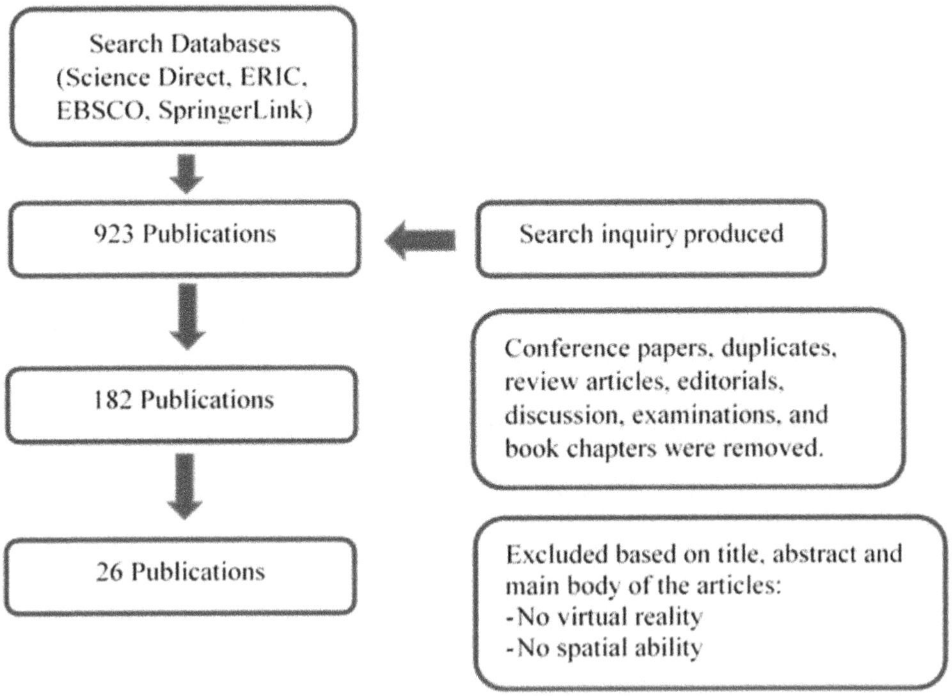

2. as a spatial task tool,
3. as a learning tool (See Figure 2).

Eleven out of 26 articles were coded as having used VR as a spatial assessment tool. For example, Negen et al. (2018) used VR to investigate children`s allocentric reasoning developing process, which is the ability to understand the locations of objects related to other objects. In several of the reviewed articles, both paper-and-pencil spatial ability and VR versions of the tests were used to create more realistic, accurate, and reliable spatial assessments (Ip et al., 2017; Parsons et al., 2004). Several studies tested spatial presence in VR environments (Coxon et al., 2016; Hedge, Weaver & Schnall, 2017; Hite et al., 2019; Seibert & Shafer, 2017). For example, Coxon et al. (2016) investigated whether a significant correlation between spatial ability and spatial presence can be made clear by using VR. Leó et al. (2018) used VR to test spatial memory and mental rotation ability, and Meade et al. (2019) used VR technology to test the difference between active and passive encoding on spatial memory.

The second most common reason for using VR was as a spatial task tool. In these studies, VR was used as a platform to perform spatial tasks including navigating, locating, and rotating objects (Astur et al., 2016; Cao, Lin & Li, 2019; Fabroyir & Teng, 2018; Liang et al., 2019). For instance, in the study of Fabroyir and Teng (2018), spatial behaviors were investigated concerning the virtual navigation preferences and performance of the individuals while navigating the VR environment. The VR environment was an urban touring system, which is a simulation of a street view. Liang et al. (2019) investigated the effect of collaboration and competition activities that are completed within a VR environment on users' navigation behavior and performance in remembering the location of the items.

Figure 2. Reasons for using VR

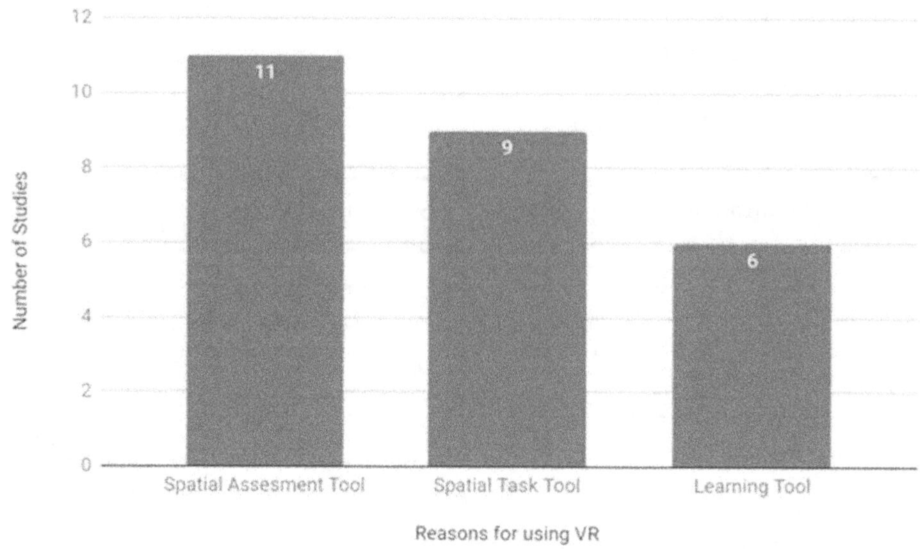

Lastly, VR technology was used as a learning tool in six studies (Abe et al., 2018; Cheng & Tsai, 2019; de la Torre-Luque, Valero-Aguayo & de la Rubia-Cuestas, 2017; Fogarty et al., 2017; Jang et al., 2017; Sun et al., 2018). In the study of Abe et al. (2018), researchers tried to find a relationship between visual spatial ability and robotic suturing skill acquisition in VR by having novices in robot-assisted surgery perform basic skill exercises in a simulated surgery. Jang et al. (2017) compared direct manipulation and passive viewing on learning anatomy using a virtual representation of the inner ear and found that the manipulation group outperformed the viewing group.

VR Environments

Four types of VR environments were mentioned in the reviewed articles:

1. virtual models of common places,
2. VR models of learning environments,
3. VR maze/treasure hunts, and
4. VR games (see Figure 3).

Fourteen studies incorporated virtual models that replicated actual places such as a virtual city (Coxon et al., 2016), shopping mall (Liang et al., 2019), rehabilitation center (de la Torre-Luque et al., 2017), and room (Leo et al., 2018). These environments were generally used for spatial recall, navigation, orientation, and route finding. Six articles mentioned using VR to create learning environments, including a VR simulation of surgery for medical students (Abe et al., 2018), a VR model of the inner ear (Jang et al., 2017), a VR environment for learning about multiple science concepts including the human heart, robotics, and dissection (Hite et al., 2019), a VR model showing buckling in steel columns

Figure 3. Types of VR environments used in the articles

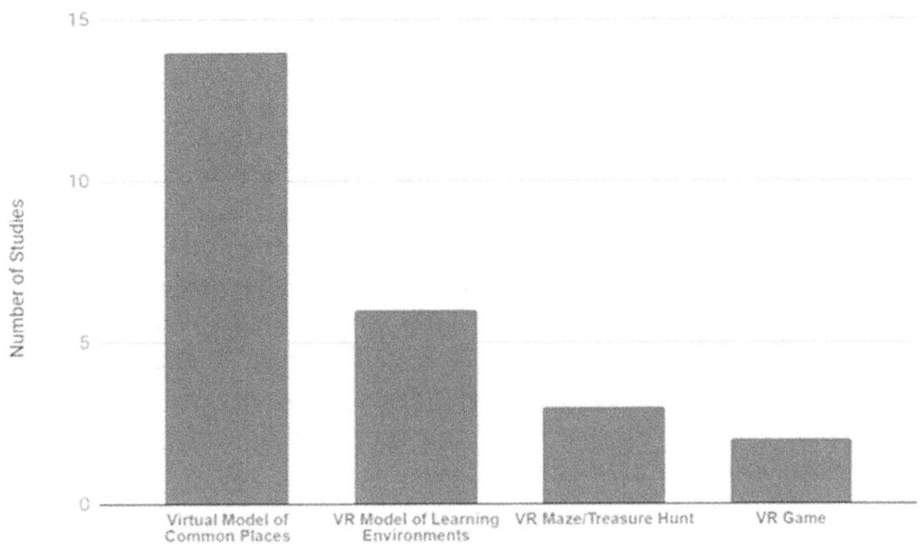

for engineering students (Fogarty et al., 2017), and VR-based modules of the solar system (Sun et al., 2018). In other studies, maze/treasure hunts were used for solving navigation problems, spatial exploration, or investigating landmark uses (Astur et al., 2016; Cao et al., 2019; Farran et al., 2016). In two of the studies, VR environments were used for games, including Bubble Poking and Balloon Poking games and a first-person shooter video game "Half-Life 2" (Ip et al., 2017; Seibert & Shafer, 2017).

Spatial Abilities

Nine types of spatial abilities emerged from the reviewed articles: 1) mental/spatial rotation ability, 2) spatial recall/object location memory, 3) spatial navigation, 4) spatial presence, 5) spatial orientation, 6) spatial visualization, 7) topological memory, and 8) spatial generalization (see Figure 4). Mental rotation, which is the ability to manipulate objects in one's mind to view them from a different perspective, was reported in eight of the twenty-seven studies. Several studies used the terms "visio-spatial ability" and "spatial rotation" synonymously. Studies used different modalities for the spatial assessments; some used paper-and-pencil tests for mental/spatial rotation (Astur et al. 2016; Coxon et al., 2016; Jang et al. 2017), some studies used website based assessment (Abe et al., 2018), and others used VR versions of the mental rotation tests (Leo et al., 2018).

The second most frequently mentioned spatial ability in the reviewed articles was spatial/object recall, which is the ability to recall the position of an object in space. In some of the reviewed articles, VR was used to create realistic environments to assess object recall. For instance, in the study of Liang et al. (2019), participants navigated in a virtual shopping mall and tried to remember the locations of specific items. Astur et al. (2016) measured participants' ability to recall the details of a virtual room. Negen et al. (2018), asked children to remember the location of targets using various cues during an immersive virtual reality task.

The third and fourth most commonly mentioned spatial abilities in the reviewed articles were spatial navigation (Astur et al., 2016; Fabroyir & Teng, 2018; Liang et al., 2019) and spatial presence (Cheng & Tsai, 2019; Coxon et al., 2016; Hedge et al., 2017; Hite et al., 2019; Seibert & Shafer, 2017). For spatial navigation, Meade et al. (2019) used VR to create similar virtual environments (four cities, four malls, four parks) for participants to navigate through both actively and passively navigate. The effects of various other variables on spatial navigation behaviors were also investigated in some reviewed articles.

These were collaboration (Liang et al., 2019), allocentric vs. egocentric navigation preference (Fabroyir & Teng, 2018), landmark use (Farran et al., 2016), and age (Ranjbar et al., 2017). VR environments that create realistic and alternative learning environments were also used for testing spatial presence. Seibert and Shafer (2017) investigated the effect of VR on video game players' feeling of spatial presence. Cheng and Tsai (2019) explored elementary school students' learning experiences in immersive educational virtual field trips, and they investigated the degree of spatial presence of learners in immersive virtual environments. The other spatial abilities mentioned in the articles were spatial orientation (Tascón et al., & Cimadevilla, 2017), spatial visualization (Meade et al., 2019), topological memory (Nori et al., 2015), and spatial generalization (Tascón et al., 2017).

Figure 4. Spatial abilities in the articles

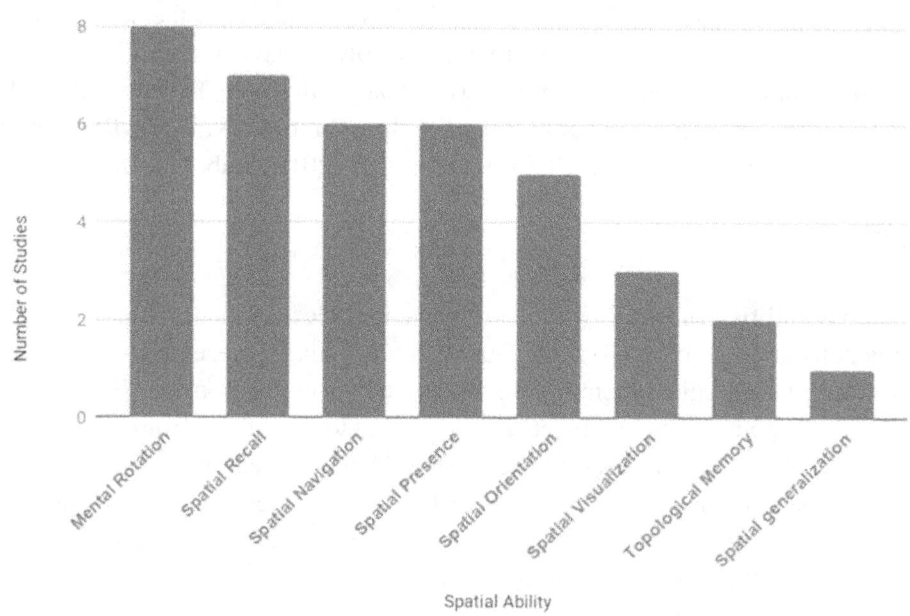

Characteristics of the Studies

The subject domains covered in the articles were divided into the following areas (see Table 1): Cognitive Science (16 articles), Surgical Skills (one article), Anatomy (one article), Engineering (one article), Disability (three articles) and Space (one article). The participants in the studies were mostly in higher

Table 1. Characteristics of the reviewed articles

Reference	Subject Domain	# of Participants	Education Level
Abe et al. (2018)	Surgical skills	21	Higher Education
Astur et al. (2016)	Cognitive Psychology	163	Higher Education
Cao et al. (2019)	Cognitive Psychology	64	Higher Education
Cheng & Tsai (2019)	Social Studies	24	Elementary
Coxon et al. (2016)	Cognitive Psychology	53	Higher Education + Adults
Liang et al. (2019)	Cognitive Psychology	25	Higher Education
Jang et al. (2017)	Anatomy	75	Higher Education
Fabroyir & Teng (2018)	Cognitive Psychology	40	Higher Education
Hedge et al. (2017)	Cognitive Psychology (Spatial)	55	Higher Education
Hite et al. (2019)	Science concepts (e.g., human heart, robotics).	75	Middle School
Fogarty et al. (2017)	Engineering	24	Higher Education
de la Torre-Luque et al. (2017)	Disability	20	People with a severe disability
Farran et al. (2016)	Disability	19	People with WS
Ip et al. (2017)	Disability	36	Kindergarten + Children with special needs
Leó et al. (2018)	Cognitive Psychology	120	Higher Education
Meade et al. (2019)	Cognitive Psychology	44	Higher Education + Adults
Negen et al. (2018)	Cognitive Psychology	21	Kindergarten
Ranjbar Pouya, et al. (2017)	Cognitive Psychology	319	Adults
Lefrançois & Messier (2019)	Cognitive Psychology	14	Higher Education
Pouliquen-Lardy et al. (2016)	Cognitive Psychology	28	Higher Education
Seibert & Shafer (2017)	Cognitive Psychology	207	Higher Education
Sun et al. (2018)	Space	32	Higher Education
Serino et al. (2015)	Cognitive Psychology	30	Higher Education
Nori et al. (2015)	Cognitive Psychology	80	Higher Education
Tascón et al. (2017)	Cognitive Psychology	108	Higher Education

education (16 articles). Others focused on people with adults (three articles), middle school students (one article), kindergarten students (two articles), and severe disabilities (three articles). Seven studies were carried out with fewer than 25 students, twelve studies were carried out with 25-75 students, two studies were carried out with 76-125 students, and three studies were carried out with more than 125 students.

Research Purposes

The research purposes of the articles could be sorted into six categories:

1. Factors affecting spatial performance in VR.
2. Effectiveness of VR on learning.

3. Exploring spatial presence in VR.
4. VR based intervention for spatial tasks for people with disabilities.
5. Developing and testing VR assessment tools for spatial abilities.
6. Testing the relationship between spatial abilities or other abilities (see Figure 5).

The most-reported research purpose was examining factors affecting spatial performance in VR, with 14 of the studies coded this way. Common factors that were investigated in VR environments included gender, spatial exploration mode, collaboration, competition, map type, and age (Leo et al., 2018; Liang et al., 2019; Meade et al., 2019). Astur et al. (2018) found that there were no differences between genders in recalling a map of the room or maze task (in the first trial). On the other hand, there was a significant difference between genders while using strategies to perform a navigational task within a VR maze, males mostly used place strategy (after rotating the maze, returning to the same direction) while solving the maze, while females did not use any strategy.

Cao et al. (2019) examined how a "spatial exploration mode" (active vs. passive) feature influenced players' wayfinding experience during a virtual building fire emergency in VR. The research had two main purposes: to investigate how different spatial exploration modes affect players` wayfinding performance, and how the stress factors affect individuals` wayfinding performance while escaping from a fire emergency. Results showed that participants in the active exploration mode (where participants explored the environment without any directions) traveled for a longer distance and spent more time during all tasks than participants in the passive exploration mode (people follow given directions).

Ranjbar Pouya, et al. (2017) explored the relationship between age and spatial updating of a target after changes in body-centered spatial relationships and they found that younger age was correlated significantly with better spatial performance and spatial updating. Five of the twenty-seven articles addressed the effectiveness of VR on learning. Cheng and Tsai (2019), studied students' learning experiences in the context of educational immersive virtual field trips (panoramic images in a VR environment). To understand how the teacher and the students interacted during the immersive trips, the instructional activities were videotaped and observed. They found four types of teacher behaviors: "instruction, asking questions, guiding for virtual field trips, and disciplining.

Additionally, they found four types of student behaviors: "observing VR content, searching for information on the Internet, a disorder in the classroom, and responding to teacher`s questions". Sun et al. (2018) compared traditional teaching methods (standard presentation) and teaching in VR. Examples of other research purposes were exploring students' perceptions of presence after they explored science concepts in a VR system (Hite et al., 2019), testing how a VR-based intervention may improve visuospatial skills of people with disabilities (de la Torre-Luque, Valero-Aguayo & de la Rubia-Cuestas, 2017), developing and testing the VR version of the Almeria Spatial Memory Recognition Test (Tascón et al., 2017), and testing the relationship between visual-spatial ability and learning surgical skills in VR environments (Abe et al., 2018).

Results of the Studies

Key results of the studies are presented separately by their research purpose. In these studies, various factors that affect spatial performance in VR were investigated (please see Table 2). The following key results were found.

Figure 5. Research Purposes

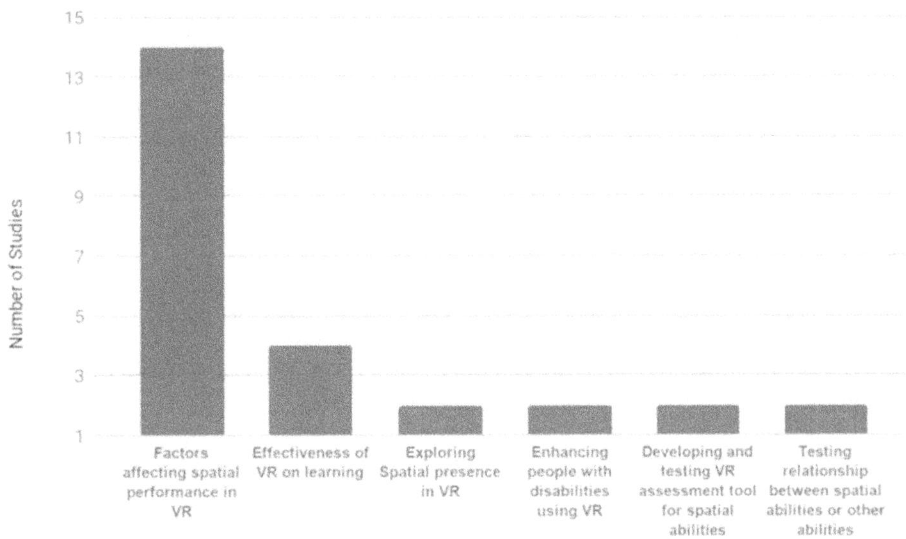

Effectiveness of VR on Learning

These studies investigated the effectiveness of VR on learning with the following key results.

Table 2. Factors Affecting Spatial Performance in VR

Independent Variables	Results
Gender	→ There were no significant differences between males and females in recalling a map of a room (Astur et al., 2016). → Males performed better on the test of survey knowledge in a full-dome (immersive VR environment designed for large audiences) compared to a large, flat-screen display, while females showed no difference (Hedge et al., 2017) → Men outperformed women in both versions (real environment vs. VR environment) in the topographical memory task (Nori et al., 2015).
Navigation/ Rotation Preference	→ Participants in an active exploration group traveled for longer distances and spent more time during a given task in VR than participants in a passive exploration group (Cao et al., 2019). → Participants mostly used egocentric strategies while orienting and navigating within a virtual environment (Fabroyir & Teng, 2018). → Active navigation was more effective than passive navigation, significantly so in older adults (Meade et al., 2019). → When manipulators moved a virtual object based on a guide's instructions, guides used significantly more "addressee-centered" and "neutral" language and noted less mental demand compared to the manipulators, who mainly used "ego-centered" language and reported more mental demand (Pouliquen-Lardy et al., 2016).
Age	→ Children's abilities were assessed in a VR environment and it was found that allocentric recall begins developing at around 4.0-4.5 years and could become more flexible over time (Negen et al., 2017). → Younger age and increased Montreal Cognitive Assessment scores were related significantly with better spatial performance and spatial updating among adults (Ranjbar Pouya et al., 2016).
Map type	→ Participants performed the best on finding a hidden target object and memorizing its location when given a small-scale aerial view that featured a larger arrow indicating their egocentric heading (Serino et al., 2015).

Table 3. Effectiveness of VR on Learning

Results
➔ Learners' motivation was enhanced by VR social studies field trips, and learners' test anxiety decreased. Teacher-student interactions (questions and answers) happened frequently during the virtual field trips (Cheng & Tsai, 2019). ➔ Learners benefited more from direct manipulation than passive viewing when learning anatomy in a VR simulation (Jang et al., 2017). ➔ Students who experienced the fully immersive environment (CAVE-like) outperformed students who experienced VR with a head-mounted display on spatial knowledge in structural engineering posttest scores (Fogarty et al., 2017). ➔ There was no difference in learning between traditional teaching methods (standard presentation) and teaching in VR (Sun et al., 2018).

In the following section, the key results of the studies that aimed to test spatial presence, enhance spatial learning in people with disabilities, develop VR assessment tools, and test relationships between abilities are presented.

DISCUSSION

This body of literature demonstrates that VR environments are used both to assess individuals' current spatial abilities and to enhance spatial abilities. The following section discusses the study findings and complementary relationship between spatial abilities and VR. Limitations of the studies and future directions will be discussed at the end of the section.

Table 4. Results of the studies with exploring spatial presence

Research Purpose	Results
Exploring Spatial Presence in VR	➔ Although students were unable to make assessments about what was and was not real, they had a feeling of spatial presence while in VR (Hite et al., 2019). ➔ Using VR significantly and positively increased spatial presence within a group of undergraduate students (Seibert & Shafer, 2017). ➔ Participants who viewed the virtual environment in a full-dome had more feeling of spatial presence than participants who viewed the virtual environment on a flat screen (Hedge et al., 2017).
Enhancing people with disabilities using VR	➔ Individuals with disabilities learned better with VR (times and errors decreased after training) and also experienced positive outcomes in real-life (de la Torre-Luque et al., 2017). ➔ Both normally developing children and individuals with Williams Syndrome (WS) were able to learn routes in just a few VR trials, but the WS group needed more trials and made more errors than the normally developing children (Farran et al., 2016).
Developing a VR Assessment tool	➔ VR technology was adopted as an assessment tool for children with Autism Spectrum Disorder (ASD). There was no significant difference between ASD and typically developing groups in the 2D paper-and-pencil test of visual attention or 3D VR tasks (Ip et al., 2017). ➔ A simple VR version of the Almeria Spatial Memory Recognition Test was developed. While performing the task, men generally did better than women, significantly so when task difficulty was increased (Tascón et al., 2017).
Testing Relationships between spatial abilities and other abilities	➔ A statistically significant correlation was found between visio-spatial ability (mental rotation) and simulator score in only one attempt after learners performed surgical skill exercises in a VR simulator (Abe et al. 2018). ➔ There was a positive correlation between self-reports of imagery and spatial presence, whereas spatial presence was not correlated to the other spatial tests (mental rotation and topographical memory) (Coxon et al., 2016).

VR environments provide more realistic assessments compared to classic assessments (Negut et al., 2016). VR immerses users in a virtual reconstruction of real-world events; users can select their viewpoints and feel a sense of complete presence (Kanade et al., 1997). Using VR significantly and positively increases spatial presence (Seibert & Shafer, 2017). In this respect, previous studies mostly used VR to perform spatial tasks like navigating by following a path or using a map, locating and rotating target objects, and also to perform spatial assessments (e.g., spatial presence, mental rotation, visuospatial imagery). Results showed that spatial abilities and VR technologies can be studied together in different subject domains including engineering, anatomy, surgery, and outer space. Each of those domains is associated with spatial abilities; for instance, a significant correlation was found between visual-spatial ability and performance in robotic surgical skills training (Abe et al., 2018).

Results of the present study showed that VR technology was also used to create learning activities including performing surgery, exploring historical places, and learning anatomy. For example, Jang et al.'s (2017) study showing that direct manipulation is better than passive viewing provides a clear design principle for future educational VR experiences. In the set of articles reviewed for this paper, VR was used to make models that allow users to learn about common places (city, mall, museum), and about the human body (inner ear, heart, and full body for surgery). Simulations of these kinds of environments allow learners to practice before they experience situations in real life. VR environments demonstrated promising results for learning. Learners` motivation was enhanced by VR social studies field trips, and learners` test anxiety decreased (Cheng & Tsai, 2019). However, significant differences could not be found between traditional teaching methods (standard presentation) and teaching in VR (Sun et al., 2018). Moreover, a significant correlation was observed between visio-spatial ability (mental rotation) and simulator score while performing surgical skills in VR simulators (Abe et al., 2018). VR can also help researchers and educators understand the types of spatial abilities that are related to learning in different domains.

Results also showed promise in spatial learning, which involves developing spatial skills and perceptions of size and scale awareness by providing learners with a context to interact with virtual objects (Hedge et al., 2017; de la Torre-Luque et al., 2017). Two examples of studies of spatial learning in this review are Hedge et al.'s (2017) study of understanding the effect of various displays in VR environments on spatial learning and Nori et al.'s (2015) study investigating differences among college students' learning of spatial information such as topographical memory between genders. Visuospatial skills of people with disabilities can be enhanced by practicing in VR environment; improved visuospatial abilities can also transfer to real-life situations (de la Torre-Luque et al, 2017).

Implications: What Makes VR and Spatial so Unique?

This review is beneficial for researchers to gain a holistic understanding of the available research regarding VR technology and spatial abilities and to understand the gaps that remain in the literature. This review also revealed a special link between spatial ability and virtual reality. Virtual reality can be both diagnostic and therapeutic for spatial skills; VR is an excellent tool for examining spatial ability in individuals and also individuals can enhance their spatial abilities through using virtual reality. Spatial skills are important in success in STEM fields (Uttal & Cohen, 2012), as well as in success in everyday activities such as wayfinding (e.g., Cao et al., 2019; Meade et al., 2019), understanding systems (e.g., Jang et al, 2017), and communication with collaborators (e.g., Pouliquen-Lardy et al., 2016). Now that this review has revealed this link, future research directions could examine how best to design VR environments for the purposes of learning and measuring spatial skills. Future studies may harness the power of design-based research in interrogating how attributes of a VR application or experience are linked to outcomes. Design-based research in learning spatial skills could investigate how to design experiences that help individuals overcome spatial problems or enhance spatial presence and immersion in VR environments. Design-based research in the assessment of spatial skills could shed light on how to convert more paper and pencil tests into VR versions to improve the validity and reliability of those tests. It is entirely likely that applications for learning spatial skills have different attributes that applications for assessing those skills, however, the increasing availability of VR technology creates an excellent opportunity for both developing and studying spatial skills.

Limitations and Future Studies

The majority of research studies (17 articles) involved students who were in higher education. This could be the result of convenience sampling, as higher education students can be an easy population to access for university-based researchers. The three studies showing the benefits of VR environments on learners with disabilities (e.g., de la Torre et al., 2017) could be expanded to investigate whether these positive benefits extend to other age groups. Conducting studies with different learners will contribute to understanding the potential value of VR technologies.

Moreover, almost all of the studies had fewer than 100 participants. Conducting research with VR technology is not an easy process, and setting up and running the study protocol for each participant is time-intensive. Unlike paper-and-pencil tests, which can be easily copied and distributed, most VR assessments require a full setup for each participant, and each setup can only be used to test one participant at a time. As technology becomes more widespread, it will become more feasible to conduct larger VR studies. Thus, future studies should replicate these studies with different education levels and more diverse groups of participants, such as learners with disabilities.

None of the studies focused on spatial unawareness, the inability to be aware of one's location in space, which is an important component of spatial ability to consider, especially in VR. Future studies can examine both spatial presence and spatial unawareness simultaneously to create design principles for VR learning environments designed to improve spatial understanding.

CONCLUSION

This review synthesizes the current research connecting spatial abilities and VR systematically into a holistic interpretation by systematically reviewing articles that have been published on VR and spatial ability. Of the 26 studies reviewed, 40% used VR to assess spatial abilities. As VR environments are more realistic than paper and pencil tests, they are likely to provide more authentic assessments compared to classic assessments (Negut et al., 2016). Results of the present study showed that VR technology was also used to enhance learning in different domains including performing surgery, exploring historical places, and learning anatomy. On the other hand, results also showed promise in spatial learning by providing learners an opportunity to interact with virtual objects (Hedge et al., 2017; de la Torre-Luque et al., 2017). 50% of the articles used the virtual model of common places (cities, malls, and parks) as VR environments. The majority of research studies (17 articles) involved fewer than 100 students who were in higher education, which could be a result of convenience sampling and the time-intensive process of transporting and setting up VR equipment.

The present study was limited to the past five years and four research databases. Future studies could build on the current work by increasing the time range, databases searched, and by doing statistical comparisons of the studies. The present study demonstrates the complementary use of VR as a learning and assessment tool, thus revealing what is so special about spatial abilities and VR. This review will help researchers to gain a holistic understanding of the previous literature regarding the use of VR technology for spatial understanding and research gaps that need further investigation.

REFERENCES

Abe, T., Raison, N., Shinohara, N., Shamim Khan, M., Ahmed, K., & Dasgupta, P. (2018). The Effect of Visual-Spatial Ability on the Learning of Robot-Assisted Surgical Skills. *Journal of Surgical Education*, *75*(2), 458–464. Advance online publication. doi:10.1016/j.jsurg.2017.08.017 PMID:28918007

Astur, R. S., Purton, A. J., Zaniewski, M. J., Cimadevilla, J., & Markus, E. J. (2016). Human sex differences in solving a virtual navigation problem. *Behavioural Brain Research*, *308*, 236–243. Advance online publication. doi:10.1016/j.bbr.2016.04.037 PMID:27108050

Atienza, R., Blonna, R., Saludares, M. I., Casimiro, J., & Fuentes, V. (2016, May). Interaction techniques using head gaze for virtual reality. In *2016 IEEE Region 10 Symposium (TENSYMP)* (pp. 110-114). IEEE. 10.1109/TENCONSpring.2016.7519387

Brown, A., & Green, T. (2016). Virtual reality: Low-cost tools and resources for the classroom. *TechTrends*, *60*(5), 517–519. doi:10.100711528-016-0102-z

Cao, L., Lin, J., & Li, N. (2019). A virtual reality based study of indoor fire evacuation after active or passive spatial exploration. *Computers in Human Behavior*, *90*, 37–45. Advance online publication. doi:10.1016/j.chb.2018.08.041

Cheng, K.-H., & Tsai, C.-C. (2019). A case study of immersive virtual field trips in an elementary classroom: Students' learning experience and teacher-student interaction behaviors. *Computers & Education*, *140*, 103600. Advance online publication. doi:10.1016/j.compedu.2019.103600

Cheng, Y. L., & Mix, K. S. (2014). Spatial training improves children's mathematics ability. *Journal of Cognition and Development*, *15*(1), 2–11. doi:10.1080/15248372.2012.725186

Cogné, M., Taillade, M., N'Kaoua, B., Tarruella, A., Klinger, E., Larrue, F., Sauzéon, H., Joseph, P. A., & Sorita, E. (2017). The contribution of virtual reality to the diagnosis of spatial navigation disorders and to the study of the role of navigational aids: A systematic literature review. *Annals of Physical and Rehabilitation Medicine*, *60*(3), 164–176. doi:10.1016/j.rehab.2015.12.004 PMID:27017533

Coxon, M., Kelly, N., & Page, S. (2016). Individual differences in virtual reality: Are spatial presence and spatial ability linked? *Virtual Reality (Waltham Cross)*, *20*(4), 203–212. doi:10.100710055-016-0292-x de la Torre-Luque, A., Valero-Aguayo, L., & de la Rubia-Cuestas, E. J. (2017). Visuospatial Orientation Learning through Virtual Reality for People with Severe Disability. *International Journal of DisablIlty, 64*(4), 420–435. doi:10.1080/1034912X.2016.1274022

Fabroyir, H., & Teng, W. C. (2018). Navigation in virtual environments using head-mounted displays: Allocentric vs. egocentric behaviors. *Computers in Human Behavior, 80*, 331–343. Advance online publication. doi:10.1016/j.chb.2017.11.033

Farran, E. K., Formby, S., Daniyal, F., Holmes, T., & Van Herwegen, J. (2016). Route-learning strategies in typical and atypical development; eye tracking reveals atypical landmark selection in Williams syndrome. *Journal of Intellectual Disability Research, 60*(10), 933–944. doi:10.1111/jir.12331 PMID:27634746

Fogarty, J., Asce, A. M., Mccormick, J., El-Tawil, S., & Asce, F. (2017). *Improving Student Understanding of Complex Spatial Arrangements with Virtual Reality*. doi:10.1061/(ASCE)EI.1943-5541.0000349

Hedge, C., Weaver, R., & Schnall, S. (2017). *Spatial Learning and Wayfinding in an Immersive Environment: The Digital Fulldome*. doi:10.1089/cyber.2016.0399

Hite, R. L., Jones, M. G., Childers, G. M., Ennes, M., Chesnutt, K., Pereyra, M., & Cayton, E. (2019). *Investigating Potential Relationships Between Adolescents' Cognitive Development and Perceptions of Presence in 3-D, Haptic-Enabled, Virtual Reality Science Instruction*. doi:10.100710956-018-9764-y

Hwang, W. Y., & Hu, S. S. (2013). Analysis of peer learning behaviors using multiple representations in virtual reality and their impacts on geometry problem solving. *Computers & Education, 62*, 308–319. doi:10.1016/j.compedu.2012.10.005

Ip, H. H., Hoi-Yan Lai, C., Wong, S. W., Tsui, J. K., Chen Li, R., Shuk-Ying Lau, K., & Chan, D. F. (2017). Visuospatial attention in children with Autism Spectrum Disorder: A comparison between 2-D and 3-D environments. *Cogent Education, 6*(1), 1307709. Advance online publication. doi:10.1080/2331186X.2017.1307709

Jang, S., Vitale, J. M., Jyung, R. W., & Black, J. B. (2017). Direct manipulation is better than passive viewing for learning anatomy in a three-dimensional virtual reality environment. *Computers & Education, 106*, 150–165. Advance online publication. doi:10.1016/j.compedu.2016.12.009

Kanade, T., Rander, P., & Narayanan, P. J. (1997). Virtualized reality: Constructing virtual worlds from real scenes. *IEEE MultiMedia, 4*(1), 34–47. doi:10.1109/93.580394

Larsen, C. R., Soerensen, J. L., Grantcharov, T. P., Dalsgaard, T., Schouenborg, L., Ottosen, C., Schroeder, T. V., & Ottesen, B. S. (2009). Effect of virtual reality training on laparoscopic surgery: Randomised controlled trial. *BMJ (Clinical Research Ed.), 338*(2), b1802. doi:10.1136/bmj.b1802 PMID:19443914

Laver, K. E., Lange, B., George, S., Deutsch, J. E., Saposnik, G., & Crotty, M. (2017). Virtual reality for stroke rehabilitation. *Cochrane Database of Systematic Reviews*, 11. PMID:29156493

Lee, E. A. L., & Wong, K. W. (2014). Learning with desktop virtual reality: Low spatial ability learners are more positively affected. *Computers & Education, 79*, 49–58. doi:10.1016/j.compedu.2014.07.010

Lefrançois, C., & Messier, J. (2019). Adaptation and spatial generalization to a triaxial visuomotor perturbation in a virtual reality environment. *Experimental Brain Research, 237*(3), 793–803. doi:10.100700221-018-05462-2 PMID:30607472

Leó, I., Tascó, L., Ortells-Pareja, J. J., Manuel, J., & Id, C. (2018). *Virtual reality assessment of walking and non-walking space in men and women with virtual reality-based tasks.* doi:10.1371/journal.pone.0204995

Liang, H. N., Lu, F., Shi, Y., Nanjappan, V., & Papangelis, K. (2019). Evaluating the effects of collaboration and competition in navigation tasks and spatial knowledge acquisition within virtual reality environments. *Future Generation Computer Systems, 95*, 855–866. Advance online publication. doi:10.1016/j.future.2018.02.029

McLay, R. N., Wood, D. P., Webb-Murphy, J. A., Spira, J. L., Wiederhold, M. D., Pyne, J. M., & Wiederhold, B. K. (2011). A randomized, controlled trial of virtual reality-graded exposure therapy for post-traumatic stress disorder in active duty service members with combat-related post-traumatic stress disorder. *Cyberpsychology, Behavior, and Social Networking, 14*(4), 223–229. doi:10.1089/cyber.2011.0003 PMID:21332375

Meade, M. E., Meade, J. G., Sauzeon, H., & Fernandes, M. A. (2019). *Active Navigation in Virtual Environments Benefits Spatial Memory in Older Adults.* doi:10.3390/brainsci9030047

Merchant, Z., Goetz, E. T., Keeney-Kennicutt, W., Cifuentes, L., Kwok, O. M., & Davis, T. J. (2013). Exploring 3-D virtual reality technology for spatial ability and chemistry achievement. *Journal of Computer Assisted Learning, 29*(6), 579–590. doi:10.1111/jcal.12018

Negen, J., Heywood-Everett, E., Roome, H. E., & Nardini, M. (2018). Development of allocentric spatial recall from new viewpoints in virtual reality. *Developmental Science, 21*(1), 12496. doi:10.1111/desc.12496 PMID:28256025

Neguţ, A., Matu, S. A., Sava, F. A., & David, D. (2016). Task difficulty of virtual reality-based assessment tools compared to classical paper-and-pencil or computerized measures: A meta-analytic approach. *Computers in Human Behavior, 54*, 414–424. doi:10.1016/j.chb.2015.08.029

Nori, R., Piccardi, L., Migliori, M., Guidazzoli, A., Frasca, F., De Luca, D., & Giusberti, F. (2015). The virtual reality Walking Corsi Test. *Computers in Human Behavior, 48*, 72–77. Advance online publication. doi:10.1016/j.chb.2015.01.035

Onyesolu, M. O., & Eze, F. U. (2011). Understanding virtual reality technology: advances and applications. Advances in Computer. *Science and Engineering*, 53-70.

Parsons, T. D., Larson, P., Kratz, K., Thiebaux, M., Bluestein, B., Buckwalter, J. G., & Rizzo, A. A. (2004). Sex differences in mental rotation and spatial rotation in a virtual environment. *Neuropsychologia, 42*(4), 555–562. Advance online publication. doi:10.1016/j.neuropsychologia.2003.08.014 PMID:14728927

Pouliquen-Lardy, L., Milleville-Pennel, I., Guillaume, F., & Mars, F. (2016). Remote collaboration in virtual reality: Asymmetrical effects of task distribution on spatial processing and mental workload. *Virtual Reality (Waltham Cross), 20*(4), 213–220. doi:10.100710055-016-0294-8

Ranjbar Pouya, O., Byagowi, A., Kelly, D. M., & Moussavi, Z. (2016). *Introducing a new age-and-cognition-sensitive measurement for assessing spatial orientation using a landmark-less virtual reality navigational task.* doi:10.1080/17470218.2016.1187181

Reger, G. M., Holloway, K. M., Candy, C., Rothbaum, B. O., Difede, J., Rizzo, A. A., & Gahm, G. A. (2011). Effectiveness of virtual reality exposure therapy for active duty soldiers in a military mental health clinic. *Journal of Traumatic Stress, 24*(1), 93–96. doi:10.1002/jts.20574 PMID:21294166

Riva, G., & Waterworth, J. A. (2014). Being present in a virtual world. The Oxford handbook of virtuality, 205-221. doi:10.1093/oxfordhb/9780199826162.013.015

Seibert, J., & Shafer, D. M. (2017). Control mapping in virtual reality: Effects on spatial presence and controller naturalness. *Virtual Reality (Waltham Cross), 22*(1), 79–88. Advance online publication. doi:10.100710055-017-0316-1

Serino, S., Mestre, D., Mallet, P., Pergandi, J. M., Cipresso, P., & Riva, G. (2015). *Do not get lost in translation: The role of egocentric heading in spatial orientation. Neuroscience Letters.* MELAT., doi:10.1016/j.neulet.2015.06.057

Sherman, W. R., & Craig, A. B. (2018). *Understanding virtual reality: Interface, application, and design.* Morgan Kaufmann.

Slater, M., & Sanchez-Vives, M. V. (2016). Enhancing our lives with immersive virtual reality. *Frontiers in Robotics and AI, 3*, 74. doi:10.3389/frobt.2016.00074

Steuer, J. (1992). Defining virtual reality: Dimensions determining telepresence. *Journal of Communication, 42*(4), 73–93. doi:10.1111/j.1460-2466.1992.tb00812.x

Sun, R., Wu, Y. J., & Cai, Q. (2018). The effect of a virtual reality learning environment on learners' spatial ability. *Virtual Reality (Waltham Cross), 1*, 3. doi:10.100710055-018-0355-2

Tascón, L., García-Moreno, L. M., & Cimadevilla, J. M. (2017). Almeria spatial memory recognition test (ASMRT): Gender differences emerged in a new passive spatial task. *Neuroscience Letters, 651*, 188–191. Advance online publication. doi:10.1016/j.neulet.2017.05.011 PMID:28499888

Tsirlin, I., Dupierrix, E., Chokron, S., Coquillart, S., & Ohlmann, T. (2009). Uses of virtual reality for diagnosis, rehabilitation and study of unilateral spatial neglect: Review and analysis. *Cyberpsychology & Behavior, 12*(2), 175–181. doi:10.1089/cpb.2008.0208 PMID:19361298

Uttal, D. H., & Cohen, C. A. (2012). Spatial thinking and STEM education: When, why, and how? *Psychology of Learning and Motivation, 57*, 147–181. doi:10.1016/B978-0-12-394293-7.00004-2

Uttal, D. H., Miller, D. I., & Newcombe, N. S. (2013). Exploring and enhancing spatial thinking: Links to achievement in Science, Technology, Engineering, and Mathematics? *Current Directions in Psychological Science, 22*(5), 367–373. doi:10.1177/0963721413484756

Wai, J., Lubinski, D., & Benbow, C. P. (2009). Spatial ability for STEM domains: Aligning over 50 years of cumulative psychological knowledge solidifies its importance. *Journal of Educational Psychology, 101*(4), 817–835. doi:10.1037/a0016127

Witmer, B. G., & Singer, M. J. (1998). Measuring presence in virtual environments: A presence questionnaire. *Presence (Cambridge, Mass.)*, *7*(3), 225–240. doi:10.1162/105474698565686

Woolgar, S. (Ed.). (2002). *Virtual society?: technology, cyberbole, reality*. OUP Oxford.

Yılmaz, H. B. (2017). On the development and measurement of spatial ability. *International Electronic Journal of Elementary Education*, *1*(2), 83–96.

ADDITIONAL READING

Hartmann, T., Wirth, W., Schramm, H., Klimmt, C., Vorderer, P., Gysbers, A., Böcking, S., Ravaja, N., Laarni, J., Saari, T., Gouveia, F., & Sacau, A. M. (2016). The spatial presence experience scale (SPES): A short self-report measure for diverse media settings. *Journal of Media Psychology*, *28*(1), 1–15. doi:10.1027/1864-1105/a000137

Ling, Y., Nefs, H. T., Brinkman, W. P., Qu, C., & Heynderickx, I. (2013). The relationship between individual characteristics and experienced presence. *Computers in Human Behavior*, *29*(4), 1519–1530. doi:10.1016/j.chb.2012.12.010

Parong, J., Pollard, K. A., Files, B. T., Oiknine, A. H., Sinatra, A. M., Moss, J. D., Passaro, A., & Khooshabeh, P. (2020). The mediating role of presence differs across types of spatial learning in immersive technologies. *Computers in Human Behavior, 107*(September 2019), 106290. doi:10.1016/j.chb.2020.106290

Seibert, J., & Shafer, D. M. (2018, March). Control mapping in virtual reality: Effects on spatial presence and controller naturalness. *Virtual Reality (Waltham Cross)*, *22*(1), 79–88. Advance online publication. doi:10.100710055-017-0316-1

Slater, M. (2018). Immersion and the illusion of presence in virtual reality. *British Journal of Psychology*, *109*(3), 431–433. doi:10.1111/bjop.12305 PMID:29781508

Weibel, D., & Wissmath, B. (2011). Immersion in computer games: The role of spatial presence and flow. *International Journal of Computer Games Technology*, *2011*, 1–14. Advance online publication. doi:10.1155/2011/282345

Wirth, W., Hartmann, T., Böcking, S., Vorderer, P., Klimmt, C., Schramm, H., Saari, T., Laarni, J., Ravaja, N., Gouveia, F. R., Biocca, F., Sacau, A., Jäncke, L., Baumgartner, T., & Jäncke, P. (2007). A process model of the formation of spatial presence experiences. *Media Psychology*, *9*(3), 493–525. doi:10.1080/15213260701283079

Yildirim, Ç., Bostan, B., & Berkman, M. İ. (2019). Impact of different immersive techniques on the perceived sense of presence measured via subjective scales. *Entertainment Computing, 31*(December 2018). doi:10.1016/j.entcom.2019.100308

Chapter 4
Unified Approach to Augmented Reality:
Taking Into Account Technological, Psychological, and Ecological Approaches

Hocine Chebi
Faculty of Electrical Engineering, Djillali Liabes University of Sidi Bel Abbes, Algeria

ABSTRACT

The authors present a new and holistic conceptualization on the feeling of presence. This consists of several components. The first two propose a new definition of presence and the identification of a fourth component of presence called presence of action. The third component consists of a unified approach to presence taking into account technological, psychological, and ecological considerations. They have developed a model that identifies the processes leading to the feeling of presence. According to the model, two unconscious phases of judgment condition the emergence of presence. The first judgment concerns the credibility of the environment, which depends on the satisfaction of the user's intellectual and perceptual expectations.

INTRODUCTION

Virtual reality needs a strong basis to distinguish itself from other media. This is why we define it as a mediated experience that immerses one or more users into an artificial environment in which the user can feel and interact in real-time via sensory-motor interfaces. The user deems the experience credible, agrees to take part in the game, and in response feels a sense of presence. We can note that this definition combines technological and cognitive considerations and does not forget to point to the experience aspect. We, therefore, do not reduce virtual reality to a set of technologies but consider it as the medium of a type of experience that leads to the feeling of presence. We want to express through this definition a strong relationship between virtual reality, presence, and user. Through this definition, we wish to emphasize the idea of focusing on the user's and sensory and cognitive capacities. In virtual reality,

DOI: 10.4018/978-1-7998-4222-4.ch004

more than in any other computerized activity, we think it crucial to adopt a human-centered approach, for the effectiveness of the experience but also to achieve the feeling of presence. We, therefore, associate virtual reality and a feeling of presence.

The latter is a multidimensional and multifactorial umbrella concept that is often the subject of quarrels in scientific areas. Is it the result of the technology implemented? Is immersion born from the emotions brought about by experience? If the feeling of presence is an object that is difficult to identify, it is even more difficult to reach it. Given this objective, it is important to have solid theoretical foundations. It is then necessary to understand the underlying processes leading to presence.

This chapter proposes to answer these multiple needs and questions and to specify the path which makes it possible to understand the feeling of presence. The identification of a complete and unified model of presence will serve as a theoretical and technical framework for the design of devices and applications in virtual reality. After describing three existing approaches including technological, psychological, and ecological, we present a new balanced approach between these three visions and then identify a fourth component of presence. We then propose a framework dedicated to the design of virtual reality applications. Finally, we present a complete and unified model of presence.

Evaluation Phase to Verify the Relevance of our Theoretical Choices

For this phase we have developed a questionnaire comprising sixty-four questions, a third of which was created for the occasion, the others come from questionnaires present in the literature (Lessiter, 2001; Schubert 2001; Slater, 1994). The context of the evaluation is a three-dimensional video game. The participants tested this game on two different visual rendering devices, a large, polarized screen offering stereoscopic vision and an autostereoscopic screen. A large part of the questions aimed to validate some of the hypotheses put forward when designing our model of presence. The limited number of pages in this article does not allow us to present the quantified results of this evaluation, so we will content ourselves with communicating the analyzes. However, the interested reader can read the details of these results (Bouvier, 2009).

It was in 1980 that Minsky (1980) introduced the concept of telepresence. It then refered to the feeling that an operator can feel during a remote operation. The operator's body is then projected onto the machine's workplace, the operator's cameras become his eyes, and the operator can therefore at that moment feel like being (tele) present in this other place. Slater (1993) proposed a definition on the concept of being elsewhere, telepresence, as (a) the user is elsewhere than where he is physically; and (b) the "elsewhere" is formed by the images, sounds, and physical sensations supplied to the senses of the user by the system generating the virtual environment. The concept of being elsewhere or of being there is essentially associated with sensory perception: the user feels there because his senses perceive stimuli describing the virtual environment and then he builds a mental representation of the environment around him. This definition of presence by the concept of being there is very common. However, this definition is exclusively dependent on stimulating the senses of the user and does not consider the role of action, and and denies the psychological and human aspect.

Following different definitions of presence, Lombard and Ditton (1997) managed to isolate the following central idea. Presence is a perceptive illusion of non-mediation. This definition indicates that presence appears when the user is no longer aware of the existence and role of interfaces. This second definition has also become a classic. It reminds us that presence is an illusion and indicates that the interfaces must be erased in order not to hinder the illusion. This definition is therefore appreciable because it points to the aspect perceptual and the property of transparency that interfaces must assume to allow presence to appear. We criticize this definition for seeming more to state a condition for successful interaction (through the choice of interfaces and interaction patterns) than to define presence. Also, once again, this exclusively highlights the perceptual aspect.

The two previous definitions focus on the technological aspect and imply that the feeling of presence depends directly and exclusively on the technical properties of the system. The better the technical qualities (better immersion, fine possibilities for interaction), the stronger the presence felt. We regret this exclusively technological orientation. Our approach, without denying the importance of technology, will point to the need for an additional cognitive dimensions.

Psychological Approach

The psychological approach can be characterized by the following observation by Biocca (2003) (known as the book's paradox). If sensorimotor immersion is the key to being present, then how do you explain the high level of presence felt by readers of a book. Books have a very low level in all the factors identified as being at the origin of the presence: quality of sensory stimulation, restitution in the first person, and possibilities of modifying the environment.

Biocca (2003) proposed to introduce, in addition to physical space and virtual space, a third aspect of imaginary space. The spatial presence felt depends on the user's reference space. It moves between the following three poles: physical, virtual, and imaginary. So, the answer to the book paradox would be imagination. The reason why a reader can feel a sense of intense presence despite poor quality immersion is due in part to the power of his imagination to transport himself into the environment (the web) of the book. The power of imaginary space could somehow compensate for the lack of sensory immersion.

To this proposition, the proponents of the technological approach (Slater, 2003; Waterworth, 2003) counter that presence should only be seen as the fruit of technology. Introducing the content (i.e., the non-technological part of an experience: scenario, artistic aspect, etc.) into this relationship risks causing confusion between presence, emotional response, and involvement. The argument is as follows: if listening to an opera disc or reading a book it is possible to feel the impression of being there, it is only due to the power of the work which, by the emotions aroused, is capable of transporting us. If the book is not good or the reader just doesn't like it, it won't work.

Still, according to the authors (Slater 2003; Waterworth 2003), the feeling of presence has nothing to do with interest or even more generally with emotions. Emotions and presence are described as orthogonal by Slater (Slater 2003). Feeling there is an opera, because the sensory stimuli describe an opera, is presence, but having the impression of being there by the sole force of the work and its power of projection is only an emotional response. The objection is also based on the observation that the book can only provoke emotional, then physiological but not behavioral responses. For advocates of the psychological approach, even if sensory realism certainly has a great influence on presence, it takes more to feel it (Heeter, 2003):

Presence is a subjective experience. Even a perfect sensory immersion cannot by itself alone arouse a strong sense of presence. Even reality cannot automatically create a strong sense of presence. For our part, we envision a balanced position between these two points of view. Like Slater (2003), we do not confuse emotional response with presence and do not consider the book as a system of virtual reality since, among other things; the book is not capable of sensually describing a place. On the other hand, we consider the content and more generally the emotions generated by the application in virtual reality but also the imagination as some of the factors allowing tending towards the presence.

Ecological Approach

The ecological approach to presence comes from the work of Gibson (1986) on visual perception. Gibson argues that the perception of the environment is not made through its appearance (defined by properties of size, shape, color, etc.) but through the possibilities of action that the user perceives in the environment. Thus, people do not perceive an environment through the senses and then deduces possible actions from it, but perceives the environment directly through the possibilities of action detected. These possibilities of action are called affordances by Gibson (1986). This term is a creation of Gibson (1986) and comes from the English verb to afford which means to offer. The affordances, therefore, define the possibilities or potentials of action offered by the environment for a given animal.

Supporters of the ecological approach, Zahorik, and Jenison (1998) propose the following definition: Presence is equivalent to successfully taking actions in the environment. The authors assert by this definition that reality is formed through the actions taken and that the reality of an experience is defined by functionality rather than appearance. Taking action successfully means that the environment's responses to user actions match the responses that they're used to in the real world. These answers then meet his expectations. Zahorik and Jenison (1998) reject that presence is associated with the concept of being there, which is based on sensory stimulation describing the virtual environment. Instead, they propose to associate presence and ability to do there.

The first strong point of this approach, it puts the couple perception-action forward (and not first the immersion then the interaction) and points to the idea that this couple should lead the design of virtual environments. More than the definition of presence proposed by Zahorik and Jenison (1998), it is the concept of affordance that interests us. So, whether it is our virtual reality application design framework or our presence model, all have a marked ecological dimension. One possible objection to the ecological approach is that it only deals with visual perception. However, with quality sound reproduction and a feedback system for interactions, a blind person can perfectly feel a sense of presence during a virtual reality experience. Furthermore, this definition denies the possibility of feeling a sense of presence in a contemplative experience. Finally, we regret that the psychological considerations of experience are left aside.

Definition of Presence

As we mentioned we define virtual reality as:

1. A mediatized experience that immerses one or more users in the heart of an artificial environment in which the user can feel and interact in real-time via sensorimotor interfaces. The user deems the experience credible, agrees to take part in the game, and in response feels a sense of presence. And we define presence as:
2. The authentic feeling of existing in a world other than the physical world where our body is located.

The feeling of presence is, therefore, like all feelings, a subjective experience lived consciously which depends on internal and external factors to the user. Immersion describes to our senses an environment, our brain then receives these stimuli and interprets them. The perceptual system does not know that all this is virtual and the brain, therefore, considers these stimuli as describing reality. This state is manifested by instinctive responses: physiological, emotional, and behavioral responses (Sanchez-Vives 2005). The intensity of the feeling of presence is not constant during the experience, it may at times disappear completely causing pauses in presence (Slater 2000).

But people are more than a simple perceptual system; we are endowed with an intelligence that enables us to interpret his perception and to have a critical mind. Thus, it is possible to have responses similar to those obtained in a real environment while at the same time being aware of the virtuality of the situation. However, although still aware of the virtuality of events, the user can feel an authentic sense of presence. It is, therefore, necessary that at some point in the experience the user goes beyond their awareness of the virtuality of the situation. If the experience is of sufficient quality (both in content and in form), has meaning for the user and the affordances are assumed then the user deems the experience credible and agrees to take part in the game. this one. For this, it does not seem necessary for us to offer a realistic experience, this is why we prefer to use the term of credibility which better translates the underlying subjectivity.

We use the verb existed rather than being because the latter is too associated with the concept of being there or elsewhere often associated with sensory stimulation. However, although we want to keep this previous aspect, we want to add to it an idea of identification, of an embodiment of the role proposed by the application. The sensory stimuli but also the possibilities of actions in the environment contribute to the feeling of existing. It seems to us that this dimension of embodiment is missing from the previous definitions. The study we conducted validates our vision and definition of presence. Indeed, it shows that the notions of existence and role incarnation are correlated to the different components of presence presented in the following section. Thus, the participants who felt a sense of existence and intense role incarnation also experienced a strong sense of presence in each of the components of presence. Furthermore, these same participants also felt more intense emotions than the average of the participants. Everything seems to indicate that the concepts of existence and role incarnation correspond well to the concept of presence as it is understood by the scientific community.

With these two inseparable definitions, we think we occupy an intermediate position between the three approaches described above. We point out the importance of technology for immersion and interaction. In this, we are close to the technological approach. However, we are deviating from it by adding an expensive cognitive dimension to the psychological approach. We do not think that presence depends exclusively on immersion or interaction. By judging the credibility of the experience and by its acceptance to take the game we clearly show that the user participates in the emergence of the presence. Always related to the psychological approach, our application design framework in virtual reality considers the emotions carried by the application as one of the factors allowing tending towards the feeling of presence. Also, from a presence perspective, leaving more room for the imagination could have a positive impact. Finally, we will see in the next chapters that affordances are at the heart of our presence model and our framework. Through the introduction of the notion of credibility and the importance given to affordances, our approach has a strong ecological dimension.

The Components of Presence

Presence is a complex concept. Want to answer the question of why and how do I feel present? makes it clear that the answer cannot be monolithic. Heeter (1992) will be the first to speak of the 3 dimensions of presence. For her, presence is a subjective (and therefore personal) feeling that encompasses the following three dimensions:

- Personal presence: this is about feeling there (in this precise place).
- Social presence: to what extent other beings (living or not) are there with you and can interact with you.
- The environmental presence: to what extent the environment seems to know that you are there.

It should be noted that the distinction between personal presence and environmental presence may seem rather blurred. Indeed, environmental presence as it is thought by Heeter seems to us more to be a method of increasing personal presence than a component of presence in its own right.

For Biocca (1997) presence breaks down through the following three components:

- Physical presence: here it is a question of answering the question where am I? the idea of being transported in an environment other than the underlying physical environment.
- Social presence: appears when the user has the feeling of being able to communicate with another entity (living or artificial).
- The presence of self intervenes when the user perceives his self (the awareness that he has of himself) as belonging to the virtual environment.

This time again we will be able to find the distinction between physical presence and presence of self quite vague. If the user can say "I am on a beach" (physical presence), it is difficult to understand that his self is not also there. Physical presence and self-presence are therefore very strongly correlated.

Lee (2004) uses the same titles as Biocca (1997) to define the components of presence but for slightly different concepts:

- Physical presence: intervenes when the objects making up the environment (and therefore the environment itself) are understood as real objects. Here, there are no underlying notions of being there or being transported into the virtual environment.
- Social presence: appears when other environmental actors (living or artificial) are accepted as real actors.
- The presence of self: the virtual self is perceived as the real. The idea of projection in the virtual environment or appropriation of the virtual representation is found in this point.

The main interest of this approach is that it differentiates physical presence and presence of self. The author insists that physical presence is not associated with the idea of being transported because it is essentially based on the immersive qualities of the device; in fact, weakly immersive devices are not excluded.

PROPOSAL FOR A FOURTH COMPONENT

We rank behind the taxonomy proposed by Lee (2004) for the following reasons. This taxonomy helps avoid confusion between physical presence and self-presence. These two components are thus separated.

Also, his desire to withdraw the idea of projection of the physical presence component allows rebalancing the weight of the different components. Indeed, the other proposals attached, it seems to us, too much importance to the physical presence which could lead to confusion between global presence (in all its dimensions) and physical presence. However, it would seem more meaningful to us to rename the physical presence in environmental presence or spatial presence because it is a question of accepting the environment as a real physical environment.

The spatial presence is often mentioned in the literature but it is mostly accompanied by the idea of projection into the environment. On the other hand, we think that there is a component missing from current taxonomy. For the moment we have the following dimensions: the presence of the environment, the social presence and the presence of self. We defined the feeling of presence as the feeling of existing in the virtual environment. We associate this feeling of existing with embodying the role that experience dedicates to the user. However, if this idea of existing is based on the three components currently identified, it seems to us that a dimension relating to the actions of the user in the environment is missing. We therefore believe that the user must be aware of his actions and their scope to fully embody his role. We call this fourth component the presence of action.

The presence of the self approaches this consideration but it is seen by the various authors (Biocca 1997; Lee 2004), only as the appropriation of the virtual representation of the user. We have identified the following three factors as potentially influencing the presence of action:

- User action must correspond to an affordance perceived and assumed by interaction patterns.
- The interaction patterns must allow a correspondence between the proprioceptive sensations of the virtual self and the proprioceptive sensations of the real self. For this, the interaction scheme must be natural.
- The causal link must be maintained between a user action and his perception of the system response.

Our study shows that the ratings obtained for the presence of action are consistent with those of the other three components. This result therefore indicates the relevance of the introduction of the presence of action. Of course, other studies targeting more particularly the presence of action and its links with assumed affordances and proprioceptive sensations remain to be conducted to confirm the validity of the presence of action dimension.

FRAMEWORK OF VIRTUAL REALITY APPLICATION DESIGN

Reading the previous sections makes it clear that creating a sense of presence in a user is a laudable goal, often relevant but difficult to achieve and maintain. Also, we prefer to speak more modestly to tend towards this feeling. Three main categories of factors participate in the emergence of the presence (IJsselsteijn, 2000): the characteristics of the system (the form), the content of the application (the background) and the characteristics of the user (Sas, 2003; Thornson, 2009).

In this section we define a framework dedicated to the design of virtual reality applications. Once identified the needs and objectives of the application as well as the typical user (we will take into account its characteristics and more particularly its motor and intellectual capacities), the designer can follow the framework to define the services and functionalities it wish to offer. Depending on the objectives, constraints, and skills present, he can rely on an optimal combination of factors. Recall that the purpose of this framework is to offer an experience that is sufficiently credible to the user so that the latter agrees to take on the game so that in return he can feel a sense of presence. The designer can therefore rely on a knowledge base on human cognition and then on four pillars called immersion, interaction, sensorimotor loop and emotions (see figure 1 for an illustration).

THE COGNITIVE FOUNDATION

We consider knowledge of human cognition as essential to develop new paradigms of interaction and immersion or simply to optimize algorithms and methods. By human cognition we mean the body of knowledge relating to perception, information extraction, the role of emotions, memorization, etc. An example of successful application of knowledge on human vision (Ferwerda, 2001) is found in computer graphics in the family of perceptual rendering algorithms. Environmental perception studies tend to focus on one direction only. It is only recently that researchers in psychology and neuroscience are studying perception through multisensory integration (Calvert, 2004).

It turns out that we perceive our environment through all senses at the same time and integrates all these multiple perceptions into unique information. If an increase in quality on a monosensory rendering (visual for example) is perceptible when only one sense is stimulated, then this may not be the case in the context of a multisensory rendering: the perceptual capacities and the attention of the user then being shared between several senses and no longer dedicated to one. Grelaud et al. (2009) take advantage of recent knowledge on the multimodal perception of materials (Bonneel, 2009) to propose an efficient method allowing rendering graphically and sounding impacts between objects. The integration of stimuli obtained via distinct senses can lead to multimodal illusions or more or less surprising effects (Alais, 2004; McGurk, 1976; Zampini 2004).

Immersion

While the feeling of presence is subjective, immersion is limited to an objective and measurable description of the technological means used to restore the virtual environment to the senses (Slater, 1997). Immersion is defined as the stimulation of the user's senses to generate the sensations that allow, sometimes through an illusion (we seek to deceive the user's senses), the perception of the virtual environment. The purpose of the immersion is multiple: immerse the user in the virtual environment, prevent the perception of the real environment to encourage the user to focus his attention on the experience, and finally offer a good understanding of the environment. The latter depends on the perception of affordances of the environment. In our opinion, immersion is part of a diegetic purpose 1. We also include in this pillar the content of the experience of neutral level, i.e., which aims for a descriptive and realistic representation of the environment regardless of the emotions potentially aroused.

Multisensory stimulation (Stein, 1993) avoids the appearance of a phenomenon of lack (Gilkey, 1995) and constitutes as much redundant information (Burr, 2006) describing the virtual environment and the events which take place there. During our evaluation phase, we notably noted that the environmental presence felt by the study participants is low compared to the global presence and the other components of the presence. However, the video game that supports the experiment offers stereoscopic vision, the environment is three-dimensional and the participants have the possibility of moving freely in the virtual

Figure 1. Our framework for designing virtual reality applications. The four pillars can build on a foundation of knowledge on human cognition

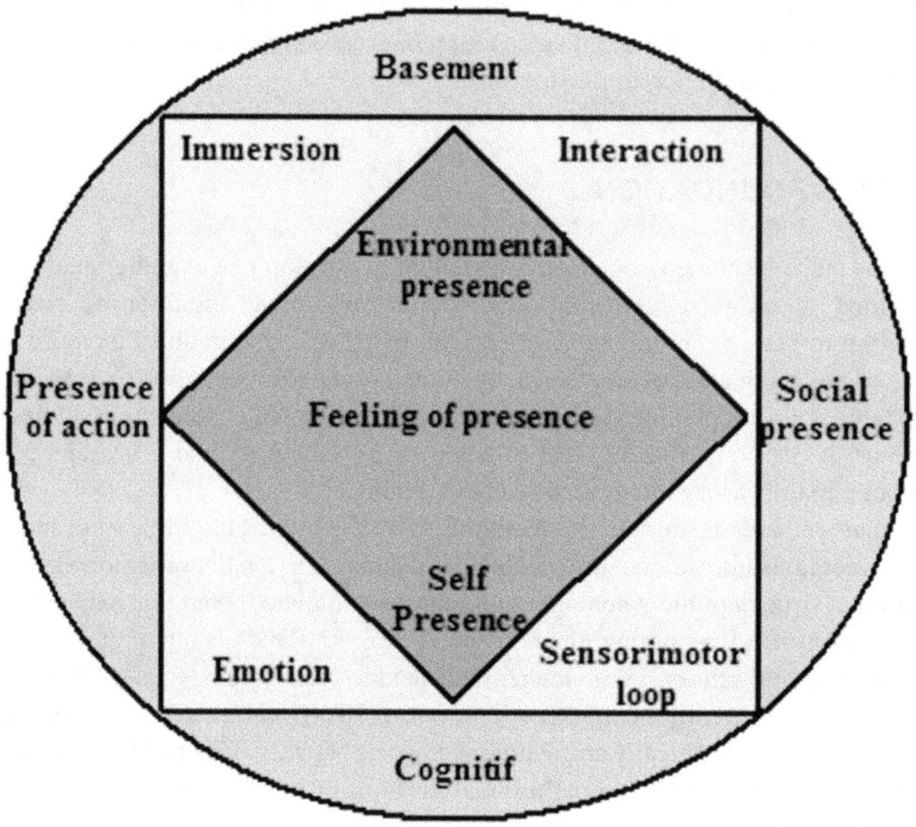

world. We think that the reason for this deficit is that the immersion is based in this case only on a visual representation. It is very likely that with a sound stimulation rendering the sounds of the explosions and the engine and by proposing as an interaction tool, a steering wheel or a joystick, the spatial presence would have been better. This result, therefore, militates for a resolutely multisensory immersion.

We believe that immersion should be bidirectional. If the immersion consists of immersing the user in the virtual environment then his simple presence must have consequences on this environment. Rendering these consequences must increase the credibility of the experience. Also, this can reduce the static and immutable aspect of the environment. Referring to the usual senses, it is important to mention the proprioceptive sense. This allows us to build a mental model associated with the arrangement of the different segments of our body (Sherrington, 1906). Its meaning status encourages the positioning of proprioception in the section dedicated to immersion. However, it must be treated separately because unlike the other senses it cannot be stimulated directly. The immersion must give an illusion of reality, but this will be more significant if the proprioceptive sensations are in accordance with the stimuli received by the other senses. So, it is considered as very important for the presence that the interaction patterns allow correspondence between the proprioceptive sensations of the virtual self and the proprioceptive sensations of the real self (Slater, 1994).

Interaction

Being able to act on the environment and the content of the experience rather than passively watching is an important factor for the emergence of the feeling of presence (Welch, 1996). The usual classification (Bowman, 1999) of possible actions in virtual reality is as follows: navigation, selection, manipulation, and control of the system. However, it seems to us wise to differentiate the possible interactions with the environment according to only the following two criteria: either the user wants to acquire information (for example via a tactile interface) or information communication (by manipulating an object or indicating a direction). Thus, our classification makes it possible to include the interactions with the other characters (alive or not) that the user can meet during his experience. This interaction will have a direct impact on social presence and therefore on the feeling of presence (Skalski, 2007).

The degree of interactivity of the experience depends on the variety of interaction modalities (Lombard, 1997), the range of freedom offered to the user, and finally the latency time between an action of the user and the response of the system. (Beigbeder, 2004). If we refer to the concept of the illusion of non-mediation (Lombard, 1997), we understand that on the one hand, the interaction tools must be as transparent as possible until they can be forgotten during the experience. On the other hand, the interaction diagrams as well as the manipulation of any interfaces must be ergonomic, easily understandable, and easy to use. The cognitive capacities of the user should not be mobilized by manipulation because otherwise, he would not be able to grasp the rest of the experience. One method supposed to be able to satisfy all of these conditions for success is direct interaction coupled with natural interaction patterns.

Direct interaction does not exploit interfaces other than the user's body. (Slater, 1994) Natural interaction patterns are similar to those used in the physical environment. They, therefore, correspond to the sensorimotor capacities of the user, and consequently, there is a perfect correspondence between the interaction patterns and the proprioceptive sensations of the user. This involves, for example, moving an object with your hand rather than with a mouse or keyboard keys. The interaction is no longer a source of disruption and the user can fully focus on the experience. The gains for presence are therefore multiple: proprioceptive feedback, illusion of non-mediation, focusing attention on experience. If the interaction scheme allows adequate proprioceptive feedback then the user is more easily identified with his virtual body. This is a very important step for the presence of self and the presence of action.

In accordance with our presence model presented in section 6.3 we consider that the affordances that the user perceives in the virtual environment must be assumed (that is to say achievable) by the interfaces and interaction schemes proposed by the virtual reality device. The affordances are assumed if a direct interaction scheme allows responding to the affordances. For example, if the environment allows the user to move by walking, the walking interaction diagram must be achievable by the user. That is to say that navigation is done by walking and not by using a joystick for example. Direct and natural interaction and assumed affordances are the keys to a successful interaction leading to the illusion of non-mediation and valid proprioceptive sensations. We can therefore conclude that when designing an experience in virtual reality it is important to ensure that a maximum of perceived agreement is assumed by the interaction patterns.

Coherence of the Sensorimotor Loop and Multimodality

This pillar is multidimensional. The first dimension concerns the maintenance of the causal link between user action and their perception of the system's responses. This dimension, therefore, constitutes a bridge between the first two pillars. It is clear that if this causal link is broken, the illusion of non-mediation will be in vain and the credibility of the experience will be null. Care must therefore be taken to implement algorithms operating in real-time and to provide sensorimotor interfaces whose display or detection frequencies are fast enough so that the user does not perceive latency.

By considering emotions as a factor in their own right to tend towards presence, we are breaking with the technological approach for which emotions and presence is orthogonal (Slater, 2003). To respond to Slater's warning, (2003) we do not confuse presence with emotional responses. We are aware that emotional responses allow you to be transported and that they can induce physiological responses. However, we also know that they cannot translate into behavioral reactions, which excludes

The presence that we defined previously as the authentic feeling of existing in a world other than the physical world where our body is located can be examined through its four components: environmental presence, social presence, presence of self and presence of action. In this section, we want to highlight the influence of the pillars on the different components of presence.

We believe that the pillars do not work in a parallel or additive fashion but rather in synergy. For example, immersion by allowing a good understanding of the scene facilitates interactions with the environment and makes it possible to perceive affordances. Likewise, an overly complex or cumbersome pattern or interaction device can penalize the perception of emotions in the environment. Examples could multiply. So, we should not consider that there is a direct and almost exclusive relationship between the level of immersion and the level of presence felt.

The study by Baños et al (2004) assesses the variations in presence felt like a function of the visual interfaces used and of the level of emotions carried by the environment. The results indicate that the level of presence varies simultaneously depending on these two factors. From a presence perspective, we believe that the pillars offset each other. That is to say that if a pillar suffers from a lower quality then an effort in one (or more) other pillars can compensate for this lack. A recent study by Banos et al (2008) shows that stereoscopic vision does have a positive impact on a neutral environment, but the impact is zero when the environment is full of emotions.

THE DIFFERENT MODELS OF PRESENCE

A presence model aims to identify and organize the underlying processes leading to the feeling of presence. It is therefore a question of understanding how and why from a virtual reality experience, a user feels - or not - a feeling of presence.

CONCLUSION

We consider virtual reality as a mediated experience that immerses one or more users in the heart of an artificial environment in which the user can feel and interact in real-time via sensory-motor interfaces. The user deems the experience credible, agrees to take part in the game, and in response feels a sense of presence. The latter consists of an authentic feeling of existing in a world other than the physical world where one's body is located. These definitions translate our global vision of virtual reality and presence. This vision is based on a phase of reflection which we hope sheds new light on presence. This consists

Figure 2. Our complete and unified model of presence.

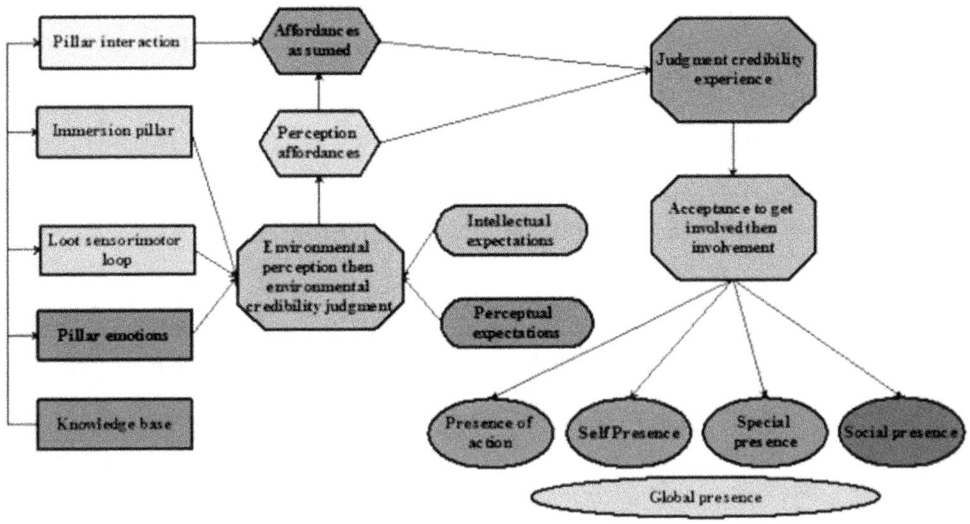

of a new definition of presence and the identification of a fourth dimension of presence called presence of action. The latter manifests itself by being aware of its actions and their scope.

As we wrote earlier, the emergence of presence cannot happen until the user agrees to take on the game of experience. Using our presence model, we have identified the processes leading to the feeling of presence. The work of the designer of experience in virtual reality will therefore consist of creating the conditions necessary for the user to accept to be caught in the game. According to our model, this acceptance depends on the credibility of the environment and the credibility of the experience in its entirety. The credibility of the environment depends on satisfying the intellectual and perceptual expectations of the user. The credibility of the experience is accepted if the affordances perceived in the environment are assumed by the interaction patterns of the experience. We insisted on talking about credibility, not realism.

REFERENCES

Alais, D., & Burr, D. (2004). The ventriloquist effect results from near-optimal bimodal integration. *Current Biology*, *14*(3), 257–262. doi:10.1016/j.cub.2004.01.029 PMID:14761661

Baños, R. M., Botella, C., Alcañiz, M., Liaño, V., Guerrero, B., & Rey, B. (2004). Immersion and emotion: Their impact on the sense of presence. *Cyberpsychology & Behavior*, *7*(6), 734–741. doi:10.1089/cpb.2004.7.734 PMID:15687809

Baños, R. M., Botella, C., Rubió, I., Quero, S., García-Palacios, A., & Alcañiz, M. (2008). Presence and emotions in virtual environments: The influence of stereoscopy. *Cyberpsychology & Behavior*, *11*(1), 1–8. doi:10.1089/cpb.2007.9936 PMID:18275306

Beigbeder, T., Coughlan, R., Lusher, C., Plunkett, J., Agu, E., & Claypool, M. (2004, August). The effects of loss and latency on user performance in unreal tournament 2003®. In *Proceedings of 3rd ACM SIGCOMM workshop on Network and system support for games* (pp. 144-151). 10.1145/1016540.1016556

Biocca, F. (1997). The cyborg's dilemma: Progressive embodiment in virtual environments. *Journal of Computer-Mediated Communication, 3*(2).

Biocca, F. (2003, May). Can we resolve the book, the physical reality, and the dream state problems? From the two-pole to a three-pole model of shifts in presence. In *EU Future and Emerging Technologies, Presence Initiative Meeting* (Vol. 12, pp. 13-69). Academic Press.

Bonneel, N., Suied, C., Viaud-Delmon, I., & Drettakis, G. (2010). Bimodal perception of audio-visual material properties for virtual environments. *ACM Transactions on Applied Perception, 7*(1), 1–16. doi:10.1145/1658349.1658350

Bouvier, P. (2009). *La présence en réalité virtuelle, une approche centrée utilisateur* (Doctoral dissertation).

Bowman, D. A. (1999). *Interaction techniques for common tasks in immersive virtual environments.* Georgia Institute of Technology.

Burr, D., & Alais, D. (2006). Combining visual and auditory information. *Progress in Brain Research, 155*, 243–258. doi:10.1016/S0079-6123(06)55014-9 PMID:17027392

Calvert, G., Spence, C., & Stein, B. E. (Eds.). (2004). *The handbook of multisensory processes.* MIT Press.

Ferwerda, J. A. (2001). Elements of early vision for computer graphics. *IEEE Computer Graphics and Applications, 21*(5), 22–33. doi:10.1109/38.946628

Gibson, J. (1986). *The Ecological Approach to Visual Perception.* Lawrence Erlbaum Associates.

Gilkey, R. H., & Weisenberger, J. M. (1995). The sense of presence for the suddenly deafened adult: Implications for virtual environments. *Presence (Cambridge, Mass.), 4*(4), 357–363.

Grelaud, D., Bonneel, N., Wimmer, M., Asselot, M., & Drettakis, G. (2009, February). Efficient and practical audio-visual rendering for games using crossmodal perception. In *Proceedings of the 2009 symposium on Interactive 3D graphics and games* (pp. 177-182). 10.1145/1507149.1507178

Heeter, C. (1992). Being there: The subjective experience of presence. *Presence (Cambridge, Mass.), 1*(2), 262–271. doi:10.1162/pres.1992.1.2.262

Heeter, C. (2003). Reflections on real presence by a virtual person. *Presence (Cambridge, Mass.), 12*(4), 335–345. doi:10.1162/105474603322391587

IJsselsteijn, W. A., De Ridder, H., Freeman, J., & Avons, S. E. (2000, June). Presence: concept, determinants, and measurement. In Human vision and electronic imaging V (Vol. 3959, pp. 520-529). International Society for Optics and Photonics.

Lee, K. M. (2004). Presence, explicated. *Communication Theory, 14*(1), 27–50. doi:10.1111/j.1468-2885.2004.tb00302.x

Lessiter, J., Freeman, J., Keogh, E., & Davidoff, J. (2001). A cross-media presence questionnaire: The ITC-Sense of Presence Inventory. *Presence (Cambridge, Mass.), 10*(3), 282–297. doi:10.1162/105474601300343612

Levine, D. N. (2007, February). "The Integrative action of the nervous system": A centennial appraisal. *Journal of the Neurological Sciences, 253*(1-2), 1–6. doi:10.1016/j.jns.2006.12.002 PMID:17223135

Lombard, M., & Ditton, T. (1997). At the heart of it all: The concept of presence. *Journal of Computer-Mediated Communication, 3*(2).

McGurk, H., & MacDonald, J. (1976). Hearing lips and seeing voices. *Nature, 264*(5588), 746–748. doi:10.1038/264746a0 PMID:1012311

Minsky, M. (1980, June). Telepresence. *OMNI Magazine*.

Sanchez-Vives, M. V., & Slater, M. (2005). From presence to consciousness through virtual reality. *Nature Reviews. Neuroscience, 6*(4), 332–339. doi:10.1038/nrn1651 PMID:15803164

Sas, C., & O'Hare, G. M. (2003). Presence equation: An investigation into cognitive factors underlying presence. *Presence (Cambridge, Mass.), 12*(5), 523–537. doi:10.1162/105474603322761315

Schubert, T., Friedmann, F., & Regenbrecht, H. (2001). The experience of presence: Factor analytic insights. *Presence (Cambridge, Mass.), 10*(3), 266–281. doi:10.1162/105474601300343603

Skalski, P., & Tamborini, R. (2007). The role of social presence in interactive agent-based persuasion. *Media Psychology, 10*(3), 385–413. doi:10.1080/15213260701533102

Slater, M. (2003). A note on presence terminology. *Presence Connect, 3*(3), 1-5.

Slater, M., & Steed, A. (2000). A virtual presence counter. *Presence (Cambridge, Mass.), 9*(5), 413–434. doi:10.1162/105474600566925

Slater, M., & Usoh, M. (1993, September). Presence in immersive virtual environments. In *Proceedings of IEEE Virtual Reality Annual International Symposium* (pp. 90-96). IEEE. 10.1109/VRAIS.1993.380793

Slater, M., & Usoh, M. (1994). Body centred interaction in immersive virtual environments. *Artificial Life and Virtual Reality, 1*(1994), 125-148.

Slater, M., Usoh, M., & Steed, A. (1994). Depth of presence in virtual environments. *Presence (Cambridge, Mass.), 3*(2), 130–144. doi:10.1162/pres.1994.3.2.130

Slater, M., & Wilbur, S. (1997). A framework for immersive virtual environments (FIVE): Speculations on the role of presence in virtual environments. *Presence (Cambridge, Mass.), 6*(6), 603–616. doi:10.1162/pres.1997.6.6.603

Stein, B. E., & Meredith, M. A. (1993). *The merging of the senses*. The MIT Press.

Thornson, C. A., Goldiez, B. F., & Le, H. (2009). Predicting presence: Constructing the tendency toward presence inventory. *International Journal of Human-Computer Studies, 67*(1), 62–78. doi:10.1016/j.ijhcs.2008.08.006

Waterworth, J. A., & Waterworth, E. L. (2003). *The meaning of presence*. Academic Press.

Welch, R. B., Blackmon, T. T., Liu, A., Mellers, B. A., & Stark, L. W. (1996). The effects of pictorial realism, delay of visual feedback, and observer interactivity on the subjective sense of presence. *Presence (Cambridge, Mass.)*, *5*(3), 263–273. doi:10.1162/pres.1996.5.3.263

Zahorik, P., & Jenison, R. L. (1998). Presence as being-in-the-world. *Presence (Cambridge, Mass.)*, *7*(1), 78–89. doi:10.1162/105474698565541

Zampini, M., & Spence, C. (2004). The role of auditory cues in modulating the perceived crispness and staleness of potato chips. *Journal of Sensory Studies*, *19*(5), 347–363. doi:10.1111/j.1745-459x.2004.080403.x

Chapter 5
Application of Augmented Reality and Virtual Reality in Education

Dharmpal Singh
JIS College of Enginnering, India

Abhishek Banerjee
Pailan College of Management and Technology, India

Ira Nath
https://orcid.org/0000-0001-9648-0819
JIS College of Engineering, India

ABSTRACT

Augmented reality (AR) and virtual reality (VR) play an important role in today's world. Due to COVID-19, we all are doing many things by online mode. In this virtual place, the importance of AR and VR increases tremendously. With AR and VR tools, students have an inimitable chance to explore historic destinations while remaining in the classroom. Moreover, AR and VR tools provide students the ability to gain deeper understandings of abstract or complex subjects and phenomena that are relatively difficult to understand only by two-dimensional text, pictures, and video. This chapter discusses the similarities and differences of AR and VR and the evaluation of the application of AR and VR into educational programs.

INTRODUCTION

Augmented Reality (AR) and Virtual Reality (VR)play an important role in today's world. Due to COVID-19, we all are doing many things by online mode. In this virtual place, the importance of AR and VR increases tremendously. With AR and VR tools, students have an inimitable chance to explore historic destinations while remaining in the classroom. Moreover, AR and VR tools provide students the

DOI: 10.4018/978-1-7998-4222-4.ch005

ability to gain deeper understandings of abstract or complex subjects and phenomena that are relatively difficult to understand only by two-dimensional text, pictures, and video.

Today students are familiar with all forms of technology and use these at school as well as at home. They have grown up with technology from a very early age and they do not have any fear or hesitation about using it. At this time, we live in a technological society. So, it is important to implement VR and AR as one of several forms of technology to educate tomorrow's citizens. Education has moved on from books, pencils, and pens to the use of interactive technologies to help impart knowledge and understanding. Computers have become an important part of everyday life that it can be difficult to remember a time when they did not exist. It has been used since the abacus approximately 5000 years ago. Computer technology in the classroom can improve teaching and learning and boost up student achievement, compared to teaching without such aids.

BACKGROUND

VR is a combination of different types of technologies that are used to visualize and provide communication with a virtual environment that belongs to 3D Space. It may be realistic, imaginary, macroscopic, or microscopic (Christou, 2010). VR may be used to make it broadly applicable to many areas in education. A key feature of VR is that it allows multi-sensory interaction with the space visualized.

VR is a realistic, collaborating 3D computer-generated environment in which we can experience our existence and interact. VR is the utilization of computer technology to develop a virtual platform. VR creates feelings or realization inside the users. VR creates an environment through which we can visualize, understand, realize, and interact with each other to explore one matter virtually (Woodford, 2020). VR is used in various fields to visualize data in the development of drugs, and in the training of pilots and the military.

AR enables the connection of the digital and physical domains. It is one of the new technologies applied to education. It has already begun to show promise in helping students learn more effectively and increase knowledge retention, relative to traditional 2D desktop interfaces. It supports the understanding of complex phenomena by providing unique visual and interactive experiences that combine real and virtual information and help communicate abstract problems to learners. AR can support knowledge of a real-world environment where the objects that exist in the real world are improved by computer-generated perceptual information, sometimes across multiple sensory modalities.

AR is when the user's physical world is added to, or augmented, with computer-generated input such as sound, video, graphics, GPS, and more. It can be defined as a system that fulfills three basic features including a combination of real and virtual worlds, real-time interactions, and accurate 3D representation of virtual and real objects. It is used to enhance natural environments or situations. In comparison to VR, AR does not create the whole artificial environment to replace real with a virtual one.

AR is connected to the interactive concept with the growth of the Internet and smartphones. It is directly projected 3D models onto physical things or focused together in real-time. AR apps typically connect digital animation to a special 'marker', or with the help of GPS in phones pinpoint the location. This technology expands our physical world, adding layers of digital information onto it. AR is view of an existing environment with sounds, videos, and graphics added to it. AR integrates digital information with real environments where everything is processed and produced in real-time.

The main difference between VR and AR is that VR uses artificial environments and AR uses the real world and adds to it with digital information. AR technology is less developed because it needs more processing power. Initially, the main applications of this technology's potential have been interior designs, video conferences, visits to malls, browsers, etc. All of these are low levels of development when taking into account what information was required in the system. However, many of the major technology multinationals have already created AR prototypes.

AR is an interactive experience for a person with a real-world environment feeling. Here objects that exist in the real world are improved by computer-generated predictive information, sometimes taking data from multiple sensory modalities, including visual, auditory, haptic, somatosensory, and olfactory. AR environments give a feeling of realistic objects that are familiar to us at a macroscopic scale. It may depict the physical world as known to science but which is not usually observable, or it may be used to visualize an entirely imaginary world.

AR is a visual and interactive experience in a real-world environment where the objects in the real-world are "augmented" by computer-generated perceptual information. AR means interaction with 3D models. where you can set the rotation, transparency, color scheme, styles, etc. These virtual enhancements in the real world can appear as something visual and auditory. Finally, there could be more advanced animations via special gadgets like holographic lenses, instead of smartphones.

Gutierrez et al. (2017) discussed how AR is implemented in many sectors like industry, education, video games, and other sectors. AR is emerging as one of the key drivers of the technology economy. AR apps, headsets, and smart glasses hold the promise to add value to virtually every industry from retail to industrial manufacturing. Major corporations are designing AR prototypes.

With the help of AR, educational designers can superimpose virtual graphics over real objects, allowing users to interact with digital content through physical manipulation. The result is a more effective demonstration of spatial and temporal concepts and it is the contextual relationships among real and virtual objects. With the help of AR, classes will turn out more interactive and allow learners to focus more on practice instead of just theory. AR adds virtual objects to the real world because AR has the potential to change the location and timing of studying, to introduce new and additional ways and methods.

VR and AR carry out two very dissimilar things in two very dissimilar ways, despite the similar designs of the devices themselves. VR replaces reality, taking you somewhere else. AR adds to reality, projecting information on top of what you're already seeing. They're both are powerful technologies that have yet to make their mark with consumers but show a lot of promise. They can completely change how we use computers in the future, but whether one or both will succeed is anyone's guess right now.

VR EDUCATION

Many designers see VR as an extension of the gaming industry. Indeed, VR has historically been dedicated to gaming, but things are changing. According to a recent survey conducted by Greenlight VR, the desire for education outweighs the desire for gaming content with 63.9 percent vs. 61 percent. VR acts as a whole new concept in educational technology with a unique student-friendly interface, gesture controls, embedded educational resources, and simple-to-use teacher controls. VR academic apps should have the following characteristics:

1. **Affect.** The developers must attempt to develop feelings among the learners while they will use VR education apps. If you develop a geography app then you have to create it in such a way so that geography will be alive in the minds of the active learners.
2. **Simple to handle:** You should reduce the necessity of learning distinct skills to handle with a VR education app. The process of controlling the VR education app will be simple and easy enough.
3. **Easy to understand and meaningful learning:** Clear understanding of any subject is the most important thing for any learner. The simple and easy explanation of any subject is essential for making any good VR educational app. The art of storytelling is an important approach for inspiring learners using VR educational apps.
4. **Adjustable and flexible:** Learners also need an environment in which they can be able to learn properly and appropriately. A VR app can provide this space to the students in such a way that they will be more motivated to learn and develop new knowledge. To make the education system more effective, the developers of VR educational apps must take feedback from the present learners, and then this valuable feedback will be required to be incorporated to develop more adaptable and efficient VR educational apps.
5. **Quantifiable:** Every VR educational app must be quantifiable. Instructors must be capable of knowing the measurement of learning responses so that they can quantify the new learning. The capability of measurement of learner response is needed in educational VR apps.

The transformation of present academics using VR has been identified in multiple sources (Singh, 2020; Bordi, 2020). In 2019, Babich (2019) discussed the effect of VR in academics for our present teaching and learning process. Babich described the main purposes of using AR in academics. Singh presented various apps for pupils with their proper utilization in academics and the current challenges of AR. Kovach (nd) described the transformation of AR in academics. She explained the potential of AR in the classroom, and training

VR technology brings a series of significant changes in multiple fields. Yoon et al. (2017) has shown how digital simulation and dynamic visualization tools have impacted productivity in multiple fields. Xu's (2020) research described how VR has been implemented in sports. As one of the key technologies of the future development of the VR application is in the field of sports teaching. It will subvert the traditional physical education thinking and unidirectional sports teaching model for physical education.

VR simulations are used for students to learn practical skills. One of the biggest benefits of training people in this way where students can learn from realistic scenarios without the risk of practicing an unfamiliar skill in an uncontrolled real-life situation. The VR simulation Apollo 11 recreates the events of the July 1969 Moon landing. It is a simulations where the learner can control and fly the command module, land the lunar lander, explore the Moon's surface, and deploy some experiments. Another graphical app from google, "Tilt Brush" is used to create art in 3D space with lots of possibilities. By using a wide range of dynamic brushes and a variety of interfaces, students can use any virtual space as a canvas to create a real work of art and share as animated gifs.

Most of the topics in geography can be taught to the learners using VR technology. Using this technology, the learner can experience trips to those places on the earth which they currently studying. One example of a VR educational app is Google Expeditions. The learners who have a smartphone with an internet connection can use this app for tours in VR. The learner can do trips to different places all over the world. These places are not possible for the learners to visit in the real world. Using VR, the learner can experience the virtual trip and increase their engagement and understanding about different place in the world.

The medical field is an also an area where VR is applicable. The anatomy part of medical science can be taught to the learners using VR. It also helps the trainer to teach the students appropriately using the three dimensional images of body parts and their connections using VR. Schools all over the world are taking the advantages of VR to teach biology in their classes. VR is also applicable in military training.

The vital portion of the teaching and learning process is receiving exposure to various fields. The instructors can use AR to provide simulated career or mentoring experiences. Often, we get this understanding through internships. VR can assist learners in extending exposure to careers. The students can get more knowledge about working in various fields including what are they doing, how they have reached this position, what are the reasons for their success in this particular field, about their job prospects, and so on using VR. It also helps the learners to build their careers. This will be only be possible using VR. VR learners can provide a link the distance between professionals and pupils. With virtual reality, remote learning can connect the professionals and pupils at the same place digitally. The professionals can teleport into the VR and lead pupils using their knowledge and expertise.

VR provides us the advantages to create a platform to connect in simulations with others all over the world. Utilizing avatars and mapped facial expressions, learners can come together to deliberate, debate, and learn from one another. The students also are more interested in this innovative learning instead of only reading textbooks. It is clear that using VR is no doubt challenging but the journey with VR in academics has started. This potential technology can be utilized in every part of academics to make education more attractive to learners. There are many challenges to make academics effective for the students using VR. These challenges must be overcome in near future.

AR EDUCATION

AR and VR are the new trends in education where AR superimposes our real-world information through the use of a device, and VR uses a computer-generated environment to interact and be immersed with VR goggles. These goggles allow you to see a different world or space with 360-degree vision.

AR is a growing field of technology where real life is modified and enhanced by computer-generated sights and sounds. Gandolfi (2020) provided an overview of AR and VR in education. Even though their role in K-12 online learning and blended environments is still at an early stage, significant efforts have been made to frame their core affordances and constraints, and potential future developments. An ordinary class will change into an engaging experience by using AR. It provides virtual examples and adds practical elements to support textbook materials

The past, present, and future of VR and AR research has been described in a meta-analysis by Cipresso et al. (2020). The ability to connect reality and digital content has been steadily improving, opening more options for teachers and students. AR devices are becoming more common with AR features with the ability to explore and learn. AR means interaction with 3D models where you can set the rotation, transparency, color scheme, styles, etc. There could be more advanced animations via special gadgets like holographic lenses, instead of smartphones.

AR maximizes students' ability to spend their time learning curricular subjects while minimizing the time spent learning how to use the new technology. It can inspire responsiveness in an individual. It offers two-dimensional methods of presenting information versus the traditional one-dimension. This combination of interactivity and engagement could enhance the ability of students to remember what they've learned and lead to faster acquisition of information and skills.

The technologies that make AR possible are much becoming more powerful and compact enough to deliver AR experiences. AR is possible on personal computers, wireless mobile devices, smartphones, and tablet PCs. It can be used to just stimulate interest and discussion in different subject areas and be the basis for class activities.AR transforms volumes of data and analytics into images or animations that are overlaid on the real world. Today most AR applications are delivered through mobile devices. Some of the reasons AR is useful in education include:

1. It deals with a more emotional and immersive experience which creates the interest of students.
2. It simplifies the learning and transmission of concepts.
3. It increases the motivation of the students which makes the classes more enjoyable and interesting.
4. It inspires the participation of all students to interact with the subject.
5. AR breaks the traditional monotony of classes where it offers incentives to learn.
6. It allows students to view the subjects and their closest reality from another perspective.
7. It prepares students for digital communication.

Naaz and Sharma (2018) described the application, challenges, and recent trends of AR. It provides students with opportunities to deepen their knowledge within five areas like reading, working with numbers, spatial concepts, playing, content writing, and real-life environments and scenarios. They can include everything from field trips to exposure to training within different professions. AR provides new opportunities for students to learn how to communicate and collaborate.

Digital simulation tools have facilitated new technological learning challenges by providing different technological frameworks. Students can acquire a more accurate concepts with the help of an AR device. Within a short period of investigation in a science museum, students can demonstrate significantly with the help of AR tools. AR affords a greater ability to visualize details and hidden information to help students learn science. AR in the education sector is a resource that offers many possibilities but still has a long way to go when it comes to future developments. AR also has some negative aspects. They are as follows:

- It is a recreational element. For this reason, it is necessary to know how to guide learning in the educational field.
- It can be a challenge for teachers to adapt and train in new methods.
- Specific teaching material and devices must be adapted to AR.
- It can be expensive to implement and some schools may not have the necessary budget.

AR training protocols are the next big thing in AR technologies. We could be using AR experiences to learn new things, train on the job, and augment everyday life. AR may be best known in the gaming industry but it has broader applications than just gaming. AR can shape our experiences of the world where new technology could create an opportunity for safer training, and build more reliable repositories for digital information.

In many cases, theoretical knowledge is not enough to obtain proper skills in professional areas. Students of technical faculties especially need practice and hands-on experience in their areas. Through interaction, AR could help students perform virtual practice sessions with augmented tutorials, digital modeling, and simulations, and acquire some experience in the end.

By incorporating AR into lessons teachers can involve students in the process of manipulating three dimensional models. It may be just a part of the lesson or the support of the main topic with extra information from a different perspective. A Canadian technology company, CASE, transformed the wall of the school gym into a ball game by adding an AR layer to it. Kids through balls onto a wall to hit floating shapes and so have fun physical exercises. Visitors of museums could access AR via smartphones and discover historical content related to objects.

AR animated content in classroom lessons could catch students' attention which motivates them to engage. Adding extra data like a short biography of a person, fun facts, historical data about sites or events, visual 3D models would give students a wider understanding of topics. While doing homework, students may scan certain elements of a book and receive text, audio, or video tips from teachers. They may find useful information about the course, a teacher, or other students which could lead to better communication. The Aurasma app is already being used in classrooms where students can view their classes via a smartphone or tablet for a richer learning environment. Students learning about astronomy might see a full map of the solar system or those in a music class might be able to see musical notes in real-time as they learn to play an instrument.

The impact of AR application on student's competency development has been shown by Lee and Shvetsovia (2020). They collected quantitative data from the interview forms which are developed by the researcher and qualitative data were analyzed using the expert method and a comparative study. A significant divergence was observed between competency development in the AR class and that in a regular class with a similar syllabus. A case study identified the effectiveness of using AR apps in teaching the English alphabet to kindergarten children (Safar et al., 2016)

A new startup Medview XR (XR designates Extended Reality comprising VR, AR and Mixed Reality technologies) has been introduced with X-ray vision while operating on patients using Microsoft HoloLens or similar AR goggles. MediView XR's technology gives surgeons the ability to peer inside patients and see their internal anatomy under the skin. That includes organs, blood vessels, bones, and other structures such as cancerous lesions. This is all thanks to a system that "fuses" sensor readings from ultrasound devices with CT or MRI scans to provide an X-ray-like view that doesn't involve repeated exposure to X-rays. The three-dimensional view means that surgeons can move around patients and continue to see their internal anatomy in the right position and from the correct angle. AR apps for medical students may be one of the ways to learn human anatomy and explore it more deeply.

The most common use of AR can be seen through mobile apps. Point your device's camera at something that the app recognizes, and it will generate a 3D animation or video superimposed over whatever is on your camera's screen. The effect makes the computer-generated item appear like it is there. By incorporating AR into lessons teachers can involve students in the process of learning with three dimensional models. It may be just a part of the lesson or the support of the main topic with extra information from a different perspective.

While teachers do not necessarily need to recruit all students into science, their goal is to get them interested in a subject. That's where AR could come in handy. The potential of combining smartphones and AR for education is immense but it still has to be fully discovered. In various ways, AR could provide students with extra digital information about any subject, and make complex information easier to understand.

AR technology can reduce objects which are hard to imagine and turn them into 3D models, thus making it easier to grasp the abstract and difficult content. This is especially good for visual learners and practically anyone to translate theoretical material into a real concept. AR technology can render objects that are hard to imagine and turn them into 3D models, thus making it easier to grasp the abstract and difficult content. This is good for visual learners and practically anyone to translate theoretical material into a real concept.

The conventional learning process has many constraints. AR has the potential to change the location and timing of studying, to present new and additional ways and methods. Capabilities of AR technology may make classes more engaging and information more accessible. Educators know that the learning process should be all about creativity and interaction. Sometimes, technology is a cool factor that encourages students to follow their passion for learning and this will lead a student to a more ground-breaking environment, but we need to keep technology's instructional benefits at the front position of our searches. Educators also need to use both AR and VR with a critical eye and try to discover how this technology can help educate our students.

Examples of educational AR apps are listed below:

1. HP Reveal: It is a simple app. The concept of this app is very simple. Make any image (a photo, graphics, text document) scannable with a smartphone or tablet (iOS or Android), and associate an action to take when the image is scanned. An action can be displayed in a movie, show an extra explanation, refer to a website, etc. This way, you enrich simple paper posters, images, QR-codes, and many more for people who use the Reveal app to look at them.
2. CoSpaces Edu: It is a content creation app for students by which students can build their own 3D objects and animate them with code. Students can explore any creations with the VR and AR view modes. The app enables students to project their virtual creations onto any surface in the real world in AR.
3. Wonderscope: It is a storytelling app that uses AR to transform ordinary places into real-time stories. Students also learn to read with the app. They ask questions to the characters in the story and listen to the characters' answers.
4. Layar: It is AR software where users can enhance flyers, postcards, packaging, or any other item with interactive content, including video messages, Web and social links, photo slideshows, music clips.
5. Shapes 3D: This AR app is used for math especially geometry. Using these apps users can create prisms, pyramids, solids of revolution, and platonic solids. This AR tool wants to enhance the teacher's capabilities and provide possibilities to show things that cannot be shown with physical tools or within the classroom.
6. Google Expeditions: Google Expeditions offers a mix between AR and VR and allows a teacher to guide students through 360° scenes and 3D objects, pointing out interesting sites and another big problem with implementing AR solutions is the technological gap between AR devices. It is one thing to design an app for a fully-fledged AR gear, and it is a completely different thing to do it for a smartphone. The majority of the target audience will not likely purchase AR gear due to its impractical and high prices - smartphones remain a preferred function and since they have certain AR app design limitations - it enters the whole point of implementing AR solution to the mix.

7. A Canadian technology company transformed the wall of the school gym into a ball game by adding an AR layer to it. Kids through balls onto a wall to hit floating shapes and so have fun physical exercises.
8. Visitors of museums could access AR via smartphones and discover historical content related to objects. Additional information about what they see, though due to space or budget limitations, not all museums and landmarks can afford this. Once AR becomes more available, there will be new great opportunities for museums. The upside is that AR is already accessible to visitors through mobile devices.
9. University of Canterbury's Human Interface Technology Laboratory researchers have created a tool that can sketch a 3D object.
10. In the field of architecture, AR is being used to create scale models of buildings.
11. VTT Technical Research Centre of Finland, a multi technological applied research organization in Northern Europe, provides high-end technology solutions that include AR.
12. Elements 4D (Android / iOS) by DAQRI studio, an app for studying chemistry. It allows combining different elements as the simulation, to see how they would react in reality. To start it special triggers on printed cards are used. On their website, you can find lesson plans suitable for high school, secondary, and elementary school programs.
13. Anatomy 4D (iOS/Android) is best suitable for medical students. By scanning printed targets, the application shows 3D models of a human body and allows users to interact with it. Users may change and adjust any part of the human body, learn more about parts, joints, functions, etc.
14. Corinth Micro Anatomy, available for Windows Mobile, is another human anatomy application that may be interesting for medical staff. Or a Human Heart 3D app with less content, but more specific – to explore the human heart in detail. 3D model of a heart completed with various animations and textual tips about it.
15. Math alive: It is developed for kids in up to 3rd grades where it connects a computer, a camera, and specially printed cards. Pupils under teacher supervision place cards in front of a camera, practicing basic counting skills. Animal Alphabet AR Flashcards is a similar AR app but for learning letters, the application brings cards "into life" by showing live animals when the answer is correct.
16. ZooKazam: ZooKazam (Android / iOS) to teach about animal species offers animated 3D models and various info-graphics about mammals, insects, fish, birds, and reptiles. Bugs 3D (Android) helps kids to know more about insects, placing quests and questions about them and showing descriptions and images to play with.
17. Quiver and Chromville: It is used to learn about plants and flora. For the smallest kids check out Pete the Cat: School Jam app – it serves "pre-education" goals, like to teach empathy for live beings, as well as creativity.
18. Google Translate (Android / iOS) is just great for studying foreign languages without a dictionary. By using Google Translate special "AR mode" you may instantly check unknown words. Works well both for students and tourists, to navigate in cities abroad.
19. Amazing Space Journey, SkyORB 3D, and Star Walk. All of them have one purpose which is to study the skies with all their secrets. Learn more about stars, constellations, planets of the Solar System, galaxies, etc.
20. ClassVR concept is an innovative new technology designed to engage students and increase knowledge retention for students of all ages. ClassVR includes VR headsets and content that can be added to your classroom experiences.

FUTURE TRENDS

AR technology is experiencing broad adoption and mass public acceptance. There is a steady flow of investments in the AR app market. Startups are popping up like mushrooms after the rain with more and more outlandish concepts at hand and many big companies are trying out various AR-related solutions.

The future of AR is in the integration of advanced technologies that becoming more common as technology evolves. The following list describes these new technologies that can be used for implementing AR:

1. Mobile devices (smartphones and tablets): Most important for AR mobile apps, ranging from pure gaming and entertainment to business analytics, sports, and social networking.
2. Special AR devices:-It is designed primarily and solely for AR experiences. It is introduced to train military fighter pilots, now such devices have applications in aviation, the automotive industry, manufacturing, sports, etc.
3. AR glasses (or smart glasses):-These units are capable of displaying notifications from your smartphone, assisting assembly line workers, access content hands-free, etc.
4. AR contact lenses (or smart lenses):- Manufacturers like Samsung and Sony have announced the development of AR lenses. Respectively, Samsung is working on lenses as the accessory to smartphones, while Sony is designing lenses as separate AR devices (with features like taking photos or storing data).
5. Virtual retinal displays (VRD):-It is creating images by projecting laser light into the human eye. Aiming at bright, high contrast and high-resolution images, such systems yet remain to be made for practical use.

Educational organizations can use the latest technology in the classroom for creating a completely different learning experience opportunity for the students. Educators are preparing the leaders of the future. Schools, educators, and educational institutions are going to find different challenges if they neglect to update themselves, their methodology, and curricula to adopt a new approaches to education. Schools need to start preparing programs that are flexible enough to be adapted and modified quickly to teach students by developing their serious thinking and problem-solving abilities. It is going to be important for young students to be able to see problems from different perspectives to make the best possible decisions. This is going to constitute one of the pillars in their future that will be shared with AI robots and Quantum computers.

Students are needs to be able acquire knowledge by doing and experiencing. Schools need to provide a suitable environment that enhances this type of learning. This type of environment requires changes and a new approach to education at all levels. Schools and colleges should get ready by creating programs of study that require deep learning with active student engagement. To be successful, students need to analyze problems for possible alternative solutions according to different viewpoints, and then make decisions based on their own personal and individual critical thinking. Providing an engaging learning experience is paramount for the success of any educational institution, and in particular, the success of the educator. The latest technologies like Augmented, Virtual, and Mixed Reality, termed Extended Reality, can incorporate AR and VR content while making learning more efficient, faster, and much more fun.

Issues and Challenges

AR technology is quickly developing and gradually expanding its scope but the problem with its use cases and the content remains. The majority of AR-related content available at App Stores is mostly a showcase of simple tricks and not much else. The goal is to present some brands as forward-looking. It is designed to be a one-off affair. AR technology is still in its beginning, but if we look at what things AR development companies are trying to pull off with more or less the same tools the solutions above seem a bit lacking.

As with all technology, AR and VR adds cost to education. It is important to identify the cost and benefit ratio when integrating new technologies. A budget is a valuation of income and expenditures over an indicated future time and is usually assembled and re-evaluated periodically. It can be made for a person, a group of people, a business, a government, or anything else that makes and devotes money. There are four stages for creating a budget.

Stage 1: Review: Reviewing is the first stage for making a budget. It is a past performance for observing the entire matter. How correct was the budget? Where did the underspends and overspends occur? These questions can help you shape your school budget and increase its accuracy. It can give us a foundation by which we can build our budget and be prompted to review expenditure. Benchmarking against similar schools can help us to understand how our spending compares and put it into context. It is always an opportunity to identify cost savings or improvements.

Stage 2: Planning: It is the second phase for creating a budget. Once we collected our historical data and carried out the benchmarking, it is time to think about our resource, staffing, and accommodation needs for the next year. This stage should not be a one-step process. It is important to promote a range of income and cost scenarios based on our most important data. For making a precise budget, planning is very much important. Few important data which is very much significant are as follows:

1. Changes in funding (revenue and capital income)
2. Number of students and their characteristics
3. Class and group sizes
4. Staffing profiles and increments
5. Pay and price increases
6. Procurement and maintenance
7. Longer-term development plans in areas such as asset management, premises, staff, and IT/ICT
8. Local Authority Plans/Central Government Plans

Stage 3: Forecasting It is the third stage of making a Budget. Forecasts should be very much important for best guesses for it to be useful. But also, it is difficult to predict changes in areas such as funding, pupil numbers, and the costs of staffing. It can be beneficial to get involved in the local community to stay abreast of developments that could impact your school. Being active within the wider education sector can also give us insight into factors most likely to affect you. You can use this knowledge and your historical data to model a range of income/cost scenarios to assess the impact of varying factors on the budget. Factors to consider include:

1. Funding over the next three years
2. Changes in pupils and their characteristics

3. Curriculum changes
4. Likely staff profiles
5. Teaching staff salary rises
6. Increase
7. Goals of the school development plan
8. Longer-term improvement and development ambitions

'What if' analysis is most useful when you model trends rather than one-off changes and apply the highest probability and impact? Forecasting is easier, quicker, and more accurate by using different software. Multi-Academy Trusts follow these same principles however there are a few more considerations – we can learn more about them in the quick guide to school budget planning.

Stage 4: Implementation and evaluation It is the last stage of making a budget. Once the budget gets sanction from the governing body the budget is applied. Monitoring and evaluation also begin. Monitoring and reviewing of our monthly budget will highlight areas of potential risk early enough acting. We know that evaluation is the final stage of the school budgeting process where it feeds back into the first stage to the last stage. Ongoing evaluation gives us a head start on the following year's review and helps inform forecasting. By keeping a close eye on the budget throughout the year, we can identify ways in which resources and budget could be used more efficiently or differently.

CONCLUSION

The VR and AR technologies have the potential to radically change education. However, it has not been implemented earlier and now a global pandemic appears to have changed the technology's potential at least in the short-term. It has been observed that VR products have been hot sellers during the Covid-19 pandemic and Facebook has the vision to make AR and VR the next communications platform. Furthermore, Apple recently confirmed that it purchased NextVR, to do live streaming events like concerts and sports contests in VR. Due to the COVID-19 pandemic, we are more aware of AR and VR benefits. AR and VR technology will be the new learning method of the future.

REFERENCES

Babich, N. (2019). *How VR in Education Will Change How We Learn and Teach.* https://xd.adobe.com/ideas/principles/emerging-technology/virtual-reality-will-change-learn-teach/

Christou, C. (2010). Virtual reality in education. In *Affective, interactive and cognitive methods for e-learning design: creating an optimal education experience* (pp. 228–243). IGI Global. doi:10.4018/978-1-60566-940-3.ch012

Cipresso, P., Giglioli, I. A. C., Raya, M. A., & Riva, G. (2018). The past, present, and future of virtual and augmented reality research: A network and cluster analysis of the literature. *Frontiers in Psychology*, *9*, 2086. doi:10.3389/fpsyg.2018.02086 PMID:30459681

Gandolfi, E. (2018). Virtual reality and augmented reality. Handbook of Research on K-12 Online and Blending Learning, 545-561.

Hee Lee, J., & Shvetsova, O. A. (2019). The Impact of VR Application on Student's Competency Development: A Comparative Study of Regular and VR Engineering Classes with Similar Competency Scopes. *Sustainability*, *11*(8), 2221. doi:10.3390u11082221

Kovach, N. (n.d.). *Augmented Reality in Education*. https://thinkmobiles.com/blog/augmented-reality-education/

Martín-Gutiérrez, J., Mora, C. E., Añorbe-Díaz, B., & González-Marrero, A. (2017). Virtual technologies trends in education. *Eurasia Journal of Mathematics, Science and Technology Education*, *13*(2), 469–486. doi:10.12973/eurasia.2017.00626a

Naaz, I., & Sharma, A. (2018). *Rise of Augmented Reality: Applications, challenges, and future trends*. Academic Press.

Pantelidis, V. S. (2010). Reasons to use virtual reality in education and training courses and a model to determine when to use virtual reality. *Themes in Science and Technology Education*, *2*(1-2), 59–70.

Safar, A. H., Al-Jafar, A. A., & Al-Yousefi, Z. H. (2016). The effectiveness of using augmented reality apps in teaching the English alphabet to kindergarten children: A case study in the State of Kuwait. *Eurasia Journal of Mathematics, Science and Technology Education*, *13*(2), 417–440. doi:10.12973/eurasia.2017.00624a

Singh, T. (2020). Augmented Reality in Education: A Way to Future. *Mobile App Daily*. https://www.mobileappdaily.com/2018/08/1/augmented-reality-in-education

Uses of Virtual Reality in Education. (n.d.). *CRISS*. https://www.crissh2020.eu/uses-of-virtual-reality-in-education/

Woodford, C. (2020). *Virtual reality. Explain that Stuff*. https://www.explainthatstuff.com/virtualreality.html#:~:text=Virtual%20reality%20(VR)%20means%20experiencing,doesn't%20sound%20especially%20new.&text=A%20believable%2C%20interactive%203D%20computer,there%2C%20both%20mentally%20and%20physically

Xu, L. (2014). Research on the effect of education quality of sports teaching mode based on virtual reality technology. *Journal of Chemical and Pharmaceutical Research*, *6*(7), 1119–1123.

Yoon, S., Anderson, E., Lin, J., & Elinich, K. (2017). How augmented reality enables conceptual understanding of challenging science content. *Journal of Educational Technology & Society*, *20*(1), 156–168.

Chapter 6
Implementing Augmented Reality Into Immersive Virtual Learning Environments:
Implementation of Augmented Reality Technologies in Immersive Education Programs

Pooja Siddharth Sukhdeve
https://orcid.org/0000-0001-5006-0878
Swami Ramanand Teeth Marathwada University, India

ABSTRACT

Technology is ever-changing and ever-growing. One of the newest developing technologies is augmented reality (AR), which can be applied to many different existing technologies, such as computers, tablets, and smartphones. This chapter discusses the immersive learning process and the usage of AR into a simulated or in an artificial environment. Discussed is the background information on how the AR use in educational industries and the design process of AR immersive learning environment. The chapter also evaluates the benefits if immersive learning and AR.

INTRODUCTION

In today's global economy, technology has become a central and important part of our lives. It has modified how we think and apply knowledge. One of the latest developing technologies is Augmented reality (AR), which can be used with computers, tablets, and smartphones. AR affords the capability to overlay images, audio, video, and text components onto images or real-world spaces. AR is the latest in immersive learning experiences and the most immersive of new technologies because AR involves learners visually, aurally, and physically in a way that no other immersive learning technique can. In the

DOI: 10.4018/978-1-7998-4222-4.ch006

future, there is the potential of creating entire virtual worlds where learners can train for various tasks in myriad educational areas.

This chapter aims to explore and examine the implementation of AR using immersive learning in an educational environment. The outcome of this examination and implementation process could be set as a baseline for further enhancement, development, or innovation. The objectiveS of this chapter is as follows:

1. To discussed immersive learning encourages the student to learn easily.
2. As discussed the background information about the AR, how it is using in the educational atmosphere and industries environment.
3. To discuss the design and implementation of AR using immersive learning education.
4. To identify the problem of AR during the implementation.

BACKGROUND

In immersive learning environments, learners receive new knowledge and skills in an environment rich in sensations, perceptions, and emotions. The major benefits of AR are the interactions between the learning context and content, physical objects, and virtual objects. AR technology has obtained a following in the different educational areas for its capability to bridge gaps and bring a more tangible technique to learning. The ultimate aim focuses on the enhancement of student results throughout the educational process.

Immersive learning adds digital experiences to education that addresses the problem in education of the lack of student excitement, attention, and engagement. Virtual learning uses simulated or artificial surroundings to create unusual learning experiences for students. Immersive learning, as the name implies, empowers students to immerse themselves in interactive digital settings. AR uses sounds, images, and other sensations to provide students a full sensory activity, causing them to develop a "feel" for the virtual space. Immersive learning techniques encourage students to experience, examine, and navigate real-world subjects otherwise not possible in traditional classrooms.

Research has shown that AR can been implemented in various fields and be useful (Wu et al., 2013). More industries are using AR technology as an innovative way of increasing productivity (Kim & Rhee, 2011; Koo & Shon, 2010; Woods et al., 2004). Research has shown that the intergration of content-based AR can enrich knowledge content and stimulate learners' motivation to learn (Li et al., 2016). Students can experience immersive virtual learning by integrating interactive AR-enriched learning content and curricula. Immersive AR learning in the classroom assures active student responses in the learning process. There are various kinds of AR structured to various models (Kiryakova, 2020). These include:

- Stationary AR systems are equipped with powerful cameras and can present an accurate perception of objects and scenes of reality. Examples of stationary systems are the virtual fitting places designed in real stores.
- Spatial AR systems are known as video mapping or projection mapping. Spatial systems project virtual content in the original dimension and proportions right onto real-world objects. Many companies from the automotive industry adopt such systems to introduce their new designs. On the other side, video mapping presentation programs are getting great concentration from consumers.

- Desktop AR systems are systems that manage the device camera to identify objects or scenes from reality and embed virtual objects, both presented on the desktop screen. Many companies adopt desktop AR to design virtual fitting rooms in their online wares.
- Mobile AR is very prevalent recently due to the prevalence of mobile gadgets (tablets, phones, and hand-held devices). Many mobile AR applications use the global positioning system (GPS) capacities of the devices to ascertain users' positions and produce and present data that is directly associated with their location. The information comes in various forms (text, images, audio, and video) and is integrated into the actual environment.
- Head-mounted displays combine hardware devices with a combined picture of the real world and virtual objects. Depending on the applied technology, the head-mounted display can be separated into optical and video see-through devices. The most popular representative of this combination of hardware devices is intelligent glasses.
- Contact lenses are the future of augmented reality. Although they are still under the development process, Bionic Lens is previously being tested.

Depending on how the objects or views from the actual world are recognized (Kiryakova, 2020). AR is divided into the sections below:

- AR applications can identify and evaluate real-world images, scenes, or objects. Vision-based AR can be markerless or marker-based. Marker-based applications apply the camera of the device to understand and interpret markers, normally white and black barcodes. The software examines the market and builds virtual objects that are shown on the device screen integrated into the identified real objects. Markerless technology applies real-world objects (photos, objects, scenes, etc.) as points and the software identifies them by explicit characteristics that differentiate them from around the environment.
- Location-based AR applications apply the GPS abilities of the devices to manage their site and produce content that is related to the current location of the users-for instance, data about restaurants, museums, hotels, and others that are near to the users.

An application of AR that is growing popular is the use of AR apps that can combine virtual objects into real-world real spaces. According to Bonner and Reinders (2018), Vuforia Chalk is an example where technicians can now present remote assistance and viewing a live sense of another user's background and drawing on objects in the other user's real space (see Figure 1).

The Ikea Place app is another instance where interior design users can combine virtual furniture to a real-world living room to recognize how it views before buying (see Figure 2).

Today, different education areas are exploring AR solutions for quicker and more efficient learning. Adopting AR in the classroom can transform a regular class into an engaging activity. AR technology gives learners the ability to experience virtual examples and adds gaming components to help the standard textbook elements. As a result, classes become more interactive. AR creates the potential for students to better retain the knowledge they've just acquired. Immersive technologies are growing more widespread and in a wider variety of environments, including the classroom. This is positive progress for teachers and students alike. Immersive technologies and game-based learning have the potential to improve learning results in ways that have not before been possible, affordable, or scalable.

Figure 1. One user drawing into another user's physical space.

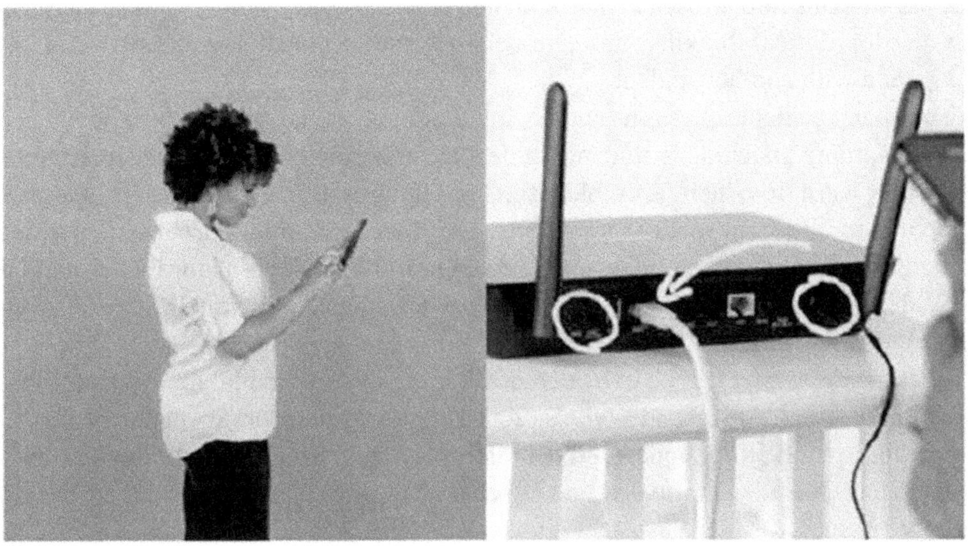

DESIGN AND IMPLEMENTATION

Immersive learning is the process of learning with the usage of a simulated or artificial environment using as many of our five senses as possible, particularly vision, sound, and touch, rather than through the traditional mechanisms of print, video, and audio. The environment allows the learners to get immersed

Figure 2. Placing location-anchored virtual objects into a real room

in the learning and in a way that feels like experiencing an authentic learning environment. Immersive technologies put students into artificial environments, where they not only obtain academic knowledge but also can develop critical thinking, problem-solving, and technical and creative skills, both singly and in participation with another student.

Rather than asking students questions and having them give an answer that's either correct or incorrect, immersive learning encourages students to develop their own questions, answers and make their conclusions so they learn from their favorable results and failures. Immersive learning spaces should also include collaboration, group formation of projects, and the co-creation in a virtual environment, such as the construction of architectural models, the recreation of historic or natural sites and other spatial renderings. With immersive technologies, educators can also create individualized experiences, that are linked to a particular curriculum or set of standards.

Immersive learning, which can be considered as an effective learning approach, is complemented by different learning styles. Auster and Wylie's (2006) context framework includes the establishment of an environment for learning that supports student interplay and engagement. Following Inks and Avila (2008), engagement is linked to the quality and effectiveness of the learning as students learn more when they are entirely engaged.

Immersion introduces to the mental status of being completely involved with an exercise. It is a robust medium for uniqueness and understanding transfer, both of which are essential parts affecting learning results. This is a system that has long been described as game-based learning (Gee, 2003), which includes choosing and engaging in a way that the student has genuine options such as improving the virtual identity and ample chance to examine the connection between new identities and old ones. Students are also provided the ability to transfer what they have acquired to later contexts. Figure 1 describes immersive learning design parameters.

Bonasio (2017) defined immersion as essential to creating efficient established learning experiences in various forms. Although it may appear counter-intuitive, necessary ideas and skills are best studied in the context of attempting approximately complex tasks that have significance to the real world (Dede, 2009). This occurs because both the arrangement and the coordinated team actions within this environment produce a wealth of embedded information. A medical student or surgical resident, for instance, will obtain and learn much more by doing tasks within the practical framework of a AR simulation room than by reading a book.

Although this is a well-recognized case, it is challenging to design such disorganized learning experiences embedded in real-world environments. Immersive experiences bypass practical limitations such as expense, logistics, volume, and risk. They tap into the potential of psychological immersion and present experiences driven by social and collaborative intercommunications, where the environment itself offers to encourage tacit skills. Sensory immersion occurs when learners can adequately "feel" themselves being the role of the virtual world, and has been used broadly for vehicle training and other procedural learning applications (Jacobson, 2013).

As discussed in Bonasio el. al. (2017), Leticia Ahumada, a primary education teacher who uses Minecraft: Education Edition described how this use of technology enhances student engagement by encouraging a sense of immersion. She described that when she asked one of her students how they experienced studying history with Minecraft, they answered that, with Minecraft, they weren't studying history, but existing in it. The narrative is an essential motivational and intellectual part of all structures of learning, and an immersive experience can trigger strong semantic correlations. In a mediated, simulated experience, immersion is the willing discontinuing of unbelief which is prompted by emotional investment in a compelling narrative. Producing strong immersion for learning, therefore, depends on a design that employs actional, social, and symbolic/narrative factors, as well as sensory motives to build game-based learning activities that are plausible from a psychological and cognitive as well as the real-world perspective(Dede, 2009). Actional immersion involves a method for the participant that directs them to use actions that have novel and intriguing consequences in the context of their own earlier experience, such as a child learning to exercise for the first time, and giving that effort their careful attention.

Figure 3. Immersion design characteristics.

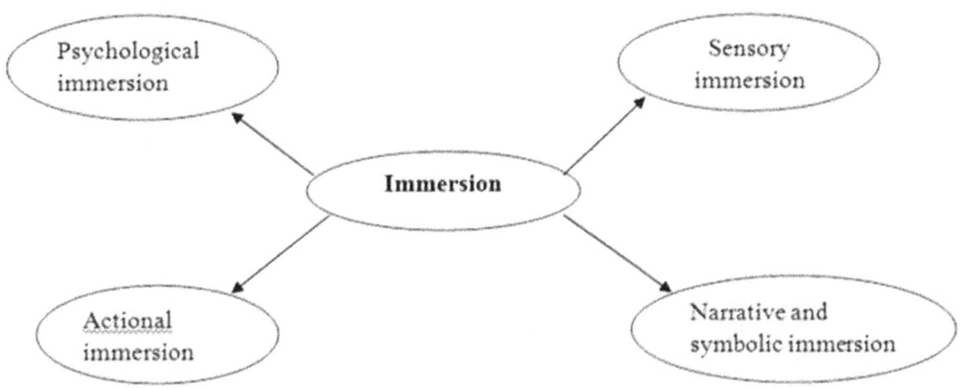

Immersive learning can make education more beneficial than ever. Immersive learning can lead to increased engagement. How hard it is to keep everyone's concentration intact, especially when learners always have their favorite smartphone by their side. The use of immersive learning can reduce all disturbances by letting learners immerse themself in a virtual world. According to Kumar (2020) starting a chapter is simple, ending it is not. This is why experts these days recommend immersive learning as it increases focused immersion. There are emotional benefits to learning in immersive environments. Since the environments designed for immersive learning are extremely engaging and practical, it improves an emotional relationship with the learners. Hence, they are more engaged in the learning process. This learning way is all about being immersed in the real context where students are encouraged to operate in a real environment simulation.

Issues, Controversies, Problems

Difficulties with the Use of AR in Education. Users of AR technology may experience usability problems and technical difficulties and some students may find this technology complex (Akçayır, & Akçayır, 2017). One of the main issues of AR applications is usability; however, ease of use is also reported as a help. There is no confirmation to recommend that usability problems are directly relevant to AR technology and may instead stem from incompetent technology experience, interface design errors, technical difficulties, or negative attitudes (Akçayır, & Akçayır, 2017). The combination of real and virtual objects may confuse as students may face challenges navigating between fiction and reality (Wu et al., 2013). The usage of AR technology within a learning ecosystem necessitates multitasking, as learners need to engage with large numbers of information and multiple technological things to accomplish complex. This may appear in cognitive overload and a perception of being surprised or misunderstood (Wu et al., 2013 Akçayır, & Akçayır, 2017). Chalimov (2020) discussed the challenges below.

- **A lack of necessary training**. Some educators might struggle to put these innovative technologies into use as their education training doesn't implement the necessary skills. Only the most open-minded educators and innovative educative institutions are willing to use AR apps in education.
- **Dependence on hardware**. Using AR in the classroom needs a certain source base as not all students have smartphones intelligent in helping AR applications.
- **Content portability issues**. The AR app creates needs to work uniformly well on all platforms and devices. However, it is practically difficult to implement the same kind of AR content on any device.

The confusion shows the authenticity of an AR system; however, this may be unprolific in a learning atmosphere as learners may lose trace of the real environment (Wu et al., 2013). Some researchers report that AR reduces cognitive load, while others report cognitive overload (2017 Wu et al., 2013). Schools may place restrictions on choosing AR technology, and educators may be resistant to use AR as this technology usually needs innovative teaching ways to be implemented.

The content accessible through AR applications is oftentimes inflexible, which reduces the teacher's control over the content and restricts modification to help student needs (Wu et al., 2013). The availability of authoring tools may solve this difficulty by allowing users to revise and create applications. Another challenge may be that the stability of mobile AR technology is not assured and problems may confront if the technology wants well-designed interfaces and direction as this may result in the technology being too complex (Wu et al., 2013; Akçayır, & Akçayır, 2017). Users may also need time to get easy and convenient with AR technology (Gopalan et al., 2016). According to the discussion, a serious problem with the unwillingness of young people to read books and textbooks is rising. Parents and teachers face challenging issues about how to encourage teens to learn more. Integrating AR into traditional books can improve solve the difficulty and form engagement and enjoyment in reading.

Lessons Learned

Immersive learning supports personalized learning as it is based on the learner-focused model. AR supports learners to learn at their pace, as they take supervised experiments to achieve proficiency in a technique, behavior, or methodology. They can respond multiple times to a simulation until they become entirely versed. Since there are fewer or no disturbances, learners are profoundly immersed in the learning method and learn at their own pace, hence, learners retain more of what they study. Immersive learning is a dynamic strategy that can enhance eLearning and revolutionize the world of education. The technique holds the excellent potential to reach the future of learning and significant goals.

The innovative medium of AR allows us unusual affordances, combining real and virtual worlds. This is the new form of shaping how we interact with this world. Without replacing the real world experiencing, this technology increases virtual information on the height of the real world with frequently, continuous, and unquestioning user restraint of the point of view and interactivity. It presents a composite look for the user with a combination of the real display viewed by the user and computer-created virtual scenes.

AR is augmentation of the real world by engaging into a place, space, thing, or event in a partially unmediated way. That can allow students seamless interaction between the real and virtual worlds by connecting AR with interfaces including the educational content. This new way improves the effectiveness and attractiveness of education and learning. The technique to cover computer-generated virtual objects onto the real world transforms the way to interact and learn that can be experienced in real-time rather than a static experience. The characteristics of AR learning environments include:

- **Learning is more accessible**. Traditional education usually depends on books or school supplies, which cost money. according to As discussed in Nijjar (2020), most nations in Europe struggle when it comes to settling on the most excellent approach to support those with less purchasing energy and even nations with free education have some difficulty making sure everyone has their supplies. With augmented reality, the school can provide everyone more access to learning elements, as long as they go to school they have their stuff there waiting for them in their classroom's AR arrangement, even if it is a comprehensive work of art like the Mona Lisa or a hard-to-get metal, which is excellent.
- **Learning Is flexible.** Another point to examine is that each educator has its teaching methodology. Not only that but each topic is taught uniquely. AR provides everyone the ability to customize their skills and improve their AR sets to specs uniting their strategies. Theoretic teachers can apply AR as a method to empower their expositions while more effective tutors can have the learners interact with the programs.
- Learning by doing. AR provides learners the opportunity to learn by doing rather than by being presented to theory classes and long speeches. Doing something instead of hearing about them or seeing someone do them increases memory retention and caters to those students who have difficulty imagining or retaining concepts through description alone.
- **Learning experiences that are possible and safe**. For education, safety is pre-eminent. Having this in mind, there are many protection and security rules in place to make sure learners are not harmed. AR can be another layer here as well, as students can perform otherwise unsafe procedures by practicing in a simulated reality through the smart usage of AR, cameras, and sensors. As an instance, students will be able to do chemical tests and experiments without the necessity for the chemicals themselves, such as experiencing potassium's effect with water through simulated experience and tests.
- **AR can improve sensory input to increase learning**. Humans observe their worlds by their senses, and it's no wonder sensory skills are normally those that are critical to successful learning. AR can add this additional layer to the development various skills that cannot be learned otherwise.
- **AR can be used to understand through simulation.** Simulation events are effective ways for learners to engage in learning. History can learned more successfully through AR. AR apps provide learners to hover significant spots in the street and see early or old pictures layered on top of it to view how it was back in historical times.

SOLUTIONS AND RECOMMENDATIONS

AR can be integrated into different ways of training. It can be used to create augmented textbooks or to develop AR educational applications. An augmented book is a traditional (paper) book with extra virtual content, which is available by appropriate hardware and software mechanisms (Altınpulluk, & Kesim, 2016). The augmented books improve traditional methods with interactive visualizations, animation, 3D Shapes, and video and audio substances. All these multimedia parts enhance reading and engage readers' concentration (Dünser et al., 2012). A very significant innovation of augmented textbooks is that support students to interact with virtual content, examine and make experiments, which prove effective learning, better and more accessible understanding, and perception of complicated and difficult concepts. It can have an assertive impact on learners' performances and approaches toward their learning (Lim & Park, 2011).

Augmented textbooks have an important benefit over other e-textbooks. the learner can study them as traditional books, but at the same time, they have access to added interactive digital content. There is no requirement to buy specific devices to use them since a smartphone or tablet is needed to imagine integrated digital content-devices that learners use every day (Kiryakova, 2020). AR provides innovative dimensions to traditional textbooks, which several digital learners examine being tedious. The technology can apply textbooks into an interactive tool that involves learners, motivates them to understand and learn, as well as interests them. Much more learning content can be involved in augmented textbooks that exceed the necessities of the curriculum. The extra content is available to anyone who has the necessity or excitement to deepen knowledge.

The augmented book joins the text-based part and interactive AR sections. Dünser et al., (2008) compared how much readers with high and low capability (teacher-provided classifications) recalled from the two media formats. From the text-based story segment, those in the high-ability category could retell notably more key story points than the low-ability category (Dünser et. al., 2008). However, the two groups showed no important difference in remembering key story points from the interactive AR segment. Arguably then, because they allow a chance for interactive substance engagement augmented books could benefit students who are less able to apprehend text-based learning content—at present the leading education medium.

Figure 4. Reading a story in the MagicBook.

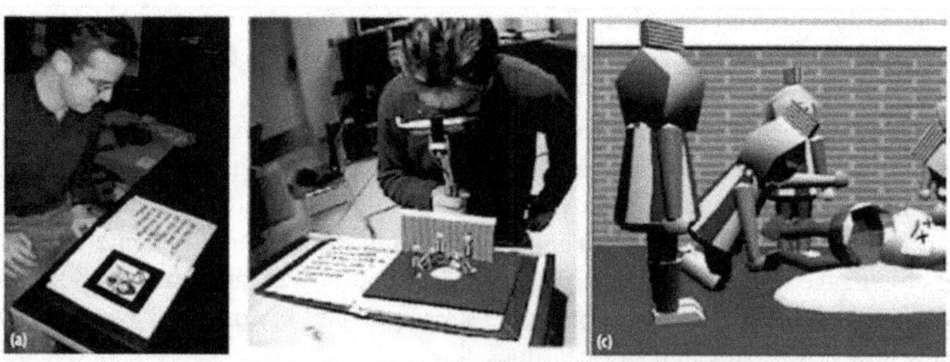

In response to the MagicBook, the reader views the page as he would in a print book. By using the handheld AR interface, the reader can view the virtual story characters in a 3D scene. The reader has "flown" into an immersive view of the battle scene. (Billinghurst & Duenser, 2012; Poupyrev el. al., 2001). AR can also be more effective in teaching topics with a strong spatial component. In a study after the reading comprehension evaluation, (Billinghurst & Dünser, 2012) stated that they differentiate learning results using a print-only text about electromagnetism and an augmented book with the same content. As per the conducted test administered immediately after presentation to the two books, the AR group responded to answer more questions accurately— both factual and inferential—with a mean count of 72%, relative to 60% for the non-AR group. In a follow-up remembrance test conducted four weeks later, the AR group again obtained significantly higher, with a 55% score, relative to 45% for the non-AR group. From these outcomes, it appears that the AR interface's added interactivity and visual design enhance subject learning (Billinghurst & Dünser, 2012)

Another way to apply AR in education is to advance AR applications. More and more products designed with AR technology are accessible in the educational applications market. Many teachers take such applications as an efficient and compelling tool to encourage students to better comprehend abstract concepts. AR can describe objects and methods that are hard to visualize and turn them into 3D shapes providing learners to interact with them. (Kiryakova, 2020) stated that complex concepts come to life and become a portion of the real world, which presents them easier to learn. AR can be applied as a powerful tool that "translates" theoretical scientific ideas into anything from the real world and everyday life, giving them understanding to learners. Kiryakova (2020) described the ways that physics, astronomy, chemistry, biology, and mathematics can support learning where AR is integrated. The different physical and chemical properties of an object can be observed and studied. Human anatomy can be observed and studied using AR.

AR animated content in classroom activities could make students' concentrate on our dynamic day and age, as well as motivate them to analyze. Adding more data, such as a brief bio of a character, fun facts, historical information about places or events, visual 3D figures, would give students a broader perception of topics. While doing homework, students may examine the essential elements of a book and collect text, audio, or video advice from teachers. Or they may obtain valuable data about the course, a teacher, or other students that could begin to effective communication (Kovach, 2019). AR technology can render things that are difficult to visualize and transform them into 3D shapes, thus presenting it simpler to grasp the abstract and complex content. This is very helpful for visual students and effectively anyone to interpret theoretical material into a real concept. For instance, the Polytechnic Institute of Leiria in Portugal integrates AR into math exercises and students record it as convenient, comfortable, and interesting (Kovach, 2019).

By combining AR into lessons teachers can involve learners in the method with 3-dimensional shapes. It may be only a part of the lesson, like a teaser, or the help of the main topic with additional information from various aspects. A Canadian technology company converted the wall of the school gym into a ball game by combining an AR screen cover. Kids throw balls onto a wall to hit floating forms and so have fun physical exercises (Kovach, 2019).AR can be very efficient in building discovery and learning solutions that immerse someone in whatever they are acquiring. Instead of being tied to a chair or desk, AR learning can assist take students in moving around and interacting with the content. When learning is engaging and experiential, the information recollection of learners develops remarkably (Banit, 2018).

AR apps for medical students may be one of the methods to study human anatomy, AND examine it more profoundly. AR means interaction with 3D shapes. And learner can set the turn, transparence, color scheme, forms, etc. Finally, there could be more advanced animations via special devices like holographic lenses (Kovach, 2019). Medical professions require a high level of proficiency and accuracy since any possible mistakes can harm patients' health and wellbeing. AR in medical education is usually applied to help learners study through interactive visual representations, create simulations and train medical students, and practice surgery or other medical procedures on virtual patients.

In many cases, theoretical information is not sufficient to acquire precise skills in professional fields. Students shouldn't be always mere listeners and passive observers. Students in technical fields especially require practice and hands-on knowledge in their fields. During the interaction, unlike AR innovations could better offer a virtual exercise with augmented tutorials, digital modeling, and simulations, and obtain some knowledge in the end. Excited and engaged students will learn a topic thoroughly and faster (Kovach, 2019).

Today many industries provide training with the helpful technology of AR in space, manufacturing, and the military. The space industry has ever been one of the primary to use advanced technologies. No wonder this industry is examining augmented reality. Technologies like AR can help astronauts with tasks like managing a space station. Using goggles, operators can obtain visual work directions without turning to guidebooks. NASA has already examined Project Sidekick, which uses HoloLens to produce virtual representations and guidance to support crew members to execute complex tasks. According to NASA, this ability has the potential to facilitate extreme training situations (Victoria, 2019).

AR technology is used to construct a background needed for training soldiers, letting them train more oftentimes. It also helps keep travel costs and reduces the need for specialized machinery, as AR can combine virtual things. Although AR can't entirely substitute traditional military training, there are already ways that exclude the need to travel to remote places and support soldiers' train without placing them at risk (Victoria, 2019).

By applying AR in distance learning, students can study also outside the classroom. Online or distance learning can be more accessible and more effective with AR-aided educative elements. For instance, Mondly, a language-learning app, has newly integrated an AR-based virtual teacher to encourage users to practice their experiences as if they were in a real-life environment. Chalimov (2020) described the potential in AR technologies for marketing and promotion, even in the education area. Many academies and universities in the USA are already applying AR tours to raise admission and encourage new learners to find their direction around campus.

It's no secret, kids are eager adopters of groundbreaking technologies like AR. Some of the most ingenious AR education apps are made for the youngest of users. Inspired by the success of PokemonGo, AR vendors are building apps that change the ways children read books, look at art and posters, learn science, and conduct classroom lab experiments. Narrator AR teaches children aged 3-5 how to write in a fun and engaging manner. The app enhances letters they write with captivating special effects and makes handwriting a truly exciting experience.

The Community College of Beaver County, Pennsylvania, uses AR to deliver various types of content, including video, audio, and digital publications. Thus, the app provides a fun and informative way to explore the campus. The app also has gamification elements to make the experience even more engaging. AR has able to displace paper textbooks, physical models, posters, printed textbooks. It offers manageable and less costly learning substances. As a result, education becomes more convenient and portable. Chalimov (2020) found that, unlike VR, AR doesn't need any costly hardware as 73% of all teens currently own a smartphone. AR technologies are directly accessible for application for the majority of the target audience. Interactive, gamified AR learning can have a significant assertive impact on students learning. It keeps them involved during the lesson and executes learning fun and easy.

AR apps allow enormous chances to change and shake up dull classes. Interactive lessons, where all learners are involved in the learning method at the same time, help enhance teamwork skills.AR in edu-

Figure 5. Paleontology The Dinosaur 4D+ app

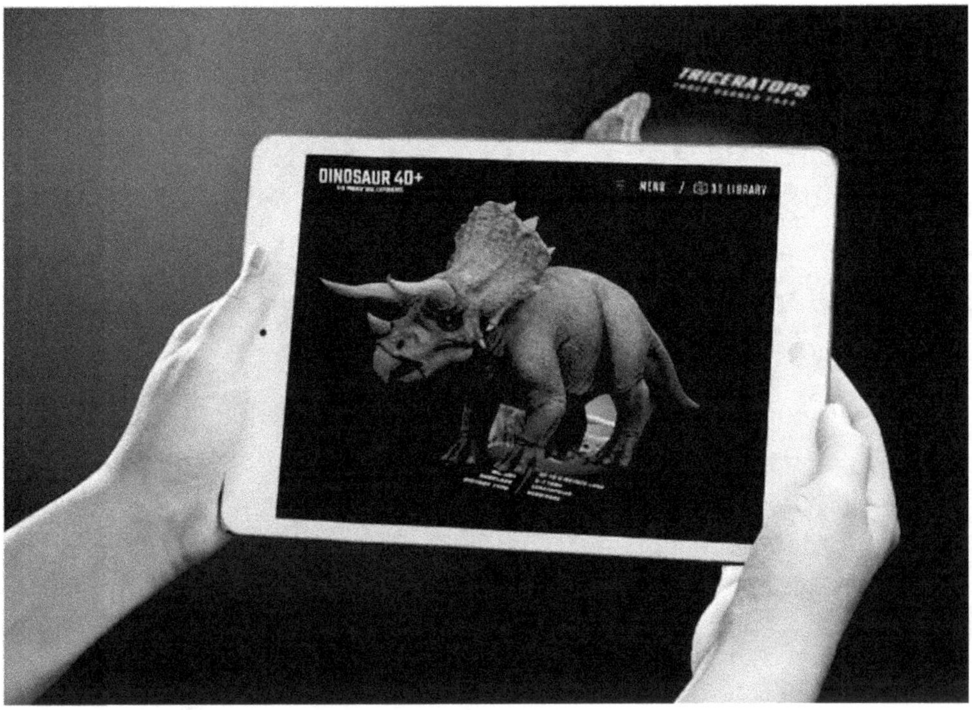

cation encourages students to achieve greater outcomes through visualization and full immersion in the topic focus. A picture is worth a thousand words, right? So, instead of the reading theory of something, learners can examine it with their own eyes, in action. Apart from schooling, professional training can also serve exceedingly from the usage of AR. For instance, the exact reproduction of in-field situations can assist understand the practical skills needed for a specific job. Be it learning games for kindergarten or on-the-job training, AR is not limited to only one use case or area of application.

Dinosaur 4D+ is an AR app and a set of flashcards. Users can scan flashcards to view 3D dinosaurs. With Dinosaur 4D+, students can observe dinosaurs in operation, turn them, and zoom in and out. The app also gives some data about each dinosaur. Elements 4D applies AR to create chemistry more playful and engaging. First, students need to get paper cubes from special component blocks. Then, they just require setting the cubes in front of their device's camera to view representations of chemical elements, their names, and their atomic weights. To explore elements, students can bring together two cubes to find out if elements react and to see the chemical reaction.

Google Expeditions presents both VR and AR tours that let teachers apply AR in education (Victoria, 2019). With AR technology and mobile devices, users can take 3D objects into the classroom, then roam throughout and explore them. Google Expeditions can be tornados, volcanos, or even DNA and includes different subjects and offers more than 100 AR Expeditions by the circulatory arrangement, history of technology, and the moon arrives. Information retention is only one component of history education, another goal of learning history is to know it so that the misconceptions of the past will not have happened again.

Figure 6. Chemistry The Elements 4D app

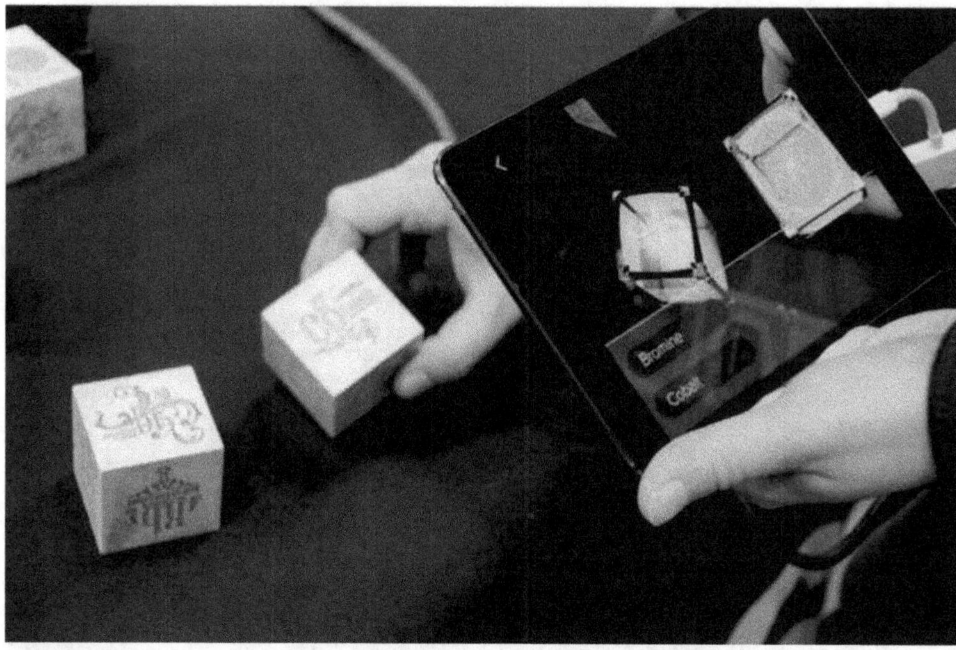

Victoria (2019) found that medical students can develop both their skills and knowledge by using the benefit of virtual and augmented reality. As further discussed, the Human Anatomy Atlas is an app that lets students examine the human body to experience how it operates. The app displays 3D models of the body and enables students to rotate and interact with them. Human Anatomy Atlas presents more than 10,000 anatomical models and some information in seven languages. The app also has a test bank for examining to help students check and Enhance their knowledge.

Figure 7. Medical The Human Anatomy Atlas app

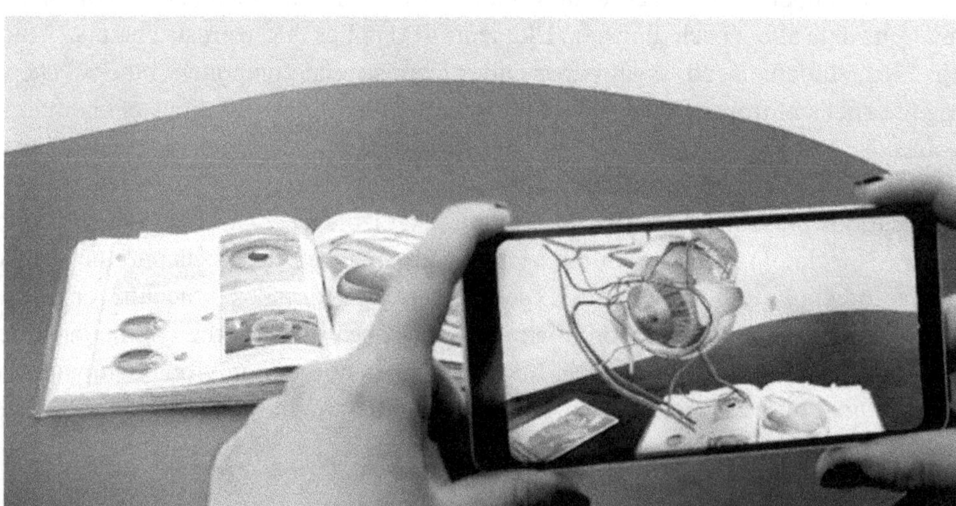

Figure 8. Historical The CityView AR application showing the history of earthquake-damaged Christchurch.

Students can also view objects from the past, people, or even performances in front of their eyes through the magic made possible by AR. The best experiences are a compound of both AR and VR, which instructs us to state these are technologies invented to work together, and the future will seemingly combine them into something different. The application uses the mobile phone's GPS and compass sensors to superimpose a virtual undamaged building on the site of the real building remains. (Billinghurst & Duenser, 2012).

AR technologies in the immersive education programs are helping and encouraging teachers and students. AR is an encouraging technology that has its place in education. The technology allows innovative models of training and learning and helps the develop new understandings when integrated into new pedagogical paradigms.

A major challenge is the unwillingness of students to read books and textbooks. Parents and teachers are facing difficult questions about how to help teens to read more. Integrating AR into traditional books can create engagement and enjoyment in reading. Recommendations to make more improvement include the following:

1. Prior to integration of AR technologies consider what type of setting is required to implement AR technology and what kind of problems and issues are in the classroom environment.
2. The teachers' role is very essential to the successful integration AR technologies. It is important to provide appropriate training to teachers.
3. The development of a management expert team to handle the issues and problems with the integration of technology is critical. This includes ongoing evaluation of the use and efficacy of the technology.

FUTURE TRENDS

AR is part of the Extended Reality (XR) with Virtual Reality and Mixed Reality. Petrov and Atanasova (2020) found that the prevalence of AR is growing because it makes elements of the virtual world into the real world, thus improving the things that the student can see, understand, and observe. Mixed reality (MR) holographs and computer-generated objects can be mixed into the real world where they can be viewed and manipulated by the learners. The XR technologies combine to create the potential to design and implement these immersive technologies into educational settings. The educational market is facing major issues without an organized way to integrate these new technologies. It is critical to understand how these technologies influence learning in immersive learning environments.

CONCLUSIONS

Immersive learning into the classroom with AR provides a hands-on approach in the learning process. With AR in immersive learning, the need for imagination is bypassed, and the student is introduced to the simulated environment as realistic as the actual world. Using AR with active problem solving and teamwork to create engaging educational experiences to teach science, math, or language skills improves student learning abilities, including critical thinking, and problem-solving.

REFERENCES

Akçayır, M., & Akçayır, G. (2017). Advantages and challenges associated with augmented reality for education: A systematic review of the literature. *Educational Research Review*, *20*, 1–11. doi:10.1016/j.edurev.2016.11.002

Altınpulluk, H., & Kesim, M. (March, 2016). The classification of augmented reality books: a literature review. *10th International Technology, Educational and Development Conference,* 10.21125/inted.2016.0200

Auster, E. R., & Wylie, K. K. (2006). Creating active learning in the classroom: A systematic approach. *Journal of Management Education*, *30*(2), 333–353. doi:10.1177/1052562905283346

Banit, M. (2018). *Using Augmented Reality (AR) for Learning and Development.* https://www.zappar.com/blog/using-ar-learning-and-development/

Billinghurst, M., & Duenser, A. (2012). *Augmented Reality in the Classroom.* https://www.researchgate.net/publication/234793015

Bonasio, A. (2017). *Immersive experiences in education.* White Paper. Microsoft Education Immersive Experiences. Retrieved from http://edudownloads.azureedge.net/msdownloads/MicrosoftEducation_Immersive_Experiences_Education_2019.pdf

Bonner, E., & Reinders, H. (2018). Augmented and virtual reality in the language classroom; Practical ideas. *Teaching English with Technology*, *18*(3), 33–53.

Chalimov, A. (2020). Augmented Reality in Education: The Hottest Edtech Trend and How to Apply it to your Business. *Eastern Peak*. Retrieved from https://easternpeak.com/blog/augmented-reality-in-education-the-hottest-edtech-trend-and-how-to-apply-it-to-your-business/

Dede, C. (2009). Immersive interfaces for engagement and learning. *Science*, *323*(5910), 66–69. doi:10.1126cience.1167311 PMID:19119219

Dünser, A., Walker, L., Horner, H., & Bentall, D. (2012). Creating interactive physics education books with augmented reality. In *Proceedings of the 24th Australian Computer-Human Interaction Conference*. (pp. 107-114). 10.1145/2414536.2414554

Gee, J. P. (2003). *What video games have to teach us about learning and literacy*. Palgrave Macmillan. doi:10.1145/950566.950595

Gopalan, V., Zulkifli, A. N., & Bakar, J. A. A. (2016, August). A study of students' motivation using the augmented reality science textbook. In. AIP Conference Proceedings: Vol. 1761. *No. 1* (p. 020040). AIP Publishing LLC. doi:10.1063/1.4960880

Inks, S. A., & Avila, R. A. (2008). Preparing the next generation of sales professionals through social, experiential, and immersive learning experiences. *Journal for Advancement of Marketing Education*, *13*(4), 47–55. http://www.mmaglobal.org/JAME-Archive/JAME-Winter-2008/JAMEWinter2008v.13p.47-55.pdf

Jacobson, J. (2013). Digital dome versus desktop display; Learning outcome assessments by domain experts. *International Journal of Virtual and Personal Learning Environments*, *4*(3), 51–65. http://publicvr.org/publications/. doi:10.4018/jvple.2013070104

Kim, Y., & Rhee, S. (2011). Augmented Reality on a Deformable Surface by Considering Self-Occlusion and Realistic Illumination. *Internet Technology.*, *12*(5), 733–740.

Kiryakova, G. (2020). The Immersive Power of Augmented Reality. In Human-Computer Interaction. doi:10.5772/intechopen.92361

Koo, B., & Shon, T. (2010). A Structural Health Monitoring Framework Using 3D Visualization and Augmented Reality in Wireless Sensor Networks. *Internet Technology, 11*(6), 801–807. Retrieved from https://jit.ndhu.edu.tw/article/view/627

Kovach, N. (2019). *Augmented Reality in Education*. Retrieved from https://thinkmobiles.com/blog/augmented-reality-education/

Kumar, J. (2020). *Everything You Need To Know About Immersive Learning*. eLearning Industry. https://elearningindustry.com/everything-need-know-about-immersive-learning

Li, K. C., Tsai, C. W., Chen, C. T., Cheng, S. Y., & Heh, J. S. (2015, August). The design of immersive English learning environment using augmented reality. In *2015 8th International Conference on Ubi-Media Computing (UMEDIA)* (pp. 174-179). IEEE. 10.1109/UMEDIA.2015.7297450

Lim, C., & Park, T. (2011). Exploring the educational use of augmented reality books. In *Proceedings of the Annual Convention of the Association for Educational Communications and Technology* (pp. 172-182). Academic Press.

Martín-Gutiérrez, J., Mora, C., Añorbe-Díaz, B., & González-Marrero, A. (2017). Virtual technologies trends in education. *Eurasia Journal of Mathematics, Science and Technology Education*, *13*(2), 469–486. https://www.ejmste.com/article/virtual-technologies-trends-in-education-4674

Nijjar, G. (2020). *7 Ways Augmented Reality Is Changing Education Industry in the UK: The Future of Learning Is Now*. AR Post. https://arpost.co/2020/03/10/7-ways-augmented-reality-education-the-uk/

Petrov, P. D., & Atanasova, T. V. (2020). The Effect of Augmented Reality on Students' Learning Performance in Stem Education. *Information (Basel)*, *11*(4), 209. doi:10.3390/info11040209

Victoria, S. (2019). *Use cases of Augmented Reality in Education and Training*. Ruby Garage. https://rubygarage.org/blog/augmented-reality-in-education-and-training#:~:text=Using%20augmented%20reality%20in%20the,information%20they's %20just%20learned.

Woods, E., Billinghurst, M., Looser, J., Aldridge, G., Brown, D., Garrie, B., & Nelles, C. (2004, June). Augmenting the science centre and museum experience. In *Proceedings of the 2nd international conference on Computer graphics and interactive techniques in Australasia and South East Asia* (pp. 230-236). 10.1145/988834.988873

Wu, H. K., Lee, S. W. Y., Chang, H., & Liang, J. C. (2013). Current status, opportunities, and challenges of augmented reality in education. *Computers & Education*, *62*, 41–49. doi:10.1016/j.compedu.2012.10.024

Section 2
Implementation of AR Into Education

These chapters are focused on the practical implementation of AR into educational programs.

Chapter 7
A Safe Space:
Practicing Teaching Skills With Avatars

Kisha L. Walker
Walden University, USA

Stacy Ness
Walden University, USA

Fran Reed
Walden University, USA

Katherine Strang
Walden University, USA

ABSTRACT

What if teacher candidates had the opportunity to practice research-based instructional strategies and the application of critical skills without fear of failure or harm to students? Would you be interested? One of the biggest challenges that teacher preparation programs face is a struggle to provide meaningful and realistic practice for pre-service teacher candidates. How do we provide practice in "real" settings with "real" students who demonstrate a depth and breadth of learning and behavioral challenges? How do we make practice sessions safe environments for both our teacher candidates and the students they serve? How do we provide needed experiences for candidates in a world where in-person learning may be curtailed by unforeseen circumstances? The purpose of this chapter is to examine the use of virtual reality simulations in education that provide scaffolded learning experiences for pre-service teachers in an online learning environment.

DOI: 10.4018/978-1-7998-4222-4.ch007

INTRODUCTION

Research has found that student teaching is one of the most beneficial components of preparing teachers for the classroom. During student teaching, teacher candidates have an opportunity to observe their assigned host/cooperating teachers as they model best practices, assess student readiness, design and implement effective lesson plans and activities, and develop rich rewarding experiences for all students. Upon completion of their programs, pre-service teachers are then expected to be able to demonstrate pedagogical content knowledge; meet the diverse learning needs of their students, academically, developmentally, and socially; and adhere to the ethical and professional responsibilities of being an educator. Within these expectations, pre-service teachers are also responsible for effectively managing classroom behavior; collaborating and communicating with parents, colleagues, and stakeholders; and keeping up with other administrative tasks.

While these requirements and expectations are the intended outcomes for most teacher preparation programs, there are times when teacher candidates are not always able to experience the intricate scenarios or details of the classroom setting. Consistent research has found pre-service preparation in classroom management to be ineffective and inadequate, providing insufficient opportunities to practice implementing evidence-based strategies during field experiences (Ficarra & Quinn, 2014; Christofferson & Sullivan, 2015). For instance, teacher candidates may not always encounter confrontational parental conferences, disagreements with colleagues, or disruptive students during their field experiences or through online discussions with other classmates. As a result, pre-service teachers often enter the profession intimidated by certain environments and situations or feeling unprepared to take on the full array of classroom responsibilities. Their lack of confidence and preparation ultimately impacts their overall classroom performance and overall student achievement and experience.

Behavioral difficulties exhibited by students was reported as one of the challenges most often experienced by new and novice teachers (Christofferson & Sullivan, 2015). While research suggests that training in classroom management is ineffective; there is little known about the specific types and sources of classroom management training offered to pre-service teachers during preparation programs. Christofferson and Sullivan (2015) conducted a study to analyze the classroom management training and resources pre-service teachers received during their teacher preparation program, along with perceptions they held about the training received. Participants included 157 pre-service teachers throughout the United States, who were enrolled in teacher preparation programs accredited by the National Council for the Accreditation of Teacher Education (NCATE). Results of the study revealed that 67% of first-year teachers reported challenges with addressing and/or managing difficult behavior.

Although participants reported multiple classroom management training sources, the most common training sources were supervised fieldwork (84%), mentoring from a licensed teacher (83.8%), course work other than classroom management (78.7%), and a lecture or presentation (74.8%) (Christofferson & Sullivan, 2015). Interestingly, survey participants reported 92% of their classroom management courses covered content, including creating and teaching rules and expectations, using reinforcement strategies, creating a community of learners, and teaching procedures.

Of the multitude of sources, participants reported greater satisfaction amongst experiential training sources like mentoring from teachers and supervised fieldwork as opposed to academic training sources (Christofferson & Sullivan, 2015). It should be noted that only 60% of survey participants received a course in classroom management (Christofferson & Sullivan, 2015). The study also identified the need for additional research to examine the gaps between teacher preparation and implementation as it relates to strategies for addressing severe misbehavior.

Similarly, Ficarra and Quinn (2014) found that teacher candidates received fewer opportunities to learn evidence-based classroom management strategies, before entering the field. While the study also examined teachers' knowledge and competency related to specific classroom management subscales, teachers overwhelmingly reported most of their experience learning about evidence-based classroom management skills were acquired during in-service experiences rather than pre-service experiences (Ficarra & Quinn, 2014). To protect privacy, teachers included in the study were not asked to reveal their teacher preparation program or the mode of training. Yet, the study revealed the need for teacher preparation programs to provide classroom management skills, both during coursework and field experiences, to prepare teacher candidates to effectively support students academically and socially (Ficarra & Quinn, 2014). Being able to effectively manage the classroom is just one of the critical roles of an educator, and it requires the acquisition of pedagogical skills, preparation, and plenty of practice.

The integration of technology has proven to be a viable option in preparation and training, affording individuals with authentic experiences in various fields of study. Virtual reality is just one of the many platforms created in which participants can engage in real-world experiences to practice strategies, techniques, and/or essential skills. With hopes of reaping the same experimental benefits, virtual reality has moved beyond the gaming industry, making its mark on several fields including business, medicine, manufacturing, architecture, and now education. Embracing this use of technology, the University of Central Florida developed a virtual platform, using a multi-component system called TeachLive, now Mursion, in which avatars helped to train future educators within a computer-generated classroom.

Using human and computational intelligence, Mursion created social and professional interactions between learners and avatars in virtual reality simulations to support learners in mastering communication skills. These virtual simulations allow unique and non-redundant responses, resulting in highly immersive and authentic interactions (Mursion, 2020). Using avatars, student teachers were granted the opportunity to practice critical skills including instructional strategies, concepts, and techniques as they prepared to become classroom teachers.

Chini et. al (2016) found that environments featuring computer simulations that offer teachers new opportunities to learn pedagogical skills as they practice with avatars have been proven to be effective for training in-service and pre-service K-12 teachers. Preparation should also include training and didactic coursework (Christofferson & Sullivan, 2015) that provide candidates with opportunities to practice so they are prepared as they take on the role of classroom teacher. Throughout this chapter, the authors will analyze the background and research of using simulations with avatars to practice teaching strategies and interpersonal skills, the overall design and implementation, support in teacher preparation, and experiences from the field.

BACKGROUND

Pre-service teacher preparation programs typically provide outcomes-driven courses coupled with methods courses and practicum field-based experiences. Field-based experiences are where candidates practice course-based learning theories. If candidates are not prepared for the rigors of field experiences, they are not likely to benefit fully from them (Hixon & So, 2009). Skill development requires practice, and pre-service candidates need multiple opportunities to practice skill sets in "low-stakes" environments (Ball & Forzani, 2009). Girod and Girod (2006, 2008) explained that the complexities of field classrooms require teachers to rapidly select what to focus on before candidates being adequately prepared to handle multiple instruction and classroom management events. Without enough time to practice, pre-service pedagogical schemas may be prone to errors that may have a positive or negative impact on real students (Kahneman, 2011).

Finding quality opportunities to practice teaching concepts can be problematic for pre-service teachers and the programs in which they are enrolled. Jones and Ryan (2014) noted that pre-service teachers' exposure to authentic teaching is "one of the aspects of teacher education that falls under much criticism due to its tendency to be disconnected from the theoretical, university-based components of teacher education courses…" (p. 133). Often, pre-service teachers do not have the opportunity to practice realistic teaching skills until they are involved in their final field experiences, which sometimes occur at schools far away from the support and guidance of their instructors.

Bridging the theory-to-practice gap requires that teacher education programs provide candidates with as many actual teaching experiences as is practical during methods classes. Pre-service candidates must have ample opportunities to practice, teach, and reflect on their teaching to develop their confidence in teaching. Critical to this process is the opportunity for pre-service candidates to hone their teaching skills in environments where "judgment and assessment are minimized to encourage risk-taking so that strong personal learning might be experienced" (Loughran, 2006, p. 161).

Thomassen and Rive (2010) suggested creating simplified contexts in which novice teachers can begin to practice skill sets and gain proficiency as classroom teachers. Contextual, practical experiences have focused on methods such as case-based instruction (Koehler et al., 2019; Malone & Langone, 2005; Yadav et al., 2009) and role-playing/microteaching (Diana, 2013; Karlström & Hamza, 2019) experiences. Case-based instruction and microteaching experiences allow pre-service educators to gain experience practicing classroom scenarios using teaching and classroom management strategies. These types of experiences are limited in realism and complexity because they do not require teachers to realistically respond to the range of behavior and academic challenges they will face in a typical classroom.

The transfer of key teaching skill sets from these experiences to actual classrooms depends on the extent to which practice opportunities match authentic situations in which the candidates are required to demonstrate acquired teaching skills (Brown et al., 1989). Using a practice already well established in the fields of aviation, military, and medicine, virtual simulations have emerged in teacher preparation programs as a way of representing and providing practice for candidates in the complexities that exist in actual classrooms (Dieker et al., 2008; Dieker et al., 2014). According to Brown and his theory of situated learning, simulation training should readily transfer to actual classrooms (Brown et al.,1989). This transfer of learning can occur using different levels of virtual environments, as discussed below, to provide teacher candidates with a wide variety of teaching and learning experiences.

Four Levels of Virtual Environments

We can look at virtual environments in terms of four levels of complexity and evolution. Mixed-reality environments can be categorized in terms of their complexity (Dieker, et al., 2014). Levels 1 and Level 2 are innovations that exist in the current education landscape; Levels 3 and 4 are works in progress. Dieker et al., provide the following descriptions (p. 57).

Level 1: Virtual reality desktop avatars. These avatars (virtual characters) help us with online chats when we're trying to get information about a service or product. We also find them in more evolved environments, such as Second Life, or in classroom-based tools…where the user can use recorded video to make any image appear to be talking.

Level 2: Mixed-reality environments. Here, immersive virtual environments, such as TeachLivE™ [i.e., TLE is now called Mursion], combine real and virtual worlds, providing users with a sense of presence or immersion. Users perceive the virtual environment as an authentic environment in which they can take action, much like in the real world.

Level 3: Immersive 3-D environments. Level 3 environments are currently in the development stage. In such an environment, the avatar would move out of 2-D space into 3-D space. Teachers could direct a robotic avatar that represented them to move around a real classroom and engage in "real" conversations with real students.

Level 4: Brain-computer interfaces. This fourth evolution might seem like science fiction, but it's already present in parts, waiting to be merged into a whole system: 5-D. In the future, the ability to look, touch, hug, see, hear, smell, and potentially taste something may occur through a remote presence. This fourth evolution is already realized in part with the emergence of robotic arms that are operated by a human brain.

The TLE TeachLivE™ simulation is a Level 2 experience and is a particularly sophisticated classroom simulation because it provides a full immersion teaching experience and represents many of the complexities that exist in a real classroom (Dieker et al., 2008; Dieker et al., 2014).

TLE/Mursion requires verbal teaching interactions in front of a classroom with life-size avatars that provide immediate verbal responses (Dieker et al., 2014). This tool is a powerful learning experience for candidates because instructors can control the complexity of the instructional environment while providing a safe setting for candidates to practice foundational teaching and management skills or more complex instructional routines. TLE/Mursion provides education departments with the ability to bridge the gap between learning and practice as well as providing realistic classroom experiences for all levels of preservice candidates.

According to Chini et al., more than 50 universities and school districts access the TeachLivE platform to support teacher professional learning (2016). The authors suggested classroom simulators as a new modality for clinal practice pedagogical skills (Chini et al., 2016). Figure 1 illustrates the upper elementary classroom setting used in teacher preparation programs. Figure 2 illustrates the high school setting, also used in teacher preparation programs. Within both simulation experiences, the avatars are controlled by a live simulation specialist, and teacher candidates can safely practice classroom management and evidence-based instructional strategies.

In a research study, funded by the Bill & Melinda Gates Foundation, the University of Central Florida in partnership with roughly 15 institutions, examined the use of virtual reality simulations for interpersonal skills with professionals (Mursion, 2020). The research experiment consisted of 300 professionals and found 90% agreeing with the accuracy of real-world people displayed by the avatars (Mursion, 2020). Overall, researchers found that virtual reality simulations improved the participants' interpersonal behaviors. Specifically, those who participated in the virtual reality simulations significantly outperformed their colleagues on all targeted measures when compared to colleagues who participated in online training of the same content (Mursion, 2020).

Figure 1. Upper elementary classroom setting used for teacher preparation programs

Hudson et al., (2018) conducted a research study to explore mixed-reality teaching experiences and participants' perceptions about managing student behavior in the classroom setting. The study consisted of 25 undergraduates in their first semester of their junior year who were pursuing a K-12 special education teaching license in special education general curriculum or adapted curriculum (Hudson et al., 2018). Participants completed three mixed-reality teaching simulations with avatars in the Mursion lab, which consisted of (a) getting to know the avatars, (b) developing classroom rules and teaching a group alert strategy, and (c) introducing a new unit of study of their choice. Upon completing their teaching experiences, they participated in a 10 group debrief with their instructor and peers to share their feed-

Figure 2. High school classroom setting used for teacher preparation programs

back along with a private reflection following their second and third simulation experiences (Hudson et al., 2018). Of the 25 participants, 19 finished all three experiences and completed their perceptions questionnaire. Overall, 10 themes were captured based on the triangulation of quantitative and qualitative data, with agreement on four themes, disagreement with four themes, and mixed agreement on two themes (Hudson et al., 2018).

Specifically, participants agreed or strongly agreed that the mixed-reality experience was like a real classroom, that they were able to practice new behavior-management skills, that they gained a deeper understanding of their teaching and behavior management practices through reflection, and they found it helpful to speak with an avatar individually. The disagreement was found in participants being aware of important behavior management skills they were missing, that it was challenging to manage disruptive behaviors positively, that they struggled with time management, and that the mixed-reality environment limited their teaching plans. A mixed agreement was found in participants gaining confidence in successfully planning and implementing a lesson plan, and benefiting from multiple mixed-reality teaching experiences. It is worth noting that the authors addressed the discrepancy in the disagreements suggesting the maturity level of the participants about being able to effectively manage the classroom and the lack of experience in delivering lessons (Hudson et al., 2018). Overall, the results of the study indicated that participants perceived that they were better prepared to teach, that the Mursion simulation experiences were an effective way to practice new skills, and that the avatars seemed like real students. Respondents also noted more confidence in managing undesired behaviors and felt like they were in a real classroom (Hudson et al., 2018).

What happens when the teacher education department is housed in an online institution? How can online universities prepare teacher candidates using Mursion simulations? As a leader in online learning, Walden University was nationally recognized in 2018 for being the first online university to use simulations within the College of Education. Using a behavior-management simulation, teacher candidates were allowed to practice research-based classroom management strategies to keep student avatars engaged and on task. Initial implementation began within the Master of Education with a specialization in Special Education program, eventually being extended to the Master of Arts in Teaching (MAT) program with a specialization in special education. The M.S. in Education is an advanced preparation program for students to enhance their teaching skills to better serve students in grades P-12 and/or to become educational leaders in the field. The MAT program with a specialization in Special Education is an initial teacher preparation licensure program that prepares candidates to teach students with exceptionalities from kindergarten through age 21.

Candidates in the M.S. in Education program are encouraged to test out their acquisition of new skills and strategies within their actual classrooms and school settings, whereas candidates in the MAT in Special Education program are acquiring content and pedagogical knowledge in the field of special education as they prepare to become special educators. Preparing candidates to teach diverse learners, classroom management, communication, and collaboration skills are just a few of the essential components embedded within the MAT program; however, student survey data revealed that many candidates rated themselves as not being quite ready to take on some of the more sensitive day-to-day responsibilities of classroom teachers and/or leaders. As shown through various research studies (Christofferson & Sullivan, 2015; Dieker et al., 2008; Dieker et al., 2014; and Ficarra & Quinn, 2014), virtual reality simulations have proven to provide a safe space to practice complexities of the classroom, classroom management strategies and skills as well as receive feedback.

DESIGN AND IMPLEMENTATION

The creation of each simulation takes careful planning and analysis of what the candidate needs to gain from the experience to write clear objectives for the experience. During the design period, the Walden University and Mursion team first identified the skills the candidates need to practice during the simulation experience. The identified skills are then aligned to teaching standards and the content of the simulation is created to meet the identified needs. The team then determines what avatar(s) will be utilized as well as the intended audience. From there the simulation experience is described in detail as to what will occur during the live event. Specific challenges are developed to ensure the candidate has opportunities to practice the identified skills. Specific "hits" and "misses" for each challenge are provided to the simulation specialist along with a suggested menu of responses for each hit or miss. For example, if the candidate has hit the objective, the avatar(s) will remain focused and engaged. When the candidate misses the objective, the avatar(s) will perform specific actions, such as become disengaged, act loudly, get upset, etc...

Once the design is finalized, it is first practiced in-house with the team and the simulation specialist. Avatars are controlled by the simulation specialist during the experience, allowing the avatars to respond in real-time to the skills exhibited by the participant. During this practice, the specialist is also able to learn the expectations of the simulation and get feedback regarding its performance. A schedule is then placed in the online course for students to set up a time to conduct their simulation experience one-to-one with the simulation specialist. During the simulation, each challenge is a fresh start, allowing candidates to get back on track to have a positive experience by the end of the simulation. The simulations are recorded and then shared with the participant. In turn, teacher candidates share their simulation recordings in the online discussion area and reflect on their experience. This allows other students and the instructor to provide valuable feedback, ask questions, or offer additional suggestions regarding the skills exhibited in the simulation, based on the identified performance objectives.

Candidates in the MAT program participate in the Behavior Management Scenario in which they have an opportunity to practice their behavior management and classroom engagement skills. For this scenario, the candidates are given a choice of three different lessons to teach the virtual students and notified that the main goal for the simulation is for them to keep the students engaged and motivated in the lesson using evidence-based practices they learned in the course or through their research. Using the preparation worksheet, candidates can write down the evidence-based strategies they could implement during their simulation. Throughout the simulation, candidates are allowed to safely practice the identified strategies to meet the expected objectives. If it is evident that the candidates are using evidence-based strategies during each of the challenges, the avatars become engaged in the lesson.

If these strategies are not evident, then the virtual students become off task, at times displaying challenging behaviors. Figure 3 illustrates an example of the simulation that shows an avatar, Will, fall asleep during the lesson, which tells the candidate that a strategy is needed to re-engage Will. Upon completion of the simulation experience, teacher candidates engage in a brief reflection with the simulation specialist, sharing their reflection of their performance. Candidates then post their videos and reflection on the course discussion board to obtain feedback from their peers and instructor.

In Walden University's Bachelor of Science in Elementary Education (BSEE), candidates view an asynchronous video of a student completing a reading inventory, featured in Figure 4 below. For the synchronous experience, candidates are provided reading data to analyze before participating in the simulation with the students' parents during a parent-teacher conference, featured in figure 5. The first

Figure 3. Example of simulation experience, demonstrating Will falling asleep

challenge in the synchronous simulation begins with the parent walking into the meeting with a negative attitude. The candidate is required to use verbal and non-verbal communication strategies to change the

Figure 4. Simulation experience of Carlos completing a reading inventory

Figure 5. Simulation experience of the parent-teacher conference

tone of the conference to positive. The candidate then needs to discuss areas in which the student did well and areas of improvement in reading while keeping the parent engaged and positive.

Issues, Controversies, Problems

After the initial design and implementation, feedback from candidates and instructors is used to enhance the simulation in preparation for the second round. Our Walden team learned many learners in the initial pilot of online simulations expressed surprise and some level of discomfort when they realized that the avatars were able to see, hear, and authentically interact at the moment with them. More than the common nervous feeling of "being in the hot seat," some participants were truly not prepared for the experience. Based on that feedback, in the second iteration of the pilot, we included an avatar facilitator named Bennett to greet the student, provide a quick overview of the simulation scenario, and answer any questions the participant may have.

Once the participant completes the simulation, Bennett returns for a feedback session in which the participant is asked three questions: "What do you think you did well? What do you think you might have done better? How might this simulation experience help you in your professional role? Figure 6 illustrates Bennett, an avatar simulator, which also is controlled by the simulation specialist. Bennett prepares the teacher candidate for the experience and provides reminders and specific information related to what the avatars can and cannot do during the simulation. Finally, to better prepare students for the experience, sample simulation recordings are provided to give a better sense of the type of interaction to expect.

Lessons Learned

Survey data were collected in four areas:

Figure 6. Bennett, is an avatar used to prepare teacher candidates for the simulation experience

1. Pre-Experience Information and Instructions,
2. Completing the Experience,
3. The Learning Experience,
4. The Avatars

Overall, the teacher candidate responses were positive, and they felt the experiences helped to strengthen their skills. Candidates found that pre-experience documents and the sample simulation video helped to prepare them for the simulation. It is also important to offer a variety of times and dates for candidates to sign up for their sessions. Candidates also found value in having the avatar, Bennett, introduce the simulation experience and walk them through the process before starting. Giving all of the directions ahead of time, as well as quickly receiving their links for posting in the course room, were also found to help alleviate the frustration candidates exhibited while completing the experience. Feedback from surveys reflected candidates are surprised at how responsive and realistic the avatars are. Candidates felt they were able to practice and strengthen their teaching skills through the simulations. Data showed that candidates felt that viewing the simulation videos of classmates and having online discussions with their peers was meaningful. As we continue to increase our use of the simulations, candidates have begun to get to know the unique personalities of each of the avatars as they plan and practice strategies.

SOLUTIONS AND RECOMMENDATIONS

When introducing the idea of mixed-reality simulations (or virtual reality simulations), some people may be skeptical and say things like: "Participants know those avatars are not real students!" and "How is this different than asking students to role-play?" Walden, as an online university, also must consider how the whole experience can be handled fully online. Previously, simulations required an on-the-ground lab where participants stood in front of a large monitor to engage with the avatars being manipulated remotely by a simulation specialist who could see and hear the participant(s). On the issue of the avatars not being "real students" (or clients, patients, etc.), participants have expressed a "suspension of disbelief" when the interaction begins and the personal connection to the avatars feels real. While traditional role-play among students can be effective, mixed-reality simulations with avatars are distinguished by the use of highly trained simulation specialists who can respond in nuanced ways that mirror unpredictable human interactions. The simulation specialists are guided by the objectives of the scenario and how they might respond to the participant(s), but each interaction is unique, offering candidates an experience closely related to what they may experience in their fields of study.

FUTURE TRENDS

The use of avatars as a safe place to practice has evolved throughout the education programs at Walden University, quickly spreading to other areas such as psychology, business, and health with preparation underway for additional simulation experiences. Students in these programs can practice their communication skills by discussing ethics and standards, responding to a company's leadership team regarding a new project, or addressing an incident that led to patient harm. Additional simulations in the education program include trauma-informed instructional strategies and practice, working with students from culturally diverse backgrounds, practicing job interviewing skills, collecting data, and participating in an Individualized Educational Planning (IEP) meeting. The addition of these unique simulations would allow candidates to feel more prepared and confident to perform these duties.

For instance, participating in IEP meetings is another critical responsibility of special educators and one that requires pertinent ethical and legal responsibilities, along with effective communication and collaboration skills. Given the delicate nature and significance of these meetings, special educators should not only be equipped with pedagogical and foundational special education knowledge and law, but they also should be savvy enough to facilitate the meeting. This is only acquired through consistent practice, repetition, and experience. Through simulation experiences, candidates will be able to practice handling crises, conducting home visits, or processing through a problem with a parent or child in real-time … all without any consequences of saying the wrong thing.

The avatar simulations are also used for training with our enrollment specialists to practice how they would talk to prospective students about different programs and respond to questions. Following the simulations, participants are provided with feedback regarding what went well and what could be done differently to have a better student experience. This type of simulation experience ensures our enrollment specialists are knowledgeable about the different programs so they can better answer potential student questions. This safe place to practice helps to build their confidence and be better prepared to help prospective students.

Virtual residencies are exploring the idea of group simulations in which one or more individuals participate in a simulation while the rest of the group observes. The participant(s) can "pause" the simulation at any time to receive feedback and coaching. Learning is scaffolded across simulation experiences, and individuals and teams have fewer opportunities to "pause" for coaching as they progress in their learning and experience.

With our in-house simulation specialists in place, the integration of avatar simulation experiences continues to be widely used throughout Walden University. The simulation center houses both adult and children avatars, with an array of environments including classroom settings, business offices, teacher break rooms, an office lobby, bar and lounge, medical exam rooms, a living room, clubhouse, and a bathroom. Leadership and faculty members can enhance programs by designing and implementing simulation experiences in a variety of settings to support the acquisition of essential skills, strategies, and techniques that adequately prepare students for their prospective field of study, advances in research, or unforeseen changes in society.

The global pandemic is just one example of a recent unforeseeable situation that caused the displacement and disruption of educational services and opportunities for millions of teachers, candidates, and students. Unfortunately, many preparation programs were forced to delay courses and field experiences for teacher candidates as a result of the pandemic. Due to our capability and success with designing and implementing avatar simulations, we were able to obtain board approval through a variance from the licensing board to allow our candidates to use simulation hours to count towards their field hour requirements. Candidates were able to continue in their educational programs, engaging in authentic and realistic field experiences using avatar simulations as well as other virtual field experiences. Simulations consisted of both synchronous and asynchronous simulation experiences, which were aligned to their course content and licensing standards, along with a reflection of their experience in which they shared with their peers.

CONCLUSION

As field experience continues to be recognized as one of the most credible sources of teacher preparation for teacher candidates, educational programs must integrate authentic, yet realistic opportunities for candidates to practice essential skills needed to perform their daily duties and responsibilities of being classroom teachers. Simulation experiences not only provide a safe place to practice professional skills, they also offer an opportunity for collaborative learning, a community of practice dialogue, and reflection. The potential for using the avatars in any type of training program is endless. Professionals in any field can use avatars to allow students or employees to practice their skills before encountering real-life situations. While this chapter highlights the value of simulations for teacher candidates, learners in all professional fields can benefit from working with avatars as a scaffolded learning experience before important interactions with real-world implications.

ACKNOWLEDGMENT

We would like to thank Walden University, Dr. Kelley Costner, and Dr. Sue Subocz for their support of our initial pilot and continued investment in our simulation center. Thanks also go to, the team of specialists who assisted us with development, scheduling, and planning: Tika Rai, Liz Taylor, David Dolinsky, Dan Billman, and Kelly Kelly. A special note of appreciation to everyone we have worked with at Mursion, especially Brentt Brown for helping us begin our journey and Carrie Straub for her support along the way and for her review of this chapter. We would also like to thank Dr. Lisa A. Dieker, who originally reached out to us and suggested that Walden be the first university to adapt and deliver live, interactive simulations in an online environment.

REFERENCES

Ball, D. L., & Forzani, F. M. (2009). The work of teaching and the challenge for teacher education. *Journal of Teacher Education*, *60*(5), 497–511. doi:10.1177/0022487109348479

Brown, J. S., Collins, A., & Duguid, P. (1989). Situated cognition and the culture of learning. *Educational Researcher*, *18*(1), 32–42. doi:10.3102/0013189X018001032

Chini, J. J., Straub, C. L., & Thomas, K. H. (2016). Learning from avatars: Learning assistance practice physics pedagogy in a classroom simulator. *Physical Review. Physics Education Research*, *12*(1), 010117. Advance online publication. doi:10.1103/PhysRevPhysEducRes.12.010117

Christofferson, M., & Sullivan, A. L. (2015). Preservice teachers' classroom management training: A survey of self-reported training experiences, content coverage, and preparedness. *Psychology in the Schools*, *52*(3), 248–264. Advance online publication. doi:10.1002/pits.21819

Diana, T. J. Jr. (2013). Microteaching revisited: Using technology to enhance the professional development of pre-service teachers. *The Clearing House: A Journal of Educational Strategies, Issues and Ideas*, *86*(4), 150–154. doi:10.1080/00098655.2013.790307

Dieker, L. A., Hynes, M., Hughes, C., & Smith, E. (2008). Implications of mixed reality and simulation technologies on special education and teacher preparation. *Focus on Exceptional Children*, *40*(6), 1–20. doi:10.17161/foec.v40i6.6877

Dieker, L. A., Rodriguez, J., Lingnugaris-Kraft, B., Hynes, M., & Hughes, C. E. (2014). The future of simulated environments in teacher education: Current potential and future possibilities. *Teacher Education and Special Education*, *37*(1), 21–33. doi:10.1177/0888406413512683

Dieker, L. A., Straub, C. L., Hughes, C. E., Hynes, M. C., & Hardin, S. (2014). Learning from virtual students. *Educational Leadership*, *71*(8), 54–58.

Ficarra, L., & Quinn, K. (2014). Teachers' facility with evidence-based classroom management practices: An investigation of teachers' preparation programmes and in-service conditions. *Journal of Teacher Education for Sustainability*, *16*(2), 71–87. doi:10.2478/jtes-2014-0012

Girod, M., & Girod, G. (2006). Exploring the efficacy of the Cook School District simulation. *Journal of Teacher Education*, *57*(5), 481–497. doi:10.1177/0022487106293742

Girod, M., & Girod, G. (2008). Simulation and the need for practice in teacher preparation. *Journal of Technology and Teacher Education*, *16*(3), 307–337.

Hixon, E., & So, H. J. (2009). Technology's role in field experiences for preservice teacher training. *Journal of Educational Technology & Society*, *12*(4), 294–304. https://www.jstor.org/stable/jeductechsoci.12.4.294

Hudson, M. E., Voytecki, K. S., & Zhang, G. (2018). Mixed-reality teaching experiences improve preservice special education students' perceptions of their ability to manage a classroom. *Journal of Virtual Worlds Research*, *11*(2), 1–17. doi:10.4101/jvwr.v11i2.7308

Jones, M., & Ryan, J. (2014). Learning in the practicum: Engaging pre-service teachers in reflective practice in the online space. *Asia-Pacific Journal of Teacher Education, 42*(2), 132–146. doi:10.1080/1359866X.2014.892058

Kahneman, D. (2011). *Thinking fast and slow*. Farrar, Straus, and Giroux.

Karlström, M., & Hamza, K. (2019). Preservice science teachers' opportunities for learning through reflection when planning a microteaching unit. *Journal of Science Teacher Education, 30*(1), 44–62. doi:10.1080/1046560X.2018.1531345

Koehler, A., Ertmer, P., & Newby, T. (2019). Instructional design skills through case-based instruction: Examining the impact of discussion format. *Journal of Teacher Education, 70*(4), 319–334. doi:10.1177/0022487118755701

Loughran, J. (2006). *Developing a pedagogy of teacher education: Understanding teaching and learning about teaching*. Routledge.

Malone, D. M., & Langone, J. (2005). Comparing general and special education preservice teachers' test performance using traditional and anchored instruction. *Journal of Early Childhood Teacher Education, 25*(2), 143–152. doi:10.1080/1090102050250207

Mursion. (2020). *Best in class leadership development: How virtual reality and avatars are changing the learning landscape* [White paper]. https://www.denasamuels.com/wp-content/uploads/2020/03/How-Virtual-Reality-and-Avatars-are-Changing-the-Learning-Landscape.pdf

Thomassen, A., & Rive, P. (2010). How to enable knowledge exchange in Second Life in design education? *Learning, Media and Technology, 35*(2), 155–169. doi:10.1080/17439884.2010.494427

Yadav, A., Bouck, E., Da Fonte, A., & Patton, S. (2009). Instructing special education pre-service teachers through literacy video cases: Teaching teachers through literacy video cases. *Teaching Education, 20*(2), 149–162. doi:10.1080/10476210902878510

KEY TERMS AND DEFINITIONS

Avatars: Virtual, lifelike figures, that are operated by simulation specialists.

Classroom Management: Actions teachers take to create an environment that supports and facilitates academic and social emotional learning.

Field-Based Experiences: Candidates practice course-based learning theories, pedagogical content knowledge, and skills within classroom and school settings.

Mixed-Reality Simulation: Combination of real and virtual environments, offering candidates a full, immersive teaching experience.

Pre-Service Teachers: Candidates pursuing teaching licenses, who have little to no experience teaching in the classroom.

Teacher Candidate: A student enrolled in a teacher preparation program.

Teacher Preparation Program: A program with the content and methods courses, including practicum and field experiences, that prepares students to become professional teachers.

Chapter 8
Immersive Virtual Reality in Sports:
Coaching and Training

Trone Jackson II
Capella University, USA

ABSTRACT

This chapter aims to show how immersive virtual reality headsets can impact sports by providing an immersive virtual learning environment that implements immersive learning, learning by doing, and immediate feedback to ensure the development of coaches and players in sports. This chapter will describe how immersive virtual reality simulations are used on virtual reality headsets and discuss the learning theories that lead to transferring skills from a virtual world to the real world. Immersive learning simulations require coaches and player to recreate live sporting events to make split decisions. This chapter will examine how creating virtual coaching and playing environments that mirror real in-game emotions, real in-game immediacy, and the pressures to make the correct split-second decisions. Additionally, the chapter reviews research of the cognitive sciences to understand how AR simulations can accelerate new skills acquisition.

INTRODUCTION

Immersive virtual reality (VR) headsets used for sports training are designed based on learning by doing model. These simulations and virtual environments use science, psychology, and technology to enhance learning and accelerate skill development. This chapter will define the core learning theories and key training concepts that make immersive virtual reality headsets an efficient way to design a simulation for sports and look at future immersive virtual reality sports trends.

Learn by doing is a learning method that allows the brain to build connections through experiences that coaches and players will face during the game. Learn by doing is a concept proven to work both in and out of the sports realm. Immersive virtual reality immerses the user into an environment where quick active decisions must be made based on the virtual environment's circumstances. The virtual environ-

DOI: 10.4018/978-1-7998-4222-4.ch008

ment must mimic the real world in-game situations that coaches experience without the risk of losing the game. Lave and Wenger (1991) refer to this as legitimate peripheral participation. The simulations of the users' experience can transfer to the real game after its completion.

Immersive virtual reality headsets have become more popular over the last few years due to technological advancement. While in immersive virtual environments three components must be adopted including,

1. Observational learning
2. Contextual interface
3. Feedback and reinforcement.

These three concepts work as the foundation during immersive simulations to create an authentic learning environment where users experience the accelerated development of new skills.

The learning that takes place during sports requires the gathering of information under a variety of conditions. Virtual environments must mimic the specific sport and skill and the environmental conditions that occur during the game. Immersive VR provides players and coaches an opportunity to transfer skills from the virtual environment to the real game. AR simulations using VR headsets are based on immersive learning concepts including learn by doing, embodiment, retrieval-based learning, transferable Training, and learning in the zone of proximal development. These aspects are critical to developing coaches and players who can respond to the immediacy of sports (Casale, 2018). This chapter aims to show how immersive virtual reality headsets used with the correct learning techniques and methodologies can lead to skill acquisition enhancement in players and promote new ways to enhance coaches' self-efficacy in-game defying moments.

BACKGROUND

Immersive learning allows the user to experience a realistic simulation. VR headsets provide 360-degree immersion with an avatar to ensure the simulated experience appears as realistic as possible. Russell (2019) found that immersion can enhance learning by allowing multiple perspectives, along with situated learning and development of the transfer of learning. Immersion works in sports as it allows coaches and athletes to be active in the learning experience. Customized virtual simulations put the users in situations that resemble the game. Immersive learning environments result in functional training.

For athletes and coaches to acquire new skills, the immersive virtual learning environment has to simulate the different movements and emotions that may occur during the game. Each learning environment requires

1. The athlete to make movements consistent with the movements made in the real-world setting.
2. Ensure that movements performed happen in various situations that all apply to the specific sport or coaching situation.
3. Provide sensory and timely feedback to encourage or correct behavior.

Interactions in virtual learning can predict the outcomes of virtual training experience. Higher levels of engagement in the virtual world lead to a higher percentage of the transfer from virtual to reality. The collaboration in a live training simulation provides a place to practice the demanding visual and perceptual-motor skills that happen during the competition (Fairly, 2019). These experiences in a virtual environment can transfer over to the real-world game. Immersive learning environments provide coaches a simulated experience where game learning can take place. The 3D avatar with 360-degree immersion makes it so the coaches' and players' movements can resemble the same movements they make in the game.

Immersive learning environments can boost the beliefs, emotions, and values of the coaches and players who use immersive VR headsets (Russell, 2019). The actions that take place during sporting events can be recreated in immersive learning environments. Technology allows players and coaches to improve their ability without the risk of injury or the need for other players to be present (Maddox, 2018). Immersive learning done correctly can improve performance accuracy and speed on a cognitive and perceptual level (Fairly, 2019). The VR headsets can provide coaches/ players an opportunity to get reps in various simulations.

The third concept of immersive learning requires users to receive timely feedback to maximize development. Athletes in immersive learning environments must receive constructive feedback in a timely matter to ensure efficient learning (Farley et al., 2019). Feedback can be received in an audio or visual form to let the athlete know when a correct decision is made. Many studies have found that receiving visual or auditory feedback can help accelerate the improvement of complex motor skills.

DESIGN AND IMPLEMENTATION

As technology becomes more prevalent in sports analysis, game-planning, and scouting, both coaches and players must use technology to strengthen their strengths and weaknesses. Over the past couple of years, significant advancements in VR technology, especially within the development of 3D and 360° virtual environments, has occurred (Farley, Spencer, & Baudinet, 2019). New advancements have created a perfect opportunity for coaches and players to take full advantage of VR headsets' many learning options. Only in virtual reality can simulations provide vital scientific principles that allow learning styles to be incorporated into training to ensure results and changed behaviors (Casale, 2018).

The benefits of virtual reality allow players and coaches to experience repetition on demand. With the headsets, players do not need a teammate to throw them a ball or rebound to get in the number of repetitions to improve their decision making. For coaches who usually could only watch a film, they can have practice or attend camps and clinics. A VR headset will allow coaches and players to experience an in-person virtual environment designed to improve learning. For virtual reality to be effective in providing coaches and players the opportunity to benefit from this technology, there are vital functions that must be included. The training protocol for coaches and players must mimic the most effective environment. Training needs to include proper speed and repetition, a variation of training concepts, and full immersion.

One of the main learning styles that make immersive virtual reality so effective is repetition learning. Repetition learning links the frequency at which two things are experienced together, with the likelihood that recall of one experience will stimulate the other's recall. Todd Maddaox (2016) states that each repetition provides an opportunity for an incremental increase in muscle memory in the basal ganglia. He states that the goal of the behavioral skills learning system and its dopamine-mediated learning mechanism in the basal ganglia is to train direct neural connections between sensory regions in the brain and motor regions in the brain. For immersive virtual reality environments to be effective, athletes and coaches must be able to get in-game repetitions from their headsets. Bonney, Jelsma, Ferguson, and Smits-Engelsman (2017) found that repetitive practice leads to better performance during the acquisition phase of training, it often impairs learners' ability to retain and transfer skills acquired in practice to other situations.

Retrieval based learning provides coaches and players with an opportunity to inter to engage in retrieving training information (Castele, 2018). Retrieval based learning allows players/ coaches to learn multiple skills along, and upon review of those skills, they can identify what they do not know and correct it. There is not enough time for coaches or trainers to revisit previously learned tasks in practice or the game situation to make sure high levels of learning occur. Immersive virtual reality headsets that provide tracking along with the ability to review the previous task can provide that quality of feedback. This helps users retain learned information along with helping them transfer skills from the virtual environment to the in-game situation.

Based on previous research there are four essential elements when it comes to the transfer of skill acquisitions from the virtual to the real world. In their research, Tirp et al. (2015) found,

1. physical conditioning elements, which relate to general physiological changes that shared between similar modes of activity (e.g., all aerobic training will promote system-wide cardiorespiratory changes)
2. movement elements, which relate to the anatomical and biomechanical similarities between tasks (e.g., overhand throwing in baseball and handball),
3. perceptual elements, which relate to the environmental information used to make performance-related decisions (e.g., the need to recognize offensive and defensive patterns of play) and (
4. conceptual elements, which relate to similarities in the strategies, rules, and guidelines governing behavior during the competition (e.g., gymnast- and diving share some conceptual elements regarding judging aesthetics of performers' movements) (Rienhoff et al., 2013, p. 1-2).

Ensuring the correct elements are implemented in an immersive virtual experience can be the difference between the user's success and the user just participating in a video game.

Issues, Controversies, Problems.

When it comes to coaching in sports, there have been no tangible ways to identify if a coach is good or not, other than the win and loss columns. It is an issue for players' coaches' families and society as a whole. The Amateur Athletic Union reports that over 700,000 youth members and 150,000 coaches participate across 41 sports programs and 55 US districts (AAU, 2020). The National Collegiate Athletic Association (NCAA) reported that in the 2017-2018 academic year nearly half a million students completed more than 19,000 teams (Schwarb,2018). With this number of coaches in America, the same emphasis that is put on developing players should be put on developing coaches. With the advancement of virtual reality technology. It will be great to see coaches receive training on managing referees, parents, and, most of all, players from different cultural and economic backgrounds.

When it comes to player development, virtual reality headsets have been used on the college and professional levels. As this technology becomes more affordable, grassroots programs should use this technology to benefit the children and teenagers who play sports. In the past, this technology was too expensive for mass adoption, but with the current advancements, it will be interesting to see the impact that virtual reality and immersive environments will have on young players and coaches' development.

Lessons Learned

Based on the research conducted for this chapter, one of the main things that the author noticed was a lack of literature that discusses how immersive virtual reality headsets can help coaches and the limited amount of movement that the virtual simulations provide. Most of the literature about virtual reality and sports focus on how to make the players better. At this point, coaches have not been studied in immersive virtual environments as much as the athletes have.

This trend is present in most of the areas of virtual reality integration. In the fields of education, business, healthcare, and other sectors, where virtual reality is present, the focus is often on the end-user. For example, many studies discuss how students can learn from immersive virtual reality environments, but there are limited studies that discuss teacher's self-efficacy when implementing virtual environments into the classroom. The main lesson learned in the production of this chapter is that the future of immersive technology is bright due to all the learning opportunities for coaches and trainers that have not been explored.

Some research has been done to investigate the psychological factors of VR. Stinson and Bowman (2014) investigated the potential of VR to train players in high-pressure situations using a penalty kick simulation in soccer. Stinson and Bowman (2014) found it was possible to induce anxiety in the VR situations they used and, in particular, there was a high influence of environment fidelity on anxiety. Adding pressured situations to training can help further prepare players for what they will experience during the game. By creating a virtual environment that incorporates the illusion of pressure, coaches can evaluate how players will perform in clutch situations. These parameters can help the coach when game planning late in games.

Several studies showed that VR offers unique features to understand how a goalkeeper retrieves information on the opponent to intercept a ball in handball (Bideau et al.,2003; Vignais et al., 2009,2015) or soccer (Brault et al., 2015 Craig et al., 2006,2009). Studies like this can be duplicated for multiple sports to gauge how coaches retrieve information on players based on body language and other factors. Below in Table 1 is a chart developed by Faure et al. (2019). It shows the relevant methodological characteristics and main results of studies. This chart identifies studies for multiple sports. This table defines the sport(s) being explored, the main goal, the study design, the VR device used, the participants' characteristics, the statistical analysis performed, and the main results obtained. Of the 30 studies included for analysis, eight focused on handball, seven on rugby, eight on soccer, four on baseball or softball, one on basketball, and the remaining three were more general works on various team sports and VR (Faure et al., 2020, pp. 4-6).

SOLUTIONS AND RECOMMENDATIONS

Immersive virtual reality headset can revolutionize the way coaches are selected from a grassroots level to a pro-level. To provide some structure to the coaching world, virtual simulations that train coaches on how to deal with different situations they may encounter in a game can be designed. Providing coaches with an immersive virtual environment where they can learn how to read body cues, work with the referees, and remain calm in pressure situations will help develop youth sport. This can also lead to more positive sports experiences for children and families on the grassroots level.

Table 1. Compilation of research of VR in sports

Reference	Sport	Main Goal	Study Design	VR Device	Participants	Main Results
Bideau et al. (2003)	Handball	To explore the potential of VR as a training tool in handball	The immersive situation of a real goalkeeper facing real thrower and virtual thrower	VR center (3 Barco 1208S video projectors and a large cylindrical screen)	One expert handball goalkeeper	A high correlation between reaction when facing real and virtual throws (*R2* between 0.97 and 1, for all kinematics parameters)
Bideau et al. (2004)	Handball	To explore the use of VR to understand visual elements taken into account by a handball goalkeeper	The immersive situation of a real goalkeeper facing virtual throws, under various visual modifications (increase in elbow angle, rotation of the trunk, or delayed ball release)	VR center (3 Barco 1208S video projectors and a large cylindrical screen)	8 expert handball goalkeepers	The significant influence of all modifications on goalkeeper's reaction/ motion
Bideau et al. (2010)	Handball & Rugby Union	To explore the use of VR to: (1) assess players' ability to detect deceptive movement in rugby and (2) assess the ability of handball goalkeeper to perceive and intercept virtual throws	(1) "Perception-only" (PO) task: players judged deceptive movement of rugby, with a "cut-off" protocol(2) "Perception-action" (PA) task: Immersive situation of a real goalkeeper physically intercepting virtual throws in handball	(1) PO task: HMD (CyberMind Visette Pro)(2) PA task: VR center (3 Barco 1208S video projectors and a large cylindrical screen)	(1) PO task: 8 novices and 8 experts rugby players(2) PA task: 2 expert handball goalkeepers	(1) PO task: experts perceived better and faster deceptive movements(2) PA task: the importance of ball trajectory over player movements to intercept the ball

The NCAA and the AAU and other grassroots organizations should use new technologies to teach coaches how to deal with players, families referees on and off the court. Each coach should be required to spend a certain amount of time in an immersed virtual environment per year. Coaches volunteering or being paid should have to go through training on how to deal with hectic situations these situations can range from player attitudes to being at the end of the game having to rally the team for one defensive stop. The more coaches can be inserted into real game like situations with no risk when situations occur in a real game. Immersive virtual reality environments can help coaches' coach from a psychological level and develop their knowledge of the game. Novice coaches and expert coaches can all benefit from the use of immersive virtual reality headsets.

FUTURE TRENDS

The future of virtual reality in sports is promising. VR startups have already implemented VR in the National Football League (NFL), Major League Baseball (MLB) and have been focused on helping players improve one aspect of the game for the National Basketball League (NBL). It is the free-throw

Table 2. (continued)

Reference	Sport	Main Goal	Study Design	VR Device	Participants	Main Results
Bootsma et al. (2016)	Soccer	To examine how soccer goalkeepers moved along the goal line to intercept long-range shots on goal in a VE	Immersive situation: goalkeepers faced virtual kicks with straight or curved trajectories	Large VR facility (CAVE (Cave Automatic Virtual Environment))	21 experienced soccer players	Straight trajectories: Effect of ball arrival position, ball departure position, and interaction between them on player position and motion. Similar results for initiation time. Curved trajectories: 12 of 16 trajectories led to reversals of movement direction during the trial → high influence of spin Movement patterns rely on combinations of optical position and velocity for straight trajectories, and optical velocity and acceleration for curving trajectories
Brault et al. (2009)	Rugby Union	To explore the relevance of Tau COM (Center Of Mass) as a variable to predict the deceptive movement of side-step in rugby	Participants judged randomized virtual movements (deceptive and non-deceptive) of side-step	HMD (CyberMind Visette Pro)	8 novices and 8 mid-level rugby players	Tau COM is a better variable than COM displacement to predict the final direction of the side-step. The mid-level group was able to pick relevant information before the novice group → better anticipation skills

visualization for the NBL, the MLB hitting visualization, and the use of visualization in the NFL that have been ahead of the curve. The company that will revolutionize immersive training is Sports Virtual Training Systems (Sports VTS) with the creation of QBSIM. Their proprietary software allows the quarterback in the NFL to take hundreds of snaps with different offenses and defenses and throw the ball.

The future of immersive virtual reality are programs that look similar to the Sports VTS simulation. According to Maddox (2017), when behavior is performed correctly (e.g., a completed pass), the relevant neural connections are strengthened, and that behavior will be more likely to occur next time. If the behavior is performed incorrectly (e.g., an incomplete pass), the relevant neural connections are weakened, and that behavior will be less likely to occur next time. Being able to use virtual reality along with game equipment allows players the opportunity to get in reps with the equipment they use in the game. This technology will revolutionize how athletes supplement their reps. In football, players use film to supplement the reps they may miss in practice because the team goal is the priority, not the players' training. The limited-time players spend with their teams on the field, or the court helps make VR headsets so crucial to player development.

VR headsets allow players to get in-game repetitions at their leisure. Quarterbacks can enter a virtual simulation and study the coverages of the teams that they may be facing at the end of the week. The extra reps that the players receive will make it, so when they see a defensive shift in the game's players will make the right reads. Players are already using VR in this capacity. In the future, players will be able to

Table 3. (continued)

Reference	Sport	Main Goal	Study Design	VR Device	Participants	Main Results
Brault et al. (2012)	Rugby Union	To understand how the dynamics of deceptive body movement influence a defending player's decision about how and when to act when facing the deceptive movement	PO task: players had to predict the final direction of a virtual opponent (cut-off protocol) PA task: players had to physically intercept a virtual opponent	HMD (CyberMind Visette Pro)	PO task: 14 experts and 14 novices rugby players PA task: 12 experts and 12 novices rugby players	PO task: Experts were more sensitive to "honest" signals(COM) than novices, performed better, and pick up relevant information earlier. Novices were more sensitive to "deceptive" signals (upper trunk yaw and out-foot placement) PA task: Experts were more sensitive to "honest" signals (COM) than novices, performed better, and waited significantly longer before moving to intercept. More movements and with higher amplitude in the wrong direction for novices
Brault et al. (2015)	Soccer	To explore the motion and performance of a goalkeeper facing a free-kick	The goalkeeper had to intercept free-kicks in VE with different conditions	Nvidia 3D vision system	11 mid-level soccer goalkeepers	Better performance when 5 defenders in the wall (compared to 4 players), and when the wall was aligned to the right goalpost
Chong and Croft (2009)	Rugby Union	To explore the capacity to build a virtual assessment/ training system for rugby lineout	Players had to perform real rugby throws, facing virtual lineout	NuView SX-2000 Stereo3D (photogrammetric system)	Rugby players (unknown number and level)	Accuracy of throw decreased when distance increased. A less accurate throw was correlated with a higher trunk flexion
Correia et al. (2012)	Rugby Union	To explore what action cues are perceived and chosen in 3 vs. 3 tasks in rugby	The Player had to make the right choice (keep the ball, short pass, long pass) according to the 3 vs. 3 situation	HMD (CyberMind Visette Pro)	9 novices, 9 recreational, 16 intermediate, and 12 professional rugby players	Influence of the position of the gaps, as well as the level of expertise on the choice made. Higher ability to perceive the affordance for oneself than for the others

combine the visualization with actual movement and equipment that will allow them to simulate game performance without the risk of injury or needing other players to participate in helping them develop.

For players, the advancement of technology will not only help in-game performance but will also help with rehabilitation and other intangibles that help players psychologically. As technology advances, there will be a shift from pro athletes and college athletes being privy to this technology, and more high school middle school, and grassroots programs will be able to use the same technology. This advancement will ensure that players develop college and pro-like skills at earlier ages. This advancement will revolutionize the efficiency with which players play the game.

One area that has not received attention is how coaches can use virtual headset technologies to advance self-efficacy. The training of coaches is often overlooked. Most coaches get better by experiencing failure in the game. This can mean that a coach must lose to get better. VR makes it possible for coaches to practice light game situations in practice and at home. So much of a coach's job is managing players' attitude and the flow of the game. With the emergence of software that teaches empathy along with communication techniques, coaches can immerse themselves in in-game situations that not only focus on the X & Os but also focus on dealing with players who are in a slump, have bad attitudes, or need positive reinforcement to help them perform in the game.

Table 4. (continued)

Reference	Sport	Main Goal	Study Design	VR Device	Participants	Main Results
Covaci et al. (2015)	Basket-Ball	To explore the feasibility of developing a free-throw simulator in basket-ball	Players were asked to perform free throws in 3 visual conditions (first person, third person, third person + guidance)	Large VR facility (CAVE)	11 novices	Underestimation of distance in VR: lower ball speed, slightly higher height of ball release, higher angle when the ball enters the basket compared to real condition. Visual feedback (*3rd* person + guidance) reduces underestimation
Craig (2013)	General discussion on VR	Interests and issues of using VR in perception-action in sport	Ø	Ø	Ø	Importance of the perception-action loop in training, but the PO task also allows participants to be "active observers". The interest of VR for both coaches and players
Craig et al. (2006)	Soccer	To assess the influence of curved free-kicks on perception and judgment	Players were asked to judge the final direction of free-kicks ("cut-off" protocol)	HMD (Cybermind HI-Res 900)	11 experts soccer field-players and 9 expert soccer goalkeepers	Influence of arrival point on judgment, and high influence of spin on a judgment. No effect of cut-off or group on performance
Craig et al. (2009)	Soccer	To identify what information is used by experts and non-experts to predict where the ball will end	Similar setup as Craig et al. (2006) with additional conditions	HMD (Cybermind Hi-Res900)	13 non-soccer players + comparison with Craig et al. (2006)'s population	Worst judgment when spin, with no influence of the position of the player. More variability in Tau information used for individual novice players

From an X & O's perspective, coaches can use virtual environments to create or re-create game situations where players may have made a mistake. Coaches can place players in the simulations that require them to make split decision reads, and the coaches can analyze the player's eyes and decision making and provide the players the necessary feedback they need to get better. For coaches, immersive VR environments will help coaches be more comfortable in their decision making in light game situations or games. Coaches can also use this software to teach their team playbook. In the future, coaches should be using VR technology as much as they watch film or coach on the floor.

The future possibilities of immersive VR in sports are endless. It is noted in many different publications that to receive mastery level understanding a person needs to spend 10,000 hours learning and doing. VR can accelerate this process because it breaks down multiple hours of training into ten and 15-minute intervals. With the emergence of more affordable VR headsets, teams, players, and coaches can now use this technology to train daily.

With the proper applications, athletes can participate in virtual environments that simulate the game from anywhere. VR allows for players to get consistent high-intensity repetitions without the risk of any injuries. VR systems allow individualization of training (Kim et al., 2013) and can be applied in everyday settings, such as when traveling, lying in bed, or working. Düking (2017) found that bio-feedback can be provided by continuous learning algorithms to athletes directly in real-time this also allows for coaches

Table 5. (continued)

Reference	Sport	Main Goal	Study Design	VR Device	Participants	Main Results
Craig et al. (2011)	Soccer	To explore the ability to judge and intercept curved ball trajectories in VR	Similar setup as Craig et al. (2009), with an interception by moving virtual effector manually controlled	HMD (Cybermind HI-Res 900)	7 recreational soccer players	Better interception performance when no spin, and for close balls compared to far balls. Many reversal movements when spin
Croft et al. (2011)	Rugby Union	To assess rugby lineout throw kinematics in a VR task	Similar setup as Chong and Croft (2009)	NuView SX-2000 Stereo3D (photogrammetric system)	8 elite rugby players	Thrower's accuracy decreased as the distance increased. Identification of 4 elements (elbow separation, front footstep, trunk flexion, arm follow-through) to assess the accuracy of lineout throw
Dessing and Craig (2010)	Soccer	To examine the ability of soccer goalkeepers to perceive and use lateral ball rotation to stop a free-kick in VR	Players were asked to manually intercept curved free-kicks	HMD (Cybermind Visette 45 SXGATM)	2 experts and 10 recreational soccer goalkeepers	Hand movement is influenced by spin. Initiation of hand movement in the wrong direction when the trajectory is curved, but the effect was less important on experts
Fink et al. (2009)	Baseball/ Softball	To explore visual control of action used by a player catching fly balls in VR	Participants had to catch flying baseball ball with normal parabolic trajectory, or perturbed trajectory. The ball ended behind ("backward balls") or ahead ("forward balls") of the player.	HMD (Cybermind Visette-Pro)	12 experienced college baseball/ softball players	Consistent prediction of Optical Acceleration Cancellation (OAC) on tan(α) over time, for normal and perturbed balls (forward AND backward balls)

to track the progression of student-athletes electronically and/or even remotely. During this pandemic student-athletes all over the country have been deprived of time with their teams. VR can provide an alternative way for coaches to coach and players to train.

CONCLUSION

This chapter discusses how immersive VR headsets can be used to provide athletes and coaches an opportunity to accelerate personal skill acquisition. The immersive learning concepts that ensure the transfer of skill acquisition from the virtual environment to the court or field are less likely to happen without specific scientific methods and learning strategies. Athletes and coaches can use a virtual environment to learn and develop new skills.

The highly interactive environment provided by immersive VR headsets allows learning to transfer from training into the game. Players' improvement has happened in multiple sports using immersive virtual reality headsets. This has already proven to accelerate skill acquisition and help athletes to perform on the court better. VR's learning efficiency can be attributed to combining over 100 years of scientific data and learning styles and incorporating them into training through the headset (Casale, 2018). To create a virtual environment where athletes can reenact sports specific movements and make split-second decisions without the possibilities of injuries. The immersive environment that the VR headsets provide becomes more of a learning environment where athletes can make mistakes without the pressure of win-

Table 6. (continued)

Reference	Sport	Main Goal	Study Design	VR Device	Participants	Main Results
McLeod et al. (2008)	Soccer	To explore the potential of OAC theory to explain how soccer players head a ball	Players had virtually head back a ball (normal parabolic trajectory, of the perturbed trajectory) in the direction which it had come, with a 1) backward/forward displacement or 2) lateral displacement	HMD (Datavisor 80)	Back/forward displacement task: 2 amateur soccer players Lateral displacement task: 4 amateur soccer players	Influence of trajectory on displacement. For both conditions, the results support that players intercepting balls use on-line strategies, and are consistent with the particular claim of OAC theory
Miles et al. (2012)	General discussion on VE as a training tool in ball sports	To propose a review on the use of VE for training in ball sports, and to assess the pros and cons of different technologies used	Ø	Ø	Ø	Several studies on training physical, perceptive, and decision skills, but also a potential tool for training strategy and tactics. Transfer from lab to field is still unclear. Importance of realism and perception-action loop in a VE
Ranganathan and Carlton (2007)	Baseball/ softball	To examine baseball batters' ability to distinguish between a fastball and a change-up in VR	Players had to judge or bat balls thrown by a VR pitcher, with different conditions of "available information"	Three-sided VE	10 novices and 10 expert baseball batters	The relation between performance and level of "available information". Experts relied more on the information picked on the ball than on the movement pattern of the pitcher. Better prediction of the type of pitch when only verbal judgment
Reference	**Sport**	**Main Goal**	**Study Design**	**VR Device**	**Participants**	**Main Results**
Rolin et al. (2018)	Baseball/ softball	To assess and improve the perception of depth in a VE when intercepting a looming object, through the use of a baseball situation	Motion-in-depth cues (size and velocity) of VR baseball were individually identified and modified to increase participants' ability to interpret movements in a baseball batting task. Participants had to hit a looming, pitched ball as directly as possible back towards the pitcher by physically making a swinging motion.	HMD (Oculus Rift CV1)	18 students without experience at a competitive level in ball sports	Better performance for slowest balls. Significant effect of depth cues modifications on performance for fastest balls ($p<0.001$), with performance improvement.
Stinson and Bowman (2014)	Soccer	To assess if a VE can induce anxiety in players, and be used as a training tool for high-pressure situations	Players had to face and stop penalty kicks in VR, under the various condition of known anxiety triggers ANX (LOW/ HIGH), the field of regard FOR (LOW/HIGH), and simulation fidelity SF (LOW/HIGH)	VisCube (CAVE like projection system)	25 students (23 of them had competitive sports experience)	Ability to induce anxiety in this VR situation. The great influence of ANX and SF on the anxiety of participants. An inverse relation between FOR and anxiety. Interaction FOR-SF on performance save

ning or losing, along with the tracking And immediate feedback, which is why virtual reality users learn at an accelerated pace. Another aspect of the potential of these virtual environments is the impact that they can make on coaches. There has been little research done on how virtual reality impacts the coach's

Table 7. (continued)

Reference	Sport	Main Goal	Study Design	VR Device	Participants	Main Results
Vignais et al. (2009b)	Handball	To analyze the influence of the degree of perception-action coupling on the performance of handball goalkeepers in a VE	Handball goalkeepers had to judge (judgment task, or perception-only task) or intercept (motor task, or perception-action task) virtual handball throw in a VE	VR center (3 Barco 1208S video projectors and a large cylindrical screen)	8 national handball goalkeepers	Better interception performance in perception-action task. Higher radial error in perception only task
Vignais et al. (2010a)	Handball	To evaluate the influence of visual conditions of a throwing action on the goalkeeper's performance in handball	Handball goalkeepers had to face virtual throws, with different conditions of available information on ball trajectory and throwing action of the attacking player	VR center (3 Barco 1208S video projectors and a large cylindrical screen)	10 elite handball goalkeepers	Better results when combining information from throwing action and ball trajectory, for both perception and perception-action task
Vignais et al. (2010b)	Handball	To evaluate the influence of the graphical levels of detail (LODs) of a virtual thrower on the perception of the movement	Goalkeepers faced virtual throws	VR center (3 Barco 1208S video projectors and a large cylindrical screen)	12 expert handball goalkeepers	The judgment made by goalkeepers when few available information was not as accurate as when more available information, especially information on the ball
Vignais et al. (2015)	Handball	To determine video or VR technologiepreferred	The similar task to Vignais et al. (2009b), with a comparison	VR center video projectorslarge cylindri	10 expert handball goalkeepers	Goalkeepers were more effective, more accurate, and started to intercept earlier when facing a virtual handball thrower than when facing the video clip

Reference	Sport	Main goal	Study design	VR device	Participants	Main results
Watson et al. (2011)	Rugby Union	To explore, through the Tau-theory, the perception of "passability" affordance of a gap between two approaching defenders in rugby	Participants had to judge (with a "cut-off" protocol) the "passability" of a gap between two virtual rugby defenders, with different conditions of starting/end gaps	HMD (Vissette Pro CyberMind)	14 non-rugby players	"S-shape" response for the % of good judgment to end gap-size, with no difference between 8 m and 12 m cuts-off. Tau-based informational quantity here accounted for more than 82% of the variance in the data
Zaal and Michaels (2003)	Baseball/ softball	To explore the potential use of VR to assess and study perception and catches of fly balls	Experiment 1: Participants had to judge (judging condition) or catch (catching condition) virtual fly balls, with different conditions of passing distance and vision Experiment 2: Similar to exp. 1, with additional conditions of initial ball distance, the maximum height of the ball, and passing distance	CAVE	Experiment 1: 10 participants Experiment 2: 8 participants Experiment 3: 8 participants	Experiment 1: Better judgment for "near" balls than "far" balls. Influence of distance on response time. Poor results in catching condition. Experiment 2: The closer the ball was to the participants, the fewer the correct responses. Less good results when balls are coming from a far distance and reaching the lowest peak in trajectory. Better response when participants are waiting longer. Experiment 3: Very good score in judging task. 47% of balls were intercepted.
Zaal and Bootsma (2011)	The general approach of VR and fly balls	To propose a critical analysis of the use of VR to study perception-action in the situation of running to catch fly balls (such as in baseball/ softball)	Ø	Ø	Ø	Importance of comparison between real task and the VR task. Importance of feedback (visual, haptic, etc.) when performing a task in VR. The question of the possible transfer from VE to a field remains unclear.

decision making. VR headsets technology can be used as a tool to develop coaches' self-efficacy. The same learning principles that make immersive VR an asset to players will make it an asset to coaches. The design of immersive virtual environments that correlates with research in the cognitive sciences allows these technologies to provide a trackable way for athletes and coaches to train anytime and anywhere.

REFERENCES

Announcing partnership between FastModel sports and synergy sports technology. (2019). Retrieved from https://corp.synergysportstech.com/2019/12/13/announcing-partnership-between-fastmodel-sports-and-synergy-sports-technology/

Belch, B., Casale, & Manuccia. (2016). *Training using virtual reality*. Strivr Labs Inc. Retrieved from https://patents.google.com/patent/US10586469B2/en

Bideau, B., Kulpa, R., Ménardais, S., Fradet, L., Multon, F., Delamarche, P., & Arnaldi, B. (2003). Real handball goalkeeper vs. virtual handball thrower. *Presence (Cambridge, Mass.)*, *12*(4), 411–421. doi:10.1162/105474603322391631

Bideau, B., Kulpa, R., Vignais, N., Brault, S., Multon, F., & Craig, C. (2009). Using virtual reality to analyze sports performance. *IEEE Computer Graphics and Applications*, *30*(2), 14–21. PMID:20650707

Bonney, E., Jelsma, L. D., Ferguson, G. D., & Smits-Engelsman, B. C. M. (2017). Learning better by repetition or variation? Is transfer at odds with task-specific training? *Plus One*, *12*(3), e0174214. doi:10.1371/journal.pone.0174214 PMID:28333997

Bootsma, R. J., Ledouit, S., Casanova, R., & Zaal, F. T. (2016). Fractional-order information in the visual control of lateral locomotor interception. *Journal of Experimental Psychology. Human Perception and Performance*, *42*(4), 517–529. doi:10.1037/xhp0000162 PMID:26569338

Brault, S., Bideau, B., Kulpa, R., & Craig, C. (2009). Detecting deceptive movement in 1 vs. 1 based on global body displacement of a rugby player. *The International Journal of Virtual Reality: a Multimedia Publication for Professionals*, *8*(4), 31–36. doi:10.20870/IJVR.2009.8.4.2746

Brault, S., Bideau, B., Kulpa, R., & Craig, C. M. (2012). Detecting deception in movement: The case of the side-step in rugby. *PLoS One*, *7*(6), e37494. doi:10.1371/journal.pone.0037494 PMID:22701569

Casale, M. (2018). *Sports training in virtual reality*. Retrieved from https://www.strivr.com/use-cases/sports/

Chong, A. K., & Croft, H. G. (2009). A photogrammetric application in virtual sport training. *The Photogrammetric Record*, *24*(125), 51–65. doi:10.1111/j.1477-9730.2009.00517.x

Correia, V., Araújo, D., Duarte, R., Travassos, B., Passos, P., & Davids, K. (2012). Changes in practice task constraints shape decision-making behaviours of team games players. *Journal of Science and Medicine in Sport*, *15*(3), 244–249. doi:10.1016/j.jsams.2011.10.004 PMID:22153899

Covaci, A., Olivier, A. H., & Multon, F. (2015). Visual perspective and feedback guidance for vr free-throw training. *IEEE Computer Graphics and Applications*, *35*(5), 55–65. doi:10.1109/MCG.2015.95 PMID:26416362

Craig, C. (2013). Understanding perception and action in sport: How can virtual reality technology help? *Sports Technology*, *6*(4), 161–169. doi:10.1080/19346182.2013.855224

Craig, C. M., Bastin, J., & Montagne, G. (2011). How information guides movement: Intercepting curved free kicks in soccer. *Human Movement Science*, *30*(5), 931–941. doi:10.1016/j.humov.2010.08.007 PMID:21414677

Craig, C. M., Berton, E., Rao, G., Fernandez, L., & Bootsma, R. J. (2006). Judging where a ball will go: The case of curved free kicks in football. *Naturwissenschaften*, *93*(2), 97–101. doi:10.100700114-005-0071-0 PMID:16450083

Craig, C. M., Goulon, C., Berton, E., Rao, G., Fernandez, L., & Bootsma, R. J. (2009). Optic variables used to judge future ball arrival position in expert and novice soccer players. *Attention, Perception & Psychophysics*, *71*(3), 515–522. doi:10.3758/APP.71.3.515 PMID:19304642

Dessing, J. C., & Craig, C. M. (2010). Bending it like Beckham: How to visually fool the goalkeeper. *PLoS One*, *5*(10), e13161. doi:10.1371/journal.pone.0013161 PMID:20949130

Düking, P., Holmberg, H. C., & Sperlich, B. (2017). Instant biofeedback provided by wearable sensor technology can help to optimize exercise and prevent injury and overuse. *Frontiers in Physiology*, *8*, 167. doi:10.3389/fphys.2017.00167 PMID:28420998

Farley, O., Spencer, K., & Baudinet, L. (2019). Virtual reality in sports coaching, skill acquisition, and application to surfing: A review. *Journal of Human Sport and Exercise*, *15*(3). Advance online publication. doi:10.14198/jhse.2020.153.06

Faure, C., Limballe, A., Bideau, B., & Kulpa, R. (2020). Virtual reality to assess and train team ball sports performance: A scoping review. *Journal of Sports Sciences*, *38*(2), 192–205. doi:10.1080/02640414.2019.1689807 PMID:31724487

Fink, A., Graif, B., & Neubauer, A. C. (2009). Brain correlates underlying creative thinking: EEG alpha activity in professional vs. novice dancers. *NeuroImage*, *46*(3), 854–862. doi:10.1016/j.neuroimage.2009.02.036 PMID:19269335

Interactive and immersive learning using 360° virtual reality contents on mobile platforms. (2018). *Mobile Information Systems*, 1-12. doi:10.1155/2018/2306031

Kim, J., Son, J., Ko, N., & Yoon, B. (2013). Unsupervised virtual reality-based exercise program improves hip muscle strength and balance control in older adults: A pilot study. *Archives of Physical Medicine and Rehabilitation*, *94*(5), 937–943. doi:10.1016/j.apmr.2012.12.010 PMID:23262158

Kulpa, R., Bideau, B., & Brault, S. (2013). Displacements in Virtual Reality for sports performance analysis. In *Human walking in virtual environments* (pp. 299–318). Springer. doi:10.1007/978-1-4419-8432-6_13

Lave, J., & Wenger, E. (1991). *Learning in doing: Social, cognitive, and computational perspectives. Situated learning: Legitimate peripheral participation*. Cambridge University Press. doi:10.1017/CBO9780511815355

Maddox, L. (2018). *The brain science of muscle memory: QBSIM and repetition*. Retrieved from https://www.sportsvts.com/media/2018/4/26/the-brain-science-of-muscle-memory-qbsim-and-repetition

Maddox, T. (n.d.). *Sports VTS leverages brain science: QBSIM optimizes quarterback training*. Retrieved from https://www.sportsvts.com/media/2018/1/29/sports-vts-leverages-brain-science-qbsim-optimizes-quarterback-training

McLeod, A. J. (2008). *The management and maintenance of second generation sand-filled synthetic sports pitches*. Academic Press.

Miles, H. C., Pop, S. R., Watt, S. J., Lawrence, G. P., & John, N. W. (2012). A review of virtual environments for training in ball sports. *Computers & Graphics*, *36*(6), 714–726. doi:10.1016/j.cag.2012.04.007

Neumann, D. L., Moffitt, R. L., Thomas, P. R., Loveday, K., Watling, D. P., & Lombard, C. L. (2017). A systematic review of the application of interactive virtual reality to sport. *Virtual Reality (Waltham Cross)*. Advance online publication. doi:10.100710055-017-0320-5

Ranganathan, R., & Carlton, L. G. (2007). Perception-action coupling and anticipatory performance in baseball batting. *Journal of Motor Behavior*, *39*(5), 369–380. doi:10.3200/JMBR.39.5.369-380 PMID:17827114

Rolin, R. A., Fooken, J., Spering, M., & Pai, D. K. (2018). Perception of looming motion in virtual reality egocentric interception tasks. *IEEE Transactions on Visualization and Computer Graphics*, *25*(10), 3042–3048. doi:10.1109/TVCG.2018.2859987 PMID:30072330

Russell, D. (2016). The Design of Immersive Virtual Learning Environments Utilizing Problem-Based Learning Templates. In Computer-Assisted Language Learning: Concepts, Methodologies, Tools, and Applications (pp. 430-449). IGI Global.

Steinberg, L. (n.d.). *Virtual reality is leading sports-tech wave*. Retrieved from https://www.forbes.com/sites/leighsteinberg/2018/07/31/virtual-reality-the-forefront-of-the-tech-wave-sweeping-over-sports/

Stinson, C., & Bowman, D. A. (2014). Feasibility of training athletes for high-pressure situations using virtual reality. *IEEE Transactions on Visualization and Computer Graphics*, *20*(4), 606–615. doi:10.1109/TVCG.2014.23 PMID:24650988

Vignais, N., Bideau, B., Craig, C., Brault, S., Multon, F., Delamarche, P., & Kulpa, R. (2009). Does the level of graphical detail of a virtual handball thrower influence a goalkeeper's motor response? *Journal of Sports Science & Medicine*, *8*(4), 501. PMID:24149589

Vignais, N., Kulpa, R., Brault, S., Presse, D., & Bideau, B. (2015). Which technology to investigate visual perception in sport: Video vs. virtual reality. *Human Movement Science*, *39*, 12–26. doi:10.1016/j.humov.2014.10.006 PMID:25461430

Vignais, N., Kulpa, R., Craig, C., & Bideau, B. (2010). Virtual thrower versus real goalkeeper: The influence of different visual conditions on performance. *Presence (Cambridge, Mass.)*, *19*(4), 281–290. doi:10.1162/PRES_a_00003

Wang, J. (2012). Research on application of virtual reality technology in competitive sports. *Procedia Engineering*, *29*, 3659–3662. doi:10.1016/j.proeng.2012.01.548

Wass, R., & Golding, C. (2014). Sharpening a tool for teaching: The zone of proximal development. *Teaching in Higher Education*, *19*(6), 671–684. doi:10.1080/13562517.2014.901958

Watson, G., Brault, S., Kulpa, R., Bideau, B., Butterfield, J., & Craig, C. (2011). Judging the 'passability' of dynamic gaps in a virtual rugby environment. *Human Movement Science*, *30*(5), 942–956. doi:10.1016/j.humov.2010.08.004 PMID:20952081

Young, J. (2019). *Atrium sports buys sports analytics provider synergy to create $100 million sports data and AI company*. Retrieved from https://www.cnbc.com/2019/12/16/sports-analytics-provider-synergy-purchased-by-atrium-sports.html

Zaal, F. T., & Bootsma, R. J. (2011). Virtual reality as a tool for the study of perception-action: The case of running to catch fly balls. *Presence (Cambridge, Mass.)*, *20*(1), 93–103. doi:10.1162/pres_a_00037

Zaal, F. T., & Michaels, C. F. (2003). The information for catching fly balls: Judging and intercepting virtual balls in a CAVE. *Journal of Experimental Psychology. Human Perception and Performance*, *29*(3), 537–555. doi:10.1037/0096-1523.29.3.537 PMID:12848325

KEY TERMS AND DEFINITIONS

Immersive Learning: The impression that one is participating in a comprehensive, realistic experience.

Immersive Learning Environment: An environment or simulation where the participant can experience or initiate actions in a virtual world.

Learn by Doing: The belief that family is central to well-being and that family members and family issues take precedence over other aspects of life.

Peripheral Participation: Putting someone into a situation where the activity mimics their real-world activities and provide a productive learning activity.

Skill Acquisition: The development of new skills through practice or repetition.

Transferable Training: Training that transfers from virtual reality to reality.

Virtual Learning Environment: An environment that is created through simulation and is not of the real world.

Zone Proximal Development: A zone that allows users to respond at their highest level without the stress of losing.

Chapter 9
Advancing Emergency Nurse Practitioner Training Using Virtual Nursing Centers

Donna Russell
Walden University, USA

Laura L. Kuensting
University of Missouri, St. Louis, USA

ABSTRACT

The purpose of this chapter is to describe the design of a live emergency room simulation for nurse practitioners using augmented reality and virtual reality. The authors describe the specific design and development procedures including (1) the design of a learning analytic system for formative and summative assessment, (2) the design of the virtual space for the live event, (3) the development of a timed script for the emergency room event, and (4) the development of the virtual world in Second Life. The authors also define all the design decisions based on research on the cognitive theories that support the development of advanced problem-based learning curriculum, research of virtual immersive learning environments, and research on virtual simulations used to develop advanced skills and knowledge.

INTRODUCTION

The purpose of this chapter is to describe the design and implementation of the Virtual Nursing Center designed to train nurses. The goal is to describe the details surrounding the design of the virtual space, the assessments, the scripts for the live events, and the learning management and learning analytic systems required in the educational space to provide holistic and systemic evaluation of the nurses' responses.

The Virtual Nursing Clinic (VNC) was designed based on a problem-based learning curriculum design model that creates live interactive events that engage learners in simulations of real-world events, in this case design, a pediatric emergency occurring in the Emergency Room in the clinic. The VNC also includes several players to increase the complexity including a mother, a Registered Nurse (RN),

DOI: 10.4018/978-1-7998-4222-4.ch009

and a pedagogical agent, a baby bot, both preprogrammed using AI to respond to specific interactions using specific tools in the simulation.

The live ER simulation includes a timer for phases of the Nurse Practitioner response to assess the level, quality, and timeliness of the nurse practitioner's interactions, communication, decision-making, evaluation, and the use of the varied tools in the simulated environment including medical devices and a simulation of an electronic medical report interface. The simulation is designed to include (a) pedagogical agents; (b) a learning analytic system; (c) a pre and post-event conference; (d) multiple players that will interact with the nurse trainee during the live event; and (e) a system of timed interactions that have medical consequences in a live event.

The learning analytic system was designed to create a Competency Map for Emergency Nurse Practitioners based on the review of national and international standards. The in-situ assessments, e.g. the timed responses for case diagnosis, the interactions within the simulation, will be included in the learning analytic system in near real-time. Additionally, there will be an expert nurse practitioner who will do observations and score the trainees. Finally, there are multiple rubrics that will be scored on the higher-order cognitive processes required by nurse practitioners. The Competency Map will then link these assessments with the selected standards to map the level of response to provide a comprehensive rubric for trainee or instructor review.

This chapter will describe the design case for this project. including the systemic design of the interactions and responses in the learning environment (Boling, 2010). Throughout this chapter, we will describe the designed artifacts and experiences as a guide for future designers in the instructional design field, which is lacking in design case examples (Boling, 2010). Instructional designers utilizing the process of design case research can provide new conceptual formats for the integration of immersive technologies into learning environments. As a result, this chapter will provide a design case with a comprehensive description of the design of the Virtual Nursing Clinic and the integration of VR technologies.

BACKGROUND

A study by John Hopkins found that 250,000 deaths per year in the U.S. are due to medical errors (Daniel, 2016). This makes medical errors the 3rd leading cause of death in the U.S. Researchers have shown that improved live training programs can prevent medical errors because of limited experience in responding to live events that replicate the types and qualities of thinking and decision-making needed by medical personnel to reduce errors in live events (Kohn et al., 2000; Shah et al., 2020).

The Institute of Medicine's 2003 Report, Health Professions Education: A Bridge to Quality, was prompted by the 2002 Health Professions Education (HPE) Summit. The Summit was organized in response to the Institute of Medicine's report To Err is Human, which revealed the chasm between quality care and patient safety in the United States. The HPE report concluded that nurses, doctors, and other allied health professionals lack the education and training necessary to meet 21st-century healthcare needs. The report urged all health professionals to develop proficiency in five common core competencies, specifically: delivering patient-centered care, working as interdisciplinary teams, practicing evidence-based medicine, focusing on quality improvement, and using information technologies (Kohn et al., 2003).

The use of simulations has increased in recent years in the nursing industry as a result of a greater emphasis on patient safety (Foronda et al., 2017). Gaba et al (1998) insisted that in an industry where human lives depend on the skill of the practitioner, one cannot wait for the unequivocal proof of the benefits of simulations before using it. Even without definitive proof that simulations work to train more effective nursing personnel the best reason for using simulations is that they do no harm and may do some good while saving lives (Gaba et al., 1998).

Studies have shown that nurses benefit from collaborative training as occurs in live simulations of emergency events. Collaborative problem-solving in live virtual simulations of real-world medical events will develop advanced problem solving and decision-making capabilities in nurses, and fill training needs to develop needed problem-solving abilities (Bradley & Postlethwaite, 2003; Stevens et al., 2006). Further, in some settings, especially in rural areas where exposure to complex situations may not be available, avatars are suggested to be an innovative way to augment nursing education and experience. This type of case-based pedagogy has been found to be a creative learning strategy and has enhanced clinician engagement, critical thinking, problem-solving, and decision-making (Flood & Commendador, 2016). In the age of COVID-19, the principle of virtual training is essential to updating medical personnel's skills to meet the demands of an ongoing pandemic.

There is also an associated need to design research that helps us understand how our educational systems can develop these skills in nursing students (Richardson & Trudeau, 2003). Based on the premise of PBL, learning experiences build on the interdependent attributes of meaningful learning which includes authentic, intentional, active, constructive, and cooperative learning while involving the meaningful application of knowledge and skills (Jonassen et al., 1999). In PBL environments, a problem triggers cognitive engagement including the psychological processes of context for engagement, curiosity, inquiry, and a quest to address a real-world issue. In productive problem-based learning environments, learners consider themselves active members of their community of learners within the context of solving the problem. This is a phenomenon Lave and Wenger call legitimate peripheral participation (LPP) (Lave & Wenger, 1991). As a result, PBL has an incredible potential to develop advanced learning and knowledge responses required for successful nurses.

Virtual 3D PBL simulations may provide a better alternative to an otherwise limited undergraduate and graduate skills training platform that results in nurses working in internships without the clinical skills training needed to perform their jobs safely. The development of advanced learning processes such as critical thinking, decision-making, and problem-solving are essential for medical trainees because of the nature of their work environment (Peugnet et al., 1998). In simulations of emergencies, for instance, trainees can learn how to communicate effectively, use the information to diagnose correctly, and act appropriately (Russell, 2009a). In Second Life, participants can train in a safe environment that allows them to learn from mistakes without a negative impact on a real patient. Additionally, the VNC can replicate extreme emergencies. The success in the use of Second Life for medical and healthcare education has been previously documented (Boulos et al., 2008). Finally, Second Life has been used for disaster simulation, nursing training, and nutrition education as an effective form of learning.

DESIGN AND IMPLEMENTATION

The purpose of this case design study is to evaluate the potential of integrating a Virtual Nursing Center (VNC) that can be used in advanced nurse training courses and continuing education to enhance curriculum goals in areas not currently developed during the traditional nurse training programs. Advanced practice nursing students and currently practicing advanced practice registered nurses (APRNs) will interact in a complex simulation of emergency room events to develop advanced problem-solving skills

Figure 1. VITL Worlds science campus

and evaluate competence in responding to a medical simulation for improving the patient outcome. The VNC was created in Second Life, a 3D virtual interactive environment designed by Virtual Immersive Technologies for Learning (VITL). An overview of VITL World Science Campus is shown in Figure 1.

The development of advanced problem-based learning (PBL) processes and their corresponding critical and evaluative decision-making skills are essential goals for nurse training programs. Virtually simulated medical training may ultimately reduce medical errors in actual clinical situations since there are several limitations in current simulation training programs. The VNC will provide opportunities for advanced practice nursing students and APRNs to engage in a complex medical situation involving interpersonal interactions and other real-world distractions that may affect decision-making.

Online virtual worlds are available 24/7 offering anytime or anywhere benefits for distance education of students and clinicians (Hansen, 2008). The traditional simulation requires high-fidelity equipment, a predetermined place, and a time for the training to occur. Often interpersonal interactions and other distractions are not replicated or are a part of the simulation; hence, comprehensive learning may be impeded. Further, the measurement of learning and skill competence may be subjective.

The VNC is a virtual social environment that allows for the design of a complex medical interaction among virtual characters called avatars. An avatar is a deity that takes on a human shape (Hansen, 2008). The advanced practice student or APRN will create their avatar for the simulation. The VNC will engage the APRN avatar in a simulation of a clinical experience including critical thinking, differential and final diagnoses, interpretations of diagnostic testing, procedural competence, and social interactions with patients, families, and other healthcare staff. As a result of their virtual interactions, these APRNs and students will be able to develop their clinical competencies without harm to the virtual patient.

The VNC was designed to develop advanced learning processes through structured interactions in a collaborative virtual learning environment through the immersion and interaction capabilities of the simulations (Bereiter, 2002). The VNC will include a virtual world scenario guide which includes a game-like problem-based scenario, a curriculum design template that includes holistic assessments, and an evaluative qualitative research program to understand the levels and qualities of the clinical knowledge and learning resulting from the virtual learning environment.

The designers created the problem-based learning curriculum guide which was used to collaboratively design the simulation. The initial pilot simulation engaged an APRN or student in a complex emergency room scenario of an infant presenting to the emergency department with a common chief complaint of "fever and vomiting". The study participant will need to perform a history and physical, determine differential diagnoses, order diagnostic tests, interpret the results, order therapeutic interventions, perform a procedure, re-evaluate patient responses to treatments, formulate a final diagnosis, and plan the disposition of the patient. All this needs to occur while interacting with multiple avatars, e.g. registered nurse (interactive AI bot), infant (pedagogical agent or baby bot), infant's mother (interactive AI bot), who have responses and behaviors that may influence the situation. Based on key decision-making points in the scenario, the case will progress to either an improved or deteriorating clinical condition of the infant. The study participant's responses will be evaluated on these points.

The researchers of this case design used a mixed-method research methodology including case study analysis and standardized metrics of proficiency at critical decision-making points in response to a medical simulation. The goal was to identify and assess the development of advanced clinical knowledge and skills in advanced practice nursing students and APRNs. The case design analysis was based on be cultural-historical activity theory (CHAT). CHAT defines the interactions that influence the development of advanced learning processes. Research analysis will define 1. The development of advanced PBL processes using holistic assessments based on Bereiter's Scheme of Knowledge (Bereiter, 2002); and 2. The development of critical thinking and productive decision-making skills using a virtual recreation of emergency room scenarios. The metric for assessment of the in-situ responses of the nurses will be the objective structured clinical examination (OSCE) test of clinical knowledge.

Virtual 3D technology gives learners the tools that allow for expanded forms of communication, analysis, and expression including visualization tools, and access to authentic issues and problems. Also, the ability for students to share work, access authentic resources, and experience opportunities to collaborate are made possible. Learning to think critically, analyze, and synthesize information to solve problems in a variety of contexts, and to work effectively in teams are essential skills for nurses.

Emergency Room Live Simulation

Using the VNC, the study participant will respond to a virtually live emergency room event. The participant will be presented with a patient who exhibits physical and non-verbal characteristics. The participant will communicate with the patient, others present in the room, perform a history and physical exam, develop a list of differential diagnoses, enter orders, perform procedures, document in the electronic health record, make a diagnosis, and decide on a disposition for the patient. The participants' levels of learning will be measured from level 2-6 on the Bereiter Scale at critical decision-making points. Some levels will require live feedback such as with the EKG monitor, heart rate, respiratory rate, and blood pressure.

This simulation will be used to evaluate competency while performing a procedure. This includes a necessary but not often performed the procedure of a suprapubic tap. The participant's avatar can choose to perform or not perform the procedure with the patient avatar who will show the response to the procedure if performed or begin to display deterioration in clinical condition if not performed. Hence, there some procedures that are therapeutic and some that are diagnostic. In this case, the procedure will be diagnostic which is critical in deciding therapeutic interventions for the patient.

The patient's avatar can display symptoms such as pain (facial grimacing, flexion of extremities, and physical findings such as the arching of the back, increased heart and respiratory rates, and more) during the procedure. This patient avatar response will elicit a response from the parent and registered nurse avatars who are also in the room. These multiple responses may affect the decision-making or performance skill in doing the procedure. This is often the difference between virtual simulation and traditional medical simulations.

This emergency medical scenario will be used to enact simulations of a real-world clinical setting that will be designed to develop advanced learning processes in APRNs and advanced practice nursing students, including decision-making skills and problem-solving processes. The design team will also create a basic curriculum for a medical training program and determine assessments of participant learning throughout the curriculum. As a result of this comprehensive approach to design and evaluation, this project has the potential to reform medical training to increase the competence and skills of medical providers. Medical errors may subsequently be reduced when virtual training modalities minimize the lack of varied clinical experiences in the current training practices for the medical professions.

Ultimately the VNC can be used by varied medical personnel and teaching institutions to develop learning goals that are not accessible through traditional simulations. The VNC provides medical personnel with the opportunity to experience challenging medical situations while removing the negative aspect of potential harm to patients. This project will also be researched in a manner that will identify the components of the training program that develop advanced learning processes and clinical skills so this project can facilitate the development of these processes in medical providers and potentially reduce medical errors while advancing the field of advanced practice nursing to enhance patient outcomes.

Description of the ER Simulation

All design case data collection will take place in the Virtual Nursing Center online forum. The VNC will be login protected, as only those with a given login will be able to access the VNC. All data will be collected in the login protected Virtual Nursing Center online data management system. Participants interact in Pre-Clinical Conference Room to learn how to move and interact through their Avatar. Participants have scheduled a live simulation in the Virtual Emergency Room Simulation is recorded as a machinima for assessment of competencies.

Practice using the Virtual Nursing Center: Participants practice until comfortable with the Virtual Nursing Center medical tools and environment. The designers are in the environment to answer questions. The participants go into the Virtual Nursing Center at their scheduled time where responses are timed throughout the simulation. The designers play signature roles in the simulation. One designer is an RN and another is the mother. The mother brings in a sick baby. The baby is an AI bot; preprogrammed to respond to specific tools at specific times in the simulation.

The script for the ER event was designed in around five critical activities with multiple events designed into the timer for the virtual event. As the nurses responded to the live event the script preloaded changes in the AI bot, the baby, which created changes in the readings on the virtual diagnostic equipment. If decisions were not made, or activities were not completed in this time range the baby's condition deteriorated until a medical doctor came in a removed the nurse from the ER, a failure of the simulation. Below in Table 1 is a script for the ER event. In Appendix A the steps for the simulation are listed and described.

Assessment Procedures

Each of the six discrete activities in the ER simulation is 'mapped' with four competency outcomes. Each competency is assessed using:

1. tracking built into the virtual space, e.g. timer on activities, interaction through the avatar with the technology, such as posting notes.
2. Observational Checklist to identify timeliness and accurate response and
3. holistic rubric for advanced cognitive processes such as critical thinking.
4. Self-reflection survey.

The first competency is Productive Communication. During the simulation, the script involves communication with the mother and the other nurse. Evaluation is through a scaled rubric using the criteria below:

1. Empathetic communication
2. Negative communications
3. Sharing relevant information with family/patient
4. Effective communication with other medical staff

The second outcome competency is Professional Interactions. These are relevant to the timeliness of interactions with a focus on critical thinking during the phases.

1. Timely interactions with family/patient
2. Timely interactions with other medical staff
3. Level of engagement with family/patient
4. Level of engagement with medical staff

The third outcome of competency is Advanced Decision-Making. These are the responses during the live simulations that identify the evaluative decision-making processes.

1. Timely decisions in response to medical events
2. Medical decisions are correct
3. Evaluate information for usefulness
4. Shared decision-making with family

The fourth outcome competency is Functional Knowledge and Skills. These are aspects of the ER built into the virtual space through interactions within the virtual space, such as the lab equipment and the technologies which are viewed and interacted with during the simulation.

1. Appropriate medical response
2. Skilled using medical technologies

Additionally, the designers created holistic rubrics for the review and evaluation of the full simulation for reflection and redirection of the trainee. Below in Table 1 is the summative competencies rubric for the simulation.

In this systemic case design of assessment procedures, there were assessments created to identify the live responses of the nurses of their interactions in the virtual ER through the learning analytic system's pre-structured response timer, the semantic identifier, and the review of the event using the observational checklist. Below in Table 2 is a checklist for reflection of the nurses to their simulation. Self-reflection on their interactions is a critical aspect of professional development.

Table 1. Holistic rubric for assessing learning

Holistic Rubric Virtual Nursing Center Pediatric Emergency Simulation				
Communication	communication is unclear minimal response to family does not listen to RN	communication is clear responds sporadically to family listens to RN	communication is clear and focused on the issue response to the family is ongoing listens to and responds to RN	Communicates clearly, effectively. Listens to RN input. Interpersonal communication with family is directed and supportive
Leadership	breaks from procedure decisions are delayed does not develop authority over RN	completes procedures decisions are appropriate interacts with RN appropriately	completes procedures promptly decisions are prompt recognizes the authority role in ER	Stayed calm and in control prompt and firm decision making recognizes authority in ER oversees the entire ER event
Resource Utilization	does not use the resources to support decision-making creates an incomplete case history creates an incomplete diagnostic	uses technology to create a case uses technology to create diagnostics	uses technology to create a case and diagnose. uses technology to input into the EMR	uses technology to support decision making uses technology effectively uses technology appropriately promptly
Situational Awareness	does not revise procedural decisions with new information	does consider new procedures but is not able to access resources to make new decisions	revises procedures in response to the new situation	avoids fixation errors reassesses and reevaluates situation when new information arises
Problem Solving	problems are not addressed promptly problem-solving is not apparent	problems are addressed sporadically problems are addressed without prioritization	problems are address procedurally problems are not addressed promptly	organized and efficient problem solving quick in implementation recognizes alternatives during the crisis

Issues, Controversies, Problems

The most important issue with the design and implementation of this VR simulation is the development of the technical expertise for the virtual space. The learning management system, the learning analytic system, and the virtual space require multiple forms of technical expertise that must be managed by the designers.

Table 2. Self-reflection survey

SELF-REFLECTION SURVEY	1 2 3 4 5
Knowledge of the environment	
The anticipation of and planning for potential problems	
Assumption of leadership role	
Communication with other team members	
Distribution of workload/delegation of responsibility	
Attention allocation	
Utilization of information	
Utilization of resources	
Recognition of limitations/call for help early enough	
Professional behavior/interpersonal skills	
Overall behavioral crisis management skills	
Additional comments	

Lessons Learned

The most critical lesson learned throughout this design process was understanding how nursing abilities are accessed in current clinical training and emergency rooms. Understanding how these skills are assessed in live ER events was critical to the design of this VR space. It guided each aspect of the curriculum, the assessments, the scripts, as well as the learning management system with the learning analytic system to provide the feedback loop needed by highly skills nurses to engage and develop their critical skills.

SOLUTIONS AND RECOMMENDATIONS

The most important practical solution that this VR program provides is the forum for repeated practice of critical nursing skills without risk to a patient. In this complex live virtual experience, the nurses can practice not only skills for diagnostics but also communication skills and leadership skills that are not possible in a normal clinical training space. By creating this live event, the designers can assess the learners' responses but also provide them with a safe forum for review and reflection on their responses. The process of review and self-reflection is advantageous to professionals in building their advanced skills and knowledge (Russell, 2009b).

FUTURE TRENDS

The future of VR and AR in nursing education will be based on the effectiveness of the training protocols that integrate these technologies. As a result, it is required that these technologies be integrated in the most effective manner possible. That is why the integration of simulations is based on the pedagogy and design methods of proven clinical experiences. The next step for integration of AR into nursing education is to develop mixed reality lenses and AR-based simulations that provide the trainees with access to increasingly complex virtual realities to practice and develop their skills without risk to patients (Hauze, et al., 209). The focus of future design and research should be on the alignment of AR technologies into credible and trustworthy training programs in place in nursing education. By linking the most effective learning qualities of clinical experiences with the most effective learning aspects of immersive technologies the future of AR technologies can be assured.

CONCLUSION

This chapter identified a practical application of advanced simulations to train nurses. The virtual world was designed to provide nurses with access to the virtual space to guide the development of critical skills in a live event. The assessment model was designed into the learning analytic system so the formative and summative assessments in the virtual space were linked to previously credentialled assessment models. It is through this alignment between the real-world clinical training procedures and the virtual world training procedures where the most benefit is gained from immersive technologies.

REFERENCES

Bereiter, C. (2002). *Education and mind in the knowledge age*. Lawrence Erlbaum Associates. http://unr.edu/homepage/luvisis/bereiter.html

Boling, E. (2010). The need for design cases: Disseminating design knowledge. *International Journal of Designs for Learning*, *1*(1). Advance online publication. doi:10.14434/ijdl.v1i1.919

Boulos, M. N., Ramloll, R., Jones, R., & Toth-Cohen, S. (2008). Web 3D for public, environmental, and occupational health: Early examples from Second Life®. *International Journal of Environmental Research and Public Health*, *5*(4), 290–317. doi:10.3390/ijerph5040290 PMID:19190358

Boulos, M. N. K., Hetherington, L., & Wheeler, S. (2007). Second Life: An overview of the potential of 3-D virtual worlds in medical and health education. *Health Information and Libraries Journal*, *24*(4), 233–245. doi:10.1111/j.1471-1842.2007.00733.x PMID:18005298

Bradley, P., & Postlethwaite, K. (2003). Simulation in clinical learning. *Medical Education*, *37*(s1), 1–5. doi:10.1046/j.1365-2923.37.s1.1.x PMID:14641632

Daniel, M. (2016). Study suggests medical errors now third leading cause of death in the US. *Johns Hopkins Medicine*, *3*. Advance online publication. doi:10.1136/bmj.i2139

Flood, J. L., & Commendador, K. (2016). Avatar case studies. A learning activity to bridge the gap between classroom and clinical practice in nursing education. *Nurse Educator*, *41*(1), 3–4. doi:10.1097/NNE.0000000000000195 PMID:26132174

Foronda, C. L., Alfes, C. M., Dev, P., Kleinheksel, A. J., Nelson, D. A., O'Donnell, J. M., & Samosky, J. T. (2017). Virtually nursing: Emerging technologies in nursing education. *Nurse Educator*, *42*(1), 14–17. doi:10.1097/NNE.0000000000000295 PMID:27454054

Gaba, D. M., Howard, S. K., Flanagan, B., Smith, B. E., Fish, K. J., & Botney, R. (1998). Assessment of clinical performance during simulated crises using both technical and behavioral ratings. *Anesthesiology: The Journal of the American Society of Anesthesiologists*, *89*(1), 8–18. doi:10.1097/00000542-199807000-00005 PMID:9667288

Hansen, M. (2008). Versatile, immersive, creative and dynamic virtual 3-D healthcare learning environments: A review of the literature. *Journal of Medical Internet Research, 10*(3), e26. doi:10.2196/jmir.1051 PMID:18762473

Jonassen, D. H., Peck, K. L., & Wilson, B. (1999). *Learning with technology: A Constructivist Perspective*. Merrill-Prentice Hall.

Kohn, L. T., Corrigan, J. M., & Donaldson, M. S. (2000). *To err is human: building a safer health system. A report of the Committee on Quality of Health Care in America*. Institute of Medicine.

Lave, J., & Wenger, E. (1991). *Situated learning: Legitimate peripheral participation*. University Press. doi:10.1017/CBO9780511815355

Peugnet, F., Dubois, P., & Rouland, J. F. (1998). Virtual reality versus conventional training in retinal photocoagulation: A first clinical assessment. *Computer Aided Surgery, 3*(1), 20–26. doi:10.3109/10929089809148124 PMID:9699075

Richardson, K., & Trudeau, K. J. (2003). A case for problem-based collaborative learning in the nursing classroom. *Nurse Educator, 28*(2), 83–88. doi:10.1097/00006223-200303000-00011 PMID:12646828

Russell, D. (2009a). Group collaboration in an online problem-based university course. *Problem-Based Learning and Creativity*, 173-192.

Russell, D. (Ed.). (2009b). *Cases on Collaboration in Virtual Learning Environments: Processes and Interactions: Processes and Interactions*. IGI Global.

Russell, D. (2016). The Design of Immersive Virtual Learning Environments Utilizing Problem-Based Learning Templates. In D. Russell & J. Laffey (Eds.), *Handbook of Research on Gaming Trends in P-12 Education* (pp. 105–123). Information Science Reference. doi:10.4018/978-1-4666-9629-7.ch005

Shah, K. P., Goyal, S., Ramachandran, V., Kohn, J. R., Go, J. A., Wiley, Z., Moturu, A., Namireddy, M., Kumar, A., Jacobs, R., Stampfl, M., Shah, J., Fu, J., Lin, W., Ho, B., Wey, G., Lin, S. Y., Caruso, A. C., Gay, L. J., ... Andrabi, S. (2020). Efficacy of quality improvement and patient safety workshops for students: A pilot study. *BMC Medical Education, 20*(1), 1–10. doi:10.118612909-020-1982-3 PMID:32326951

Stevens, A., Hernandez, J., Johnsen, K., Dickerson, R., Raij, A., Harrison, C., & Jackson, J. (2006). The use of virtual patients to teach medical students history taking and communication skills. *American Journal of Surgery, 191*(6), 806–811. doi:10.1016/j.amjsurg.2006.03.002 PMID:16720154

ADDITIONAL READING

Russell, D. (Ed.). (2009). *Cases on collaboration in virtual learning environments: processes and interactions: Processes and interactions*. IGI Global.

Russell, D. (Ed.). (2015). *Handbook of Research on Gaming Trends in P-12 Education*. IGI Global.

Russell, D., Davies, M., & Totten, I. (2008, November). Geoworlds: Utilizing second life to develop advanced geosciences knowledge. In *2008 Second IEEE International Conference on Digital Game and Intelligent Toy Enhanced Learning* (pp. 93-97). IEEE. 10.1109/DIGITEL.2008.50

Russell, D., & Wallis, S. E. (2016). Designing a learning analytic system for assessing immersive virtual learning environments. In *Handbook of Research on Gaming Trends in P-12 Education* (pp. 502–526). IGI Global. doi:10.4018/978-1-4666-9629-7.ch024

Russell, D. L., & Schneiderheinze, A. (2005). Understanding innovation in education using activity theory. *Journal of Educational Technology & Society*, *8*(1), 38–53.

KEY TERMS AND DEFINITIONS

Advanced Decision Making: The learner response to the information deemed critical and involves the integration of critical thinking and the advanced knowledge or skills required to be successful.

Critical Thinking: A cognitive process that requires the learner to consider the information and make decisions concerning it's relevance in their response to the problem or issue.

Immersive Learning Environment: A learning setting where students engage in live learning events without direct instruction.

Problem-Based Learning: A learning model that is designed to engage learners in responding to a problem or issue designed to develop advanced cognitive skills.

Chapter 10
Teaching and Learning Mandarin Chinese:
Gamification and Simulation in an Early Childhood Classroom

Francesca Pugh-Opher
Walden University, USA

ABSTRACT

The advancement of new technologies in K-12 educational settings has the potential for new learner experiences and outcomes. The integration of gamification and simulation into second language learning classrooms has the potential to support language learning for young learners. This chapter explores effective ways to introduce instructional models and technological tools for immersing early childhood learners in the second language learning process. In this chapter, the author describes the need for gamified and simulated virtual technologies to facilitate the learning of Mandarin Chinese in an early childhood setting.

INTRODUCTION

Second language learning is a critical component of global and cultural awareness (Baker, 2015; Murphy, 2014). Although English and Spanish are the fastest-growing second language options in many American schools (Pinter, 2017), the United States has demonstrated a need for highly developed competencies in other world languages. Languages such as Arabic and Mandarin Chinese have gained popularity throughout American high schools and colleges (Liu & Wang, 2018). Although most of the language learning opportunities in Mandarin Chinese are in high schools and colleges (He, 2017; Liu & Wang, 2018), several early childhood and elementary education programs offer second languages such as Chinese (Asia Society, 2012). The enrollment of Mandarin Chinese as a second language has increased in early childhood and elementary school settings throughout the United States (American Councils for International Education, 2017). As the interest in learning Mandarin Chinese grows, it is essential to

DOI: 10.4018/978-1-7998-4222-4.ch010

explore technology integration and innovative instructional pedagogy, especially in an early childhood language learning environment.

Teachers play a vital role in integrating technology into classroom environments (Lu et al., 2014). As a result of COVID-19, the use of technology and innovative instructional practices are at the forefront of education. As many educational settings are resorting to online learning, educators must know how to shift from a traditional classroom to a virtual classroom by incorporating a virtual immersive learning environment in the Mandarin Chinese classroom. Educators are introducing students to virtual environments such as augmented reality, mixed reality, and virtual reality. Virtual environments provide useful and engaging learning experiences. Technological advances make it possible for these tools and resources to integrate the education field, specifically early childhood education. When working with young children, effective gamification and simulation activities positively impact second language development and learning. Therefore, educators need practical ways to implement gamification and simulation in early childhood classrooms.

However, noticeable gaps in second language learning in early childhood revealed a need for research advancements in pedagogical methods in Mandarin Chinese as a second language and the use of technological resources to facilitate the learning process. Bridging the gaps in second language learning may allow Mandarin Chinese language educators to increase their knowledge and understanding of integrating technology, pedagogy, and content knowledge in Mandarin Chinese for early childhood learners.

As young children are rapidly learning and developing in a digital age, early childhood educators need to integrate technology into their classrooms. The National Association for the Education of Young Children (NAEYC) (2012) stated that technology in early childhood classrooms supports learning and development if appropriately used. Instructional methods, tools, and technology are important to use in language learning classrooms. Language learning activities immersed in virtual reality technology promote the use of educational resources that stimulate visual, auditory, and kinesthetic learning styles to encourage students to learn a new language (Pugh-Opher, 2019). As educators shift from traditional-based learning tasks to more technology-based learning tasks, it is crucial to grasp a solid understanding of the theoretical perspective that promotes learning through experiences and play, especially for young children.

From a sociocultural perspective, the language learning classroom allows students to learn in a social context to construct knowledge (Vygotsky, 1978). The conceptual framework of Vygotsky's sociocultural theory is used as a lens to understand children's learning processes in a Mandarin Chinese language learning environment related to social activities through the use of virtual technologies. The use of a sociocultural lens in this chapter facilitates understanding social interactions and immersive technological and instructional methods that shape second language learning in an early childhood setting. In essence, learning in these environments requires the learner to solve problems, think critically, and apply knowledge to maximize their learning through virtual worlds.

In this chapter, the author explores the role of gamification and simulation in an early childhood second language learning setting. The following sections describe the fundamentals of teaching and learning a second language in an early childhood setting, focusing on Mandarin Chinese. The author explores the language learning process through Vygotsky's sociocultural lens to determine how gamification and simulated technologies help educators with virtual lessons and activities.

BACKGROUND

The core focus of early childhood pedagogy is providing opportunities for play-based learning. Play is an important concept in child development. Early childhood education exposes children to social interactions, developmental growth, and academic success (Lamrani & Abdelwahed, 2019). Many early childhood educators create learning opportunities where students enjoy informal play during instruction. Many early childhood educators are aware that traditional education can decrease interaction and engagement. Most early childhood educators incorporate play-based learning in their classrooms. Although learning through play supports growth and development in all learners, play-based education is a critical learning tool in early childhood education. Play enhances language skills, logical thinking, imagination, and development. Play-based activities strengthen learning experiences that promote growth and development through problem-solving, critical thought, and socialization. Regarding second language learning, play-based activities allow the learner to use the target language in interactive ways.

Alpar (2013) studied the effects of play on elementary school students in a foreign language setting. His study aimed to determine if play-based instruction increased vocabulary and other cognitive-based learning skills. Alpar (2013) found that language development in the target language increased when educators used play-based instruction. However, Alpar (2013) found a slight increase in vocabulary knowledge amongst traditional class students. Nonetheless, the game-based group demonstrated a significant increase in test scores compared to the traditional groups. Alpar (2013) concluded that game-based play contributed to language learning. This study also revealed that students were less stressed about learning a new language during play-based and game-based education. Alpar (2013) also discovered that student motivation increased along with the improvement of test scores.

One important form of play and interaction in the early childhood classroom is the use of technology. Young children are using diverse types of technology to engage in play and learning. If appropriately used, technology can play a vital role in young children's learning process and development. For young children, teachers need to integrate technology with play-based learning experiences (Edwards, 2016). Although the emergence of advanced technologies has allowed educators to provide game-based platforms in a second language learning environment, it is still a challenge for early childhood educators to find age-appropriate resources to teach and learn a second language. A study conducted by Pugh-Opher (2019) found a lack of educational and technological resources for early childhood educators who taught Mandarin Chinese as a second language. Although there is limited research on teaching and learning Mandarin Chinese in early childhood education in the United States, I hope this chapter can provide insight into what Mandarin Chinese language teachers require to implement gamified and simulated activities.

As we examine the idea of a play-based environment, which includes immersion of technology and digital media, it is important to understand the scope of Vygotsky's (1978) sociocultural learning theory in terms of second language learning. The sociocultural theory focuses on the importance of social interaction and cognitive development. From a sociocultural perspective, the language learning classroom allows students to construct knowledge (Vygotsky, 1978). Using a sociocultural lens helped the researcher understand how social interactions, immersive play embedded in the curriculum, and technological and instructional methods shaped second language learning in an early childhood setting. The sociocultural learning theory focuses on the learners' ability to learn a second language in a social and meaningful environment. Sociocultural learning allows the learner to gain knowledge by actively constructing meaning through interaction with peers and adults (Yang, 2012). Social interactions play a vital role in the learning process, especially in second language learning, not only for the students but also for the teacher. Social interactions are equally important for the cognitive development of children and adults.

Two fundamental components of the sociocultural theory are scaffolding and the zone of proximal development. Vygotsky (1978) believed that social interactions and cultural constructs influenced language learning. Teachers introduce these social and cultural constructs to increase student learning potential. Vygotsky explained that scaffolding acted as an instructional strategy that supported learning and development. Vygotsky referred to the zone of proximal development as an instructional method that moves students from a dependent learning state to an independent learning state.

The zone of proximal development is the concept of what a student can accomplish independently compared to what the student can achieve with help from a teacher or a more skilled peer (Lantolf et al., 2015). Teachers use the zone of proximal development to encourage and motivate students to learn in an "independent and voluntary manner" (Veraksa et al., 2016, p. 222). Vygotsky's zone of proximal development problem solving with the guidance of an adult or more skilled peer. The zone of proximal development (ZPD), coined by Vygotsky (1978), is defined as the "the distance between the actual developmental level as determined by independent problem solving and the level of potential development as determined through problem-solving under adult guidance or in collaboration with more capable peers" (p. 86).

Nemati and Arabmofrad (2014) defined the zone of proximal development as the range between what a student can achieve alone and what a student can achieve with assistance. Wass and Golding (2014) asserted that the ZPD is a useful teaching tool in the learning process. Nemati and Arabmofrad (2014) explained that the role of ZPD is to facilitate a student's potential while helping the student complete a task on their own. As the student moves toward their potential development, the student gains the ability and confidence to complete the task. The teacher can withdraw support (scaffolding) as the student gains independence and confidence. The teacher will move the student's zone of proximal development to decide if the student can move to the next task (Nemati & Arabmofrad, 2014).

The concept of Vygotsky's zone of proximal development encourages the student to perform tasks independently. Scaffolding enables teachers to use instructional pedagogy to strengthen constructive learning outcomes. In the following sections, I provided a detailed synthesis of the zone of proximal development and scaffolding. According to Nemati and Arabmofrad (2014), scaffolding is the ability to solve a problem or complete a task with support from a more experienced individual. Teachers use scaffolding to withdraw support as the student gains confidence and competence (Nemati & Arabmofrad, 2014). The concept of scaffolding is the ability to move the student to the next task effectively. Philip, et al. (2017) asserted that children learning an unfamiliar language need teacher and peer support. In second language learning, scaffolding encourages positive development and growth. Therefore, scaffolding in second language learning for children is vital for language development and growth. Children need an environment where they can flourish through positive interactions, play, and observations.

Linguistic scaffolding suggests that language teachers need to support students as they learn complex language learning tasks. As Lucero (2014) described, linguistic scaffolding is the support teachers provide to their students to increase or improve language development. Munoz (2014) discussed the importance of promoting and supporting linguistic diversity. Munoz (2014) explained that teachers and students have a limited time for foreign language interaction in most classroom settings. Most students do not have the opportunity to extend their learning outside of the classroom. Therefore, the quality of instruction must take priority.

Second Language Learning

All individuals can learn a language (Lenneberg, 1967). According to Krashen (2013), young children learn their first language effortlessly. Krashen (2013) continued by explaining that learning a first or native language is involuntary. Through his research on second language learning, Krashen (2013) described two types of language learning methods: second language acquisition and second language learning. Second language acquisition is a "subconscious process" (Krashen, 2013, p.1) of learning a language; second language learning refers to a formal process of learning a language. This process is evident through structured learning environments such as traditional classroom settings or online language learning courses. In addition to the differences in language learning methods, children and adults may experience language learning variances.

Researchers have suggested that children and adults have different educational experiences while learning a second language (Philip, Borowczyk, & Mackey, 2017). Children who learn a second language are known to have successful, long-term benefits instead of adults (Bialystok & Hakuta, 1999; Murphy, 2014). Many researchers found that second language learning offers positive cognitive benefits for children (Bialystok & Hakuta, 1999). Therefore, children need to have the opportunity to learn a second language (Murphy, 2014) to increase life-long benefits. Ananiandou and Claro (as cited in Murphy, 2014) stated that many countries had stressed the importance of foreign language learning in the primary years. Murphy (2014) asserted that second language learning encourages 21st-century skills such as "global citizenry, communication skills, and intercultural sensitivity" (p. 132). As a result, some countries are lowering the starting age for second language learning to include children as young as preschool (Maad, 2016; Murphy, 2014). Moreover, many countries are spearheading progressive second language education programs by implementing less commonly taught languages to the curriculum.

The Center for Advanced Research on Language Acquisition (2017) defined less commonly taught languages as languages that do not include English, French, Spanish, and German. Furthermore, many less commonly taught languages do not share the same alphabetic script as English. Most K–12 institutions offer standard language learning options. Common options are usually French, Spanish, or German. Significantly few schools in the United States incorporate the less commonly taught languages such as Arabic, Chinese, and Japanese (Asia Society, 2012). However, the United States Department of Education (2008) expressed the need for American students to study and demonstrate proficiency in less commonly taught languages.

To aid this need, the United States government increased the education budget in 2007 to include progressive avenues for second language education (U.S. Department of Education, 2008). The United States is trying to provide opportunities for students to increase, enhance, and improve their second language learning skills in less commonly taught languages. However, most of these opportunities were for high school and college students. Very few schools across the United States offer early childhood students the ability to learn less commonly taught languages. Lu and Lavadenz (2014) believed that the lack of language learning opportunities for young students lies in the absence of innovative instructional methods, qualified faculty, curriculum policies, and research. This study was important because it allowed me to understand Mandarin Chinese teachers' experiences and perceptions who integrated technology and instructional methods to teach Mandarin Chinese to early childhood learners.

Researchers have asserted that exposure to second language learning produces positive outcomes for young learners (Bialystok, 2017; Nicolay & Poncelet, 2015; Ramirez & Kuhl, 2017). One study found that exposing children to second languages can increase expressive and receptive language skills

(Kaushanaskaya et al., 2014). Researchers Nicolay and Poncelet (2015) also found that second language skills increased oral language and vocabulary skills.

Also, Bialystok (2017) found that young children enhanced cognitive development during second language learning. A rationale for researching language learning in early childhood is that early childhood learners are underrepresented in many second language studies. Another justification for exploring young learners is young children would have the time to learn a foreign language long-term to achieve positive outcomes (Bialystok, 2017). Long-term exposure increases cognitive development (Bialystok, 2017), verbal working memory (Kaushanaskaya et al., 2014), and pronunciation and fluency (Prosic-Santovac, 2016). Younger children should be exposed to languages to promote life-long learning and enhance receptive and expressive communication skills and cognitive abilities (Murphy, 2014; Ramirez & Kuhl, 2017).

A study conducted by Bankovic and Sollars (2017) examined how teachers' practices in English as a second language kindergarten class in Malta can affect second language learning. The researchers deemed that the quality of foreign language education in early childhood is important to increase receptive and expressive communication skills. However, while conducting observations, the researchers found that active play, coupled with learning, was not integrated into English as a second language classroom. The researchers found that the children in this study did not have the opportunity to use English through play and meaningful interactions with the teachers and their peers (Bankovic & Sollars, 2017). The teachers used a teacher-centered approach to learning. After their research, Bankovic and Sollars (2017) recommended that the teachers implement child-centered teaching and learning approaches. Child-centered pedagogy increases learning and development through play and social interactions (Dewey, 1938). The researchers suggested that child-centered pedagogy will allow the students to expand their cognitive and linguistic abilities in English (Bankovic & Sollars, 2017).

Game-Based Learning and Gamification

Game-based learning has gained the attention of many early childhood educators. Game-based language learning is considered vital in second language learning, especially in early childhood education (Meyer, 2013). Ryder and Machajewski (2017) conducted a study examining a German gamification app for second language learners. The authors explained that gamification is a "use of game mechanics in a non-game context to engage users" (p.2). Based on their study, the authors found that gaming apps increased their participants' attention and motivation. Sandanayake (2016) introduced new and innovative approaches to virtual learning to enhance technology-based learning. Virtual learning environments are interactive and collaborative. The author asserted that group learning appears to be more effective than individual learning. Future trends in virtual education will be to enhance learning through interactive, collaborative, multimedia technologies.

The implementation of technology-supported instruction has helped learners enhance second language skills. Technology can be a powerful resource tool in an educational setting, especially in learning oral language and vocabulary instruction. Researchers have found that integrating technology in a language learning classroom offers many opportunities for growth and development. Ahmad (2016) and Lu et al. (2014) found that the use of technology outweighed the benefits of traditional-based learning in a language learning classroom. Technology enhances language learning outcomes (Lu et al., 2014). Liu and Olmanson (2016) found that technology integration supported native English speakers, Chinese character acquisition. Although teachers play a crucial role in using technology to enhance learning in the classroom (Hsu et al., 2017). Nikolopoulou and Gialamas (2015) found that their study participants had difficulty implementing technology in their classrooms. The participants noted several barriers: lack of funding, lack of resources, and lack of support.

However, implementing technology in a second language learning environment can improve second language development. Various technology tools may support children's academic and social development by enhancing social interaction and communication with peers (Hsin et al., 2014). The implementation of technology is shaping the way young children learn second languages. Research has shown that implementing technology into a second language classroom can increase motivation and engagement (Asia Society, 2012; Butler, 2015), improve receptive and expressive language and writing skills, and introduce students to native speech (Pemba et al., 2016).

There have been new advancements and initiatives in technology-based education. Educators gamify tasks to stimulate engagement and motivation (Dehghanzadeh et al., 2019). As motivation and engagement are critical for second language learning, educators have found that game-based activities are effective methods to motivate and engage learners, especially in second language learning. Gamification has reshaped the educational experience for both students and educators. Research has found that gamification increases student motivation and engagement. Digital gaming is an ideal resource tool for educators to enhance engagement and motivation. Gamification uses game elements and game design techniques in non-game contexts (Werbach & Hunter, 2012). Gamification uses incentives such as badges, achievements, and rewards to motivate and engage learners. According to Lamrani and Abdelwahed (2019), digital-gamed based technologies has increased in education. Gamified elements in the classroom encourage learners to achieve goals and complete learning objectives. Gamification is used to motivate and engage learners of all ages.

Game-based learning is an innovative learning tool that promotes learning. Hsu et al. (2017) stated that game-based learning is used to enhance learning and support instruction. The researchers found that elementary school teachers were more likely to use game-based learning. They had higher levels of confidence and motivation in game-based education as an instructional tool. Rawendy et al. (2017) asserted that game-based learning increases motivation. It encourages students to participate in the activity/task actively. Chinese character learning to improve vocabulary can decrease motivation for younger children (Rawendy et al., 2017). Educators can redesign the learning experience by adding gamified activities to the second language classroom by introducing digital games such as Quizlet, ClassDojo, Kahoot. Teachers can design games to introduce a new topic, review existing information, or complete a formative assessment. Although there are several gaming resources for middle school, high school, and college, early childhood education lacks early childhood learners' digital gaming activities.

Simulations

Simulations are used in the military, aeronautics, and medical fields. Simulations are activities that produce conditions similar to real environments (Sharifi et al., 2017). There are three simulated approaches to teaching and learning. Live simulations allow real people to use simulated equipment in the real world. Virtual simulations will enable learners to use simulated equipment in a virtual environment. A constructive simulation involves simulated people in simulated environments. Simulations have also been instrumental in education, specifically second language learning. Great learning potentials are creating simulated activities for young learners in a second language learning setting. Simulated activities are very motivating and engaging. In their study, Li and Topolewski (2002) described a simulated game called Zip and Terry. The game was designed for native Chinese speaking children to learn English. The simulated game created a realistic environment for children to practice English through automated speech recognition, conversation modes, vocabulary development, and activities that promote listening and speaking skills. Simulations are viewed as innovative technological resources for teachers to enhance engagement, interests, and second language learning in an early childhood classroom.

The use of simulation is a tool to support second language learning. Simulations are effective methods to motivate and increase engagement in second language learning for early childhood learners. By integrating simulation into second language learning environments for early childhood learners, educators can provide young learners with the most effective instructional model for immersing early childhood learners in the learning process. Simulations are interactive as it allows students to use the target language.

Due to the impact of COVID-19 educational settings are experiencing a shift from the traditional classroom setting to the home. As some schools prepare for the new 2020-2021 school year, many parents select a virtual/remote learning setting. However, the educational background for this chapter supports an early childhood classroom environment. Moreover, it helps native English-speaking children learning Mandarin Chinese in an early childhood setting. This chapter provides educators with a learning platform that can be conducted in the classroom or at home based on the educator's and learner's access to technology. The next section will describe what many educators are currently employing based on the author's dissertation study.

DESIGN AND IMPLEMENTATION

Researchers have found that technology increases student engagement and motivation (Ahmad, 2016; Alpar, 2013; Ryder & Machajewski, 2017). In a dissertation study conducted by Pugh-Opher (2019), the participants agreed that technology was useful and beneficial in supporting language learning because it increased student engagement and motivation, which increased the student's willingness to learn. Traditional learning environments lack the perceptual, visual, and sensory features from simulated learning situations (Legault et al., 2019). Many Mandarin Chinese language teachers use technology and innovative instructional methods to teach Mandarin Chinese to early childhood learners in preschool through 3rd grade.

However, the current design in many Mandarin Chinese language learning classrooms for early childhood learners consists of teacher-created games and materials, minimal use of gaming apps in Mandarin Chinese, and limited resources for innovative technology such as digital gamification apps and simulation. The teachers used technological resources such as iPads, projectors, laptops, and smartboards to engage students in songs, videos, movement, and games. Teachers need to create and develop meaningful gamified activities and authentic real-life simulations to immerse young learners in the second language learning process.

Language learning activities, instructional methods, and technology should promote the use of traditional and high-tech educational resources that stimulate visual, auditory, and kinesthetic means to encourage students to communicate orally and use newly learned vocabulary. Recent research proved that the use of instructional methods enhanced learning in a second language classroom. For example, Snow (2017) found an instructional approach that increased vocabulary development. Children acquired larger vocabularies with "responsive interactions" (p. 7) in the classroom with teachers and classmates.

Responsive interaction is an instructional method that includes speaking, listening, and collaborating through discussions and interactive play.

A study conducted by Prosic-Santovac (2016) examined the effects of an instructional method that used popular animated videos and cartoons to promote English as a second language for preschool learners. The animated videos and films increased vocabulary, grammar, pronunciation, and fluency through interactive play and dialogue. The study results found that animated cartoons and videos were effective in developing second language skills.

After reviewing the literature about Mandarin Chinese language teachers, early childhood learners, instructional methods, and technology, empirical research lacked Mandarin Chinese as a second language in the early childhood education context. Most notably, with the demands of 21st-century technology skills, the research into the teaching and learning Mandarin Chinese through the integration of technology was necessary. The need for age-appropriate language learning materials is essential for these teachers and their colleagues. A recommendation for practice would be creating software, apps, and other instructional materials specifically for young English-speakers who are learning Mandarin Chinese as a second language.

Issues, Controversies, Problems

An increase in technology presence in education has presented advantages and challenges in teaching and learning (Byker, 2014). Preparing teachers for technology integration in an early childhood education setting can be challenging. In a study conducted by Pugh-Opher (2019), the researcher found several challenges of integrating digital technology and simulations in an early childhood second language learning classroom including:

1. A lack of innovative technology resources
2. Affordability
3. Limited access to technology
4. Self-efficacy

There is an abundance of technological resources and apps to promote gamification and simulation in commonly taught languages such as English and Spanish. However, there is a lack of gamified and simulated activities for teaching and learning Mandarin Chinese. Mandarin Chinese teachers need to advocate for age-appropriate technology for native English speakers learning Mandarin Chinese, especially in an early childhood setting.

New and innovative technology in second language learning may be costly for some schools and school districts. However, schools that offer second language education should invest in state-of-the-art technology to promote motivation and engagement. Schools should take advantage of available grants to ensure that students and teachers get the technology needed to learn a second language. The lack of technology access may limit an educator's ability to integrate technology effectively in the classroom. By restricting the use of technology in the school, students and teachers do not have access to meaningful online resources. Therefore, access to Wi-Fi should be paramount in all schools.

On the other hand, some early childhood educators grappled with integrating technology in an early childhood classroom due to the learners' age and level. A study conducted by Aldhafeeri et al. (2016) found that Kindergarten teachers in Kuwaiti schools believed play-based pedagogy was more beneficial to young children than technology-based instruction. In Ludgate's (2015) study, preschool teachers thought preschool children were too young for technology. However, this sentiment was not consistent with the other participants who welcomed technology in their early childhood classrooms. Nikolopoulou and Gialamas (2015) found that the lack of funding, technology, and support were many barriers teachers faced in their classroom. Teachers should have ample access to technology to facilitate student learning.

Self-efficacy as a problem Bandura's (1994) theory of self-efficacy emerged to provide additional support to understand and identify teacher self-efficacy, technology acceptance, and teacher confidence while integrating TPACK. The lack of knowledge and teacher confidence. The lack of knowledge and enthusiasm can hinder technology integration in the classroom. Teacher's self-efficacy beliefs about technology and their experiences using technology are significant. Teachers who experienced effortless ways to implement new technology perceived technology as beneficial in their classroom (Nikolopoulou & Gialamas, 2015). Teachers need to believe that the technology they are implementing is meaningful and will promote positive learning experiences.

Lessons Learned

The connection between second language learning and teaching has become more technology-based. There is a need for games-based learning, gamification, and simulation in Mandarin Chinese as a second language. Even more so for young children who learn through play-based activities. However, more research is required to ensure that Mandarin Chinese language educators are well-equipped with effective and efficient games-based learning, gamification, and simulation resources. One important lesson learned is providing the necessary professional development for teachers. Technology that employs digital gaming and simulation requires a great deal of professional development and training to ensure that teachers are knowledgeable and comfortable with the technology. Therefore, self-efficacy plays a significant role in how comfortable teachers are with innovative technology to teach the concepts and facilitate the learning process through a game or simulation. Moreover, effective professional development can alleviate the feeling of helplessness and combat technology avoidance.

SOLUTIONS AND RECOMMENDATIONS

As our global society increases with immigration, international security, and foreign economic advancements, there is a strong demand for second language learning skills. Research has demonstrated that learning a second language positively impacts academic and cognitive development (Bialystok, 2017). Looking at immersive reality learning environments through a conceptual framework lens, it is evident that teachers need a moderate to a high level of technological, pedagogical, content knowledge to be effective in the classroom. By implementing immersive technology and other innovative instructional methods, teachers will provide students with unlimited opportunities to be active participants in the second language learning classroom.

The education field is experiencing a complicated time due to the impact of COVID-19. Educators and parents are grappling with providing a substantial educational experience for their students and children and finding ways to stay safe and healthy. Therefore, a future exploration into immersive virtual reality in gamification and simulations is needed to stay abreast of second language education's technological advances. In a study conducted by Pugh-Opher (2019), teachers voiced the need for more technological resources because technology positively impacted language learning. They all agreed that technical resources are needed to prepare engaging lessons and activities for young learners. Therefore, the need for age-appropriate language learning materials is essential for these teachers and their colleagues. A recommendation for practice would be creating software, apps, and other instructional materials specifically for young English-speakers who are learning Mandarin Chinese as a second language. New opportunities to develop and create gamified and simulated activities for young second language learners is essential.

Research about Mandarin Chinese as a second language in early childhood education is minimal. Further research on teaching and learning Mandarin Chinese as a second language in early childhood education is necessary. A longitudinal study relating to immersive game-based learning, gamification, and simulation in Mandarin Chinese language learning includes quantitative and qualitative data to assess student growth. It is essential to evaluate student performance by using benchmark assessments, classroom observations, and teacher and student interviews to examine the impact and influence of learning Mandarin Chinese through game-based learning, gamification, and simulation over a long period.

FUTURE TRENDS

Education is an agent for social change. As an agent for social change, education continues to evolve to meet the needs of learners. Not only does education promote intellectual and academic growth, but also social, emotional, and cultural evolution. Moreover, the development of a second language in American schools can produce many social change implications. Second language learners develop a flexible thought process to view the world through a different lens. A flexible thought process can influence the way learners perceive the world. Second language learning can increase the opportunity for global and cultural awareness (Baker, 2015). Most importantly, second language learning can encourage learners to advance their 21st-century competency skills to increase interpersonal and communication skills in another language and the possibilities for life-long learning and career opportunities. In addition to acquiring competency skills, technology is a crucial aspect of teaching and learning.

As technology's role in education continues to evolve, it has become an emerging trend in the early childhood classroom. The role of technology in second language learning has become an essential aspect of motivation and engagement. Many second language educators are experiencing a shift in educational methods as the number of computer-assisted language learning software increases. However, there is little empirical research on how early childhood teachers implement technology, specifically in early childhood second language classrooms. Young children are digital natives who are very familiar with using technology inside and outside of the school.

As educators think of future trends in the use of technology in second language education, it is critical to assess the impact of game-based learning, gamification, and simulations. As stated above, there is a lack of Mandarin Chinese resources for second language resources for early childhood learners. There is a strong need for language educators, instructional designers, and technology specialists to develop efficient and effective technological resources for Mandarin Chinese educators who teach Mandarin Chinese in an early childhood setting.

The use of immersive tools in response to the impact of COVID-19 is critical to help educators. The simulated online app should help early childhood learners between the ages of 4 and 8. The app should consist of illustrations, vocabulary, short stories, and task-based activities for children to review prior learning skills. To gamify the activities, children can earn incentives such as badges, rewards, or gems to collect. Also, when students complete a certain number of tasks, they can move up to different levels. Each level should increase in difficulty level based on the student's ability.

Simulations facilitate play. In this context, simulations can be achievement-focused for young children, which contains educational and fun activities. Teachers can create simple simulations with less complicated tasks for younger students. Children may feel comfortable simulating familiar environments such as a classroom, house, or playground setting. For example, a teacher can create a simulated environment within the school by incorporating classroom centers. A housekeeping or kitchen center can allow students to play and communicate in the target language. Students can use the vocabulary learned from previous lessons. Therefore, teachers need to provide ample time for students to gain comprehensible vocabulary and phrases. A housekeeping center can produce knowledge of Mandarin Chinese vocabulary of foods, family members, kitchen appliances, and other meaningful items within a home. A dramatic play center can cultivate creativity and imagination. Teachers can change dramatic play centers each month to encourage students to use new vocabulary. For example, a dramatic play center set up as a post office can encourage children to write Mandarin Chinese characters. Children can learn numbers, addresses, and simple directions in Mandarin. Since many early childhood teachers make their activities, Mandarin Chinese language teachers must create high-quality resources to stimulate young children's minds.

The rapid advancement of technology has provided educators with supplemental teaching and learning resources. Educators who would like to use technology can use a game-based platform, which would allow students to learn Mandarin Chinese. The game-based app can feature simulated environments while focusing on vocabulary, short sentences and phrases, and proper pronunciation. To use gamification and simulation in a Mandarin Chinese classroom, early childhood learners can learn the target language through motivation and engagement. Teachers need to establish meaningful activities that provide context and real life-situations in the target language. Students learning Mandarin Chinese in gamified or simulated environments thrive while learning vocabulary, meaningful phrases and sentences, pronunciation, and Chinese culture.

Second language teachers need to find resources that meet the needs of young children in second language classrooms. Teachers need to understand the role technology plays in the early childhood classroom, specifically in second language learning and how to use the technology during instruction. Second language teachers who introduce play-based education through games and activities increase motivation and engagement in young students. One way to introduce play-based instruction is to integrate technology into the learner-centered classroom. Students will have the opportunity to interact with the teacher, classmates, and technology to increase positive student language learning outcomes.

Young language learners can effectively learn a second language by participating in engaging and fun activities with teachers and fellow students. Movement can act as an instructional method that allows students to learn through a kinesthetic learning style. The total physical response is an instructional method used by some educators. Total physical response (TPR) is a language teaching method developed by James Asher (Al Harrasi, 2014). TPR combines language learning with whole-body movements to increase students' ability to learn and retain information (Asher, as cited in Al Harrasi, 2014). Participants who used movement such as TPR and gestures in their classroom experienced an enhancement of their lessons.

Virtual reality systems design to promote learning a second language produce a more effective second language learning environment. Games such as Second Life provide virtual immersion environments for the learner. The Microsoft Kinect features a camera, sensor, full-body 3D motion capture, facial and voice recognition, which allows learners to control and interact with the app using movements, gestures, and spoken commands. Kinect uses a hands-free device to reduce the use of a computer or mouse. A laptop or mouse for younger students thwarts interaction and engagement (KOL, 2015). Microsoft's Kinect uses body movements and gestures to get learners to participate in the learning process. Kinect and headsets allow children to learn with their bodies. It is an active way to promote motivation and engagement. Second language educators need to collaborate with IT specialists to create a simulation designed for children to learn Mandarin Chinese. The design must be interactive with learners' opportunities to practice or increase vocabulary development, distinguish tones, listen and speak, and comprehend.

CONCLUSION

The implementation of technology is shaping the way young children learn second languages. The teaching of second language learning is vital to the development of 21st-century language skills and competencies. The learning of languages that do not share the same alphabetic script as English has grown in popularity. As the United States pushes second language educational reforms on secondary and higher education, there is little early childhood progression. Early childhood is a critical learning period. Early childhood learners experience rapid growth of language and cognitive skills. A rich linguistic environment with useful instructional materials and technology can help teach and learn a new language in early childhood education.

Teaching Mandarin Chinese in an early childhood setting can seem overwhelming to the novice and experienced educator. Early childhood learners have little to no exposure to Mandarin Chinese. Research has proven that many educators who teach Mandarin Chinese to young children do not have age-appropriate language learning resources deemed sufficient or adequate. Second language learning requires a lot of practice inside and outside of the classroom. There are challenges for educators in engaging young children in learning Mandarin Chinese. Therefore, technological developments are incorporated into the second language learning environment for optimal learning and progress. Create virtual environments for students to engage in second language learning. The use of VR, such as Kinect, can motivate and engage young students. Embedding language activities that include task-based and goal-oriented skills will help students learn.

REFERENCES

Ahmad, J. (2016). Technology-assisted language learning is a silver bullet for enhancing language competence and performance: A case study. *International Journal of Applied Linguistics and English Literature*, *5*(7), 118–131. doi:10.7575/aiac.ijalel.v.5n.7p.118

Al Harrasi, K. T. S. (2014). Using "Total Physical Response" With Young Learners in Oman. *Childhood Education*, *90*(1), 36–42. doi:10.1080/00094056.2014.872513

Aldhafeeri, F., Palaiologou, I., & Folorunsho, A. (2016). Integration of digital technologies into play-based pedagogy in Kuwait early childhood education: Teacher's views, attitudes, and aptitudes. *International Journal of Early Years Education*, *24*(3), 342–360. doi:10.1080/09669760.2016.1172477

Alpar, M. (2013). The importance of games in foreign languages to children. *Educational Research Review*, *8*(15), 1247–1255. doi:10.5897/ERR2013.1494

American Councils for International Education. (2017). *The national K-12 foreign language enrollment survey report*. https://www.americancouncils.org/sites/default/files/FLE-report-June17.pdf

Asia Society. (2012). *Chinese language learning in the early grades: A handbook of resources and best practices for Mandarin immersion*. http://asiasociety.org/files/chinese-earlylanguage.pdf

Baker, W. (2015). Research into practice: Cultural and intercultural awareness. *Language Teaching*, *48*(1), 130–141. doi:10.1017/S0261444814000287

Bandura, A. (1994). Self-efficacy. In V. S. Ramachaudran (Ed.), *Encyclopedia of human behavior* (Vol. 4, pp. 71–81). Academic Press.

Bankovic, I., & Sollars, V. (2017). English as a second language in a Maltese early years setting. *An Leanbh Óg: The OMEP Ireland Journal of Early Childhood Studies*, *11*, 61–69.

Bialystok, E. (2017). The bilingual adaptation: How minds accommodate experience. *Psychological Bulletin*, *143*(3), 233–262. doi:10.1037/bul0000099 PMID:28230411

Bialystok, E., & Hakuta, K. (1999). *Confounded age: Linguistic and cognitive factors in age differences for second language acquisition*. http://citeseerx.ist.psu.edu/viewdoc/download?doi=10.1.1.475.3365&rep=rep1&type=pdf

Butler, Y. G. (2015). The use of computer games as foreign language learning tasks for digital natives. *System*, *54*, 91–102. doi:10.1016/j.system.2014.10.010

Byker, E. J. (2014). Needing TPACK without Knowing It: Integrating Educational Technology in Social Studies. *Social Studies Research & Practice*, *9*(3).

Center for Advanced Research on Language Acquisition. (2017). *Less commonly taught languages*. https://carla.umn.edu/lctl/index.html

Dehghanzadeh, H., Fardanesh, H., Hatami, J., Talaee, E., & Noroozi, O. (2019). Using gamification to support learning English as a second language: A systematic review. *Computer Assisted Language Learning*, *1*(24), 1–24. Advance online publication. doi:10.1080/09588221.2019.1648298

Dewey, J. (1938). *Experience and Education*. Macmillan.

Edwards, S. (2016). New concepts of play and the problem of technology, digital media and popular-culture integration with play-based learning in early childhood education. *Technology, Pedagogy and Education*, *25*(4), 513–532. doi:10.1080/1475939X.2015.1108929

He, H. (2017). Analysis of the Reasons of Public High School Students in United States Choosing Chinese as a Foreign Language–The Case of Nevada. *International Journal of Emerging Technologies in Learning*, *12*(06), 140–148. doi:10.3991/ijet.v12i06.7092

Hsin, C. T., Li, M. C., & Tsai, C. C. (2014). The influence of young children's use of technology on their learning: A review. *Journal of Educational Technology & Society*, *17*(4), 85–99.

Hsu, C. Y., Tsai, M. J., Chang, Y. H., & Liang, J. C. (2017). Surveying in-service teachers' beliefs about game-based learning and perceptions of technological pedagogical and content knowledge of games. *Journal of Educational Technology & Society*, *20*(1), 134–143.

KOL, S. (2015). Computer Perceptions of Children in Early Childhood period. *International Online Journal of Educational Sciences*, *7*(2).

Krashen, S. (2013). *Second language Acquisition: Theory, applications, and some conjectures*. Cambridge University Press.

Lamrani, R., & Abdelwahed, E. (2019). Game-based learning and gamification to improve skills in early childhood education. *Computer Science and Information Systems*, *17*(1), 339–356. doi:10.2298/CSIS190511043L

Lantolf, J., Thorne, S. L., & Poehner, M. (2015). Sociocultural Theory and Second Language Development. In B. van Patten & J. Williams (Eds.), *Theories in Second Language Acquisition* (pp. 207–226). Routledge.

Legault, J., Zhao, J., Chi, Y.-A., Chen, W., Klippel, A., & Li, P. (2019). Immersive Virtual Reality as an Effective Tool for Second Language Vocabulary Learning. *Languages*, *4*(1), 13. doi:10.3390/languages4010013

Lenneberg, E. H. (1967). *Biological foundations of language*. Wiley & Sons. doi:10.1080/21548331.1967.11707799

Li, R., & Topolewski, D. (2002). Zip and Terry: A new attempt at designing language learning simulation. *Simulation & Gaming*, *33*(2), 181–186. doi:10.1177/1046878102332006

Liu, S., & Wang, F. (2018). A qualitative study on learning trajectories of non-native Chinese instructors as successful Chinese language learners. *Asian-Pacific Journal of Second and Foreign Lang Education*, *3*(2), 1–21. doi:10.118640862-018-0043-5

Liu, X., & Olmanson, J. (2016). A technology-supported learning experience to facilitate Chinese character acquisition. *The Nebraska Educator: A Student-Led Journal, 30*, 87-107.

Lü, C., & Lavadenz, M. (2014). Native Chinese-Speaking K-12 Language Teachers' Beliefs and Practices. *Foreign Language Annals*, *47*(4), 630–652. doi:10.1111/flan.12111

Lu, J., Meng, S., & Tam, V. (2014). Learning Chinese characters via mobile technology in a primary school classroom. *Educational Media International*, *51*(3), 166–184. doi:10.1080/09523987.2014.968448

Lucero, A. (2014). Teachers' use of linguistic scaffolding to support the academic language development of first-grade emergent bilingual students. *Journal of Early Childhood Literacy*, *14*(4), 534–561. doi:10.1177/1468798413512848

Ludgate, S. (2015). *Pre-School Children's Experiences with Touchscreen Technologies: Early Findings from Survey Results*. TACTYC Conference, Birmingham, UK.

Maad, M. R. (2016). Awakening young children to foreign languages: Openness to diversity highlighted. *Language, Culture and Curriculum*, *29*(3), 319–336. doi:10.1080/07908318.2016.1184679

Meyer, B. (2013). Game-based language learning for pre-school children: A design perspective. *The Electronic Journal of e-Learning, 11*(1), 39-48.

Munoz, C. (2014). Contrasting effects of starting age and input on the oral performance of foreign language learners. *Applied Linguistics, 35*(4), 1–21. doi:10.1093/applin/amu024

Murphy, V. A. (2014). *Second language learning in the early school years: Trends and contexts*. Oxford University Press.

NAEYC. (2012). *Technology and Media*. https://www.naeyc.org/sites/default/files/globally-shared/downloads/PDFs/resources/topics/PS_technology_WEB.pdf

Nemati, M., & Arabmofrad, A. (2014). Development of interlanguage pragmatic competence: Input- and output-based instruction in the zone of proximal development. *Theory and Practice in Language Studies, 4*(2), 262–270. doi:10.4304/tpls.4.2.262-270

Nicolay, A., & Poncelet, M. (2015). Cognitive benefits in children enrolled in an early bilingual immersion school: A follow up study. *Bilingualism: Language and Cognition, 18*(4), 789–795. doi:10.1017/S1366728914000868

Nikolopoulou, K., & Gialamas, V. (2015). Barriers to the integration of computers in early childhood settings: Teachers' perceptions. *Education and Information Technologies, 20*(2), 285–301. doi:10.100710639-013-9281-9

Pemba, D., Mann, V., Sarkar, T., & Azartash, K. (2016). Learning English in China: A tablet-based app using the voices of native speakers. *Open Journal of Social Sciences, 4*(07), 85–91. doi:10.4236/jss.2016.47014

Philip, J., Borowczyk, M., & Mackey, A. (2017). Exploring the Uniqueness of Child Second Language Acquisition (SLA): Learning, Teaching, Assessment, and Practice. *Annual Review of Applied Linguistics, 37*, 1–13. doi:10.1017/S0267190517000174

Pinter, A. (2017). *Teaching young language learners* (2nd ed.). Oxford University Press.

Prosic-Santovac, D. (2016). Popular video cartoons and associated branded toys in teaching English to very young learners: A case study. *Language Teaching Research*, 1–21. doi:10.1177/1362168816639758

Pugh-Opher, F. (2019). *Mandarin Teachers' Experiences Using Technological Pedagogical Content Knowledge in Early Childhood Classrooms* [Unpublished doctoral dissertation]. Walden University.

Ramirez, N. F., & Kuhl, P. (2017). *The brain science of bilingualism*. http://ilabs.uw.edu/sites/default/files/2017_FerjanRamirez_Kuhl_NAEYC.pdf

Rawendy, D., Ying, Y., Arifin, Y., & Rosalin, K. (2017). Design and development game Chinese language learning with gamification and using mnemonic method. *Procedia Computer Science, 116*, 61–67. doi:10.1016/j.procs.2017.10.009

Ryder, R., & Machajewski, S. (2017). The "UIC German" game app for the enhancement of foreign language learning - case study. *International Journal of Educational Technology, 4*(1), 1–16.

Sandanayake, T. (2016). Upcoming trends in virtual learning to enhance technology-based learning. *International Journal of Applied Engineering Research: IJAER, 11*(23), 11454–11460.

Sharifi, A., Ghanizadeh, A., & Jahedizadeh, S. (2017). The effect of simulation on middle school students' perception of classroom activities and their foreign language achievement: A mixed-methods approach. *International Electronic Journal of Elementary Education, 9*(3), 667–680.

Snow, C. E. (2017). The role of vocabulary versus knowledge in children's language learning: A fifty-year perspective. *Journal for the Study of Education and Development, 40*(1), 1–18. doi:10.1080/02103702.2016.1263449

United States Department of Education. (2008). *Enhancing foreign language proficiency in the United States: Preliminary results of the national security language initiative.* https://nsep.gov/sites/default/files/nsli-preliminary-results.pdf

Veraksa, N., Shiyan, O., Shiyan, I., Pramling, N., & Pramling-Samuelson, I. (2016). Communication between teacher and child in early child education. *Vygotskian Theory and Educational, 39*(2), 221-243. doi:10.1080/02103702.2015.1133091

Vygotsky, L. S. (1978). *Mind in society: The development of higher psychological processes.* Harvard University Press.

Wass, R., & Golding, C. (2014). Sharpening a tool for teaching: The zone of proximal development. *Teaching in Higher Education, 19*(6), 671–684. doi:10.1080/13562517.2014.901958

Werbach, K., & Hunter, D. (2012). *For the win: How game thinking can revolutionize your business.* School Press.

Yang, S. H. (2012). Social interaction in second language learning. *English Teaching, 67*(1), 131–156. doi:10.15858/engtea.67.1.201203.131

ADDITIONAL READING

Cahill, G. (2020). Why game-based learning? https://thelearningcounsel.com/article/why-game-based-learning

Dalim, C. S. C., Sunar, M. S., Dey, A., & Billinghurst, M. (2020). Using augmented reality with speech input for non-native children's language learning. *International Journal of Human-Computer Studies, 134*, 44–64. doi:10.1016/j.ijhcs.2019.10.002

Fan, M., Antle, A. N., & Warren, J. L. (2020). Augmented Reality for Early Language Learning: A Systematic Review of Augmented Reality Application Design, Instructional Strategies, and Evaluation Outcomes. *Journal of Educational Computing Research, 58*(6), 1059–1100. doi:10.1177/0735633120927489

Hanim, N., Sim, M. S., Khin, L. S., & Shy, F. P. (2020). Experiential Learning in Mandarin Classrooms: The case for simulation. *International Journal of Asian Social Science, 10*(4), 171–180. doi:10.18488/journal.1.2020.104.171.180

Meyer, B. (2013). Game-based language learning for pre-school children: A design perspective. *The Electronic Journal of e-Learning, 11*(1), 39-48.

Miller, C. R. (2020). *How to use games to build community in distance learning*. https://www.edutopia.org/article/how-use-games-build-community-distance-learning

KEY TERMS AND DEFINITIONS

Constructivism: Constructing meaning through social interactions.

Early Childhood Education: Young learners between the ages of birth to 8 years old.

Game-Based Learning: the interaction of game play with educational content.

Gamification: Using game-based elements to engage, motivate, and promote learning.

Less Commonly Taught Languages: Languages that are seldom taught in schools due to availability and complexity of the language.

Mandarin Chinese: Mandarin Chinese is the predominate language spoken in China and Taiwan.

Scaffolding: The ability to solve a problem or complete a task with support from a more experienced individual.

Second Language Learning: Learning a language other than the student's native language in an educational setting.

Simulation: The imitation of a real world situation.

Sociocultural Learning Theory: The theoretical development of social and cultural connections.

Target Language: A foreign language which a person want to learn.

Chapter 11
Integrating Augmented Reality Into the Workshop Model Remote Learning Classroom

Patience Ndidi Onyegwara
Independent Researcher, USA

ABSTRACT

The global pandemic has forced schools across the globe to go to online learning environments. This chapter describes the potential of integrating augmented reality technologies into a virtual immersive workshop model of instruction. Effective utilization and integration of these immersive tools in the workshop model has the potential to develop learners' 21st century skills to be decision makers, problem solvers, lifelong learners, creators, innovators, and to think critically in solving problems.

INTRODUCTION

Today K-12 educational system are implementing remote learning incorporating an augmented reality (AR) approach and virtualization to supplement the normal face-to-face teaching. The contemporary switch to the use of AR immersive virtual technologies in remote learning Workshop Model (WSM) classroom is crucial to education stakeholders. Earlier on, most large and small school districts across the nation have launched some effective technologies to enhance various instructional programs designed to assist young adults to develop 21st century required skills. Remote learning is a form of distance education or online learning that allows content dissemination for continued education through the application of information technology and Internet technology. The purpose of this chapter is to summarize how the application of innovative immersive technologies into the WSM remote classroom can be used to promote classroom interactive learning within an immersive AR and virtual reality (VR) system. Productive learning depends on how well one understands how immersive resources of AR and VR work to provide quality interactive learning in today's WSM classroom.

The purpose of this chapter is to define the design and implementation of innovative educational programs using AR simulations in today's remote learning WSM classroom. Most K-12 educational

DOI: 10.4018/978-1-7998-4222-4.ch011

settings adopted remote or virtual learning as a pedagogical means to continue learning and disseminate content through the application of information and internet technology.

BACKGROUND

Changes from COVID-19 sparked educational settings to adopt a blended or online content delivery approaches. This rapid shift to remote or virtual learning became a prevalent alternative to face to face classroom instruction that is not realistic due to COVID-19 limitations to in person instruction. School districts modified their instructional plan and curriculum to meet the learning standards using new technologies.

As a result of this change, educators in K-12 educational settings were expected to continue the quality and explicit teaching and learning process of all content areas using online or blended classrooms. In response, teachers face the challenges of adopting best practices to foster 21st-century learning for every student. Koh et al. (2017) described twenty-first-century knowledge as the learning experiences that help students to promote the sociocultural, cognitive, metacognitive, productive, and technological competencies to function in a 21st-century workplace. Educators face the task to redesign and implement innovative learning environments that support student development toward a more dynamic, interactive, and global society.

Furthermore, the development of advanced 21st-century knowledge workers is critical in the present economy. Dole et al. (2016a) study found that the U. S. educational system requires new constructivist and differentiated pedagogies to prepare diverse students with required 21st-century skills. To attain this goal, teachers must adopt an innovative approach to change to a constructivist project-based learning environment (Dole et al., 2016b; Fullan & Langworthy, 2013). As a result, educators face the task of shifting their traditional teacher-centered method of instruction to constructivist learner-centered pedagogy to increase their students' readiness to succeed beyond k12 education.

Research by Liang and Akiba (2015) found that students who learn in constructivist environments tend to have more positive cognitive outcomes compared with students learning in a traditional learning environment. A constructivist learning environment is characterized with features such as (a) knowledge is shared between teachers and students; (b) teachers and students will share authority; (c) the teacher's role is one of a facilitator or guide and; (d) learning groups will consist of small numbers of heterogeneous students. This instructional approach allows students to construct their knowledge through investigation, collaboration, and reflection (Liang & Akiba, 2015).

Given that the traditional method of instruction does little in helping students develop confidence, ownership, and beliefs in their abilities and learning, teachers in today's educational settings need to provide student-centered instruction (Bautista et al., 2018). Studies have examined the effectiveness of utilizing innovative student-centered instructional approach in K-12 grade classroom (Casey et al., 2016; Bautista et al., 2018; Calkins & Tolan, 2010; Ciampa, 2016; Hattie et al., 2017; Hemmeter et al., 2016; Leu et al., 2017; Porath, 2016; Russell, 2012; Sand, 2018; Tomlinson, 2017).

The trend has necessitated a change in the instructional approach from traditional or teacher-directed didactic method to a student-centered approach which places the learner at the heart of the teaching process while the teacher designs the instruction to address the students' ideas, interests, and needs (Bautista et al., 2018). Student-centered instruction allows teachers to nurture the autonomy of the learner as well as assist students in developing key 21st century competencies such as collaboration, critical thinking, high student engagement, self-directed learning, and communication skills to become life- long learners (Sharp et al., 2019). This necessitates a switch to active engagement through project-based learning.

Workshop Model of Instruction (WSM)

The WSM is an example of a reform model implemented to support the development of 21st-century learning. Koh et al. (2017) identified 21st-century learning as the engagement of students in collaborative work and real-world problem solving through effective exploitation of information and communications technologies (ICT). The WSM is a constructivist project-based learning environment that engages the learners in developing projects in groups (Williams, 2015). Research has supported the underlying precepts of the WSM, such as self-directed learning activities, including extensive reading and writing opportunities (Porath, 2016).

The WSM is a differentiated instructional model that is based on constructivist learning principles. The WSM is designed to support diverse learners through a differentiated, problem-based learning environment. To implement the WSM, teachers must design and implement a new curriculum, a new instructional model, and integrate new technologies into their middle school classrooms (Porath, 2016). This non-traditional instructional model is being implemented in various school districts across the U.S. to promote essential 21st-century skills of problem-solving, critical thinking, collaboration, and communication skills. The WSM classroom allows educators to use a learner-centered pedagogical approach to differentiate and maximize instruction to meet individual students learning needs (Calkins & Tolan, 2010).

Unlike the traditional method of instruction where students are passive and disconnected from learning, the WSM of instruction promotes students' active participation. In a WSM classroom, students have a choice and authority for their learning. The WSM student-centered pedagogy prepares students to succeed in a future where information is ever-changing. Students in the WSM classroom have the opportunity to engage in classroom discussions and dialogue with group members to share opinions and thoughts regarding class tasks (Tomlinson, 2017). Educators implementing the WSM of instruction act as a coach, or guide that facilitate the learning process through conferencing, small group instruction, and station teaching of specific areas of needs to foster individual student's learning need.

Alt (2015) found that teachers using the WSM in their classrooms were able to increase students' motivation to learn, increase students' comprehension skills, and improved students' opportunities for authentic experiences. The results of these studies highlighted the effectiveness of utilizing student-centered instructional strategies to improve learning. Based on the literature reviewed, the WSM connects differentiated instruction in a way that is aligned with the Common Core State Standards. Teachers implementing the WSM design a collaborative learning model that engages the learners in developing projects in response to problems identified in their workshops. Additionally, the WSM includes the integration of an online workspace creating a blended model of learning.

The WSM is a problem-based learning instructional model that relates to constructivist learning principles. Research on the WSM has shown positive results, such as active collaborative learning and fostering students attaining 21st. Century skills. Research has found that the WSM classroom provides a conducive environment for students to develop essential 21st. Century skills of critical thinking, problem-solving, communication, creativity, and collaboration. The WSM includes an integrated literacy approach that focuses on both content literacy and technological literacy.

The WSM is designed as a constructivist instructional model to develop advanced learning skills and content knowledge required by new standards and the increasingly diverse students. Kwan and Wong

(2015) found that instructional approaches that emphasized creating a constructivist environment and promoting active learners or a learner-centered culture can develop students' critical thinking. Classrooms based on constructivism principles presuppose that active learners can investigate further and can construct knowledge for themselves (Vygotsky, 1978). According to Bruner (1961), the purpose of education is not to impart knowledge, but instead to facilitate a child's thinking and problem-solving skills which can then be transferred to a range of situations.

Educators are capable to change mindsets and embrace new concepts in learning. They embrace a certain innovative instructional approach of teaching, such as the WSM, to ensure that students get prepared to succeed in a future where information is ever-changing. To achieve this goal, present-day educators must create meaningful learning experiences that allow students to develop the 21st-century skills of creativity, critical thinking, communication, collaboration, and innovation (Bishop, 2013) that will provide the educated citizens of the future. Currently, most schools across the globe implement remote learning to provide quality interactive teaching and learning process. In effect, the application of AR and VR tools are evolving in the education platform.

AR and VR Technologies

Educators implementing student-centered instruction require new understandings of how to integrate appropriate technology because of the rapid technology growth and changes in today's classroom (Koh et al., 2018). Previous research findings have revealed that technology integration supports constructivist pedagogy, students' individualized, and exploratory learning. Furthermore, appropriate technology integration increased students' active participation in learning leading to an increase in the production of knowledge. Similarly, teachers' use of digital app and techniques promote innovative pedagogical practices in both face-to-face and blended learning classroom setting. Generally, the application of technology tools to learning allows students to use technology to explore new concepts and optimize their understanding.

AR is an advanced technology developed to combine digital information with a real environment, unlike VR where the entire experience is composed of digital information. Integration of AR technologies in the WSM classroom are relevant to enhance pedagogies that allow for greater enthusiasm on the part of the student. Additionally, AR technologies provide significant benefits including. creativity, innovation, participation, and especially in the motivation of participants' maximum immersive experience of remote or virtual learning. Research has noted that AR offers many new opportunities for innovation in the teaching and learning process.

AR is one of the emerging technologies that can impact the education field. Research has proven that AR-based activities improve the teaching and learning processes. Integration of AR tools has enormous potential for increasing the efficiency of the independent work of students in the WSM remote learning classroom. Also, the use of this type of technology in the classroom facilitates the understanding of contents from different areas as Language Arts, Mathematics, or Science (Daher et al., 2018).

VR and AR immersive technologies have become popular with today's modern human life undergoing changes and modifications. Although these immersive technologies have existed for years, researchers have emphasized the increase in VR and AR popularity as well as application in various fields including education via our mobile devices. VR technology's popularity is attributed to advances in both hardware and software resources in various fields such as health, education, sports, and entertainment.

VR offers new possibilities for the user to acquire knowledge through the application of the immersive visualization of a 3D object.

Thus, AR technologies are an important part of the learning process for users in a remote learning environment. AR technology has potential in present-day WSM remote learning classrooms because the tool simulates a visual classroom space to match the real-world classroom setting. Additionally, the new AR technology application offers the possibility for users to acquire knowledge through playful interaction within a virtual classroom environment. The rapid changes in today's world with advancements in technology have developed the potential to integrate immersive technologies such as AR into immersive learning environments such as the WSM.

DESIGN AND IMPLEMENTATION

This chapter provides a new practice into the regular teaching and learning processes. Specifically the design of WSM that moves instruction beyond the established instructional plan and programs usually employed to teach basic concepts in the WSM classroom. The application of these innovative instructional tools places interactive techniques within a constructivist discovery-based pedagogy learning environment. As most school districts adopt the remote or virtual learning method with the help of mobile devices, the application of immersive technologies are useful potential tools in the WSM remote classroom. AR technologies are popular tools for learning in STEM classrooms. AR provides valuable apps that promote synergistic interaction and collaboration between students and teachers. Similarly, AR tools empower students to become active participants in their learning which enhances students' development of 21st-century essential skills.

MERGE Cube and COSPACES are novel AR technologies that have the potential for supplementing real interactive teaching and learning processes in a STEM WSM remote learning environment. Integration of AR tools like MERGE Cube and COSPACES in our K-12 STEM have enormous potential for increasing students' interactivity and project-based learning. Research has identified that MERGE Cube and COSPACES have the potential to develop a simulation platform to teach the water cycle process for learners. Similarly, effective utilization and integration of these immersive tools in WSM remote learning environment would develop learners' 21st-century skills to be decision-makers, problem solvers, lifelong learners, creators, innovators, and to think critically in solving problems (Salanger et al., 2020)

Merge Cube

Merge Cube is a new form of AR immersive technology developed to promote active learning using an inquiry-based approach. Merge Cube Explorer is compatible with Smartphones, tablets, iPad, Android, and Windows 10. The new tool of Merge Cube enables students to hold virtual 3D objects and learn by interacting with the digital world. Students can engage with digital content naturally and intuitively using visual, auditory, kinesthetic, and tactile senses, for more memorable and impactful learning. Merge Cube tool allows students to exercise spatial intelligence by manipulating and inspecting digital 3D objects. Students with strong spatial abilities excel in STEM fields, allowing them to go further. Merge Cube works with 3D creation software like Paint 3D and Tinker card use. This allows students to hold the 3D design in their hand or preview a creation before 3D printing, allowing faster design and easier collaboration in a remote learning environment. There is an additional tool of Merge Headset students can use to experience the full power of immersive technology.

Merge Cube works with Merge EDU, an educational platform with primary-intermediate standards-aligned STEM for students' learning and creation. Merge EDU has the Object Viewer and Merge Explorer apps that have free and paid options. The Merge Explorer is a science Merge EDU App that is aligned to STEM standards for primary and middle-grade levels. This app enables students to learn and explore various science concepts with interactive hands-on science lessons using Merge Cube. Object Viewer App allows students to upload view and share 3D objects on the Merge Cube. Also, students can create 3D models of math, social studies, science, and other content areas into virtual objects that one can hold and inspect from every section of the cube.

The Merge Education App. is the platform allows students to experience learning in multiple ways such as visual, auditory, kinesthetic, and tactile senses. Students are privileged to experience meaningful learning in the remote learning environment. This platform gives students access to upload their 3D objects into the Merge Cube and collaborate with teachers and peers. Additionally, the Merge Education apps platform allows students to touch and hold science lessons, interact with STEM concepts, and engage in fun activities designed by teachers to enhance lessons. Learners immerse completely into inquiry learning to explore and understand complex science concepts using a hands-on digital learning tool combined with Merge EDU apps.

This innovative approach evokes a sense of wonder and amazement, accelerates understanding, deepens engagement, and lets students discover learning in a fun meaningful way remotely. Merge EDU work in close alliance with educators around the world to create curriculum-aligned, standard-based lessons and step-by-step activity plans students can follow in a remote learning environment or the classroom at school. The activity plan includes classroom and remote learning resources for both students and teachers. Teacher dashboard, and student progress tracking resources are included. There are assessment options and extension ideas that students may explore to take learning further at the end of each activity (https://mergeedu.com/cube).

CoSpaces

CoSpaces is a good development AR/VR tool that helps students to create an infographic, with a grid canvas to align objects. For example, charts can be created in CoSpaces using the various building blocks available in the library. CoSpaces creation tools, allow students to build a house or apartment in 3D. CoSpaces Edu offers a proper solution for beginners who are getting started with coding. Students can discover 3D creation and modeling through the construction and architecture of a virtual house or apartment. For example, the floor plan image can be imported from the upload section and used as the basis on which to build a house or apartment.

AR provides benefits and advantages centered on pedagogies that allow for greater enthusiasm on the part of the students, with significant advantages in creativity, innovation, participation, and especially in the motivation of participants (Kersten et al., 2020) Furthermore, AR offers many advantages for education. It expands the usefulness of the cell phone, a device that is already very popular with students and the public. A marker-based program can be developed for minimal cost, which is an important consideration at a time when finances are so tight for all types of institutions.

The breadth of the program can be adjusted based on available staff time. Such a program lends itself to being phased in over a period of time or deployed all at once. It provides new connections between the public and the archives and other collections that already exist at many libraries and museums. AR offers many new opportunities for innovation and meshes well with the current public interest in social networks. Perhaps most important, it builds on the natural curiosity of the students and the public, so it is more about individual learning than restricted programs (Al-Gindy et al., 2020).

Issues, Controversies, Problems

A previous study on real-world experiences of teachers implementing innovative instructional models in their classrooms with technology integration revealed that the U.S. is struggling to implement reform designed to support diverse learners. A study by Onyegwara (2020) found some challenges that hindered the effective implementation of new reform in the middle-grade classroom. The study found that the restrictions on teachers' instructional scheduling limited their flexibility to proper implementation. Similarly, the difficulties related to lack of professional development may pose problems to the effective application of immersive technology in the WSM remote classroom. Furthermore, the integration of technology into classrooms, a key component of the WSM remote classroom could be hindered primarily by the lack of external technology-specific support and by the lack of consistent access to the technology involved.

Additionally, researchers Daher et al. (2018) pointed out that teachers are often reluctant to use Information and Communication Technology (ICT) even with the availability of ICT tools and their awareness of the numerous benefits. Given that the Merge Cube app is an emerging AR in the field of education there could be possible barriers that may hinder the effective application of this innovative learning tool in WSM remote classrooms. According to Rogers (2004) diffusion of innovation framework and Hall and Hord (2015) the decision to adopt innovation, rate of learning to develop the skill, and the competence to use innovative practices depends on the individual and strong relationship within a group. Rogers's (2004) theory suggests that teachers' belief and attitude in the adoption of the Merge Cube app into their WSM remote learning environment is an important factor to consider. Some teachers may be unmotivated and lack the confidence to adopt Cube MERGE technology in their remote learning classroom.

Time constraints in completing a class project involving the MERGE Cube app may pose a problem for effective application. Other barriers include insufficient Professional development opportunities for a specific application of AR immersive technology projects that limit teachers' knowledge. Koh et al. (2017) and Althauser's (2015) assertions that professional development improves teachers' confidence in designing curriculum as well as their instructional self-efficacy for implementing reforms.

Inadequate technical support to coach and follow-up teachers and students to ensure effective application. and lack of AR devices at the school level; lack of teachers' knowledge about ways to integrate ICT to enhance the curriculum; difficulty in integrating and using different ICT tools in a single lesson. Trumper and Eldar (2015) posited that professional development increases teachers' effective instructional practices and beliefs about their ability to implement new instructional practices. Limited availability of resources at home with parents' lack of knowledge of the immersive technology for the students to access the necessary educational materials could pose a challenge in the application of AR technology. Finally, the age of the teachers could pose a barrier in the application of AR tools such as the Merge Cube app. Younger teachers who are digital natives tend to adopt the immersive technology as innovators and early adopters while their older colleagues would be late adopter and laggards (Rogers, 2004)

Lessons Learned

Although most teachers in present-day classroom imaginatively and effectively integrate laptops, iPad, smartboards, video clips, Google Classroom, and flip grids to their instruction to foster student learning. However, they would become more effective with improved knowledge, training, and guidance in the application of AR, VR, or mixed reality tool functions. Cengiz's (2015) noted that educators in present-day classrooms lack the competency and application knowledge to use technology in their practice even with the increased availability and awareness of technology in the educational setting. It is worthy of note that most teachers in the K-12 educational setting have experiences implementing the innovative blended WSM designed based on constructivist learning concepts utilizing differentiated instructional model with technology integration. Additionally, technology integration has become part of the instructional plan in most school districts in the US. However, merging technology integration with the immersive constructivist instructional model like the WSM is not currently happening in education. The application of AR, VR 3D apps into immersive learning environments like the WSM holds great potential in today's virtual learning environment.

SOLUTIONS AND RECOMMENDATIONS

Findings from the literature on innovation reform implementation of technologies indicated that it enhanced students' active participation in learning, promoted personalized learning, and helping students become autonomous learners. Furthermore, it offered teachers the opportunity for an innovative teaching approach needed to foster their students' learning in today's virtual learning environment. However, more support from the administrative level is required to provide implementation resources, flexible scheduling, effective and specific professional development, and adequate technology training of teachers on effective application of AR, VR, and mixed reality in WSM remote learning classrooms to ensure maximum utilization of the potentials these immersive tools have to offer (Onyegwara, 2020).

Policymakers at the district level must consider providing more training, reduce the emphasis on standardized testing, provide consistent technical support and access to technology to empower educators with better implementation techniques and strategies that they need to overcome AR immersive technology implementation challenges. All the educational stakeholders must consider the identified specific areas of concern during the application of this innovative immersive technology of Merge Cube Apps and COSPACES

FUTURE TRENDS

The rapid advancement in technology has brought a major change in the educational setting. Educators in K-12 have perceived that it is time to change their practice in today's remote learning environment. The normal physical classroom interactions between students and students, teachers, and students are impossible. Most science instructions and lab activities are now taught through google meet or zoom meeting live session remotely. This new shift of practice is posing a great challenge to the teaching and learning process. Educators have to adopt a new approach to ensure that quality and explicit instruction is provided to students in today's remote learning environment. The integration and application of AR tools of Merge Cube and CoSpaces have the potential to provide a realistic environment that can stimulate an actual classroom space where students can continue to learn complex science topics, engage in lab activities, and interact with peers and teachers effectively.

CONCLUSION

The application of immersive technologies into a remote learning environment is critical in today's school system. Schools are indeed integrating technology in their normal physical classroom instruction. However, the global pandemic pushed educators into online or blended learning environments. Educators started using Google meets and zoom meetings to teach live session instructions remotely. There are limitations to students' learning due to the absence of real classroom interactions between students and teachers as well as students with their peers. These limitations can be remedied by the application of novel AR and VR immersive tools of Merge Cube and CoSpaces to increase students' engagement in learning and interactions.

REFERENCES

Al-Gindy, A., Felix, C., Ahmed, A., Matoug, A., & Alkhidir, M. (2020). Virtual Reality: Development of an Integrated Learning Environment for Education. *International Journal of Information and Education Technology (IJIET)*, *10*(3), 171–175. doi:10.18178/ijiet.2020.10.3.1358

Alt, D. (2015). Assessing the contribution of a constructivist learning environment to academic self-efficacy in higher education. *Learning Environments Research*, *18*(1), 47–67. doi:10.100710984-015-9174-5

Althauser, K. (2015). Job-embedded professional development: Its impact on teacher self-efficacy and student performance. *Teacher Development*, *19*(2), 210–225. doi:10.1080/13664530.2015.1011346

Bautista, A., Toh, G. Z., & Wong, J. (2018). Primary school music teachers' professional development motivations, needs, and preferences: Does specialization make a difference? *Musicae Scientiae*, *22*(2), 196–223. doi:10.1177/1029864916678654

Bishop, J. (2013). *Partnership for 21st Century Skills (P21)*. Retrieved from https://www.imls.gov/assets/1/AssetManager/Bishop%20Pre-Con%202.pdf

Bruner, J. S. (1961). The act of discovery. *Harvard Educational Review*.

Calkins, L., & Tolan, K. (2010). *Units of study for teaching reading, grades 3–5: A curriculum for the reading workshop*. FirstHand Heinemann.

Casey, A., Goodyear, V. A., & Armour, K. M. (Eds.). (2016). *Digital technologies and learning in physical education: Pedagogical cases*. Taylor & Francis. doi:10.4324/9781315670164

Cengiz, C. (2015). The development of TPACK, technology integrated self-efficacy and instructional technology outcome expectations of pre-service physical education teachers. *Asia-Pacific Journal of Teacher Education*, *43*(5), 411–422. doi:10.1080/1359866X.2014.932332

Ciampa, K. K. (2016). Implementing a digital reading and writing Workshops Model for content literacy instruction in an urban elementary (K-8) school. *Reading Teacher,* 70(3), 295-306. doi: .1514 doi:10.1002/trtr

Daher, W., Baya'a, N., & Anabousy, R. (2018). In-service mathematics teachers' integration of ICT as innovative practice. *International Journal of Research in Education and Science*, *4*(2), 534–543. doi:10.21890/ijres.428945

Dole, S., Bloom, L., & Kowalske, K. (2016b). Transforming pedagogy: Changing perspectives from teacher-centered to learner-centered. *The Interdisciplinary Journal of Problem-Based Learning*, *10*(1), 1.

Dole, S. F., Bloom, L. A., & Doss, K. K. (2016a). Rocket to creativity: A field experience in problem-based and project-based learning. *Global Education Review*, *3*(4).

Hall, G. E., & Hord, S. (2015). *Implementing change: Patterns, principles, and potholes* (4th ed.). Pearson Education.

Hattie, J., Fisher, D., Frey, N., Gojak, L., Moore, S., & Mellman, W. (2017). *Visible leaning for mathematics*. Corwin.

Hemmeter, M. L., Snyder, P. A., Fox, L., & Algina, J. (2016). Evaluating the implementation of the Pyramid Model for promoting social-emotional competence in early childhood classrooms. *Topics in Early Childhood Special Education*, *36*(3), 133–146. doi:10.1177/0271121416653386

KerstenT. P.TrauD.TschirschwitzF. (2020). The Four-Masted Barque Peking in Virtual Reality as a New Form of Knowledge Transfer. *ISPRS Annals of the Photogrammetry, Remote Sensing and Spatial Information Sciences, 4,* 155-162. https://doi-org.proxy1.ncu.edu/10.5194/isprs-annals-V-4-2020-155-2020

Koh, J. H. L., Chai, C. S., Hong, H. Y., & Tsai, C.-C. (2017). A survey to examine teachers' perceptions of design dispositions, lesson design practices and their relationships with technological pedagogical content knowledge (TPACK). *Asia-Pacific Journal of Teacher Education*, *43*(5), 378–391. doi:10.1080/1359866X.2014.941280

Kwan, Y. W., & Wong, A. F. (2015). Effects of the constructivist learning environment on students' critical thinking ability: Cognitive and motivational variables as mediators. *International Journal of Educational Research*, *70*, 68–79. doi:10.1016/j.ijer.2015.02.006

Leu, D. J., Kinzer, C. K., Coiro, J., Castek, J., & Henry, L. A. (2017). New literacies: A dual-level theory of the changing nature of literacy, instruction, and assessment. *Journal of Education*, *197*(2), 1–18. doi:10.1177/002205741719700202

Liang, G., & Akiba, M. (2015). Teacher evaluation, performance-related pay, and constructivist instruction. *Educational Policy*, *29*(2), 375–401. doi:10.1177/0895904813492379

Onyegwara, P. (2020). *Middle School Teachers' Experiences Implementing the Workshop Model in Their Classroom* (Doctoral dissertation). Walden University.

Porath, S. L. (2016). Conceptual, pedagogical, cultural, and political dilemmas of implementing a constructivist workshop approach to teaching literacy. *Teachers and Teaching*, *22*(7), 1–13. doi:10.1080/13540602.2016.1185822

Rogers, E. M. (2004). A prospective and retrospective look at the diffusion model. *Journal of Health Communication*, *9*(sup1, S1), 13–19. doi:10.1080/10810730490271449 PMID:14960401

Russell, D. (2012). *Inquiry into Mediated Action: Understanding Collaborative Online Professional Development*. Lambert Academic Publishing.

Salanger, M., Lewis, D., Vallier, T., McDermott, T., & Dergan, A. (2020). Applying Virtual Reality to Audiovisual Speech Perception Tasks in Children. *American Journal of Audiology*, *29*(2), 244–258. doi:10.1044/2020_AJA-19-00004 PMID:32250641

Sand, A. (2018). The Math WSM and the Effect on Students' Academic Achievement and Mindset in Sixth-Grade Mathematics. Ed.D. Dissertations. 178.

Sharp, L. A., Bonjour, G. L., & Cox, E. (2019). Implementing the Math Workshop Approach: An Examination of Perspectives among Elementary, Middle, and High School Teachers. *International Journal of Instruction*, *12*(1), 69–82. doi:10.29333/iji.2019.1215a

Tomlinson, C. (2017). *How to differentiate instruction in academically diverse classrooms*. ASCD.

Trumper, R., & Eldar, O. (2015). The effect of a MEd program in science education on teachers' professional development: An Israeli case study. *Professional Development in Education*, *41*(5), 826–848. doi:10.1080/19415257.2014.958244

Vygotsky, L. (1978). *Mind in society: The development of higher psychological processes*. Harvard University Press.

Williams, J. A. (2015). Reading every single day. *The Reading Teacher*, *68*(7), 530–538. doi:10.1002/trtr.1349

Chapter 12
Delivering Interventions to Individuals With Trauma-Induced Behaviors Through Immersive Virtual Learning Environments

Robin E. Ruiz
Walden University, USA

ABSTRACT

The purpose of this chapter is to provide information on immersive virtual interventions for children with behavioral problems. The closing of all schools in March 2020 due to a global pandemic exposed children with negative attributed childhood experiences to more trauma. The mental health services provided by their schools stopped. Although the international community gained insight into how schools were unprepared to educate students during a pandemic, schools were also unable to deliver mental health services. This chapter reviews research on a new generation of tools using XR in learning environments. The goal is to examine educational tools that are used to help trauma (violence, poverty, drugs, abuse) in people, specifically children. This chapter will seek to discuss augmented environments in student learning that may promote self-reflection, mindfulness, and meditation.

INTRODUCTION

This chapter's general perspective will be to define the causes of childhood trauma and identify the augmented reality (AR) technologies that can help these people. The objectives of this chapter are (a) to understand the history of these technologies; (b) to describe what technologies are being used now; (c) to define what future technologies are discoverable, and (d) evaluate if they will work. This chapter will describe AR applications that will reduce stress and anxiety and create mindfulness in children and adolescents with behavior disorders.

DOI: 10.4018/978-1-7998-4222-4.ch012

BACKGROUND

Adverse childhood experiences (ACE) can have lasting, adverse effects on health, wellbeing, and opportunity. According to Merrick et al. (2019), these indicators include emotional, physical, or sexual abuse, neglect, witnessing violence, parents addiction to alcohol or other substances, family members' mental illness, divorce, jailed family member, involvement with the foster care system, living in an unsafe neighborhood, bullying, experiencing racism, and poverty. Merrick et al. (2019) found these experiences can create health problems, change brain development, and affect learning. Children growing up with toxic trauma stress may have difficulty forming healthy relationships, have unstable work histories as adults, and struggle throughout their lives. The effects of ongoing traumas and the impact of poverty result from limited educational and economic opportunities. Merrick et.al. (2019) stated these children are at a greater risk for high school noncompletion, unemployment, and poverty.

COVID 19 has caused social isolation from school and society. The disease disrupted the economy as many businesses shut down and increased the number of jobless households. These traumatic times can trigger existing mental illnesses or cause new psychological symptoms (Fegert et al., 2020). Many students receive their mental health services from the schools. Ali et al. (2019) used a study from the National Survey on Drug Use and Health and found that 13.2% or three million adolescents received mental health services from the school setting. Ali et al. found many of these children are on public assistance from low-income households and a minority group (2019). Lux and Escobar (2019) examined the increasing numbers of mental health disorders because of natural disasters (earthquakes, tsunamis, hurricanes) and COVID19.

This chapter describes the need to provide students lessons in mental health, wellbeing, self-management, relationship skills, and social awareness. This chapter will discuss the tools available to assist adolescents with trauma caused by attributed childhood experiences. The chapter will be organized into types or tools using AR, MR, VR, or XR in an immersive environment.

DESIGN AND IMPLEMENTATION

Although there is still not enough evidence to fully understand how the curriculum will integrate with AR and VR programs or what will be needed in the adoption process (Meredith et al., 2018). Tzima et al., (2019) surveyed teachers asking if they had heard or read about augmented reality. Fifty percent responded with yes, and 50% answered no to the question. Data from Tzima et al.'s (2019) research indicate the learning process, motivation, and effectiveness of teaching increases when augmented reality is applied in education. In contrast, 100% of the teachers responded, they have never used augmented reality applications in teaching (Tzima et al., 2019).

From early childhood to the universities, all levels of education have researched AR and VR for educational purposes. AR and VR are being explored by Stanford Virtual Human Interaction Lab and Virtual Reality Lab, Oxford Virtual Reality Lab for mental health, Virtual Embodiment Lab, MIT Play labs, and Harvard Innovation Lab. AR and VR have the possibility of becoming the norm education (2019). In search of applications that would meet this chapter's requirements as the potential to support students with mental health issues, I found a lack of information in educational technology specific to this study that would benefit children and adolescents with trauma-induced behavioral disorders. Furthermore, the literature search confused the specific technical terms used to describe immersive educational environments. A review of the literature resulted in clarification of the technical terms presented in this chapter.

Commonly confused words between technology terms provide needed conceptual clarity for researchers and educators. Girvan (2018) explains that educational literature complicates the varied terms used to identify and describe the technology. Furthermore, Girvan makes a point that "terms operating as buzzwords or fuzzwords" limit these technologies' development, thus limiting the impact on education (2018, p.1089). The plethora of terms is not limited to the virtual world, virtual environment, and immersive technologies such as immersive virtual world, immersive world, immersive online environment, 3D virtual learning environment, and virtual learning environment. Girvan argues that virtual worlds are designed to provide supported teacher elements. However, educational virtual worlds can be used for other purposes by its inhabitants, an example is Second Life.

What leads to the notion of immersion is a sense of presence. Immersion is a product of the purpose of reality. Immersive environments using AR, VR are not a virtual world with avatars (Girvan, 2018). A comparison of terms related to this study provides clarity. Southgate (2018) describes immersive virtual reality as immersive technologies that immerse users in an environment that uses augmented reality AR to put objects in a real environment. Mixed reality adds virtual objects that users interact within the natural environment. Southgate (2018) agrees there is no accepted definition of immersive reality. Southgate (2018) found that the technologies create a sense of presence and a feeling that what is happening in the virtual space seems real. This study is critical because AR can elicit deep emotional and physiological responses beyond everyday experience. Southgate points out different types of AR influence the developmental stages of child growth (2018).

Arguably most important, students can understand modern problems that would be difficult to conceptualize otherwise using regular text. In effect, AR can encourage empathy in students in the application called InCell2, as they can perceive how a virus takes over healthy cells. The year is 2134 and a robot named, Your Highness explains what you need to do to beat the virus. There are games in the application (arcade games) that allow the students to try to outrun the virus and have fun. Learning facts and scientific vocabulary can be possible either with a virtual reality headset or switching the App to VR and holding the IPad or phone in your hands. This App helped my students understand how the coronavirus takes over healthy cells.

These are a few of the applications that introduced into an academic subject to let students create a positive outcome while learning. I used the AR apps below with Google Cardboard to teach science.

- **InMind** is a short scientific adventure that allows the player to enter the brain searching for the neurons that cause mental disorder. According to the Russian creator, this immersive experience enters into the human mind's microworld.
- **InMind VR2** InMind VR2 is a scientific journey with John. John is becoming an adult. Once inside the human brain's chemistry that creates emotions, the player will help John shape his future by triggering emotions and critical moments of his life.
- **InCell VR** InCell is a racing VR game that takes you into a human cell's micro world. The player can stop a virus from advancing.
- **Edgenuity**. More than 20,000 schools use Edgenuity in twenty of the largest school districts in the United States (Coyle, 2020). Edgenuity did not offer social skills and social-emotional courses at that time. The social skills classes were taught face-to-face using the web resource's social skills curriculum.

Mikropoulos and Natsis (2011) found that AR supports constructive social theory through first-person experiences because the user can manipulate the size of objects into the microcosm or macrocosm space and has the potential to act as an empathy machine. Google Cardboard was the entry-level of AR and came after desktop VR. Oculus Rift, a wearable headgear, became available in the year, 2016. Southgate's study found that millions of school-age children use Google Expeditions and PlayStation VR (2018). Although, AR in schools is not a substitute for hands-on experiences (2018).

SOLUTIONS AND RECOMMENDATIONS

In researching potential AR apps that support mental health for children who have experienced trauma, I identified multiple settings where AR was used to support children who are undergoing trauma or have experienced trauma in the past. These apps are a category titled mental health elearning applications. Through personal research in social-emotional learning and the COVID19, I found Elsevier, which provides a page on mental health resources on wellness.

UNVR is the United Nations Virtual Reality platform. The power of immersive storytelling inspires viewers. The 360 and VR films provide students with a realistic view of people's lives in challenging global crisis. The movies support empathy, action, and positive social change. An example of one film is Clouds Over Sidra (Milk et al., 2015). Clouds Over Sidra (2015) was filmed in December 2014 in the Zaatari Refugee Camp in Jordan. Sidra is a young girl who lived in the Camp, made up of 130,000 Syrian refugees. Fifty percent of the population are children. This film helped my students learn about resilience in the social skills class.

The VR Film Platforms are specifically designed for immersive purposes. UNVR is a platform that gives an in-depth understanding of our global world and the unique challenges of other countries, including our own. During the COVID19, many of my classes featured contrasting films and thought-provoking discussions that supported empathy and compassion, built awareness of self and others, and positive collaborations on problem-solving. UNVR uses the power of immersive storytelling to help others create positive social change.

WITHIN is another immersive storytelling platform that creates, acquires, and distributes AR, VR experiences across the web using mobile devices and headsets. The films include documentaries, animation, music, and horror films. An example for this study is BreathePeace World. A baby panda bear, Aya, meditates in a magical forest world while snow falls all around. Breathe Peace has taught several students how to calm their anger and aggression. It is more effective than "stop and think" and "count to ten." Within can be found on the web and is an IOS App.

WITHIN was created by Chris Milk in 2014. Milk wanted to activate the minds and hearts of people through immersive experiences. There are workout products on this platform, augmented reality iOS apps for children, and stories and documentaries. Within supports major headsets, smartphones, oculus, and PlayStation for virtual and augmented reality learning, fitness, and entertainment. You can view the web with no headset, use a mobile headset like google cardboard, or go high-tech with Oculus Rift, Windows MR, HTC, or PlayStation VR. The films feature animation, music, documentary, experimental, and horror. Sanctuaries of silence, which features an ecologist in the Olympic national park, is one of my favorites. Its panoramic views with sounds of nature calm students, especially after a long week or two of off-campus learning due to a shutdown from contact with the COVID.

Google Cardboard was the entry-level of IVR. Google Daydream views a step-up from the original cardboard, sold at Walmart with higher-priced Oculus, Lenova, and HTC VR headgear. In 2014, I was the recipient of 20 free Google cardboard VR for my classroom. Google Expeditions is a VR and AR app on IOS and Android. A classroom kit can be purchased to view over 200 sites around the world. Google Expeditions is a powerful tool that allows children to think about their potential in the global world. Google Arts and History explore AR with objects like a sea star you can place on your desk to have a closer look or ancient creatures set in your living room.

In Google Arts and History, you can tour 200 art museums in VR or understand what machine learning is; take part in a poem using artificial intelligence and human collaboration in one of many Google Arts and History lab experiments. The following Apps use VR headsets or a version of the Google cardboard. Apps and films are examples of technologies that meet the notions of mental health, wellbeing, and emotions like empathy and compassion.

Starlight Virtual Reality, a technology program created in 2018, delivered 1,300 Starlight virtual reality headsets to hospitals for over 18,000 children at 300 hospitals. The VR headsets help distract children undergoing complicated procedures or who have serious illnesses. Starlight virtual reality foundation impacts giving hospitalized children playtime: structured and non-structured games, and immersive outdoor environments like fishing. Entertainments impact this program by making education fun in age-appropriate learning during a child's hospitalization. One child patient said, "I like that I can be in the ocean without having to be there!"

AR technology normalizes the hospital stay from scary to safe and fun. The technology headgear is used to prescribe medications for anxiety and pain for transfusions, wound cleaning, and medical care for broken wounds for procedural support. The Starlight VR headgear impacts pain management to reduce pain through distraction and offer children alternative virtual reality physical therapy that may be impossible in the real setting. Starlight's goal is to equip every pediatric ward and children's hospital with starlight technologies. Starlight web site also has resources during the COVID 19 for families and schooling

In an educational setting, AR allows students to learn in new ways. The application InMind and In-Mind2 are designed to help students develop an understanding of feelings and understand mental health by examining the brain's inside, which is not easily accomplished by reading a textbook. A critical benefit of adding extended reality to the educational mix is that it captures the student's attention. I could teach middle school students about the solar system or show high school students how epidemiologists and biologists work together to discover new ways to treat viruses.

Southgate (2018) stated AR manufacturers issue safety guidelines with age limits, but there is little known about the effects of long-term usage of IVR. More critical is the children's physical, cognitive, emotional, and social/moral development stages when considering introducing AR in the educational setting. The immersive virtual environments can feel so real. The question that arises is when does a child move from concrete thinking to abstract thinking? Although markers indicate average age development in different domains, there is evidence that children believe in fairies and fantasy. Exposure to AR is a concern at a psychological level for children who cannot distinguish fantasy from reality (Southgate, 2018). Also, manufacturers of the devices collect biometric data and impede the privacy rights of students.

Checkpointorg.com (2020) emphasizes the psychological benefits of video games. Mental health professionals and game industry professionals created CheckPoint to help people with mental health problems. The researchers for this website are dedicated to using games to treat mental health (2020).

Checkpoint.org provides gamers with a gaming community, digital mental health resources, mindful breathing exercises, a Checkpoint Coping Companion, and positive gaming resources.

The games listed for mental health are rated for relaxation, story, immersion and escapism, character relatedness, and challenge. An example, Hollow Knight is rated for connectivity to depression and wellbeing. The game can be found in Google Play and is rated for its immersion in relaxing music and atmosphere. The research in games that treat anxiety in adolescents is limited but findings suggest that games such as MindLight can reduce anxiety levels in adolescents (Barnes, S., & Prescott, J., 2018). Barnes and Prescott (2018) studied the use of CheckPointorg.com to further the research and gamification effects in adolescents.

Luc (2017) on the Checkpoint website talked about the game Zelda: Breath of the Wild, which has wellbeing scores in checkpointorg.com for relaxation and challenges 60%, story 100%, and 75% for impressiveness, escapism, and relatedness.

The day to day experiences of playing video games to process emotions. Games can calm us, as much as they do to frustrate us and make us cry. They can be meditative, and soothing. Recently, I've seen a lot of people experiencing this with Breath of the Wild. It's a combination of ambient noise and the breathtaking landscape. What makes a game meditative, for the most part, is our connection to it. How we, as an individual, feel when we play.

FUTURE TRENDS

Lux and Escobar (2018) reported mental health disorders are an urgent worldwide concern. The world health organization predicted that these disorders in children and adolescents would surpass HIV by 2030. Mental disorders among children aged 5 through 14 were third among the causes of disease in 2000 and 2nd in 2015 (2018). According to Lux and Escobar (2018), eLearning is a promising and necessary intervention to address the growing epidemic of mental health issues worldwide.

Mental Health eLearning provides screening, intervention, and treatment to improve health care with apps, email, and internet monitoring systems. Oxford University developed True Colors for children with bipolar disorder. True Color is an example of an MH (mental health) ELearning App for self-management. The App monitors symptoms and plans activities based upon input by the patient. Lux and Escobar's study included web-based treatment programs and cognitive behavioral therapy platforms that teach patients several skills. Their study estimated 15 million children and adolescents require an expert, but there are only 8300 child psychiatrists practicing in the United States. Research regarding the MH ELearning platform is a necessary intervention to address global education challenges regarding the millions of children with mental health problems (Lux & Escobar, 2018).

CONCLUSION

Much needs to be accomplished in education to help the millions of students with mental health concerns through the integration of mental health AR technologies. First, establish a multi-discipline approach with collaborative partnerships, including mental health professionals and educational systems. Then partner up with giant tech companies like UNITY. Education needs think tanks to develop solutions that will renovate and innovate the educational system to support the millions of children who have mental health problems. AR technologies have the potential to accomplish this.

REFERENCES

AC Experiences (ACEs). (2019). Retrieved from https://www.cdc.gov/violenceprevention/acestudy/index.html

Ali, M., West, K., Teic, J., Lynch, S., Mutter, R., & Dubenitz, J. (2019). Utilization of mental health services in educational settings by adolescents in the United States. *The Journal of School Health*, *89*(5), 393–401. doi:10.1111/josh.12753 PMID:30883761

Barnes, S., & Prescott, J. (2018). Empirical evidence for the outcomes of therapeutic video games for adolescents with anxiety disorders: Systematic review. *JMIR Serious Games*, *6*(1), e3. doi:10.2196/games.9530 PMID:29490893

Checkpointorg.com. (2020). *Analyzing Our heroes (and Villains): Video Game Psychology*. Retrieved from https://checkpointorg.com/character-analysis/

Coyle, A. (2020). *Edgenuity announces recognitions from tech and learning, CODiE, and EdTech Digest, and Tech Edvocate 2020 Award Programs*. PR Web Online Visibility from Vocus. Retrieved from https://www.prweb.com/pdfdownload/17363014.pdf

Fegert, J., Vitiello, B., Plener, P., & Clemens, V. (2020). Challenges and burden of the Coronavirus 2019 (COVID-19) pandemic for child and adolescent mental health: A narrative review to highlight clinical and research needs in the acute phase and the long return to normality. *Child and Adolescent Psychiatry and Mental Health*, *14*(1), 20. doi:10.118613034-020-00329-3 PMID:32419840

Girvan, C. (2018). What is a virtual world? Definition and classification. *Education Tech Research Dev*, *66*, 1087–1100. https://connect.iste.org/blogs/kae-novak/2018/05/04/virtual-connected-educator-for-week-of-may-2 doi:10.100711423-018-9577-y

Golberstein, E., Wen, H., & Miller, B. (2020). Coronavirus Disease 2019 (COVID-19) and Mental Health for Children and Adolescents. *JAMA Pediatrics*, *174*(9), 819. Advance online publication. doi:10.1001/jamapediatrics.2020.1456 PMID:32286618

Lloyd, L. (2017). *Getting Over It: finding stillness in chaos*. CheckPointorg.com. Retrieved from https://checkpointorg.com/getting-over-it-finding-stillness-in-chaos/

Lux, M. E., & Escobar, J. M. (2019). Where Technology Meets Psychology: Improving Global Mental Health. In Technology and Child Mental Health. IntechOpen. doi:10.5772/intechopen.88174

Meredith, P., Yeates, H., Greaves, A., Taylor, M., Slattery, M., Charters, M., & Hill, M. (2018). Preparing mental health professionals for new directions in mental health practice: Evaluating the sensible approaches e-learning training package. *International Journal of Mental Health Nursing*, *27*(1), 106–115. doi:10.1111/inm.12299 PMID:28042908

Merrick, M. T., Ford, D., Ports, K. A., Guinn, A. S., Chen, J., Klevens, J., Metzler, M., Jones, C. M., Simon, T. R., Daniel, V. M., Ottley, P., & Mercy, J. A. (2019). Vital Signs: Estimated Proportion of Adult Health Problems Attributable to Adverse Childhood Experiences and Implications for Prevention — 25 States, 2015–2017. *MMWR. Morbidity and Mortality Weekly Report*, *68*(44), 999–1005. doi:10.15585/mmwr.mm6844e1 PMID:31697656

Mikropoulos, T. A., & Natsis, A. (2011). Educational virtual environments: A ten-year review of empirical research (1999–2009). *Computers & Education*, *56*(3), 769–780. doi:10.1016/j.compedu.2010.10.020

Milk, C., & Arora, G. (Writer, Producer). Pousman. B., Arora, G. (Director). (2015). *Clouds over sidra* [Film]. WithIn. Retrieved from https://www.with.in/watch/clouds-over-sidra/

Southgate, E. (2018). *Immersive virtual reality, children and school education: A literature review for teachers* (DICE Report Series Number 6). Newcastle: DICE Research. Retrieved from http://dice.newcastle.edu.au/DRS_6_2018.pdf

Tzima, S., Styliaras, G., & Bassounas, A. (2019). Augmented reality applications in education: Teachers point of view. *Edu. Sci.*, *9*(99), 1–18. doi:10.3390/educsci9020099

ADDITIONAL READING

Gackenbach, J., & Bown, J. (2017). *Boundaries of Self and reality Online: Implications of Digitally Constructed Realities*. Academic Press.

Tzima, S., Styliaras, G., & Bassounas, A. (2019). Augmented reality applications in education teachers' point of view. *Educ. Sci.*, *9*(99). https://www.starlight.org/stories/covid-19-resources-for-families-and-schooling/

Van Krevelen, D., & Poelman, R. (2010). A survey of augmented reality technologies, applications, and limitations. *The International Journal of Virtual Reality: a Multimedia Publication for Professionals*, *9*(2), 1–20. doi:10.20870/IJVR.2010.9.2.2767

Won, A., Bailey, J., Bailenson, J., Tataru, C., Yoon, I. A., & Golianu, B. (2017). Immersive Virtual Reality for Pediatric Pain. *Children (Basel, Switzerland)*, *4*(7), 52. doi:10.3390/children4070052 PMID:28644422

Chapter 13
Mobile Tablet Integration Using Augmented Reality

Regina Malz
Independent Researcher, USA

ABSTRACT

The purpose of this chapter is to help educators successfully integrate mobile tablets in their classrooms. Research has shown that mobile tablet integration can increase learning of students. Integrating advanced technologies in classrooms will support learners and advance all students' learning experiences in ways that cannot be done without mobile tablets. This chapter provides educators with transformative tools to improve their in-person lessons and their lessons through augmented reality. This chapter also includes a set of resources educators can use to obtain augmented reality apps that will enhance their lessons, a list of ways to improve their curriculum, and how to engage students via virtual reality when home learning is necessary.

INTRODUCTION

There has been a rapid integration of new technologies into U.S. classrooms. According to Education Market Research, there are approximately 13.2 million computing devices in K-12 U.S. schools (Perez-Sanagustin et al., 2017). This 13.2 million includes 4.7 million desktop computers, 3.9 million laptop computers, and 2.3 million mobile tablets. Project Tomorrow's report stated that one-third of U.S. public school students used mobile devices for schoolwork in 2014 (Nagel, 2016). Mobile tablet purchases by schools increased by 8.6% during the 2014-2015 school year (Perez-Sanagustin et al., 2017). According to a study by Futuresource Consulting Ltd, half of all U.S. public school students during the 2015-2016 school year had the opportunity to work one-on-one with mobile devices during the day (Bonninger, et al., 2017).

Additionally, there is an increasing number of students who have special needs. During the 1990-1991 school year, 4.7 million students received special education services. In other words, 11% of all public-school students between the ages of three to 21 years old (National Center for Education Statistics, 2015). During the 2012-2013 school year, 6.4 million students received special education services, which

DOI: 10.4018/978-1-7998-4222-4.ch013

amounted to about 13% of all public-school students between the ages of three to 21 years old (National Center for Education Statistics, 2015).

The productive integration of new technologies depends on understanding multiple issues of reform, such as aspects of teacher professional development and the real-world practical act of using the technology in the classrooms to support diverse learners. The purpose of this chapter is to provide educators with the tools necessary to implement mobile tablets successfully. The purpose of this chapter is to identify how to use mobile tablets and augmented reality (AR) apps to enhance lessons in ways that would not be possible without mobile tablets. This chapter also includes a list of augmented AR apps that can be used to supplement student learning objectives.

BACKGROUND

Educational technology is defined as a component used to help teach students in a way that could not be done without that specific technology. Technology integration is defined as the act of incorporating technology into the classroom to help the students learn in a way that could not be done without that technology (Aziz et al., 2010). The focus of this chapter is the integration of AR apps with mobile devices. Students who are learning from home can benefit from lessons on mobile tablets because it allows them to participate in hands-on lessons that engage all learning styles.

Studies by Eichenlaub et al. (2011), McKenna et al. (2015), Musti-Rao et al. (2015), and Lowman and Dressler (2016) showed that mobile tablets helped students to reach achievement levels that they were unable to achieve without the mobile tablets. Studies have shown that mobile tablet apps could support learning (Carr, 2012; Chen, 2013; Eichenlaub et al., 2011; Lowman & Dressler, 2016; Riley, 2013; Shih-Hwa & Gwo-Guang, 2013).

Soykan and Ozdamli (2016) conducted a quantitative study, which showed that teachers' integrating mobile learning apps increased test scores. During the study, mobile tablets were integrated for 10 weeks. Teachers created lessons that were carried out digitally and students participated in projects using mobile tablets. The study showed an increase in the students' success using mobile tablets.

Mobile tablets, such as the iPad, have a touch-screen interface that allows students who lack hand-eye coordination to practice their letters independently (Flewitt et al., 2014). The research showed that students could use the iPads to communicate ideas in a variety of ways that were not possible without the iPads. For example, a student who cannot generate words and write them on a piece of paper to create a story could use the iPad to draw, take pictures, and record verbal descriptions to create a story (Flewitt et al., 2014, p. 110).

In the special education classroom, the number one goal is always to lessen the achievement gap between students without disabilities and those with disabilities (U.S. Department of Education, 2004). Integrating new technologies has the potential to close that gap for special education students if teachers can integrate these new technologies to their potential (Spaulding, 2014). Students with special needs require a different type of teaching and learning to reach their potential. When these students' learning needs cannot be met in a regular education classroom, they need modifications to their environment and teaching to succeed. A study by Malz (2019) found that understanding that how teachers are integrating mobile tablets with AR apps can support the learning of students with disabilities. This real-world perspective may provide new understandings of practical implications of using new technologies to support special needs learners.

Herbert (2010) found that if each student has their iPad, the students can work on various subjects at the same time. Kelly (2011) found that iPad apps allow students to collaborate with other students easily and document their progress. There was a significant focus on children with special needs and how the iPad can document, both through work samples and video, the students' progress to be shared with parents.

Studies have shown that mobile tablets using AR apps can support student learning across grade levels and student abilities. However, the integration of these new technologies is difficult and complex and requires careful, insightful decisions about how these technologies change the learning environment, the professional development of the teachers, and the roles of the teachers and students in the classroom.

DESIGN AND IMPLEMENTATION

Mobile tables using AR apps can be integrated into multiple educational settings. Mobile tablets come in all different types and brands of mobile tablets. It is recommended that students use the same type as the teacher because not all AR Apps are available on all mobile tablets, and the interfaces can look differently. The instructional design should be created with mobile tablets in mind rather than taking the current unit or lesson plans and including the mobile tablet.

Hesser and Schwartz (2013) explored the results of a qualitative study when iPads were integrated into a science laboratory for Chemistry Honors at the University of New Haven. The study took place during the fall of 2012, and 20 students were studied. Apps were chosen and loaded to the iPads before distribution. The apps were chosen based on which ones could be best used in the science lab to eliminate the need for paper (p. 6). There were fast and cheap ways to make the iPads safer to use in an environment with exposed liquids. The students could place the iPads into a zip-lock plastic bag (p. 6). The iPads can still be used while in the bags, and the bags protected the iPads from the liquid.

Reese et al., (2016) examined music teachers' experiences integrating mobile tablets into their curriculum. Most teachers reported feeling tension while they were trying to integrate into their curriculum. Some of this tension caused them to change their current practices to accommodate meaningful mobile tablet integration. Others found it too difficult to adopt and ended up disregarding the mobile tablets (p. 102). Teachers explained that tensions were caused by inabilities to get an App to do what they were wanted it to do, and/or when Apps would crash and require re-installation, and/or when differences in student needs required different use of the mobile tablets.

In a study by Kaur et al. (2017) teachers' instructional designs were entirely forfeited when one iPad was distributed to each child in the classroom. Teachers needed to use the mathematics apps available to teach lessons, and if students had difficulty understand the work, the teachers used the step-by-step instructions in the app. Teachers noted that the iPads were appropriate for all different types of learners and the headphone option was great for students who were easily distracted and/or were auditory learners. Students were not required to use the same apps but worked on the same skills using various apps.

This was very different from a study by Anderson et al. (2017), where teachers reported that although the apps were useful, they could not use them for a whole lesson. The teachers used the apps for a few days. One way was to represent information, such as showing a picture, another was for repetition, and the third was to assess students' progress (Anderson et al., 2017). The teachers also found that writing lesson plans to integrate the iPads were more complicated and time-consuming than if they had written a lesson without them. The study also showed that teachers engaged in two teaching strategies when integrating the iPads: planning and in-the-moment decisions, which would occur while teachers observed student interactions with the apps. Some teachers reported that they could not find apps that successfully supplemented the lesson, and other teachers reported using as many as 30 apps during one lesson (Anderson et al., 2017).

There are several definitive studies related to the integration of mobile tablets in the classroom. Liu et al. (2016) conducted a study to see how 342 teachers chose to use mobile tablets in their classrooms. Their school district gave these teachers iPads. The study examined teachers' comfort levels and perceptions during the time they integrated and how they used iPads to support their instruction. The district required that all teachers take workshops conducted by instructional technology staff. They participated in this professional development, both in-person and on-line. All teachers were required to demonstrate full competency using the iPad before using it in their classrooms. Competency was defined by their ability to ace a proficiency plan, which involved simple tasks, such as turning it on/off, adding apps, utilizing email, and so forth.

However, they also had to attend three different one-hour training on what to do with it in the classroom, 20 free iPad apps that teachers should use, and 15 great iPad tips for teachers. Additionally, the district also provided more professional development throughout the year the iPads were integrated (Liu et al., 2016). The study showed that novice teachers were significantly more comfortable implementing than veteran teachers, but that veteran teachers' comfort level increased as the year went on. Novice teachers also showed a higher level of excitement to implement than veteran teachers, but all teachers had a drop of excitement towards the middle of the school year. The enthusiasm was reported as increased by the end of the year. More novice teachers than veteran teachers agreed with the statement that mobile technology is vital in their classroom.

More novice teachers than veteran teachers also decided that the iPad changed the way they teach (Liu et al., 2016). Teachers also noted logistical challenges when it came to finding sufficient time for each student to use the iPad because the iPads had to be shared. They also found there was not sufficient time to integrate. In this study, teachers used the iPads for group work, such as having the students write their answers on the iPad and pass it rather than using a piece of paper. Classroom management apps, such as ClassDojo, was used to record student behaviors and performances.

Issues, Controversies, Problems

A major issue identified in the research is the need for effective professional development programs. This includes the integration of AR apps into a redesigned curriculum that matches the immersive learning processes requiring active student engagement and the focus on independent student responses using the AR apps. Hesser and Schwartz (2013) noted that if teachers want to implement iPads into their science labs, they need to put forth a lot of effort before starting the course. This is because apps need to be researched, evaluated, and tested to determine the best for the course. Additionally, time needs to be considered to teach students how to use iPad apps if they are unfamiliar. The study showed that although motivated to use the iPads, students still needed instruction on how to use the apps selected. Several students also reported that they had difficulty writing on the tablet with the stylus due to the amount of time they needed to zoom in and out to complete tasks (Hesser & Schwartz, 2013).

Instructors reported issues for retrieving the files for grading and then delivering the files back. Recovering the Dropbox files meant having to open them in the app they came from, then deleting the current files from the Dropbox, and then uploading the graded project. It was concluded that over 120 pieces of paper per student were saved throughout one semester by switching to iPads. The iPad is less expensive than a laptop, there were more apps available, and it is easier to transport them throughout lessons because they are smaller (Hesser & Schwartz, 2013).

In another study, teachers attended an Apple workshop on using iPads in their classroom, but they chose to participate independently; the school did not mandate it (O'Malley, et al., 2013). Despite doing this, teachers remarked that the integration took a great deal of time. Additionally, this study showed that students benefited the most by using the iPads to reinforce skills they were already taught before using the iPad. For example, they participated in innovative ways to increase their mathematical skills and promote independence, but the iPads were not used to teach new skills (O'Malley et al., 2013).

Hesser and Schwartz (2013) and Eichenlaub et al. (2011) studied teachers' abilities to integrate mobile tablets without changing their instructional design. Both studies found that student learning was not changed if the tablets were integrated without instructional design changes. Therefore, the mobile tablets were ineffective if the new technology was integrated into an already functioning instructional design. Cuban (2001) pointed out that unless the technology is integrated successfully and instructional practices change to use this technology to its utmost potential, there is no true value to integrating the technology (p. 60).

In a study by Mourlam and Montgomery (2015), teachers reported that they allowed the apps on the iPads to dictate their instructional design. It was also noted that even after five months of integrating the iPads, many of the teachers were still using it as a glorified projector: to show videos, pictures, and simple documents. During a mid-year professional development session in which teachers were taught to reinvent ways to use the iPads, some teachers thought of drawing an idea instead of writing, recording audio instead of writing, and doing research.

Graybeal's (2013) study focused on teacher experiences with iPads and indirectly on their learning. Graybeal explored how mathematics teachers have been ill-prepared to implement the Common Core Standards in their classrooms. Graybeal discovered the need to help teachers become more knowledgeable about mathematical procedures and practices. An iPad App was created to help teachers learn the procedures and document their students' progress with the Common Core Standards. The study found that 17 of the 22 participants increased their understanding of the Common Core Standards. Understanding how teachers in an innovative private school teaching special needs learners integrate mobile devices may help other teachers develop effective practices for integrating mobile devices.

Lessons Learned

A mixed-methods study by Al-Husain and Hammo (2017) examined the results of a semester-long professional development training for technology to international teachers from developing nations. The course was designed based on Shulman's (1986) concepts regarding pedagogical content knowledge. Dalal et al. (2017) used Shulman's theoretical framework and its relation to teaching to design a professional development course that included pedagogical knowledge, technological knowledge, and content knowledge (p. 119). Their study showed that results from coursework during an entire semester improved international teachers' understanding of how to integrate technology. The study also showed that even when teachers know how to create student-centered lesson plans with technology integration, limited access to technology in the classroom influences what happens when the technology is integrated. Additionally, survey results showed that teaching abilities across all the domains showed an improvement (Dalal et al., 2017, p. 128).

In a study by Maich and Hall (2016) the teachers were asked to look at the iPadagogy Wheel, an extensive graphic that shows the five categories of Bloom's Cognitive Domain Categories, action verbs that describe them, and activities that come from those, and then the apps that can be used for those categories. It was described that participants were stunned at the ideas presented. The iPadagogy Wheel can come in handy because many teachers struggle with identifying apps. Not all apps are appropriate for all students, and it takes a long time to search through every app's effectiveness (Maich & Hall, 2016).

Hesser and Schwartz (2013) wrote that if teachers wanted to implement the iPads, they would need to spend a lot of time determining which apps would work for their course, they made the statement that teachers would look for iPad apps that could fit into their current instructional design. Apps needed to be researched, evaluated, and tested to determine which would be the best for the course. Additionally, the study showed how students used the iPads to replace ways they commonly used paper during science experiments. For example, UPAD was an app chosen to replace paper notebooks that were typically used in experiments. Therefore, the apps were used to supplement the lesson to eliminate the need to use paper. It seemed that during the process of choosing the apps, the teachers became experienced with the apps. However, time for teachers and students to learn the technology was required for this program to be successful. This would need to be considered when planning the curriculum because class time would be necessary to teach the students how to use the apps.

Teachers in a study by Flewitt et al. (2015) reported using iPads across various subjects and settings. Still, they explained that it took time to integrate successfully. Lessons needed to be well-planned with apps carefully selected that helped to increase student motivation and concentration. Some teachers noted that their students' self-image improved because they saw how successful they were completing the lessons using the iPad. There are a few tasks that students can use on a mobile tablet that cannot be completed without the mobile tablet. For example, the students could read websites and iBooks while commuting to and from school, whereas before they could not. One student, Bonita, used an app called iBrainstorm to organize all of her notes. She could scan in handouts, draw pictures, and type notes to save everything in one neat place on her iPad. Another student, Kris, used apps Mendeley, iAnnotate, and Instapaper to take notes on PDF files, save websites without advertisements, and include personal notes (p. 19). The third student, Ashley, liked using myPANTONE to create and retrieve colors for printing assignments. The last student, Sarah, stated that she could learn more information at a quicker pace while studying from the iPad (p. 19). All four of the students concluded that conducting long-term research projects, and it would be better to use a computer because of the larger screen and the option to switch between multiple windows at the same time (p. 20).

McKenna et al. (2015) conducted a college study with students from the Integration of Technology in Second Pedagogy program. The students kept recorded journals on their experiences throughout the integration process, and it was noted that most of their frustrations were built around technical problems. For example, internet bandwidth cannot accommodate all the iPads using the internet at the same time. Additionally, because the lessons were planned solely on the iPads, and when the iPads were not used, such as the internet being down or because another class was using some of the iPads, it meant instructors could not teach the lesson planned for the day. There were many reports on students showing their cooperating teachers how to use the iPad to enhance lessons in their classrooms or how they discovered a tool to use on the iPad that helped them in another class. From this standpoint, it can be concluded that iPads did increase student involvement and achievement. The studies also noted that although many resources provide instruction for implementing the iPads, it is important to understand which app will benefit each specific classroom.

SOLUTIONS AND RECOMMENDATIONS

Both studies by Hesser and Schwartz (2013) and Eichenlaub, et al. (2011) involved integrating the iPads without changing the instructional design. Both studies showed that the iPads enhanced learning, but the iPads were being used as glorified notebooks. The studies showed that the students improved learning due to having better organization skills, note-taking opportunities, and could learn better from the notes. To implement mobile devices effectively with AR apps, educators should create instructional designs that would not be possible without the use of mobile tablets. In other words, if educators can name a replacement technology that could be used as effectively as a tablet during the lesson, that instructional design is not meaningful for tablets.

The study by O'Malley et al. (2013) showed that there was an improvement in the focused skill area of mathematics due to iPad integration. It is implied that instructional design had to change to accommodate the intensive one-on-one use for which the students would be using the iPads. It is also implied because of the amount of professional development that was needed before and during iPad integration. However, it does not clearly state that teachers' instructional designs were changed nor does it state how the iPads were used in correlation to lessons. Through his research, Spaulding (2014) explains that teachers' perceptions are influenced by their experiences and these perceptions provide valuable information on the beliefs that the teachers hold (p. 2868).

The study by Cuban (2001) showed that computers were not easily integrated because teachers did not change their instructional designs. Teachers were not learning how to integrate computers and were simply just adding them to the classroom. The study by Judson (2006) showed teachers who were truly motivated to integrate technology into their classrooms and tried to change their instructional designs and teaching objectives to encompass the opportunities the iPad allows to enhance lessons. It appeared that teachers were using the principles of constructivism to change their classroom, but when Judson (2006) examined the results thoroughly it was determined that constructivism was not being used.

Mobile tablets are a valuable source to students and teachers in the classroom and through remote learning. Appendix A includes a brief description of AR apps arranged by subject area. This list is a quick guide for teachers or parents wanting to add AR apps. Additionally, the following table explains when, why, and how mobile tablets can be integrated into the classroom and at home. The table also includes which activities are available on-line and off-line regarding Internet connectivity.

FUTURE TRENDS

There is an emerging tread related to Augmentative Reality (AR). Parents and school administrators have been considering online learning due to the rising number of dangers involved with having students sitting in a brick and mortar classroom for long hours each day. School shootings, bullying, as well as the current pandemic, all add to these concerns. AR is a great alternative to in-person learning because it can accommodate every learning need. AR, when used in an immersive virtual learning environment, will increase the learning potential of students. The best AR curriculum involves students interacting physically while watching and hearing. Using a variety of Apps, teacher-made lesson plans and units, and video chat can help students reach their highest academic potential.

Table 1. Differences between mobile tablet integration in the classroom and mobile tablet AR experiences

	Mobile Tablet Classroom Integration	Mobile Tablet Home Integration Via AR
When	• During every lesson • Used to supplement skills taught prior • Used to teach a lesson • Used when work is completed to expand knowledge on other skills	• Used exclusively throughout the entire lesson
Why	• Research shows there is an increase in student motivation and achievement when mobile tablets are integrated	• Students have the greatest chance of participating in hands-on lessons that utilize all learning styles if home lessons occur through mobile tablets • Research shows there is an increase in student motivation and achievement when mobile tablets are integrated
How	• The mobile tablets are used during lessons to enable students to participate in activities that would not otherwise be possible; for example, Google's Science Journal App enables data recording tools for light, sound pressure, and motions	• Students are guided through lessons via the Apps and directions from the teachers via live Internet video streaming or from pre-recorded lessons and videos
Online	• The Internet is a requirement for some Apps and lessons, but some work can be loaded prior so that a live Internet connection is not required	• The Internet is required for live lessons, but teachers can preload videos and work for students who will be without the Internet
Offline	• Apps that do not require the Internet	• Apps that do not require the Internet, lessons pre-made through slide shows and videos

CONCLUSION

To increase the effectiveness of integrating new technologies into the classroom teachers need to be proficient at the use and capabilities of tablets. Being able to use a tablet at home is not the same as being able to effectively use it in the classroom. Teachers need to understand how a variety of different AR apps, as well as the different features of an iPad, can reach the learning needs of all students in the classroom while providing tactile, auditory, and visual learners with opportunities that are not possible without the tablets.

The research reviewed in this chapter showed that there are studies detailing student achievement and motivation when technology is integrated. There is also research to study their needs, concerns, and success in regards to mobile tablet integration. However, there is not significant research about teachers' experiences when mobile tablets are integrated. The high-quality research that was reviewed shed insight on the characteristics of successful integration of AR apps using mobile tablets and the less successful integration of these technologies into educational settings.

For future effective integration of AR apps, educators need to become proficient in the operating systems and create a concrete list of apps that help teach their students the skills needed for success. The Appendix A includes a list of apps that can enhance several different subjects, but if teachers are interested in including more apps in their teaching they can use free trials to evaluate apps. Then, they can publish brief notes on these apps in a shared file in their school so other teachers can access and review before purchasing or requesting a purchase order from their school.

REFERENCES

Anderson, S., Griffith, R., & Crawford, L. (2017). TPACK in special education: Preservice teacher decision making while integrating iPads into instruction. *Contemporary Issues in Technology & Teacher Education, 17*(1), 97–127.

Aziz, T., Khan, M. B., & Singh, R. (2010). Effects of information technology usage on student learning: An empirical study in the United States. *International Journal of Management, 27*(2), 205.

Boninger, F., Molnar, A., & Murray, K. (2017). *Asleep at the Switch: Schoolhouse Commercialism, Student Privacy, and the Failure of Policymaking. The Nineteenth Annual Report on Schoolhouse Commercializing Trends, 2017*. National Education Policy Center.

Carr, J. M. (2012). Does math achievement "h'APP'en" when iPads and game-based learning are incorporated into fifth-grade mathematics instruction? *Journal of Information Technology Education, 11*, 269–286. doi:10.28945/1725

Chen, L. L. (2013). iPad integration strategies for teaching and learning. In T. Bastiaens & G. Marks (Eds.), *Proceedings of E-Learn: World Conference on E-Learning in Corporate, Government, Healthcare, and Higher Education 2013* (pp. 631-634). Chesapeake, VA: Association for the Advancement of Computing in Education (AACE). http://www.editlib.org.ezp.waldenulibrary.org/p/114908/

Cuban, L. (2001). *Oversold and Underused: Computers in the Classroom*. Harvard University Press. http://www.urosario.edu.co/CGTIC/Documentos/Cuban_article_oversold.pdf

Dalal, M., Archambault, L., & Shelton, C. (2017). Professional development for international teachers: Examining TPACK and technology integration decision making. *Journal of Research on Technology in Education, 49*(3-4), 117–133. doi:10.1080/15391523.2017.1314780

Eichenlaub, N., Gabel, L., Jakubek, D., & McCarthy, G. (2011). Project iPad investigation tablet integration in learning and libraries at Ryerson University. *Computers in Libraries*, 17–21. www.infotoday.com/cilmag/

Flewitt, R., Messer, D., & Kucirkova, N. (2015). New directions for early literacy in a digital age: The iPad. *Journal of Early Childhood Literacy, 15*(3), 289–310. doi:10.1177/1468798414533560

Graybeal, C. (2013). Learning to look for the standards for mathematical practice. *SRATE Journal, 22*(2), 8-13. http://apbrwww5.apsu.edu/SRATE/

Hesser, T. L., & Schwartz, P. M. (2013). iPads in the science laboratory: Experience in designing and implementing a paperless chemistry laboratory course. *Journal of STEM Education: Innovations and Research, 14*(2), 5–9. www.jstem.org

Kaur, D., Koval, A., & Chaney, H. (2017). Potential of Using iPad as a Supplement to Teach Math to Students with Learning Disabilities. *International Journal of Research in Education and Science, 3*(1), 114–121.

Kelly, A. (2011). Involve, prepare, apply, and develop: iPads in the classroom. *Technology and Learning*. Retrieved from: http://www.techlearning.com/article/Involve-Prepare-Apply-and-Develop-iPads-in-the-Classroom/47763

Liu, M., Navarrete, C. C., Scordino, R., Kang, J., Ko, Y., & Lim, M. (2016). Examining teachers' use of iPads: Comfort level, perception, and use. *Journal of Research on Technology in Education*, *48*(3), 159–180. doi:10.1080/15391523.2016.1175853

Lowman, J. J., & Dressler, E. V. (2016). Effects of explicit vocabulary videos delivered through iPods on students with language impairments. *Journal of Special Education Technology*, *31*(4), 195–206. doi:10.1177/0162643416673914

Maich, K., & Hall, C. (2016). Implementing iPads in the inclusive classroom setting. *Intervention in School and Clinic*, *51*(3), 145–150. doi:10.1177/1053451215585793

Malz, R. (2020). *Special Education Teachers' Experiences Integrating Mobile Devices in their Classroom* [Doctoral dissertation, Walden University]. Scholarworks.waldenu.edu

McKenna, K., Schulz, L., Otieno, C., Wang, X., & Williams, M. (2015). Multiple perspective account of iPad integration. In D. Slykhuis & G. Marks (Eds.), *Proceedings of Society for Information Technology and Teacher Education International Conference 2015* (pp. 1672-1678). Chesapeake, VA: Association for the Advancement of Computing in Education (AACE). http://www.editlib.org.ezp.waldenulibrary.org/p/150223/

Mourlam, D. J., & Montgomery, S. E. (2015). iPads and teacher education: Exploring a 1: 1 initiative in a professional development school partnership. *Journal of Digital Learning in Teacher Education*, *31*(3), 107–116. doi:10.1080/21532974.2015.1021981

Musti-Rao, S., Cartledge, G., Bennett, J. G., & Council, M. (2015). Literacy instruction using technology with primary-age culturally and linguistically diverse learners. *Intervention in School and Clinic*, *50*(4), 195–202. doi:10.1177/1053451214546404

Nagel, D. (2016). How teachers leverage mobile technology. *T.H.E. Journal*, *43*(6), 34.

National Center for Education Statistics. (2015). *Children and youth with disabilities*. Retrieved from: https://nces.ed.gov/programs/coe/indicator_cgg.asp

O'Malley, P., Jenkins, S., Wesley, B., Donehower, C., Rabuck, D., & Lewis, M. (2013). *Effectiveness of using iPads to build math fluency*. Kennedy Krieger Institute. www.kennedyrieger.org

Pérez-Sanagustín, M., Nussbaum, M., Hilliger, I., Alario-Hoyos, C., Heller, R. S., Twining, P., & Tsai, C. C. (2017). Research on ICT in K-12 schools e A review of experimental and survey-based studies in computers & education 2011 to 2015. *Computers & Education*, *104*, A1–A15. doi:10.1016/j.compedu.2016.09.006

Reese, J. (2016). Virtual mentoring of preservice teachers: Mentors' perceptions. *Journal of Music Teacher Education*, *25*(3), 39–52. doi:10.1177/1057083715577793

Riley, P. (2013). *Teaching, learning and living with iPads*. National Association for Music Education., doi:10.1177/0027432113489152

Shih-Hwa, L., & Gwo-Guang, L. (2013). iPad infuse creativity in solid geometry teaching. *The Turkish Online Journal of Educational Technology*, *12*(2), 177–192. www.tojet.net

Shulman, L. S. (1986). Those who understand: Knowledge growth in teaching. \. *Educational Researcher*, *15*(2), 4–14. doi:10.3102/0013189X015002004

Soykan, E., & Ozdamli, F. (2016). The Impact of M-Learning Activities on the IT Success and M-Learning Capabilities of the Special Education Teacher Candidates. *World Journal on Educational Technology: Current Issues*, *8*(3), 267–276. doi:10.18844/wjet.v8i3.1019

Spaulding, M. (2014). In-service teachers' perceptions toward iPad integration. In M. Searson & M. Ochoa (Eds.), *Proceedings of Society for Information Technology & Teacher Education International Conference 2014* (pp. 2974-2982). Association for the Advancement of Computing in Education (AACE). http://www.editlib.org.ezp.waldenulibrary.org/p/131262/

U.S. Department of Education. (2004). *Elementary and Secondary Education Act*. Retrieved from: https://www.ed.gov/esea

KEY TERMS AND DEFINITIONS

App: Abbreviation for the word application, which is downloadable from a mobile device.

Educational Technology: Is defined as a component used to help teach students in a way that could not be done without that specific technology. The educational technology being referred to in this report is the mobile tablet, such as the Apple iPad or Android-based systems.

Professional Development: Is defined as the educational opportunities provided to teachers in order to assist them in technology education.

Special Education: Is defined as special education-specific schools in which every student has developmental disabilities and all teachers are certified special education teachers.

Technology Integration: Is defined as the act of incorporating technology into the classroom to help the students learn in a way that could not be done without that technology.

APPENDIX A: AR APPS FOR MOBILE TABLETS

AR Science Lessons

Curiscope is available on iOS and Android. The App is free, but requires the use of a t-shirt and posters that must be purchased. Students use the App to point at a t-shirt, called a Virtuali-Tee, which is meant to be worn by the student, with a series of different boxes and symbols on it. Students point the mobile tablet at the t-shirt to learn about different organs and bodily functions. Students use the App to point to one of the posters depicting a planet. There are posters for Earth, the moon, Mars, and the Solar System. The App gives information about space through the mobile tablet.

Merge Explorer is available on iOs and Android. There is a free trial for the App, but the Merge Cube must be purchased. If students are using a cellular phone instead of a mobile tablet the Object Viewer can also be purchased. The focus of these K-8 STEM lessons are mathematics, engineering, art, physical sciences, Earth and space science, and life sciences. Students have the opportunity to view objects in 3D through the use of the Merge Cube. For example, they can turn on the App to the solar system and hold the Merge Cube on the other side of it. The Solar System would appear in 3D and as they turn the Merge Cube, the planets turn with it. Another example would be how the students can dissect an animal using the mobile tablet and the Merge Cube. There are activity plans that come with each lesson that include student objectives, questions for students to answer as they are guided through the lesson, and an assessment at the end to see if they retained the information.

The UPad is available on iOs. It must be purchased. This App can be used for all subjects but is especially great for recording information during science lessons. Students can write notes during lectures or lessons. They can change the color of their writing, highlight or circle important information, and make it larger for easier reading. Pictures can be added and graphs, maps, or anything from the Internet can be clipped and added into the notes at any time. The notes can be sent to the teacher for review. Students also have the opportunity to type if they do not want to write and can keep multiple applications open at the same time.

The Google Science Journal is available on iOs and Android phones. It is free to download. This is a unique recording tool that students can use to increase participation in teacher-made lessons recording light, sound, pressure, and motion. The cell phones utilizing this App uses external sensors over Bluetooth to gather data. Data can then be exported and opened in other programs, such as a spreadsheet.

The Wolfram Alpha app is available on iOS and Android. This is the ultimate money saver because students will not need to purchase a graphing calculator. Additionally, it does more than graph mathematical and science formulas. This app can also list properties of elements, create star maps, make a chart of information with Earth's geological layers, and convert units of measurement. The calculator covers over 50 topics from Math, Science and Technology, Society and Culture, and Everyday Life.

The Elements is an app available on iOs. Each element of the Periodic Table is displayed in a 3D way to help build students' interest. Students can see the physical appearance of the elements, rotate them, and learn all the details about them.

History/ Social Sciences

For history, and social studies lessons there is the ERH (Experience Real History) available on IOs and Android. Must be purchased along with Board and Card activity sets; bulk discounts are available. This App is considered a living textbook for history because it portrays the past through 3D stories that include pictures and sound. Students do not read about a battle, they see it first-hand. Currently, the app features information about the Alamo.

Ancient Rome for Kids is available on iOs. It includes short lessons, videos, and interactive games about Ancient Rome.

The Art Authority for iPad is available on iOs. Students can learn about over 1,500 artists. This includes ancient art history and present-day. There are pictures of over 100,000 paintings and sculptures, which are organized in the App in an eight-period specific museum.

The Historical Calendar app is on Android and Today is History is on iOs. Students learn quick facts related to different dates on the calendar.

World History for Kids app is available on iOs. Students can use this App to learn about WWI, WW2, the French Revolution, the Industrial Revolution, Ancient Egypt, Ancient Greece, and the Ancient Romans. Each lesson starts with an audio recording that is accompanied by animation, maps, charts, and interactive clues. Students use the interactive timeline to travel back and forth in time.

Timeline – World History is available on iOs and Android. Students can explore an in-depth timeline covering all aspects of history. This App is great for the visual learner as it includes extensive illustrations as well as basic text.

Geography

Stack the States is an app available on iOs. Students work to place the states in their correct location, just like in a puzzle. The states come to life in a colorful musical way during lessons and games about the state capitals, their geographic locations, flags, and more. Four bonus games are revealed once students earn higher levels.

Barefoot World Atlas is available on iOs.Students search the globe and learn facts through text and pictures about different countries and states. Quizzes are also included.

Ansel and Claire Adventures in Africa is available on iOs and Android. Students explore Africa in this interactive App with a few animated characters.

Math Lessons: Early Elementary School

Moose Math is available on iOs and Android. Students practice their counting skills while following numerical recipes. They add a specific number of fruits to a blender to make a smoothie. This fun game helps students reinforce the skills they learned.

Calculords is available on iOs and Android. This is a game that requires students to work on adding, subtraction, and multiplication to earn cards and avenge the Earth. It is a good opportunity to reinforce skills while playing a game.

Math vs. Zombies is available on iOs. Students solve addition, subtraction, and multiplication equations during a zombie fighting game. Their results get filed onto an in-App report card that can be shared with parents and teachers. This helps pinpoint the students' weaknesses in mathematics.

Chalkboard Math is available on iOs. Students play a hangman-type game while solving addition, subtraction, multiplication, and division problems. This App also speaks out the problems, which is beneficial for auditory learners.

Rocket Math is available on iOs and Android. Students participate in a variety of games while reinforcing basic math facts they previously learned. Additionally, when needing to make a correction the student is immediately notified. Another great benefit of this App is that if a student stalls for three seconds, the App provides the answer to the student. The student then does side work to prove that he/she understands the problem. There is a dashboard that allows teachers and parents to monitor the students' progress.

Monster Math is available on iOs and Android. This is a game in which a monster named Maxx reinforces basic addition, subtraction, multiplication, and division. Students practice solving these problems while fighting enemies and saving Dextra. Students can also compete against other players who are logged in on-line.

SplashLearn is available on iOs and Android. This game is the best for visual learners as it provides a visual representation of all mathematical problems in a fun and colorful way. There are virtual awards and a progress dashboard.

Elephant Learning is available on iOs and Android. This App is appropriate for ages 2 through 16. The App platform guarantees that students will learn a year's worth of math in three months if they use it for at least 30 minutes per week.

Pizza Fractions is available on iOs. This App uses pizzas to teach students about fractions and how to break down fractions.

Math Lessons: Middle School/High School

My Script Calculator is an app available on iOs and Android. This app enables students to write equations down in their handwriting using a stylus or their finger and the handwriting recognition system transcribes the equation into text. The app is programmed to recognize logarithms, square roots, trigonometry, and arithmetic. It also provides the answer.

PhotoMath is available on iOs and Android. Similar to the My Script Calculator, this App allows you to write down your equations, but this time the student can do so on a piece of paper. Then, the student takes a picture of it and the App transcribes the equation to text and the calculator provides an answer along with step-by-step solutions to solve.

Mathway is available on iOs and Android. Similar to the PhotoMath app, this App provides a step by step explanation to the final answer and can interpret calculus and statistics as well.

Desmos Graphing Calculator is available on iOs and Android. This App replaces the costly graphing calculator and has the same functions. Students can also use it without a Wifi connection. This App plots points and has options for parametric coordinate systems and has an output and input table.

Mathspace is available on iOs and Android. This App provides teachers with more than 20,000 interactive problems that require step by step solving. Additionally, it has handwriting recognition software so students do not have to type their answers. In addition to the problems, this App includes video lessons and teacher feedback tools so that students can learn while completing the problems. This App is a good replacement for the traditional textbook.

Prodigy Game is available on iOs and Android. This App provides mathematics games as well as diagnostic tests to provide teachers and parents with student progress. Students can work on addition, subtraction, multiplication, and division.

Dragon Box Math 12+ is available on iOs and Android. This App covers 12+ different mathematical concepts. It is one of the few Apps that helps students work on problems with parentheses, like terms, and factorization.

Art Lessons

Drawing Pad is available on iOs. Students can draw freehand, color in pictures, and apply stickers to drawings all on the tablet.

Lazoo: Squiggles is available on iOs. Students follow directions and drawing prompts to create an image. Once it is finished they press "go" and the drawing comes to life.

Toontastic is available on iOs. Students write, draw, and animate their cartoons. There is even an opportunity to record voice-overs.

Book Creator is available on iOs and Android. Students write and illustrate their books using this App. Books can be published as iBooks for them to share with others.

How to Draw is available on iOs. Students follow step-by-step instructions to learn how to draw different images.

Reading/Writing

Scrivener is an app available on iOs. Students can use this app to organize longer writing pieces. They can organize topics to quickly reach the page or paragraph they need.

Reading Trainer is available on iOs. This App has 12 different activities to improve reading speed, word recognition, comprehension, and word retention. The App gives scores so students have a goal for next time.

iMindMap is available on iOs and Android. Students can use this App to create mind maps after reading books and/or articles. This is a great resource to learn how to take notes and how to increase writing skills.

Rainbow Sentences is available on iOs. Students learn to construct sentences based on the presented pictures. Completing sentences earns rewards for further levels to open.

Evernote is available on iOs. Students can use this App to record notes, both through text and audio, while reading. Additionally, the App will transcribe verbal words into written words so students can read over their notes later.

Kids Reading Comprehension 1 is available on iOs. Students are given a library of short stories inside the App. They read the stories and answer questions at the end to improve reading comprehension.

Story Builder for iPad is available on iOs. Students build sentences and paragraphs based on illustrations. After creating their sentences, they can record their voice reading the sentences. They can then playback the full story.

Reading Comprehension Grades 2-3 is available on iOs. This is a basic comprehension App in which the student is provided a short story and must answer questions after reading a paragraph. There is immediate feedback to alert the student to right/wrong answers.

Misc.

ABC Mouse is an app available on iOs and Android. This App provides games, lessons, books, puzzles, songs, and activities for students to learn beginner reading, mathematics, science, art, and much more.

Khan Academy is available on iOs and Android. This App provides lessons in ELA, mathematics, the sciences, social studies (history, government, politics), economics and finance, politics, and much more. It even includes interactive exercises. The lessons come in the form of videos, articles, and interactive lessons.

Questimate is a trivia game that helps students learn information about the Olympics, Geography, History, science, and animals.

BrainPop is available on iOs and Android. There are multiple BrainPop apps for a variety of subjects: science, social studies, art, movies, etc. Each one provides lessons, videos, and games for students to learn more about the given topic.

Adventure Academy is available on iOs and Android. Learners can explore different subjects, such as reading and writing while improving all-around academic skills. This App also has lessons in science and history.

Chapter 14
Introduction to Augmented Reality Training in the Industrial Environment

Hocine Chebi
Faculty of Electrical Engineering, Djillali Liabes University of Sidi Bel Abbes, Algeria

ABSTRACT

Faced with technological development and that of new information and communication technologies (NICTs), organizations' service structures and their processes have become increasingly flexible, interactive, and virtual. Industrial maintenance is one of the features that can take advantage of this change based on NICTs. The objective is to improve the reliability and availability of industrial equipment and installations, as well as to maintain a knowledge base allowing the capitalization of human skills. This makes it possible to keep production equipment at a distance and quickly by relying on remote maintenance and e-maintenance platforms. This allows real-time management between operators around industrial problems related to maintenance. In this chapter, the authors describe the change in the maintenance function between the classic strategy and the modern strategy, explaining the contribution of augmented reality to help solve problems in a remote maintenance or industrial e-maintenance task.

INTRODUCTION

Industrial maintenance is confronted with multiple constraints of cost optimization, improvement of the quality of interventions, availability and maintainability, accessibility to industrial sites. Added to this is the complexity and diversity of industrial equipment and installations, without forgetting the various maintenance problems often thrown into the background in the face of the imperatives involved in production concerns. During this decade, with technological development and that of NTIC (New Information and Communication Technologies), and faced with new socio-economic challenges, profound international changes resulting from globalization and globalization as well as the new competitive environment, industrial companies wish to take advantage of this to speed up the interventions of maintenance agents on the sites.

DOI: 10.4018/978-1-7998-4222-4.ch014

This situation makes it possible to reduce the idle time of their machines and installations on the one hand, and to build a knowledge base to keep track of their work on the other hand. This allows industrial equipment to be kept at a remote production site. Such maintenance must be supported on e-service platforms (electronic service via the Internet). In this article, we will present the mutation of the maintenance function between the classic strategy and the modern strategy, while giving the contribution of augmented reality in terms of exchange and transfer of videos and view them on 3D smart glasses for remote control in an industrial remote maintenance training tasks.

BACKGROUND

Industrial maintenance has long played the curative role, the sole objective of which was to reduce the downtime of industrial machines and installations. According to the AFNOR standard, maintenance is defined as being: all of the technical, administrative and management actions carried out during the life cycle of an asset and intended to maintain or restore it in a state in which it can perform the required function (AFNOR, 2001). Once curative, maintenance becomes preventive, contributes to improving the reliability of equipment and the quality of products. This maintenance results in the definition of action plans and interventions on the equipment, by the replacement of certain parts in the process of deterioration. Indeed, this is done by greasing or cleaning certain installations. In fact, these actions were initially carried out systematically according to predefined timetables.

Thanks to the evolution of diagnostic and control methods, new maintenance has been created. Such maintenance aims to use fault forecasting techniques such as vibration analysis. This maintenance is said to be conditional preventive allowing the parts to be replaced just before they break. Maintenance has thus evolved towards the proactive concept (Cocheteux, 2010) which results in the application of means of monitoring and continuous controls on the primary problems which cause the failure of the system, while being based on methods of optimization such as Total Productive Maintenance TPM (Bufferne, 2008), Maintenance Based on Reliability (MBF) (Cotaina et al., 1997), Expert Systems (SE) (Blanc et al., 1989). The following figure shows the evolution of the maintenance function within the framework of a classic production:

The unrestrained competition and the race for competitiveness encourage companies to seek the total quality of the product, and especially the reduction of costs, the maintenance function has thus become one of the important functions in companies. In the next section we present the evolution of maintenance in a modern production context. With the development of competition and the race for competitiveness and with the increasing complexity and automation of processes, industrial maintenance has become one of the strategic functions of the company. Far from being stabilized today, it is evolving according to New Information and Communication Technologies (NTIC), the introduction of new management methods, as well as the technological development of production tools. (Rachidi et al., 2014)

These factors have changed the communication strategy and the information between maintenance operators. Indeed, in the past information was entered manually on paper, and also was exchanged verbally between operators. On the other hand, the information is quite different, it has become structured and formalized in order to be manipulated by computer systems (Computer-Aided Maintenance Management). (Rachidi et al., 2013a). Industrial companies are looking to improve the current maintenance system through two strategic levels: outsourcing and outsourcing. (Alali, 2010).

Figure 1. The evolution of maintenance in the context of conventional production

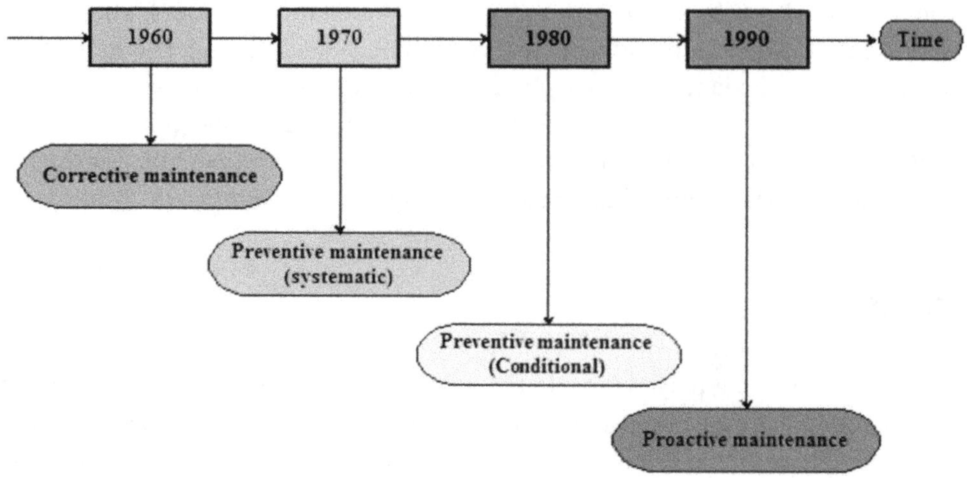

DESIGN AND IMPLEMENTATION

The current trend is to outsource, in part, the Maintenance function. This outsourcing leads us to evolve in a distributed and virtual domain (Rachidi et al., 2013b) which has modified information systems. Thanks to NICTs and the emergence of Web technologies and the Internet, the tasks of maintenance services and checks can be performed automatically remotely, hence the birth of remote maintenance. Two architectures exist including the remote maintenance and E-maintenance (see figure 2):

These new forms of maintenance are supported by technologies for access, data processing, information or knowledge and exchange between remote actors. (c, Rachidi et al., 2014). To maintain equipment at a distance, several resources are involved, whether material such as repair tools, maintenance workshop, smartphones, smart tablets, etc., or immaterial such as human resources, Groupeware, internet,

Figure 2. Different remote maintenance architectures (b, Rachidi et al., 2013)

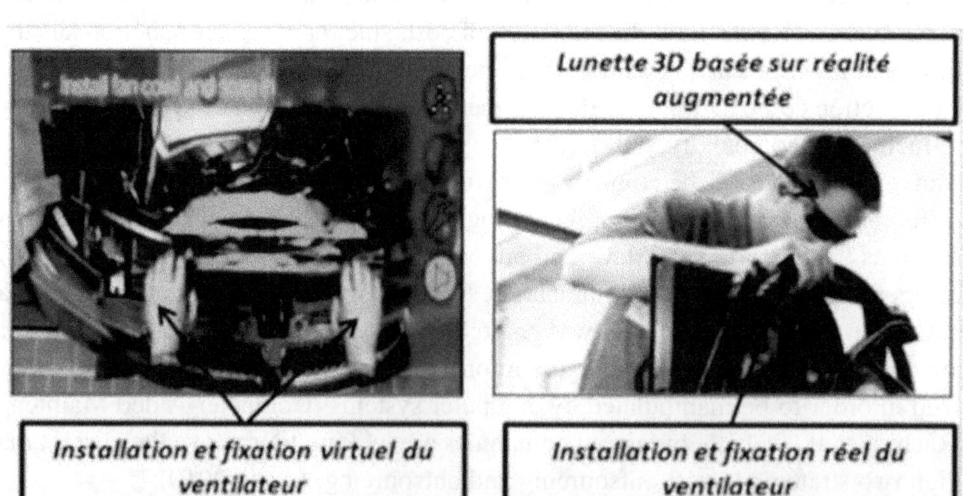

man-machine interface (Rachidi et al., 2014). In the literature, there are several remote maintenance and E-maintenance platforms such as the MIMOSA platform (Kahn, 2003), TELMA (Levrat et al., 2005), PROTEUS (Bangemann et al., 2006), TEMIC (Garcia and al., 2004), NEMOSYS (Bressy et al., 2005), as well as our platform IndusRCMW (c, Rachidi et al., 2014). In our contribution, we will choose the industrial remote maintenance platform Indus-RCMW (Industrial Remote Collaboration Maintenance Work).

To pilot this Indus-RCMW platform, the site technician contains a virtual workspace on which he can perform his corrective or preventive maintenance tasks on industrial equipment (Rachidi et al., 2014). This is done in real time. If the maintenance agent finds it difficult to resolve the fault, he collaborates with the local expert center (group of senior technicians with expertise and knowledge for solving maintenance problems) in order to provide documentation and instructions necessary to solve the problem encountered (Rachidi et al., 2014). The site technician and the local group of experts form a couple piloting a local remote maintenance, but if this couple finds it difficult to diagnose the problem encountered, they collaborate with an external expert on behalf of the equipment supplier. That this guide the couple (site technician / local group of experts) to correct the anomaly. (See figure 3). These different collaborations are made thanks to a messaging space in the Indus-RCMW platform.

Each resource contains a workspace (Figure 4) relating to the exercise of its function; the following figure shows the different workspaces for each maintenance staff.

The Indus-RCMW (Industrial Remote Collaboration Maintenance Work) platform can remotely manage the various maintenance tasks, whether preventive or corrective (Rachidi et al., 2014). It also allows the efficient management of Park machine while keeping a mixed remote maintenance based on the triad (do-do, do-together, and do internally) (Kaffel, 2001). Also, the Indus-RCMW platform provides robust monitoring of knowledge and know-how related to the management of the skills of maintenance agents (Rachidi et al., 2014). Our contribution lies in transforming the various static information relating to preventive or corrective maintenance (plan, diagram, maintenance operating mode, etc.) into animated 3D information in order to provide the maintenance operator with instructions and flexible and flexible instructions in its maintenance work, while being based on Augmented Reality technology.

SOLUTIONS AND RECOMMENDATIONS

Augmented reality is defined as: any computer system that makes it possible to superimpose a 3D / 2D virtual model on the perception of having natural reality and this in real time. (Azuma, 1997). Augmented reality is characterized by the fact that it enriches the real world instead of replacing it. The first applications of augmented reality were reserved for the military field for the display of virtual information on the visors of the helmets of airplane pilots, and subsequently it diverged in the 90s, towards other fields. Such as cultural (Ciccotelli et al., 2005), medical (Bockholt et al., 2003), industrial (Pentenrider et al., 2006), etc.

There are two main families of AR systems, the one with markers (Rekimoto et al., 2000) and the one without markers (Harald et al., 2005). These are the two principles allowing finding the point of view of the user (position and trajectory) in order to match the perspective of the virtual object with that of the real scene and, thus obtain in real time an image real.

The maintenance operator integrates his work space under the Indus-RCMW platform, on which he searches in the technical file section of the equipment (see figure 5). The technician follows the instruc-

Figure 3. Remote management between human resources around the various maintenance works (b, Rachidi et al., 2014)

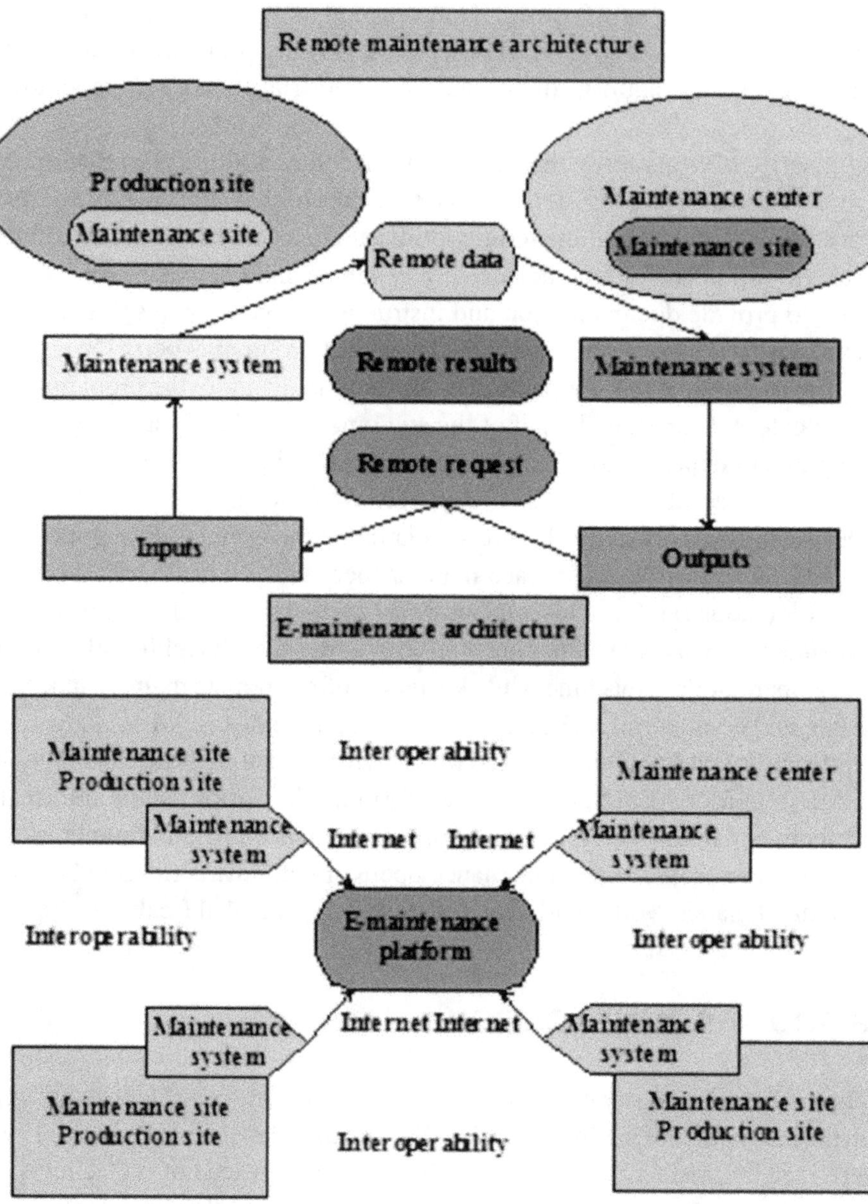

tions and steps for carrying out the maintenance task on digital documentation. The accomplishment of its tasks depends, of course, on a high capacity for knowledge and know-how in order to be able to follow static instructions on the remote maintenance platform based on an NTIC tool (Smartphone, smart tablet, etc.) (Rachidi et al., 2014).

Competence therefore remains an important link for carrying out remote maintenance and E-maintenance work (Rachidi et al. 2013). On the other hand, the existence of RA technology in maintenance work contributes positively to the decrease in the number of errors (Marsot et al., 2009) (risk manage-

Figure 4. Different workspaces in the Indus-RCMW platform (c, Rachidi et al., 2014)

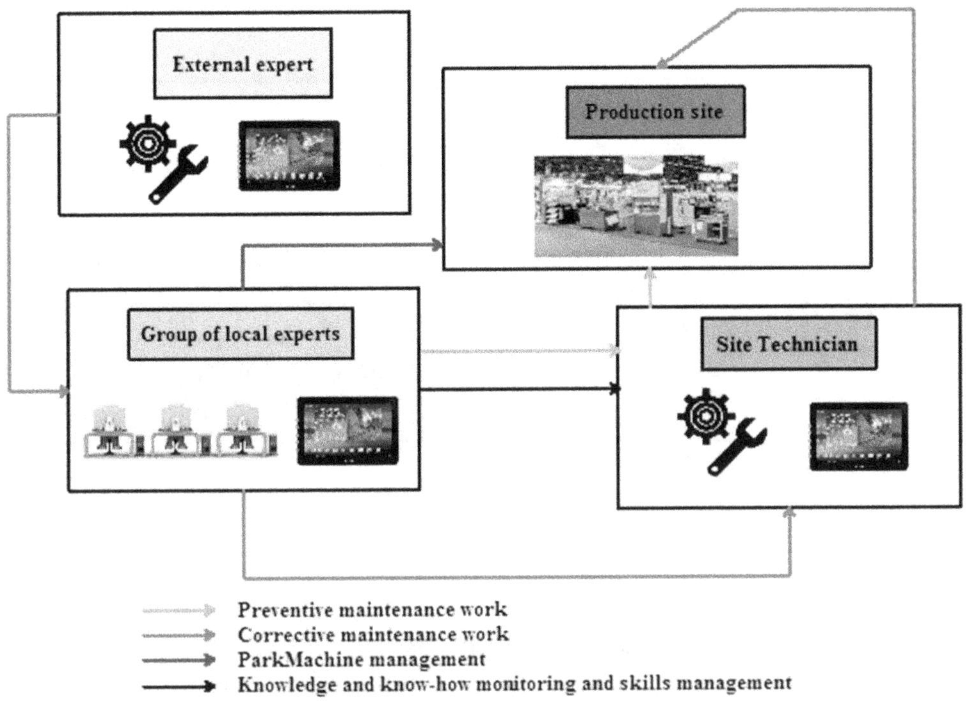

ment linked to maintenance works). The following figure shows the corrective maintenance work space in the Indus-RCMW platform.

In the box of the equipment technical file, the maintenance operator chooses the mechanical part on which he selects the ventilation device, then the assembly and disassembly operation. Automatically and on his 3D glasses, the instructions and steps for carrying out maintenance are displayed (there is

Figure 5. Site technician corrective workspace

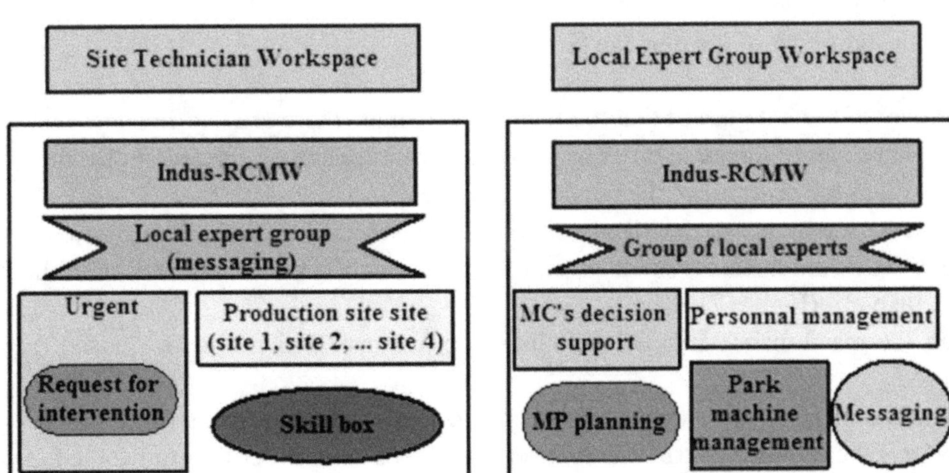

Figure 6. Loosening the fixing screws of the fan cage

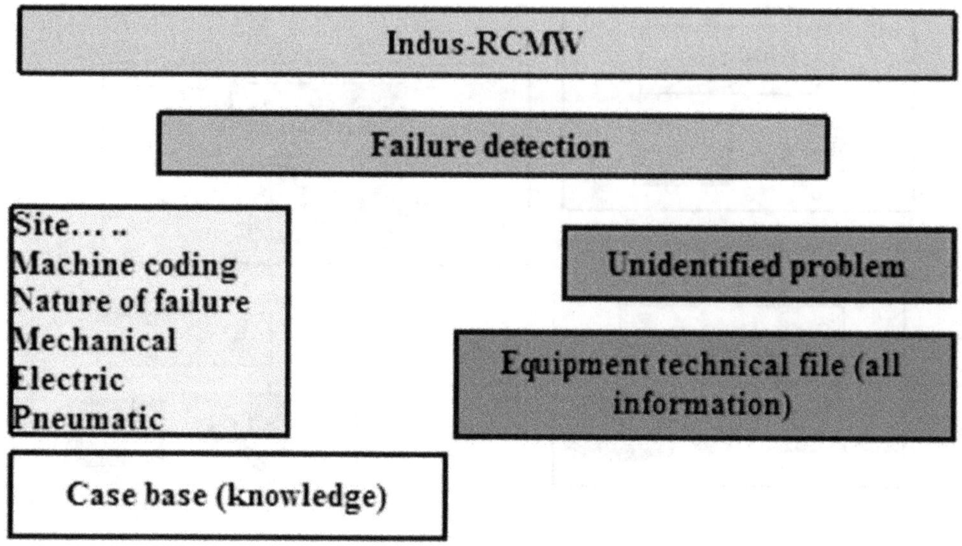

synchronization of the Indus-RCMW platform with the 3D glasses) while ensuring a superimposition of virtual images that the technician must follow. and the actual image to provide the repair.

The concept of augmented reality is used to provide the maintenance worker with the various stages of carrying out the task in the form of flash animation. Studies have been carried out through tests confirm the interest of augmented reality technology, namely the reduction in the number of errors in the performance of procedures. This does not require the notion of expertise for the maintenance operator in certain tasks. In the following part we present the exploitation of the AR for the change of a ventilator.

During a corrective maintenance task and more particularly the change of an automobile fan. The maintenance agent must perform the following steps:

- Loosen the fan cage screws
- Removal of the intake duct
- Loosen the fan screws
- Installation and fixing of the new fan

On the display of the 3D glasses that the technician brings, there are two images (real and virtual) which coincide on a single screen in order to give the instructions to be carried out for the loosening of the screws as well as the removal of the fan cage. (Figure.6).

Once the first task is finished, the 3D glasses display the second task which relates to the removal of the intake duct, so the maintenance operator will have information on the orientation of the intake duct in order to 'to take off. (Figure 7)

Thereafter, the maintenance technician follows the 3rd task which aims to loosen the fan fixing screws. (Figure.8)

After loosening the fixing screws, the next task is to remove the fan. In the figure, we notice that the technician follows the removal instruction in a vertical direction in order to remove the fan.

Figure 7. Removal of the intake duct

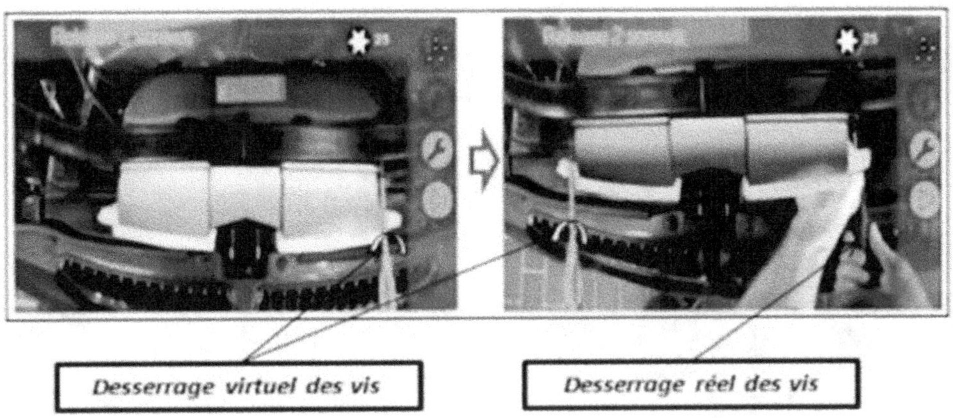

Finally, the technician brings in a new fan, and installs it according to the instructions that are displayed in the 3D glasses. (Figure10).

Figure 8. Loosening the fixing screws

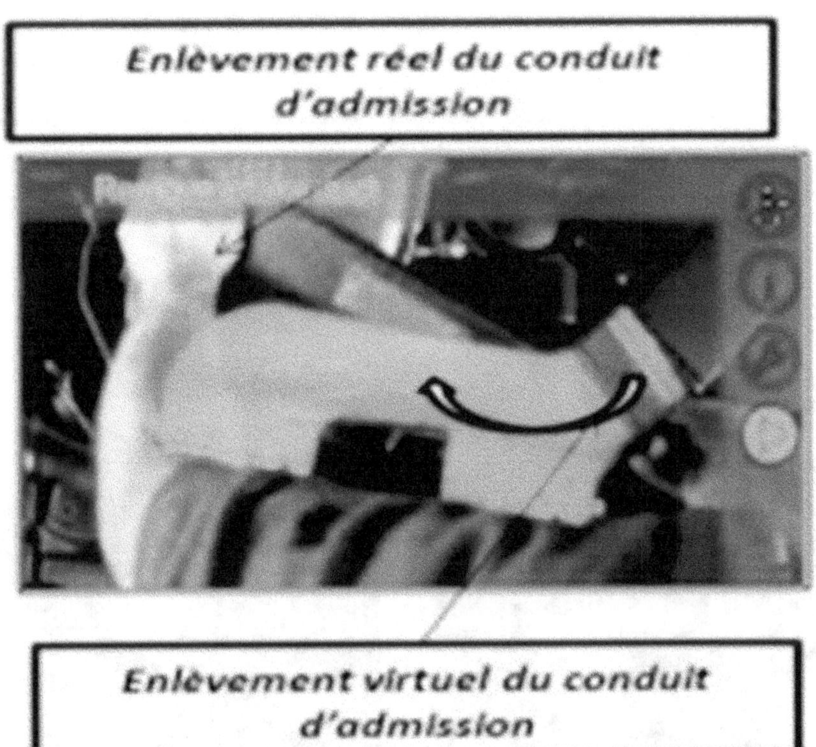

Figure 9. Removing the fan

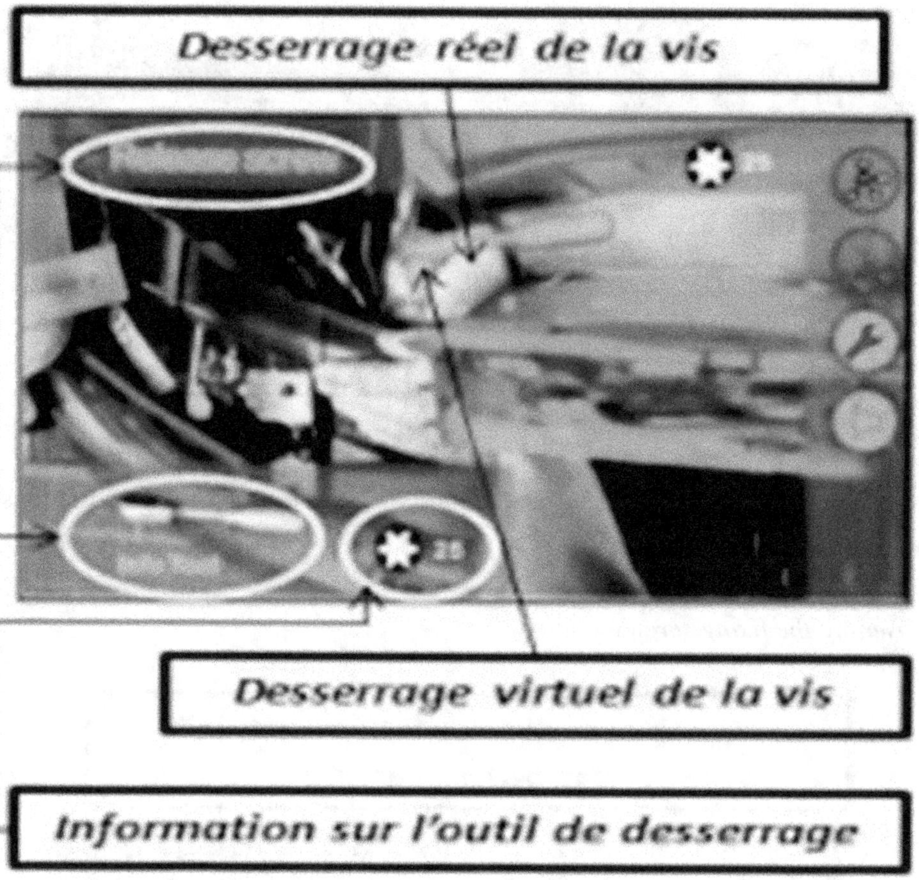

Once the repair task has been carried out, the maintenance operator transfers using the messaging

Figure 10. Installation and fixing of a new fan

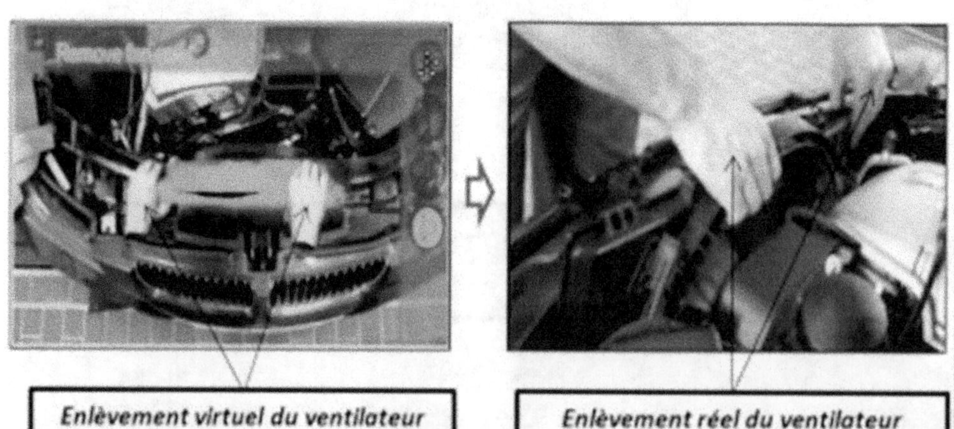

service on the Indus-RCMW platform a report of its activity to the local center of experts for validation and registration. These new forms of maintenance will have a direct impact on the development of the skills of the personnel who operate in this field. Indeed, the degree of knowledge and know-how must be increasingly required, given their knowledge in technical fields such as mechanics, electricity, and automation, maintenance personnel must have interoperability extreme with NTIC tools. This interoperability requires the development of predictive management of trades and skills by integrating new functionalities (handling computers, smartphones, etc.) in terms of processing digital documents, searching for information, communication, and obtaining '' a service (Rachidi et al., 2013b).

CONCLUSION

Augmented reality has a positive impact on the maintenance operation, which results in the reduction of the overall mission time by providing the use of conventional supports, whether paper or static supports on the Indus-RCMW platform., which leads to a reduction in the number of errors for carrying out the task. AR also has a positive impact on operators and maintenance technicians, which results in a reduction in the use of paper media. Indeed, this reduction allows the maintenance operator to use both hands for his activities. Also, AR allows the construction of real-time knowledge equivalent to training. (The mixture of real and virtual will ensure a better understanding of theoretical concepts).

REFERENCES

Azuma, R. (1997). A survey of augmented reality. *Presence (Cambridge, Mass.)*, *6*(4), 355–385. doi:10.1162/pres.1997.6.4.355

Bangemann, T., Rebeuf, X., Reboul, D., Schulze, A., Szymanski, J., Thomesse, J. P., Thron, M., & Zerhouni, N. (2006). PROTEUS—Creating distributed maintenance systems through an integration platform. *Computers in Industry*, *57*(6), 539–551. doi:10.1016/j.compind.2006.02.018

Bargar, W. L., Bauer, A., & Börner, M. (1998). Primary and Revision Total Hip Replacement Using the Robodoc (R) System. *Clinical Orthopaedics and Related Research*, *354*, 82-91.

Blanc, M., Charron, E., & Freyssenet, M. (1989). *The development of expert systems in companies*. GIP Industrial change.

Bockholt, U., Bisler, A., Becker, M., Muller-Wittig, W., & Voss, G. (2003, March). Augmented reality for enhancement of endoscopic interventions. In IEEE Virtual Reality, 2003. Proceedings (pp. 97-101). IEEE. doi:10.1109/VR.2003.1191126

Bressy, P., Zerhouni, N., Allemand, C., & Leger, J.-B. (2005). *Application du concept de emaintenance à un système naval de défense: NEMOSYS*. In 2e Colloque international francophone sur la Performance et les Nouvelles TechnOlogies en Maintenance (PENTOM'05), Marrakech.

Bufferne, J. (2008). la TPM: un système de production. Technologie (SCEREN-CNDP)–Revue Française de gestion Industrielle.

Ciccotelli, J., & Marsot, J. (2005). PR 17-Point of reference-Virtual reality and prevention-Contributions and trends. *Cahiers de Notes Documentaires-Hygiene et Securite du Travail*, (199), 99–112.

Cocheteux, P. (2010). *Contribution à la maintenance proactive par la formalisation du processus de pronostic des performances de systèmes industriels* (Doctoral dissertation).

Cotaina, N., Gabriel, M., Richet, D., & O'Reilly, K. (1997). Utilisation de la Maintenance Basee sur la Fiabilite (MBF) pour developper et optimiser les politiques de maintenance des scieries. *Revue Française de Gestion Industrielle*, 47-66.

Garcia, E., Guyennet, H., Lapayre, J. C., & Zerhouni, N. (2004). A new industrial cooperative tele-maintenance platform. *Computers & Industrial Engineering*, *46*(4), 851–864. doi:10.1016/j.cie.2004.05.019

Kaffel, H. (2001). *Distributed maintenance: concept, evaluation and implementation*. Academic Press.

Kahn, J. (2003). Overview of MIMOSA and the Open System Architecture for Enterprise Application Integration. In *Proc. of COMADEM 2003* (pp. 661-670). Växjö University.

Levrat, E., Salzemann, B., Clanché, F., & Bron, J. Y. (2006). TELMA Plate-forme d'intégration de télémaintenance pour l'enseignement et la recherche. *J3eA, 5*, 17.

Marsot, J., Gardeux, F., & Govaere, V. (2009). Réalité augmentée et prévention des risques: apports et limites. Hygiène et sécurité du travail, (214), 15-23.

Pentenrieder, K., & Meier, P. (2006, October). The need for accuracy statements in industrial Augmented Reality applications. In *5th IEEE and ACM International Symposium on Mixed and Augmented Reality*. University of California at Santa Barbara (USA).

Rachidi, A., Dakkak, B., Talbi, A., & Khatory. A., (2013). *Augmented Reality for remote maintenance and industrial E-maintenance*. Academic Press.

Rachidi, A., Khatory, A., & Talbi, A. (2014). Toward an automation increasingly interconnecting. *International Journal of Scientific & Engineering Research.*

Rachidi, A., Talbi, A., & Khatory, A. (2013, October). The positioning of the industrial maintenance and its interaction with the NICT (case study). In *Proceedings of 2013 International Conference on Industrial Engineering and Systems Management (IESM)* (pp. 1-7). IEEE.

Rachidi, A., Talbi, A., & Khatory, A. (2013a). The concept of the virtuality in the company: what strategy for change can facilitate the integration of this concept? *International Journal of Multidisciplinary Sciences and Engineering.*

Rachidi, A., Talbi, A., & Khatory, A. (2013b). The new forms of industrial maintenance: which impact on the performance of the industrial companies?(Case study). *International Journal of Engineering and Advanced Technology.*

Rekimoto, J., & Ayatsuka, Y. (2000, April). CyberCode: designing augmented reality environments with visual tags. In *Proceedings of DARE 2000 on Designing augmented reality environments* (pp. 1-10). 10.1145/354666.354667

Wuest, H., Vial, F., & Strieker, D. (2005, October). Adaptive line tracking with multiple hypotheses for augmented reality. In *Fourth IEEE and ACM International Symposium on Mixed and Augmented Reality (ISMAR'05)* (pp. 62-69). IEEE. 10.1109/ISMAR.2005.8

Compilation of References

Abe, T., Raison, N., Shinohara, N., Shamim Khan, M., Ahmed, K., & Dasgupta, P. (2018). The Effect of Visual-Spatial Ability on the Learning of Robot-Assisted Surgical Skills. *Journal of Surgical Education*, *75*(2), 458–464. Advance online publication. doi:10.1016/j.jsurg.2017.08.017 PMID:28918007

AC Experiences (ACEs). (2019). Retrieved from https://www.cdc.gov/violenceprevention/acestudy/index.html

Ahmad, J. (2016). Technology-assisted language learning is a silver bullet for enhancing language competence and performance: A case study. *International Journal of Applied Linguistics and English Literature*, *5*(7), 118–131. doi:10.7575/aiac.ijalel.v.5n.7p.118

Akçayır, M., & Akçayır, G. (2017). Advantages and challenges associated with augmented reality for education: A systematic review of the literature. *Educational Research Review*, *20*, 1–11. doi:10.1016/j.edurev.2016.11.002

Al Harrasi, K. T. S. (2014). Using "Total Physical Response" With Young Learners in Oman. *Childhood Education*, *90*(1), 36–42. doi:10.1080/00094056.2014.872513

Alais, D., & Burr, D. (2004). The ventriloquist effect results from near-optimal bimodal integration. *Current Biology*, *14*(3), 257–262. doi:10.1016/j.cub.2004.01.029 PMID:14761661

Aldhafeeri, F., Palaiologou, I., & Folorunsho, A. (2016). Integration of digital technologies into play-based pedagogy in Kuwait early childhood education: Teacher's views, attitudes, and aptitudes. *International Journal of Early Years Education*, *24*(3), 342–360. doi:10.1080/09669760.2016.1172477

Al-Gindy, A., Felix, C., Ahmed, A., Matoug, A., & Alkhidir, M. (2020). Virtual Reality: Development of an Integrated Learning Environment for Education. *International Journal of Information and Education Technology (IJIET)*, *10*(3), 171–175. doi:10.18178/ijiet.2020.10.3.1358

Ali, M., West, K., Teic, J., Lynch, S., Mutter, R., & Dubenitz, J. (2019). Utilization of mental health services in educational settings by adolescents in the United States. *The Journal of School Health*, *89*(5), 393–401. doi:10.1111/josh.12753 PMID:30883761

Alpar, M. (2013). The importance of games in foreign languages to children. *Educational Research Review*, *8*(15), 1247–1255. doi:10.5897/ERR2013.1494

Alt, D. (2015). Assessing the contribution of a constructivist learning environment to academic self-efficacy in higher education. *Learning Environments Research*, *18*(1), 47–67. doi:10.100710984-015-9174-5

Althauser, K. (2015). Job-embedded professional development: Its impact on teacher self-efficacy and student performance. *Teacher Development*, *19*(2), 210–225. doi:10.1080/13664530.2015.1011346

Altınpulluk, H., & Kesim, M. (March, 2016). The classification of augmented reality books: a literature review. *10th International Technology, Educational and Development Conference,* 10.21125/inted.2016.0200

American Councils for International Education. (2017). *The national K-12 foreign language enrollment survey report.* https://www.americancouncils.org/sites/default/files/FLE-report-June17.pdf

Amir, M. F., Fediyanto, N., Rudyanto, H. E., Afifah, D. S. N., & Tortop, H. S. (2020). Elementary students' perceptions of 3Dmetric: A cross-sectional study. *Heliyon, 6*(6), e04052. doi:10.1016/j.heliyon.2020.e04052 PMID:32577547

Anderson, S., Griffith, R., & Crawford, L. (2017). TPACK in special education: Preservice teacher decision making while integrating iPads into instruction. *Contemporary Issues in Technology & Teacher Education, 17*(1), 97–127.

Announcing partnership between FastModel sports and synergy sports technology. (2019). Retrieved from https://corp.synergysportstech.com/2019/12/13/announcing-partnership-between-fastmodel-sports-and-synergy-sports-technology/

Arvanitis, T. N., Petrou, A., Knight, J. F., Savas, S., Sotiriou, S., Gargalakos, M., & Gialouri, E. (2009). Human factors and qualitative pedagogical evaluation of a mobile augmented reality system for science education used by learners with physical disabilities. *Personal and Ubiquitous Computing, 13*(3), 243–250. doi:10.100700779-007-0187-7

Asia Society. (2012). *Chinese language learning in the early grades: A handbook of resources and best practices for Mandarin immersion.* http://asiasociety.org/files/chinese-earlylanguage.pdf

Astur, R. S., Purton, A. J., Zaniewski, M. J., Cimadevilla, J., & Markus, E. J. (2016). Human sex differences in solving a virtual navigation problem. *Behavioural Brain Research, 308*, 236–243. Advance online publication. doi:10.1016/j.bbr.2016.04.037 PMID:27108050

Atienza, R., Blonna, R., Saludares, M. I., Casimiro, J., & Fuentes, V. (2016, May). Interaction techniques using head gaze for virtual reality. In *2016 IEEE Region 10 Symposium (TENSYMP)* (pp. 110-114). IEEE. 10.1109/TENCON-Spring.2016.7519387

Auster, E. R., & Wylie, K. K. (2006). Creating active learning in the classroom: A systematic approach. *Journal of Management Education, 30*(2), 333–353. doi:10.1177/1052562905283346

Aziz, T., Khan, M. B., & Singh, R. (2010). Effects of information technology usage on student learning: An empirical study in the United States. *International Journal of Management, 27*(2), 205.

Azuma, R. (1997). A survey of augmented reality. *Presence (Cambridge, Mass.), 6*(4), 355–385. doi:10.1162/pres.1997.6.4.355

Babich, N. (2019). *How VR in Education Will Change How We Learn and Teach.* https://xd.adobe.com/ideas/principles/emerging-technology/virtual-reality-will-change-learn-teach/

Bacca-Acosta, J. L., Baldiris, S. M., Fabregat, R., & Graf, S., & Kinshuk. (2014). Augmented reality trends in education: A systematic review of research and applications. *Journal of Educational Technology & Society, 17*(4), 133–149.

Baker, W. (2015). Research into practice: Cultural and intercultural awareness. *Language Teaching, 48*(1), 130–141. doi:10.1017/S0261444814000287

Ball, D. L., & Forzani, F. M. (2009). The work of teaching and the challenge for teacher education. *Journal of Teacher Education, 60*(5), 497–511. doi:10.1177/0022487109348479

Bandura, A. (1994). Self-efficacy. In V. S. Ramachaudran (Ed.), *Encyclopedia of human behavior* (Vol. 4, pp. 71–81). Academic Press.

Bangemann, T., Rebeuf, X., Reboul, D., Schulze, A., Szymanski, J., Thomesse, J. P., Thron, M., & Zerhouni, N. (2006). PROTEUS—Creating distributed maintenance systems through an integration platform. *Computers in Industry*, *57*(6), 539–551. doi:10.1016/j.compind.2006.02.018

Banit, M. (2018). *Using Augmented Reality (AR) for Learning and Development.* https://www.zappar.com/blog/using-ar-learning-and-development/

Bankovic, I., & Sollars, V. (2017). English as a second language in a Maltese early years setting. *An Leanbh Óg: The OMEP Ireland Journal of Early Childhood Studies*, *11*, 61–69.

Baños, R. M., Botella, C., Alcañiz, M., Liaño, V., Guerrero, B., & Rey, B. (2004). Immersion and emotion: Their impact on the sense of presence. *Cyberpsychology & Behavior*, *7*(6), 734–741. doi:10.1089/cpb.2004.7.734 PMID:15687809

Baños, R. M., Botella, C., Rubió, I., Quero, S., García-Palacios, A., & Alcañiz, M. (2008). Presence and emotions in virtual environments: The influence of stereoscopy. *Cyberpsychology & Behavior*, *11*(1), 1–8. doi:10.1089/cpb.2007.9936 PMID:18275306

Bargar, W. L., Bauer, A., & Börner, M. (1998). Primary and Revision Total Hip Replacement Using the Robodoc (R) System. *Clinical Orthopaedics and Related Research, 354*, 82-91.

Barnes, S., & Prescott, J. (2018). Empirical evidence for the outcomes of therapeutic video games for adolescents with anxiety disorders: Systematic review. *JMIR Serious Games*, *6*(1), e3. doi:10.2196/games.9530 PMID:29490893

Barrett, T. J., & Hegarty, M. (2016). Effects of interface and spatial ability on manipulation of virtual models in a STEM domain. *Computers in Human Behavior*, *65*, 220–231. doi:10.1016/j.chb.2016.06.026

Bautista, A., Toh, G. Z., & Wong, J. (2018). Primary school music teachers' professional development motivations, needs, and preferences: Does specialization make a difference? *Musicae Scientiae*, *22*(2), 196–223. doi:10.1177/1029864916678654

Beigbeder, T., Coughlan, R., Lusher, C., Plunkett, J., Agu, E., & Claypool, M. (2004, August). The effects of loss and latency on user performance in unreal tournament 2003®. In *Proceedings of 3rd ACM SIGCOMM workshop on Network and system support for games* (pp. 144-151). 10.1145/1016540.1016556

Belch, B., Casale, & Manuccia. (2016). *Training using virtual reality.* Strivr Labs Inc. Retrieved from https://patents.google.com/patent/US10586469B2/en

Bereiter, C. (2002). *Education and mind in the knowledge age.* Lawrence Erlbaum Associates. http://unr.edu/homepage/luvisis/bereiter.html

Bialystok, E., & Hakuta, K. (1999). *Confounded age: Linguistic and cognitive factors in age differences for second language acquisition.* http://citeseerx.ist.psu.edu/viewdoc/download?doi=10.1.1.475.3365&rep=rep1&type=pdf

Bialystok, E. (2017). The bilingual adaptation: How minds accommodate experience. *Psychological Bulletin*, *143*(3), 233–262. doi:10.1037/bul0000099 PMID:28230411

Bideau, B., Kulpa, R., Ménardais, S., Fradet, L., Multon, F., Delamarche, P., & Arnaldi, B. (2003). Real handball goal-keeper vs. virtual handball thrower. *Presence (Cambridge, Mass.)*, *12*(4), 411–421. doi:10.1162/105474603322391631

Bideau, B., Kulpa, R., Vignais, N., Brault, S., Multon, F., & Craig, C. (2009). Using virtual reality to analyze sports performance. *IEEE Computer Graphics and Applications*, *30*(2), 14–21. PMID:20650707

Billinghurst, M., & Duenser, A. (2012). *Augmented Reality in the Classroom.* https://www.researchgate.net/publication/234793015

Billinghurst, M., Kato, H., & Poupyrev, I. (2001). The MagicBook: A transitional AR interface. *Computers & Graphics, 25*(5), 745–753. doi:10.1016/S0097-8493(01)00117-0

Biocca, F. (1997). The cyborg's dilemma: Progressive embodiment in virtual environments. *Journal of Computer-Mediated Communication, 3*(2).

Biocca, F. (2003, May). Can we resolve the book, the physical reality, and the dream state problems? From the two-pole to a three-pole model of shifts in presence. In *EU Future and Emerging Technologies, Presence Initiative Meeting* (Vol. 12, pp. 13-69). Academic Press.

Bishop, J. (2013). *Partnership for 21st Century Skills (P21).* Retrieved from https://www.imls.gov/assets/1/AssetManager/Bishop%20Pre-Con%202.pdf

Blake, C. (2009). Potential of text-based Internet chats for improving oral fluency in a second language. *Modern Language Journal, 93*(2), 227–240. doi:10.1111/j.1540-4781.2009.00858.x

Blanc, M., Charron, E., & Freyssenet, M. (1989). *The development of expert systems in companies.* GIP Industrial change.

Bockholt, U., Bisler, A., Becker, M., Muller-Wittig, W., & Voss, G. (2003, March). Augmented reality for enhancement of endoscopic interventions. In IEEE Virtual Reality, 2003. Proceedings (pp. 97-101). IEEE. doi:10.1109/VR.2003.1191126

Boling, E. (2010). The need for design cases: Disseminating design knowledge. *International Journal of Designs for Learning, 1*(1). Advance online publication. doi:10.14434/ijdl.v1i1.919

Bonasio, A. (2017). *Immersive experiences in education.* White Paper. Microsoft Education Immersive Experiences. Retrieved from http://edudownloads.azureedge.net/msdownloads/MicrosoftEducation_Immersive_Experiences_Education_2019.pdf

Boninger, F., Molnar, A., & Murray, K. (2017). *Asleep at the Switch: Schoolhouse Commercialism, Student Privacy, and the Failure of Policymaking. The Nineteenth Annual Report on Schoolhouse Commercializing Trends, 2017.* National Education Policy Center.

Bonneel, N., Suied, C., Viaud-Delmon, I., & Drettakis, G. (2010). Bimodal perception of audio-visual material properties for virtual environments. *ACM Transactions on Applied Perception, 7*(1), 1–16. doi:10.1145/1658349.1658350

Bonner, E., & Reinders, H. (2018). Augmented and virtual reality in the language classroom; Practical ideas. *Teaching English with Technology, 18*(3), 33–53.

Bonney, E., Jelsma, L. D., Ferguson, G. D., & Smits-Engelsman, B. C. M. (2017). Learning better by repetition or variation? Is transfer at odds with task-specific training? *Plus One, 12*(3), e0174214. doi:10.1371/journal.pone.0174214 PMID:28333997

Bootsma, R. J., Ledouit, S., Casanova, R., & Zaal, F. T. (2016). Fractional-order information in the visual control of lateral locomotor interception. *Journal of Experimental Psychology. Human Perception and Performance, 42*(4), 517–529. doi:10.1037/xhp0000162 PMID:26569338

Boulos, M. N. K., Hetherington, L., & Wheeler, S. (2007). Second Life: An overview of the potential of 3-D virtual worlds in medical and health education. *Health Information and Libraries Journal, 24*(4), 233–245. doi:10.1111/j.1471-1842.2007.00733.x PMID:18005298

Boulos, M. N., Ramloll, R., Jones, R., & Toth-Cohen, S. (2008). Web 3D for public, environmental, and occupational health: Early examples from Second Life®. *International Journal of Environmental Research and Public Health, 5*(4), 290–317. doi:10.3390/ijerph5040290 PMID:19190358

Bouvier, P. (2009). *La présence en réalité virtuelle, une approche centrée utilisateur* (Doctoral dissertation).

Bowman, D. A. (1999). *Interaction techniques for common tasks in immersive virtual environments*. Georgia Institute of Technology.

Bradley, P., & Postlethwaite, K. (2003). Simulation in clinical learning. *Medical Education*, *37*(s1), 1–5. doi:10.1046/j.1365-2923.37.s1.1.x PMID:14641632

Brault, S., Bideau, B., Kulpa, R., & Craig, C. (2009). Detecting deceptive movement in 1 vs. 1 based on global body displacement of a rugby player. *The International Journal of Virtual Reality: a Multimedia Publication for Professionals*, *8*(4), 31–36. doi:10.20870/IJVR.2009.8.4.2746

Brault, S., Bideau, B., Kulpa, R., & Craig, C. M. (2012). Detecting deception in movement: The case of the side-step in rugby. *PLoS One*, *7*(6), e37494. doi:10.1371/journal.pone.0037494 PMID:22701569

Breen, M. P. (2009). Learner contributions to the task design. In K. Van den Branden, M. Bygate, & J. M. Norris (Eds.), *Task-based language teaching: A reader* (pp. 333–356). John Benjamins.

Bressy, P., Zerhouni, N., Allemand, C., & Leger, J.-B. (2005). *Application du concept de emaintenance à un système naval de défense: NEMOSYS*. In 2e Colloque international francophone sur la Performance et les Nouvelles TechnOlogies en Maintenance (PENTOM'05), Marrakech.

Brown, A., & Green, T. (2016). Virtual reality: Low-cost tools and resources for the classroom. *TechTrends*, *60*(5), 517–519. doi:10.100711528-016-0102-z

Brown, J. S., Collins, A., & Duguid, P. (1989). Situated cognition and the culture of learning. *Educational Researcher*, *18*(1), 32–42. doi:10.3102/0013189X018001032

Bruner, J. S. (1961). The act of discovery. *Harvard Educational Review*.

Brush, T., & Saye, J. (2006, April). *Scaffolding critical reasoning in history and social studies: Tools to support problem-based historical inquiry*. Presented as part of the Symposium, Scaffolding Disciplined Inquiry in Science and Social Studies: A Comparison to the Instructional Technology SIG.

Bufferne, J. (2008). la TPM: un système de production. Technologie (SCEREN-CNDP)–Revue Française de gestion Industrielle.

Bujak, K. R., Radu, I., Catrambone, R., MacIntyre, B., Zheng, R., & Golubski, G. (2013). A psychological perspective on augmented reality in the mathematics classroom. *Computers & Education*, *68*, 536–544. doi:10.1016/j.compedu.2013.02.017

Burr, D., & Alais, D. (2006). Combining visual and auditory information. *Progress in Brain Research*, *155*, 243–258. doi:10.1016/S0079-6123(06)55014-9 PMID:17027392

Butler, Y. G. (2015). The use of computer games as foreign language learning tasks for digital natives. *System*, *54*, 91–102. doi:10.1016/j.system.2014.10.010

Byker, E. J. (2014). Needing TPACK without Knowing It: Integrating Educational Technology in Social Studies. *Social Studies Research & Practice*, *9*(3).

Cai, S., Liu, E., Yang, Y., & Liang, J. C. (2019). Tablet-based AR technology: Impacts on students' conceptions and approaches to learning mathematics according to their self-efficacy. *British Journal of Educational Technology*, *50*(1), 248–263. doi:10.1111/bjet.12718

Calkins, L., & Tolan, K. (2010). *Units of study for teaching reading, grades 3–5: A curriculum for the reading workshop*. FirstHand Heinemann.

Calvert, G., Spence, C., & Stein, B. E. (Eds.). (2004). *The handbook of multisensory processes*. MIT Press.

Cao, L., Lin, J., & Li, N. (2019). A virtual reality based study of indoor fire evacuation after active or passive spatial exploration. *Computers in Human Behavior*, *90*, 37–45. Advance online publication. doi:10.1016/j.chb.2018.08.041

Carreon, A., Smith, S. J., & Rowland, A. (2019). Augmented reality: Creating and implementing digital classroom supports. *Journal of Special Education Technology*, *35*(2), 109–115. doi:10.1177/0162643419882423

Carr, J. M. (2012). Does math achievement "h'APP'en" when iPads and game-based learning are incorporated into fifth-grade mathematics instruction? *Journal of Information Technology Education*, *11*, 269–286. doi:10.28945/1725

Casale, M. (2018). *Sports training in virtual reality*. Retrieved from https://www.strivr.com/use-cases/sports/

Cascales, A., Laguna, I., Pérez-López, D., Perona, P., & Contero, M. (2013, July). An experience on natural sciences augmented reality contents for preschoolers. In R. Shumaker (Ed.), *International Conference on Virtual, Augmented and Mixed Reality* (pp. 103-112). Berlin: Springer. 10.1007/978-3-642-39420-1_12

CASEL. (n.d.). *What is SEL*. https://casel.org/what-is-SEL/

Casey, A., Goodyear, V. A., & Armour, K. M. (Eds.). (2016). *Digital technologies and learning in physical education: Pedagogical cases*. Taylor & Francis. doi:10.4324/9781315670164

Cengiz, C. (2015). The development of TPACK, technology integrated self-efficacy and instructional technology outcome expectations of pre-service physical education teachers. *Asia-Pacific Journal of Teacher Education*, *43*(5), 411–422. doi:10.1080/1359866X.2014.932332

Center for Advanced Research on Language Acquisition. (2017). *Less commonly taught languages*. https://carla.umn.edu/lctl/index.html

Chalimov, A. (2020). Augmented Reality in Education: The Hottest Edtech Trend and How to Apply it to your Business. *Eastern Peak*. Retrieved from https://easternpeak.com/blog/augmented-reality-in-education-the-hottest-edtech-trend-and-how-to-apply-it-to-your-business/

Chang, H. Y., Hsu, Y. S., & Wu, H. K. (2016). A comparison study of augmented reality versus interactive simulation technology to support student learning of a socio-scientific issue. *Interactive Learning Environments*, *24*(6), 1148–1161. doi:10.1080/10494820.2014.961486

Chang, H. Y., Lin, Y. K., Fang, R. J., & Lu, Y. T. (2017). Errata: A situated cultural festival learning system based on motion sensing. *Eurasia Journal of Mathematics, Science and Technology Education*, *13*(5), 1411–1411. doi:10.12973/eurasia.2017.00677a

Chapelle, C. A. (2003). *English language learning and technology: Lectures on applied linguistics in the age of information and communication technology*. John Benjamins. doi:10.1075/lllt.7

Checkpointorg.com. (2020). *Analyzing Our heroes (and Villains): Video Game Psychology*. Retrieved from https://checkpointorg.com/character-analysis/

Chen, L. L. (2013). iPad integration strategies for teaching and learning. In T. Bastiaens & G. Marks (Eds.), *Proceedings of E-Learn: World Conference on E-Learning in Corporate, Government, Healthcare, and Higher Education 2013* (pp. 631-634). Chesapeake, VA: Association for the Advancement of Computing in Education (AACE). http://www.editlib.org.ezp.waldenulibrary.org/p/114908/

Chen, C., Huang, C., & Chou, Y. (2019). Effects of augmented reality-based multidimensional concept maps on students' learning achievement, motivation and c. *Universal Access in the Information Society*, *18*(2), 257–268. doi:10.100710209-017-0595-z

Cheng, K. H. (2017). Reading an augmented reality book: An exploration of learners' cognitive load, motivation, and attitudes. *Australasian Journal of Educational Technology*, *33*(4).

Cheng, K.-H., & Tsai, C.-C. (2019). A case study of immersive virtual field trips in an elementary classroom: Students' learning experience and teacher-student interaction behaviors. *Computers & Education*, *140*, 103600. Advance online publication. doi:10.1016/j.compedu.2019.103600

Cheng, Y. L., & Mix, K. S. (2014). Spatial training improves children's mathematics ability. *Journal of Cognition and Development*, *15*(1), 2–11. doi:10.1080/15248372.2012.725186

Cheng, Y. W., Wang, Y., Cheng, I. L., & Chen, N. S. (2019). An in-depth analysis of the interaction transitions in a collaborative augmented reality-based mathematic game. *Interactive Learning Environments*, *27*(5-6), 782–796. doi:10.1080/10494820.2019.1610448

Chini, J. J., Straub, C. L., & Thomas, K. H. (2016). Learning from avatars: Learning assistance practice physics pedagogy in a classroom simulator. *Physical Review. Physics Education Research*, *12*(1), 010117. Advance online publication. doi:10.1103/PhysRevPhysEducRes.12.010117

Chmielewski, D. C. (2017, November 3). *Apple's Tim Cook says augmented reality will "change everything"*. https://deadline.com/2017/11/apple-tim-cook-augmented-reality-fourth-quarter-2017-earnings-1202200710/

Chong, A. K., & Croft, H. G. (2009). A photogrammetric application in virtual sport training. *The Photogrammetric Record*, *24*(125), 51–65. doi:10.1111/j.1477-9730.2009.00517.x

Christofferson, M., & Sullivan, A. L. (2015). Preservice teachers' classroom management training: A survey of self-reported training experiences, content coverage, and preparedness. *Psychology in the Schools*, *52*(3), 248–264. Advance online publication. doi:10.1002/pits.21819

Christou, C. (2010). Virtual reality in education. In *Affective, interactive and cognitive methods for e-learning design: creating an optimal education experience* (pp. 228–243). IGI Global. doi:10.4018/978-1-60566-940-3.ch012

Ciampa, K. K. (2016). Implementing a digital reading and writing Workshops Model for content literacy instruction in an urban elementary (K-8) school. *Reading Teacher,* 70(3), 295-306. doi: .1514 doi:10.1002/trtr

Ciccotelli, J., & Marsot, J. (2005). PR 17-Point of reference-Virtual reality and prevention-Contributions and trends. *Cahiers de Notes Documentaires-Hygiene et Securite du Travail*, (199), 99–112.

Cipresso, P., Giglioli, I. A. C., Raya, M. A., & Riva, G. (2018). The past, present, and future of virtual and augmented reality research: A network and cluster analysis of the literature. *Frontiers in Psychology*, *9*, 2086. doi:10.3389/fpsyg.2018.02086 PMID:30459681

Cocheteux, P. (2010). *Contribution à la maintenance proactive par la formalisation du processus de pronostic des performances de systèmes industriels* (Doctoral dissertation).

Cochrane, T., Antonczak, L., Keegan, H., & Narayan, V. (2014). Riding the Wave of BYOD: Developing a Framework for Creative Pedagogies. *Research in Learning Technology*, *22*(1). Advance online publication. doi:10.3402/rlt.v22.24637

Cogné, M., Taillade, M., N'Kaoua, B., Tarruella, A., Klinger, E., Larrue, F., Sauzéon, H., Joseph, P. A., & Sorita, E. (2017). The contribution of virtual reality to the diagnosis of spatial navigation disorders and to the study of the role of navigational aids: A systematic literature review. *Annals of Physical and Rehabilitation Medicine*, *60*(3), 164–176. doi:10.1016/j.rehab.2015.12.004 PMID:27017533

Collentine, K. (2011). Learner autonomy in a task-based 3D world and production. *Language Learning & Technology*, *15*(3), 50–67.

Cooke-Plagwitz, J. (2008). New directions in CALL: An objective introduction to Second Life. *CALICO Journal*, *25*(3), 547–557. doi:10.1558/cj.v25i3.547-557

Cook, M. J. (2019). Augmented reality: Examining its value in a music technology classroom. Practice and potential. *Waikato Journal of Education*, *24*(2), 23–38. doi:10.15663/wje.v24i2.687

Cornille, F., Thorne, S. L., & Desmet, P. (2012). Digital games for language learning: From hype to insight? *ReCALL Journal*, *24*(3), 243–356. doi:10.1017/S0958344012000134

Correia, V., Araújo, D., Duarte, R., Travassos, B., Passos, P., & Davids, K. (2012). Changes in practice task constraints shape decision-making behaviours of team games players. *Journal of Science and Medicine in Sport*, *15*(3), 244–249. doi:10.1016/j.jsams.2011.10.004 PMID:22153899

Cotaina, N., Gabriel, M., Richet, D., & O'Reilly, K. (1997). Utilisation de la Maintenance Basee sur la Fiabilite (MBF) pour developper et optimiser les politiques de maintenance des scieries. *Revue Française de Gestion Industrielle*, 47-66.

Covaci, A., Olivier, A. H., & Multon, F. (2015). Visual perspective and feedback guidance for vr free-throw training. *IEEE Computer Graphics and Applications*, *35*(5), 55–65. doi:10.1109/MCG.2015.95 PMID:26416362

Coxon, M., Kelly, N., & Page, S. (2016). Individual differences in virtual reality: Are spatial presence and spatial ability linked*? Virtual Reality (Waltham Cross)*, *20*(4), 203–212. doi:10.100710055-016-0292-x

Coyle, A. (2020). *Edgenuity announces recognitions from tech and learning, CODiE, and EdTech Digest, and Tech Edvocate 2020 Award Programs*. PR Web Online Visibility from Vocus. Retrieved from https://www.prweb.com/pdf-download/17363014.pdf

Craig, C. (2013). Understanding perception and action in sport: How can virtual reality technology help? *Sports Technology*, *6*(4), 161–169. doi:10.1080/19346182.2013.855224

Craig, C. M., Bastin, J., & Montagne, G. (2011). How information guides movement: Intercepting curved free kicks in soccer. *Human Movement Science*, *30*(5), 931–941. doi:10.1016/j.humov.2010.08.007 PMID:21414677

Craig, C. M., Berton, E., Rao, G., Fernandez, L., & Bootsma, R. J. (2006). Judging where a ball will go: The case of curved free kicks in football. *Naturwissenschaften*, *93*(2), 97–101. doi:10.100700114-005-0071-0 PMID:16450083

Craig, C. M., Goulon, C., Berton, E., Rao, G., Fernandez, L., & Bootsma, R. J. (2009). Optic variables used to judge future ball arrival position in expert and novice soccer players. *Attention, Perception & Psychophysics*, *71*(3), 515–522. doi:10.3758/APP.71.3.515 PMID:19304642

Csikszentmihalyi, M. (1975). *Beyond boredom and anxiety*. Jossey-Bass.

Cuban, L. (2001). *Oversold and Underused: Computers in the Classroom*. Harvard University Press. http://www.urosario.edu.co/CGTIC/Documentos/Cuban_article_oversold.pdf

Dabbagh, N. H., Jonassen, D. H., Yueh, H.-P., & Samouilova, M. (2008). Assessing a problem-based learning approach to an introductory instructional design course: A case study. *Performance Improvement Quarterly*, *13*(3), 60–83. doi:10.1111/j.1937-8327.2000.tb00176.x

Daher, W., Baya'a, N., & Anabousy, R. (2018). In-service mathematics teachers' integration of ICT as innovative practice. *International Journal of Research in Education and Science*, *4*(2), 534–543. doi:10.21890/ijres.428945

Dalal, M., Archambault, L., & Shelton, C. (2017). Professional development for international teachers: Examining TPACK and technology integration decision making. *Journal of Research on Technology in Education*, *49*(3-4), 117–133. doi: 10.1080/15391523.2017.1314780

Dalton, G., & Devitt, A. (2016). Irish in a 3D world: Engaging primary school children. *Language Learning & Technology*, *20*(1), 21–33.

Daniel, M. (2016). Study suggests medical errors now third leading cause of death in the US. *Johns Hopkins Medicine*, *3*. Advance online publication. doi:10.1136/bmj.i2139

de la Torre-Luque, A., Valero-Aguayo, L., & de la Rubia-Cuestas, E. J. (2017). Visuospatial Orientation Learning through Virtual Reality for People with Severe Disability. *International Journal of DisabIlIty*, *64*(4), 420–435. doi:10.1080/1034912X.2016.1274022

Dede, C. (2009). Immersive interfaces for engagement and learning. *Science*, *323*(5910), 66–69. doi:10.1126cience.1167311 PMID:19119219

Dehghanzadeh, H., Fardanesh, H., Hatami, J., Talaee, E., & Noroozi, O. (2019). Using gamification to support learning English as a second language: A systematic review. *Computer Assisted Language Learning*, *1*(24), 1–24. Advance online publication. doi:10.1080/09588221.2019.1648298

Dessing, J. C., & Craig, C. M. (2010). Bending it like Beckham: How to visually fool the goalkeeper. *PLoS One*, *5*(10), e13161. doi:10.1371/journal.pone.0013161 PMID:20949130

Deutschmann, M., Panichi, L., & Molka-Danielsen, J. (2009). Designing oral participation in Second Life: A comparative study of two language proficiency courses. *ReCALL Journal*, *21*(2), 206–226. doi:10.1017/S0958344009000196

Dewey, J. (1938). *Experience and Education*. Macmillan.

Diana, T. J. Jr. (2013). Microteaching revisited: Using technology to enhance the professional development of pre-service teachers. *The Clearing House: A Journal of Educational Strategies, Issues and Ideas*, *86*(4), 150–154. doi:10.1080/00098655.2013.790307

Dieker, L. A., Hynes, M., Hughes, C., & Smith, E. (2008). Implications of mixed reality and simulation technologies on special education and teacher preparation. *Focus on Exceptional Children*, *40*(6), 1–20. doi:10.17161/foec.v40i6.6877

Dieker, L. A., Rodriguez, J., Lingnugaris-Kraft, B., Hynes, M., & Hughes, C. E. (2014). The future of simulated environments in teacher education: Current potential and future possibilities. *Teacher Education and Special Education*, *37*(1), 21–33. doi:10.1177/0888406413512683

Dieker, L. A., Straub, C. L., Hughes, C. E., Hynes, M. C., & Hardin, S. (2014). Learning from virtual students. *Educational Leadership*, *71*(8), 54–58.

Dole, S. F., Bloom, L. A., & Doss, K. K. (2016a). Rocket to creativity: A field experience in problem-based and project-based learning. *Global Education Review*, *3*(4).

Dole, S., Bloom, L., & Kowalske, K. (2016b). Transforming pedagogy: Changing perspectives from teacher-centered to learner-centered. *The Interdisciplinary Journal of Problem-Based Learning*, *10*(1), 1.

Donato, R. (2004). Aspects of collaboration in pedagogical discourse. *Annual Review of Applied Linguistics*, *24*, 284–302. doi:10.1017/S026719050400011X

Dreamson, N. (2019). *Critical understandings of digital technology in education: Meta-connective pedagogy*. Taylor & Francis. doi:10.4324/9780429277528

Düking, P., Holmberg, H. C., & Sperlich, B. (2017). Instant biofeedback provided by wearable sensor technology can help to optimize exercise and prevent injury and overuse. *Frontiers in Physiology*, *8*, 167. doi:10.3389/fphys.2017.00167 PMID:28420998

Dunleavy, M., Dede, C., & Mitchell, R. (2009). Affordances and limitations of immersive participatory augmented reality simulations for teaching and learning. *Journal of Science Education and Technology*, *18*(1), 7–22. doi:10.100710956-008-9119-1

Dünser, A., Walker, L., Horner, H., & Bentall, D. (2012). Creating interactive physics education books with augmented reality. In V. Farrell (Ed.), *Proceedings of the 24th Australian Computer-Human Interaction Conference* (pp. 107-114). Melbourne, Australia: ACM. 10.1145/2414536.2414554

Edwards, S. (2016). New concepts of play and the problem of technology, digital media and popular-culture integration with play-based learning in early childhood education. *Technology, Pedagogy and Education*, *25*(4), 513–532. doi:10.1080/1475939X.2015.1108929

Edwards-Stewart, A., Hoyt, T., & Reger, G. (2016). Classifying different types of augmented reality technology. *Annual Review of Cybertherapy and Telemedicine*, *14*, 199–202.

Efstathiou, I., Kyza, E. A., & Georgiou, Y. (2018). An inquiry-based augmented reality mobile learning approach to fostering primary school students' historical reasoning in non-formal settings. *Interactive Learning Environments*, *26*(1), 22–41. doi:10.1080/10494820.2016.1276076

Eichenlaub, N., Gabel, L., Jakubek, D., & McCarthy, G. (2011). Project iPad investigation tablet integration in learning and libraries at Ryerson University. *Computers in Libraries*, 17–21. www.infotoday.com/cilmag/

El Kouzi, M., Mao, A., & Zambrano, D. (2019, March). An educational augmented reality application for elementary school students focusing on the human skeletal system. In *2019 IEEE Conference on Virtual Reality and 3D User Interfaces (VR)* (pp. 1594-1599). IEEE. 10.1109/VR.2019.8798058

Ellis, R. (2003). *Task-based Language Learning and Teaching*. Oxford University Press.

Ellis, R. (2009). Task-based research and language pedagogy. In K. Van den Branden, M. Bygate, & J. M. Norris (Eds.), *Task-based language teaching: A reader* (pp. 109–129). John Benjamins.

Ellis, R., Skehan, P., Li, S., Shintani, N., & Lambert, C. (2020). *Task-based language teaching: Theory and practice*. Cambridge University Press.

Ewais, A., & Troyer, O. D. (2019). A usability and acceptance evaluation of the use of augmented reality for learning atoms and molecules reaction by primary school female students in Palestine. *Journal of Educational Computing Research*, *57*(7), 1643–1670. doi:10.1177/0735633119855609

Fabroyir, H., & Teng, W. C. (2018). Navigation in virtual environments using head-mounted displays: Allocentric vs. egocentric behaviors. *Computers in Human Behavior*, *80*, 331–343. Advance online publication. doi:10.1016/j.chb.2017.11.033

Farley, O., Spencer, K., & Baudinet, L. (2019). Virtual reality in sports coaching, skill acquisition, and application to surfing: A review. *Journal of Human Sport and Exercise*, *15*(3). Advance online publication. doi:10.14198/jhse.2020.153.06

Farran, E. K., Formby, S., Daniyal, F., Holmes, T., & Van Herwegen, J. (2016). Route-learning strategies in typical and atypical development; eye tracking reveals atypical landmark selection in Williams syndrome. *Journal of Intellectual Disability Research*, *60*(10), 933–944. doi:10.1111/jir.12331 PMID:27634746

Faure, C., Limballe, A., Bideau, B., & Kulpa, R. (2020). Virtual reality to assess and train team ball sports performance: A scoping review. *Journal of Sports Sciences*, *38*(2), 192–205. doi:10.1080/02640414.2019.1689807 PMID:31724487

Fegert, J., Vitiello, B., Plener, P., & Clemens, V. (2020). Challenges and burden of the Coronavirus 2019 (COVID-19) pandemic for child and adolescent mental health: A narrative review to highlight clinical and research needs in the acute phase and the long return to normality. *Child and Adolescent Psychiatry and Mental Health*, *14*(1), 20. doi:10.118613034-020-00329-3 PMID:32419840

Ferwerda, J. A. (2001). Elements of early vision for computer graphics. *IEEE Computer Graphics and Applications*, *21*(5), 22–33. doi:10.1109/38.946628

Ficarra, L., & Quinn, K. (2014). Teachers' facility with evidence-based classroom management practices: An investigation of teachers' preparation programmes and in-service conditions. *Journal of Teacher Education for Sustainability*, *16*(2), 71–87. doi:10.2478/jtes-2014-0012

Fink, A., Graif, B., & Neubauer, A. C. (2009). Brain correlates underlying creative thinking: EEG alpha activity in professional vs. novice dancers. *NeuroImage*, *46*(3), 854–862. doi:10.1016/j.neuroimage.2009.02.036 PMID:19269335

Flewitt, R., Messer, D., & Kucirkova, N. (2015). New directions for early literacy in a digital age: The iPad. *Journal of Early Childhood Literacy*, *15*(3), 289–310. doi:10.1177/1468798414533560

Flood, J. L., & Commendador, K. (2016). Avatar case studies. A learning activity to bridge the gap between classroom and clinical practice in nursing education. *Nurse Educator*, *41*(1), 3–4. doi:10.1097/NNE.0000000000000195 PMID:26132174

Fogarty, J., Asce, A. M., Mccormick, J., El-Tawil, S., & Asce, F. (2017). *Improving Student Understanding of Complex Spatial Arrangements with Virtual Reality*. doi:10.1061/(ASCE)EI.1943-5541.0000349

Fokides, E., & Mastrokoukou, A. (2018). Results from a study for teaching human body systems to primary school students using tablets. *Contemporary Educational Technology*, *9*(2), 154–170. doi:10.30935/cet.414808

Foronda, C. L., Alfes, C. M., Dev, P., Kleinheksel, A. J., Nelson, D. A., O'Donnell, J. M., & Samosky, J. T. (2017). Virtually nursing: Emerging technologies in nursing education. *Nurse Educator*, *42*(1), 14–17. doi:10.1097/NNE.0000000000000295 PMID:27454054

Furdu, I., Tomozei, C., & Köse, U. (2017). Pros and cons gamification and gaming in classroom. *Broad Research in Artificial Intelligence and Neuroscience*, *8*(2), 56–62.

Gaba, D. M., Howard, S. K., Flanagan, B., Smith, B. E., Fish, K. J., & Botney, R. (1998). Assessment of clinical performance during simulated crises using both technical and behavioral ratings. *Anesthesiology: The Journal of the American Society of Anesthesiologists*, *89*(1), 8–18. doi:10.1097/00000542-199807000-00005 PMID:9667288

Gagnier, K., & Fisher, K. (2016). *Spatial thinking: A missing building block in STEM education*. John Hopkins Institute for Educational Policy.

Gandolfi, E. (2018). Virtual reality and augmented reality. Handbook of Research on K-12 Online and Blending Learning, 545-561.

Gánem-Gutiérrez, G. A. (2014). The third dimension: A sociocultural theory approach to the design and evaluation of 3D virtual worlds tasks. In M. Gonzalez-Lloret & L. Ortega (Eds.), *Technology-mediated TBLT: Researching technology and tasks* (pp. 213–237). John Benjamins. doi:10.1075/tblt.6.08gan

Gánem-Gutiérrez, G. A. (2018). Collaborative activity in the digital world. In J. P. Lantolf, M. E. Poehner, & M. Swain (Eds.), *The Routledge handbook of sociocultural theory and second language development* (pp. 391–408). Routledge. doi:10.4324/9781315624747-25

Garcia, E., Guyennet, H., Lapayre, J. C., & Zerhouni, N. (2004). A new industrial cooperative tele-maintenance platform. *Computers & Industrial Engineering*, *46*(4), 851–864. doi:10.1016/j.cie.2004.05.019

Gardeli, A., & Vosinakis, S. (2019, September). ARQuest: A tangible augmented reality approach to developing computational thinking skills. In *11th International Conference on Virtual Worlds and Games for Serious Applications (VS-Games)* (pp. 1-8). IEEE. 10.1109/VS-Games.2019.8864603

Gee, J. P. (2003). *What video games have to teach us about learning and literacy.* Palgrave Macmillan. doi:10.1145/950566.950595

Gerhard, M., Moore, D., & Hobbs, D. (2004). Embodiment and copresence in collaborative interfaces. *Human-Computer Studies*, *61*(4), 453–480. doi:10.1016/j.ijhcs.2003.12.014

Gerstein, J. S. (2019). *Learning in the making: How to plan, execute, and assess powerful makerspace lessons.* ASCD.

Gibson, J. (1986). *The Ecological Approach to Visual Perception.* Lawrence Erlbaum Associates.

Gilkey, R. H., & Weisenberger, J. M. (1995). The sense of presence for the suddenly deafened adult: Implications for virtual environments. *Presence (Cambridge, Mass.)*, *4*(4), 357–363.

Girod, M., & Girod, G. (2006). Exploring the efficacy of the Cook School District simulation. *Journal of Teacher Education*, *57*(5), 481–497. doi:10.1177/0022487106293742

Girod, M., & Girod, G. (2008). Simulation and the need for practice in teacher preparation. *Journal of Technology and Teacher Education*, *16*(3), 307–337.

Girvan, C. (2018). What is a virtual world? Definition and classification. *Education Tech Research Dev*, *66*, 1087–1100. https://connect.iste.org/blogs/kae-novak/2018/05/04/virtual-connected-educator-for-week-of-may-2 doi:10.100711423-018-9577-y

Golberstein, E., Wen, H., & Miller, B. (2020). Coronavirus Disease 2019 (COVID-19) and Mental Health for Children and Adolescents. *JAMA Pediatrics*, *174*(9), 819. Advance online publication. doi:10.1001/jamapediatrics.2020.1456 PMID:32286618

Gonzalez-Lloret, M., & Ortega, L. (2014). *Towards technology-mediated TBLT: An introduction. Technology-mediated TBLT: Researching technology and tasks.* John Benjamins. doi:10.1075/tblt.6

Gopalan, V., Zulkifli, A. N., & Bakar, J. A. A. (2016, August). A study of students' motivation using the augmented reality science textbook. In. AIP Conference Proceedings: Vol. 1761. *No. 1* (p. 020040). AIP Publishing LLC. doi:10.1063/1.4960880

Gough, D., Oliver, S., & Thomas, J. (2017). *An introduction to systematic reviews.* SAGE.

Graybeal, C. (2013). Learning to look for the standards for mathematical practice. *SRATE Journal*, *22*(2), 8-13. http://apbrwww5.apsu.edu/SRATE/

Green, M., McNair, L., Pierce, C., & Harvey, C. (2019). An investigation of augmented reality picture books: Meaningful experiences or missed opportunities? *Journal of Educational Multimedia and Hypermedia*, *28*(4), 357–380.

Grelaud, D., Bonneel, N., Wimmer, M., Asselot, M., & Drettakis, G. (2009, February). Efficient and practical audio-visual rendering for games using crossmodal perception. In *Proceedings of the 2009 symposium on Interactive 3D graphics and games* (pp. 177-182). 10.1145/1507149.1507178

Haines, K. J. (2015). Learning to identify and actualize affordances in a new tool. *Language Learning & Technology, 19*(1), 165–180.

Hall, G. E., & Hord, S. (2015). *Implementing change: Patterns, principles, and potholes* (4th ed.). Pearson Education.

Hampel, R. (2006). Rethinking task design for the digital age: A framework for language teaching and learning in a synchronous online environment. *ReCALL Journal, 18*(1), 101–121. doi:10.1017/S0958344006000711

Hampel, R. (2010). Task design for a virtual learning environment in a distance language course. In M. Thomas & H. Reinders (Eds.), *Task-Based language learning and teaching with technology* (pp. 131–153). Continuum.

Hansen, M. (2008). Versatile, immersive, creative and dynamic virtual 3-D healthcare learning environments: A review of the literature. *Journal of Medical Internet Research, 10*(3), e26. doi:10.2196/jmir.1051 PMID:18762473

Hartwick, P., & Savaskan Nowlan, N. (2018). Integrating virtual spaces: Connecting affordances of 3D virtual learning environments to design for twenty-first century learning. In Y. Qian (Ed.), *Integrating multi-user virtual environments in modern classrooms* (pp. 111–136). IGI Global. doi:10.4018/978-1-5225-3719-9.ch006

Hashim, H. (2018). Application of technology in the digital era education. *International Journal of Research in Counseling and Education, 2*(1), 1–5. doi:10.24036/002za0002

Hattie, J., Fisher, D., Frey, N., Gojak, L., Moore, S., & Mellman, W. (2017). *Visible leaning for mathematics*. Corwin.

Hedge, C., Weaver, R., & Schnall, S. (2017). *Spatial Learning and Wayfinding in an Immersive Environment: The Digital Fulldome*. doi:10.1089/cyber.2016.0399

Hee Lee, J., & Shvetsova, O. A. (2019). The Impact of VR Application on Student's Competency Development: A Comparative Study of Regular and VR Engineering Classes with Similar Competency Scopes. *Sustainability, 11*(8), 2221. doi:10.3390u11082221

Heeter, C. (1992). Being there: The subjective experience of presence. *Presence (Cambridge, Mass.), 1*(2), 262–271. doi:10.1162/pres.1992.1.2.262

Heeter, C. (2003). Reflections on real presence by a virtual person. *Presence (Cambridge, Mass.), 12*(4), 335–345. doi:10.1162/105474603322391587

He, H. (2017). Analysis of the Reasons of Public High School Students in United States Choosing Chinese as a Foreign Language–The Case of Nevada. *International Journal of Emerging Technologies in Learning, 12*(06), 140–148. doi:10.3991/ijet.v12i06.7092

Heinzen, T. E., Gordon, M. S., Landrum, R. E., Gurung, R. A. R., Dunn, D. S., & Richman, S. (2015). A parallel universes psychological science in the language of game design. In T. Reiners & L. C. Wood (Eds.), *Gamification in education and business* (pp. 133–151). Springer. doi:10.1007/978-3-319-10208-5_7

Hemmeter, M. L., Snyder, P. A., Fox, L., & Algina, J. (2016). Evaluating the implementation of the Pyramid Model for promoting social-emotional competence in early childhood classrooms. *Topics in Early Childhood Special Education, 36*(3), 133–146. doi:10.1177/0271121416653386

Hennel, P., Schmidt-Kraepelin, M., van den Eynden, S., & Basten, D. (2015). Benefits of augmented reality in educational environments – A systematic literature review. *Benefits, 3*(6), 1542–1556.

Hesser, T. L., & Schwartz, P. M. (2013). iPads in the science laboratory: Experience in designing and implementing a paperless chemistry laboratory course. *Journal of STEM Education: Innovations and Research*, *14*(2), 5–9. www.jstem.org

Hite, R. L., Jones, M. G., Childers, G. M., Ennes, M., Chesnutt, K., Pereyra, M., & Cayton, E. (2019). *Investigating Potential Relationships Between Adolescents' Cognitive Development and Perceptions of Presence in 3-D, Haptic-Enabled, Virtual Reality Science Instruction*. doi:10.100710956-018-9764-y

Hixon, E., & So, H. J. (2009). Technology's role in field experiences for preservice teacher training. *Journal of Educational Technology & Society*, *12*(4), 294–304. https://www.jstor.org/stable/jeductechsoci.12.4.294

Hmelo-Silver, C. E., Bridges, S. M., & McKeown, J. M. (2019). Facilitating problem-based learning. In M. Moalem, W. Hung, & N. Daggagh (Eds.), *The Wiley handbook of problem-based learning* (pp. 297–319). Wiley. doi:10.1002/9781119173243.ch13

Hsin, C. T., Li, M. C., & Tsai, C. C. (2014). The influence of young children's use of technology on their learning: A review. *Journal of Educational Technology & Society*, *17*(4), 85–99.

Hsu, C. Y., Tsai, M. J., Chang, Y. H., & Liang, J. C. (2017). Surveying in-service teachers' beliefs about game-based learning and perceptions of technological pedagogical and content knowledge of games. *Journal of Educational Technology & Society*, *20*(1), 134–143.

Hsu, T. C. (2019). Effects of gender and different augmented reality learning systems on English vocabulary learning of elementary school students. *Universal Access in the Information Society*, *18*(2), 315–325. doi:10.100710209-017-0593-1

Hudson, M. E., Voytecki, K. S., & Zhang, G. (2018). Mixed-reality teaching experiences improve preservice special education students' perceptions of their ability to manage a classroom. *Journal of Virtual Worlds Research*, *11*(2), 1–17. doi:10.4101/jvwr.v11i2.7308

Hu, J., Kim, J., Song, K., Lockee, B., & Burton, J. (2018). *Gamification in learning and education: Enjoy learning like gaming*. Springer.

Hwang, W. Y., & Hu, S. S. (2013). Analysis of peer learning behaviors using multiple representations in virtual reality and their impacts on geometry problem solving. *Computers & Education*, *62*, 308–319. doi:10.1016/j.compedu.2012.10.005

Ifenthaler, D., & Eseryel, D. (2013). Facilitating complex learning by mobile augmented reality learning environments. In R. H. Kinshuk, J. M. Spector, & Kinshuk (Eds.), Reshaping learning: Frontiers of learning technology in a global context (pp. 415-438). New York, NY: Springer. doi:10.1007/978-3-642-32301-0_18

IJsselsteijn, W. A., De Ridder, H., Freeman, J., & Avons, S. E. (2000, June). Presence: concept, determinants, and measurement. In Human vision and electronic imaging V (Vol. 3959, pp. 520-529). International Society for Optics and Photonics.

Inks, S. A., & Avila, R. A. (2008). Preparing the next generation of sales professionals through social, experiential, and immersive learning experiences. *Journal for Advancement of Marketing Education*, *13*(4), 47–55. http://www.mmaglobal.org/JAME-Archive/JAME-Winter-2008/JAMEWinter2008v.13p.47-55.pdf

Interactive and immersive learning using 360° virtual reality contents on mobile platforms. (2018). *Mobile Information Systems*, 1-12. doi:10.1155/2018/2306031

Ip, H. H., Hoi-Yan Lai, C., Wong, S. W., Tsui, J. K., Chen Li, R., Shuk-Ying Lau, K., & Chan, D. F. (2017). Visuospatial attention in children with Autism Spectrum Disorder: A comparison between 2-D and 3-D environments. *Cogent Education*, *6*(1), 1307709. Advance online publication. doi:10.1080/2331186X.2017.1307709

Jacobson, J. (2013). Digital dome versus desktop display; Learning outcome assessments by domain experts. *International Journal of Virtual and Personal Learning Environments*, *4*(3), 51–65. http://publicvr.org/publications/. doi:10.4018/jvple.2013070104

Jang, S., Vitale, J. M., Jyung, R. W., & Black, J. B. (2017). Direct manipulation is better than passive viewing for learning anatomy in a three-dimensional virtual reality environment. *Computers & Education*, *106*, 150–165. Advance online publication. doi:10.1016/j.compedu.2016.12.009

Johnson, K. (2003). *Designing Language Teaching Tasks*. Palgrave Macmillian. doi:10.1057/9780230596672

Jonassen, D. H. (2010, September). Research issues in problem solving. In *11th International Conference on Education Research*. New Educational Paradigm for Learning and Instruction. https://www.aect.org/publications/whitepapers/2010/JonassenICER.pdf

Jonassen, D. H., Peck, K. L., & Wilson, B. (1999). *Learning with technology: A Constructivist Perspective*. Merrill-Prentice Hall.

Jones, M., & Ryan, J. (2014). Learning in the practicum: Engaging pre-service teachers in reflective practice in the online space. *Asia-Pacific Journal of Teacher Education*, *42*(2), 132–146. doi:10.1080/1359866X.2014.892058

Kaffel, H. (2001). *Distributed maintenance: concept, evaluation and implementation*. Academic Press.

Kahneman, D. (2011). *Thinking fast and slow*. Farrar, Straus, and Giroux.

Kahn, J. (2003). Overview of MIMOSA and the Open System Architecture for Enterprise Application Integration. In *Proc. of COMADEM 2003* (pp. 661-670). Växjö University.

Kanade, T., Rander, P., & Narayanan, P. J. (1997). Virtualized reality: Constructing virtual worlds from real scenes. *IEEE MultiMedia*, *4*(1), 34–47. doi:10.1109/93.580394

Kang, Y., & Yang, K. C. (2020). Employing digital reality technologies in art exhibitions and museums: A global survey of best practices and implications. In *Virtual and augmented reality in education, art, and museums* (pp. 139–161). IGI Global. doi:10.4018/978-1-7998-1796-3.ch008

Kapp, K. M. (2012). *The gamification of learning and instruction: Game-based methods and strategies for training and education*. Pfeiffer.

Karagozlu, D. (2018). Determination of the impact of augmented reality application on the success and problem-solving skills of students. *Quality & Quantity*, *52*(5), 2393–2402. doi:10.100711135-017-0674-5

Karlström, M., & Hamza, K. (2019). Preservice science teachers' opportunities for learning through reflection when planning a microteaching unit. *Journal of Science Teacher Education*, *30*(1), 44–62. doi:10.1080/1046560X.2018.1531345

Kaufmann, H., Schmalstieg, D., & Wagner, M. (2000). Construct3D: A virtual reality application for mathematics and geometry education. *Education and Information Technologies*, *5*(4), 263–276. doi:10.1023/A:1012049406877

Kaur, D., Koval, A., & Chaney, H. (2017). Potential of Using iPad as a Supplement to Teach Math to Students with Learning Disabilities. *International Journal of Research in Education and Science*, *3*(1), 114–121.

Kelly, A. (2011). Involve, prepare, apply, and develop: iPads in the classroom. *Technology and Learning*. Retrieved from: http://www.techlearning.com/article/Involve-Prepare-Apply-and-Develop-iPads-in-the-Classroom/47763

KerstenT. P.TrauD.TschirschwitzF. (2020). The Four-Masted Barque Peking in Virtual Reality as a New Form of Knowledge Transfer. *ISPRS Annals of the Photogrammetry, Remote Sensing and Spatial Information Sciences, 4,* 155-162. https://doi-org.proxy1.ncu.edu/10.5194/isprs-annals-V-4-2020-155-2020

Kim, J., Son, J., Ko, N., & Yoon, B. (2013). Unsupervised virtual reality-based exercise program improves hip muscle strength and balance control in older adults: A pilot study. *Archives of Physical Medicine and Rehabilitation*, *94*(5), 937–943. doi:10.1016/j.apmr.2012.12.010 PMID:23262158

Kim, Y., & Rhee, S. (2011). Augmented Reality on a Deformable Surface by Considering Self-Occlusion and Realistic Illumination. *Internet Technology.*, *12*(5), 733–740.

Kiryakova, G. (2020). The Immersive Power of Augmented Reality. In Human-Computer Interaction. doi:10.5772/intechopen.92361

Klopfer, E., & Squire, K. (2008). Environmental detectives—The development of an augmented reality platform for environmental simulations. *Educational Technology Research and Development*, *56*(2), 203–228. doi:10.100711423-007-9037-6

Koehler, A., Ertmer, P., & Newby, T. (2019). Instructional design skills through case-based instruction: Examining the impact of discussion format. *Journal of Teacher Education*, *70*(4), 319–334. doi:10.1177/0022487118755701

Koh, J. H. L., Chai, C. S., Hong, H. Y., & Tsai, C.-C. (2017). A survey to examine teachers' perceptions of design dispositions, lesson design practices and their relationships with technological pedagogical content knowledge (TPACK). *Asia-Pacific Journal of Teacher Education*, *43*(5), 378–391. doi:10.1080/1359866X.2014.941280

Kohn, L. T., Corrigan, J. M., & Donaldson, M. S. (2000). *To err is human: building a safer health system. A report of the Committee on Quality of Health Care in America*. Institute of Medicine.

KOL, S. (2015). Computer Perceptions of Children in Early Childhood period. *International Online Journal of Educational Sciences*, *7*(2).

Koo, B., & Shon, T. (2010). A Structural Health Monitoring Framework Using 3D Visualization and Augmented Reality in Wireless Sensor Networks. *Internet Technology*, *11*(6), 801–807. Retrieved from https://jit.ndhu.edu.tw/article/view/627

Kovach, N. (2019). *Augmented Reality in Education*. Retrieved from https://thinkmobiles.com/blog/augmented-reality-education/

Kovach, N. (n.d.). *Augmented Reality in Education*. https://thinkmobiles.com/blog/augmented-reality-education/

Kozlova, I. (2018a). Factors affecting learner collaboration in 3D virtual worlds. In M. Kruk (Ed.), *Assessing the effectiveness of virtual technologies in foreign and second language instruction* (pp. 26–60). IGI Global.

Kozlova, I. (2018b). Task-based language learning and learner autonomy in 3D virtual worlds. In Y. Qian (Ed.), *Integrating multi-user virtual environments in modern classrooms* (pp. 50–73). IGI Global. doi:10.4018/978-1-5225-3719-9.ch003

Kozlova, I., & Priven, D. (2015). ESL teacher training in 3D virtual worlds. *Language Learning & Technology*, *19*(1), 83–101.

Krashen, S. (2013). *Second language Acquisition: Theory, applications, and some conjectures*. Cambridge University Press.

Kulpa, R., Bideau, B., & Brault, S. (2013). Displacements in Virtual Reality for sports performance analysis. In *Human walking in virtual environments* (pp. 299–318). Springer. doi:10.1007/978-1-4419-8432-6_13

Kumar, J. (2020). *Everything You Need To Know About Immersive Learning*. eLearning Industry. https://elearningindustry.com/everything-need-know-about-immersive-learning

Kwan, Y. W., & Wong, A. F. (2015). Effects of the constructivist learning environment on students' critical thinking ability: Cognitive and motivational variables as mediators. *International Journal of Educational Research*, *70*, 68–79. doi:10.1016/j.ijer.2015.02.006

Lamrani, R., & Abdelwahed, E. (2019). Game-based learning and gamification to improve skills in early childhood education. *Computer Science and Information Systems*, *17*(1), 339–356. doi:10.2298/CSIS190511043L

Lantolf, J. P. (2000). Introducing sociocultural theory. In J. P. Lantolf (Ed.), *Sociocultural theory and second language learning* (pp. 1–26). Oxford University Press.

Lantolf, J., Thorne, S. L., & Poehner, M. (2015). Sociocultural Theory and Second Language Development. In B. van Patten & J. Williams (Eds.), *Theories in Second Language Acquisition* (pp. 207–226). Routledge.

Lan, Y. J., Kan, Y. H., Sung, Y. T., & Chung, K. E. (2016). Oral performance language tasks for CSL beginners in Second Life. *Language Learning & Technology*, *20*(3), 60–79.

Larsen, C. R., Soerensen, J. L., Grantcharov, T. P., Dalsgaard, T., Schouenborg, L., Ottosen, C., Schroeder, T. V., & Ottesen, B. S. (2009). Effect of virtual reality training on laparoscopic surgery: Randomised controlled trial. *BMJ (Clinical Research Ed.)*, *338*(2), b1802. doi:10.1136/bmj.b1802 PMID:19443914

Lave, J., & Wenger, E. (1991). *Learning in doing: Social, cognitive, and computational perspectives.Situated learning: Legitimate peripheral participation*. Cambridge University Press. doi:10.1017/CBO9780511815355

Laver, K. E., Lange, B., George, S., Deutsch, J. E., Saposnik, G., & Crotty, M. (2017). Virtual reality for stroke rehabilitation. *Cochrane Database of Systematic Reviews*, 11. PMID:29156493

Lee, E. A. L., & Wong, K. W. (2014). Learning with desktop virtual reality: Low spatial ability learners are more positively affected. *Computers & Education*, *79*, 49–58. doi:10.1016/j.compedu.2014.07.010

Lee, K. M. (2004). Presence, explicated. *Communication Theory*, *14*(1), 27–50. doi:10.1111/j.1468-2885.2004.tb00302.x

Lefrançois, C., & Messier, J. (2019). Adaptation and spatial generalization to a triaxial visuomotor perturbation in a virtual reality environment. *Experimental Brain Research*, *237*(3), 793–803. doi:10.100700221-018-05462-2 PMID:30607472

Legault, J., Zhao, J., Chi, Y.-A., Chen, W., Klippel, A., & Li, P. (2019). Immersive Virtual Reality as an Effective Tool for Second Language Vocabulary Learning. *Languages*, *4*(1), 13. doi:10.3390/languages4010013

Lenneberg, E. H. (1967). *Biological foundations of language*. Wiley & Sons. doi:10.1080/21548331.1967.11707799

Leó, I., Tascó, L., Ortells-Pareja, J. J., Manuel, J., & Id, C. (2018). *Virtual reality assessment of walking and non-walking space in men and women with virtual reality-based tasks*. doi:10.1371/journal.pone.0204995

Lessiter, J., Freeman, J., Keogh, E., & Davidoff, J. (2001). A cross-media presence questionnaire: The ITC-Sense of Presence Inventory. *Presence (Cambridge, Mass.)*, *10*(3), 282–297. doi:10.1162/105474601300343612

Leu, D. J., Kinzer, C. K., Coiro, J., Castek, J., & Henry, L. A. (2017). New literacies: A dual-level theory of the changing nature of literacy, instruction, and assessment. *Journal of Education*, *197*(2), 1–18. doi:10.1177/002205741719700202

Levine, D. N. (2007, February). "The Integrative action of the nervous system": A centennial appraisal. *Journal of the Neurological Sciences*, *253*(1-2), 1–6. doi:10.1016/j.jns.2006.12.002 PMID:17223135

Levrat, E., Salzemann, B., Clanché, F., & Bron, J. Y. (2006). TELMA Plate-forme d'intégration de télémaintenance pour l'enseignement et la recherche. *J3eA, 5*, 17.

Li, K. C., Tsai, C. W., Chen, C. T., Cheng, S. Y., & Heh, J. S. (2015, August). The design of immersive English learning environment using augmented reality. In *2015 8th International Conference on Ubi-Media Computing (UMEDIA)* (pp. 174-179). IEEE. 10.1109/UMEDIA.2015.7297450

Liang, G., & Akiba, M. (2015). Teacher evaluation, performance-related pay, and constructivist instruction. *Educational Policy, 29*(2), 375–401. doi:10.1177/0895904813492379

Liang, H. N., Lu, F., Shi, Y., Nanjappan, V., & Papangelis, K. (2019). Evaluating the effects of collaboration and competition in navigation tasks and spatial knowledge acquisition within virtual reality environments. *Future Generation Computer Systems, 95*, 855–866. Advance online publication. doi:10.1016/j.future.2018.02.029

Lim, C., & Park, T. (2011). Exploring the educational use of augmented reality books. In *Proceedings of the Annual Convention of the Association for Educational Communications and Technology* (pp. 172-182). Academic Press.

Limelight Networks. (2020). *The state of online gaming 2020*. https://www.limelight.com/resources/white-paper/state-of-online-gaming-2020/

Lin, T., Wang, S., Grant, S., Chien, C., & Lan, Y. (2014). Task-based teaching approaches of Chinese as a foreign language in Second Life through teachers' perspectives. *Procedia Technology, 13*, 16–22. doi:10.1016/j.protcy.2014.02.004

Li, R., & Topolewski, D. (2002). Zip and Terry: A new attempt at designing language learning simulation. *Simulation & Gaming, 33*(2), 181–186. doi:10.1177/1046878102332006

Liu, X., & Olmanson, J. (2016). A technology-supported learning experience to facilitate Chinese character acquisition. *The Nebraska Educator: A Student-Led Journal, 30*, 87-107.

Liu, M., Navarrete, C. C., Scordino, R., Kang, J., Ko, Y., & Lim, M. (2016). Examining teachers' use of iPads: Comfort level, perception, and use. *Journal of Research on Technology in Education, 48*(3), 159–180. doi:10.1080/15391523.2016.1175853

Liu, S., & Wang, F. (2018). A qualitative study on learning trajectories of non-native Chinese instructors as successful Chinese language learners. *Asian-Pacific Journal of Second and Foreign Lang Education, 3*(2), 1–21. doi:10.118640862-018-0043-5

Lloyd, L. (2017). *Getting Over It: finding stillness in chaos*. CheckPointorg.com. Retrieved from https://checkpointorg.com/getting-over-it-finding-stillness-in-chaos/

Lombard, M., & Ditton, T. (1997). At the heart of it all: The concept of presence. *Journal of Computer-Mediated Communication, 3*(2).

López-Faican, L., & Jaen, J. (2020). Emofindar: Evaluation of a mobile multiplayer augmented reality game for primary school children. *Computers & Education, 149*, 103814. doi:10.1016/j.compedu.2020.103814

Loughran, J. (2006). *Developing a pedagogy of teacher education: Understanding teaching and learning about teaching*. Routledge.

Lowman, J. J., & Dressler, E. V. (2016). Effects of explicit vocabulary videos delivered through iPods on students with language impairments. *Journal of Special Education Technology, 31*(4), 195–206. doi:10.1177/0162643416673914

Lü, C., & Lavadenz, M. (2014). Native Chinese-Speaking K-12 Language Teachers' Beliefs and Practices. *Foreign Language Annals, 47*(4), 630–652. doi:10.1111/flan.12111

Lucero, A. (2014). Teachers' use of linguistic scaffolding to support the academic language development of first-grade emergent bilingual students. *Journal of Early Childhood Literacy, 14*(4), 534–561. doi:10.1177/1468798413512848

Ludgate, S. (2015). *Pre-School Children's Experiences with Touchscreen Technologies: Early Findings from Survey Results*. TACTYC Conference, Birmingham, UK.

Luis, C. E. M., Mellado, R. C., & Díaz, B. A. (2013, January). PBL methodologies with embedded augmented reality in higher maritime education: Augmented project definitions for chemistry practices. In J. Martin-Gutierrez & E. Ginters (Eds.), *VARE* (pp. 402–405). Elsevier. doi:10.1016/j.procs.2013.11.050

Lu, J., Meng, S., & Tam, V. (2014). Learning Chinese characters via mobile technology in a primary school classroom. *Educational Media International*, *51*(3), 166–184. doi:10.1080/09523987.2014.968448

Lu, S. J., Liu, Y. C., Chen, P. J., & Hsieh, M. R. (2020). Evaluation of AR embedded physical puzzle game on students' learning achievement and motivation on elementary natural science. *Interactive Learning Environments*, *28*(4), 451–463. doi:10.1080/10494820.2018.1541908

Lux, M. E., & Escobar, J. M. (2019). Where Technology Meets Psychology: Improving Global Mental Health. In Technology and Child Mental Health. IntechOpen. doi:10.5772/intechopen.88174

Maad, M. R. (2016). Awakening young children to foreign languages: Openness to diversity highlighted. *Language, Culture and Curriculum*, *29*(3), 319–336. doi:10.1080/07908318.2016.1184679

Maddox, L. (2018). *The brain science of muscle memory: QBSIM and repetition*. Retrieved from https://www.sportsvts.com/media/2018/4/26/the-brain-science-of-muscle-memory-qbsim-and-repetition

Maddox, T. (n.d.). *Sports VTS leverages brain science: QBSIM optimizes quarterback training*. Retrieved from https://www.sportsvts.com/media/2018/1/29/sports-vts-leverages-brain-science-qbsim-optimizes-quarterback-training

Maich, K., & Hall, C. (2016). Implementing iPads in the inclusive classroom setting. *Intervention in School and Clinic*, *51*(3), 145–150. doi:10.1177/1053451215585793

Malone, D. M., & Langone, J. (2005). Comparing general and special education preservice teachers' test performance using traditional and anchored instruction. *Journal of Early Childhood Teacher Education*, *25*(2), 143–152. doi:10.1080/1090102050250207

Malz, R. (2020). *Special Education Teachers' Experiences Integrating Mobile Devices in their Classroom* [Doctoral dissertation, Walden University]. Scholarworks.waldenu.edu

Marsot, J., Gardeux, F., & Govaere, V. (2009). Réalité augmentée et prévention des risques: apports et limites. Hygiène et sécurité du travail, (214), 15-23.

Martín-Gutiérrez, J., Mora, C. E., Añorbe-Díaz, B., & González-Marrero, A. (2017). Virtual technologies trends in education. *Eurasia Journal of Mathematics, Science and Technology Education*, *13*(2), 469–486. doi:10.12973/eurasia.2017.00626a

McGee, M. G. (1979). Human spatial abilities: Psychometric studies and environmental, genetic, hormonal, and neurological influences. *Psychological Bulletin*, *86*(5), 889–918. doi:10.1037/0033-2909.86.5.889 PMID:386403

McGurk, H., & MacDonald, J. (1976). Hearing lips and seeing voices. *Nature*, *264*(5588), 746–748. doi:10.1038/264746a0 PMID:1012311

McKenna, K., Schulz, L., Otieno, C., Wang, X., & Williams, M. (2015). Multiple perspective account of iPad integration. In D. Slykhuis & G. Marks (Eds.), *Proceedings of Society for Information Technology and Teacher Education International Conference 2015* (pp. 1672-1678). Chesapeake, VA: Association for the Advancement of Computing in Education (AACE). http://www.editlib.org.ezp.waldenulibrary.org/p/150223/

McLay, R. N., Wood, D. P., Webb-Murphy, J. A., Spira, J. L., Wiederhold, M. D., Pyne, J. M., & Wiederhold, B. K. (2011). A randomized, controlled trial of virtual reality-graded exposure therapy for post-traumatic stress disorder in active duty service members with combat-related post-traumatic stress disorder. *Cyberpsychology, Behavior, and Social Networking*, *14*(4), 223–229. doi:10.1089/cyber.2011.0003 PMID:21332375

McLeod, A. J. (2008). *The management and maintenance of second generation sand-filled synthetic sports pitches.* Academic Press.

Meade, M. E., Meade, J. G., Sauzeon, H., & Fernandes, M. A. (2019). *Active Navigation in Virtual Environments Benefits Spatial Memory in Older Adults.* doi:10.3390/brainsci9030047

Merchant, Z., Goetz, E. T., Keeney-Kennicutt, W., Cifuentes, L., Kwok, O. M., & Davis, T. J. (2013). Exploring 3-D virtual reality technology for spatial ability and chemistry achievement. *Journal of Computer Assisted Learning, 29*(6), 579–590. doi:10.1111/jcal.12018

Meredith, P., Yeates, H., Greaves, A., Taylor, M., Slattery, M., Charters, M., & Hill, M. (2018). Preparing mental health professionals for new directions in mental health practice: Evaluating the sensible approaches e-learning training package. *International Journal of Mental Health Nursing, 27*(1), 106–115. doi:10.1111/inm.12299 PMID:28042908

Merriam-Webster. (n.d.). Design. In *Merriam-Webster.com dictionary.* Retrieved September 28, 2020 from https://www.merriam-webster.com/dictionary/design

Merrick, M. T., Ford, D., Ports, K. A., Guinn, A. S., Chen, J., Klevens, J., Metzler, M., Jones, C. M., Simon, T. R., Daniel, V. M., Ottley, P., & Mercy, J. A. (2019). Vital Signs: Estimated Proportion of Adult Health Problems Attributable to Adverse Childhood Experiences and Implications for Prevention — 25 States, 2015–2017. *MMWR. Morbidity and Mortality Weekly Report, 68*(44), 999–1005. doi:10.15585/mmwr.mm6844e1 PMID:31697656

Meyer, B. (2013). Game-based language learning for pre-school children: A design perspective. *The Electronic Journal of e-Learning, 11*(1), 39-48.

Mikropoulos, T. A., & Natsis, A. (2011). Educational virtual environments: A ten-year review of empirical research (1999–2009). *Computers & Education, 56*(3), 769–780. doi:10.1016/j.compedu.2010.10.020

Miles, H. C., Pop, S. R., Watt, S. J., Lawrence, G. P., & John, N. W. (2012). A review of virtual environments for training in ball sports. *Computers & Graphics, 36*(6), 714–726. doi:10.1016/j.cag.2012.04.007

Milk, C., & Arora, G. (Writer, Producer). Pousman. B., Arora, G. (Director). (2015). *Clouds over sidra* [Film]. WithIn. Retrieved from https://www.with.in/watch/clouds-over-sidra/

Minsky, M. (1980, June). Telepresence. *OMNI Magazine.*

Moreno, R., & Mayer, R. E. (1999). Cognitive principles of multimedia learning: The role of modality and contiguity. *Journal of Educational Psychology, 91*(2), 358–368. doi:10.1037/0022-0663.91.2.358

Mori, J. (2002). Task design, plan, and development of talk-in-interaction: An analysis of a small group activity in a Japanese language classroom. *Applied Linguistics, 23*(3), 323–347. doi:10.1093/applin/23.3.323

Mourlam, D. J., & Montgomery, S. E. (2015). iPads and teacher education: Exploring a 1: 1 initiative in a professional development school partnership. *Journal of Digital Learning in Teacher Education, 31*(3), 107–116. doi:10.1080/21532974.2015.1021981

Munoz, C. (2014). Contrasting effects of starting age and input on the oral performance of foreign language learners. *Applied Linguistics, 35*(4), 1–21. doi:10.1093/applin/amu024

Murphy, V. A. (2014). *Second language learning in the early school years: Trends and contexts.* Oxford University Press.

Mursion. (2020). *Best in class leadership development: How virtual reality and avatars are changing the learning landscape* [White paper]. https://www.denasamuels.com/wp-content/uploads/2020/03/How-Virtual-Reality-and-Avatars-are-Changing-the-Learning-Landscape.pdf

Musti-Rao, S., Cartledge, G., Bennett, J. G., & Council, M. (2015). Literacy instruction using technology with primary-age culturally and linguistically diverse learners. *Intervention in School and Clinic*, *50*(4), 195–202. doi:10.1177/1053451214546404

Naaz, I., & Sharma, A. (2018). *Rise of Augmented Reality: Applications, challenges, and future trends*. Academic Press.

NAEYC. (2012). *Technology and Media*. https://www.naeyc.org/sites/default/files/globally-shared/downloads/PDFs/resources/topics/PS_technology_WEB.pdf

Nagel, D. (2016). How teachers leverage mobile technology. *T.H.E. Journal*, *43*(6), 34.

National Center for Education Statistics. (2015). *Children and youth with disabilities*. Retrieved from: https://nces.ed.gov/programs/coe/indicator_cgg.asp

Negen, J., Heywood-Everett, E., Roome, H. E., & Nardini, M. (2018). Development of allocentric spatial recall from new viewpoints in virtual reality. *Developmental Science*, *21*(1), 12496. doi:10.1111/desc.12496 PMID:28256025

Neguţ, A., Matu, S. A., Sava, F. A., & David, D. (2016). Task difficulty of virtual reality-based assessment tools compared to classical paper-and-pencil or computerized measures: A meta-analytic approach. *Computers in Human Behavior*, *54*, 414–424. doi:10.1016/j.chb.2015.08.029

Nemati, M., & Arabmofrad, A. (2014). Development of interlanguage pragmatic competence: Input- and output-based instruction in the zone of proximal development. *Theory and Practice in Language Studies*, *4*(2), 262–270. doi:10.4304/tpls.4.2.262-270

Neumann, D. L., Moffitt, R. L., Thomas, P. R., Loveday, K., Watling, D. P., & Lombard, C. L. (2017). A systematic review of the application of interactive virtual reality to sport. *Virtual Reality (Waltham Cross)*. Advance online publication. doi:10.100710055-017-0320-5

Newcombe, N. S. (2016). Thinking spatially in the science classroom. *Current Opinion in Behavioral Sciences*, *10*, 1–6. doi:10.1016/j.cobeha.2016.04.010

Nicolay, A., & Poncelet, M. (2015). Cognitive benefits in children enrolled in an early bilingual immersion school: A follow up study. *Bilingualism: Language and Cognition*, *18*(4), 789–795. doi:10.1017/S1366728914000868

Nijjar, G. (2020). *7 Ways Augmented Reality Is Changing Education Industry in the UK: The Future of Learning Is Now*. AR Post. https://arpost.co/2020/03/10/7-ways-augmented-reality-education-the-uk/

Nikolopoulou, K., & Gialamas, V. (2015). Barriers to the integration of computers in early childhood settings: Teachers' perceptions. *Education and Information Technologies*, *20*(2), 285–301. doi:10.100710639-013-9281-9

Niu, B., Liu, C., Liu, J., Deng, Y., Wan, Q., & Ma, N. (2019, October). Impacts of Different Types of Scaffolding on Academic Performance, Cognitive Load and Satisfaction in Scientific Inquiry Activities Based on Augmented Reality. In *2019 Eighth International Conference on Educational Innovation through Technology (EITT)* (pp. 239-244). IEEE. 10.1109/EITT.2019.00053

Nori, R., Piccardi, L., Migliori, M., Guidazzoli, A., Frasca, F., De Luca, D., & Giusberti, F. (2015). The virtual reality Walking Corsi Test. *Computers in Human Behavior*, *48*, 72–77. Advance online publication. doi:10.1016/j.chb.2015.01.035

Ntuli, E. (2019). Augmented reality in early learning: Experiences of K-3 teachers with merge cubes. In S. Carliner (Ed.), *Proceedings of e-learn: World conference on e-learning in corporate, government, healthcare, and higher education* (pp. 557-560). New Orleans, LA: Association for the Advancement of Computing in Education (AACE).

Nunan, D. (1997). Designing and adapting materials to encourage learner autonomy. In P. Benson & P. Voller (Eds.), *Autonomy and independence in language learning* (pp. 192–203). Longman.

Nunan, D. (2004). *Task-based language teaching*. Cambridge University Press. doi:10.1017/CBO9780511667336

O'Brien, N. P., & Collins, J. W. (2011). *The Greenwood dictionary of education* (2nd ed.). ABC-CLIO.

O'Malley, P., Jenkins, S., Wesley, B., Donehower, C., Rabuck, D., & Lewis, M. (2013). *Effectiveness of using iPads to build math fluency*. Kennedy Krieger Institute. www.kennedyrieger.org

O'Shea, P., Mitchell, R., Johnston, C., & Dede, C. (2009). Lessons learned about designing augmented realities. *International Journal of Gaming and Computer-Mediated Simulations*, *1*(1).

Onyegwara, P. (2020). *Middle School Teachers' Experiences Implementing the Workshop Model in Their Classroom* (Doctoral dissertation). Walden University.

Onyesolu, M. O., & Eze, F. U. (2011). Understanding virtual reality technology: advances and applications. Advances in Computer. *Science and Engineering*, 53-70.

Oxford, R. (2006). Task-based language teaching and learning: An overview. *Asian EFL Journal*, *8*(3), 94–121.

Panichi, L., & Deutschmann, M. (2012). Language learning in virtual worlds: Research issues and methods. In M. Dooly & R. O'Dowd (Eds.), *Researching online foreign language interaction and exchange: Theories, methods and challenges* (pp. 205–231). Peter Lang.

Pantelidis, V. S. (2010). Reasons to use virtual reality in education and training courses and a model to determine when to use virtual reality. *Themes in Science and Technology Education*, *2*(1-2), 59–70.

Papert, S. A. (1980). *MINDSTORMS: Children, computers, and powerful ideas*. BASIC Books.

Parsons, T. D., Larson, P., Kratz, K., Thiebaux, M., Bluestein, B., Buckwalter, J. G., & Rizzo, A. A. (2004). Sex differences in mental rotation and spatial rotation in a virtual environment. *Neuropsychologia*, *42*(4), 555–562. Advance online publication. doi:10.1016/j.neuropsychologia.2003.08.014 PMID:14728927

Pedaste, M., Mäeots, M., Siiman, L. A., de Jong, T., van Riesen, S. A., Kamp, E. T., Manoli, C. C., Zacharia, Z. C., & Tsourlidaki, E. (2015). Phases of inquiry-based learning: Definitions and the inquiry cycle. *Educational Research Review*, *14*, 47–61. doi:10.1016/j.edurev.2015.02.003

Pedaste, M., Mitt, G., & Jürivete, T. (2020). What is the effect of using mobile augmented reality in K12 inquiry-based learning? *Education Sciences*, *10*(4), 94. doi:10.3390/educsci10040094

Pellas, N., Fotaris, P., Kazanidis, I., & Wells, D. (2019). Augmenting the learning experience in primary and secondary school education: A systematic review of recent trends in augmented reality game-based learning. *Virtual Reality (Waltham Cross)*, *23*(4), 329–346. doi:10.100710055-018-0347-2

Pemba, D., Mann, V., Sarkar, T., & Azartash, K. (2016). Learning English in China: A tablet-based app using the voices of native speakers. *Open Journal of Social Sciences*, *4*(07), 85–91. doi:10.4236/jss.2016.47014

Pentenrieder, K., & Meier, P. (2006, October). The need for accuracy statements in industrial Augmented Reality applications. In *5th IEEE and ACM International Symposium on Mixed and Augmented Reality*. University of California at Santa Barbara (USA).

Pepper, C. (2009). Problem based learning in science. *Issues in Educational Research*, *19*(2), 128.

Pérez-Sanagustín, M., Nussbaum, M., Hilliger, I., Alario-Hoyos, C., Heller, R. S., Twining, P., & Tsai, C. C. (2017). Research on ICT in K-12 schools e A review of experimental and survey-based studies in computers & education 2011 to 2015. *Computers & Education*, *104*, A1–A15. doi:10.1016/j.compedu.2016.09.006

Perrin, A. (2020, May 30). *5 facts about Americans and video games*. https://www.pewresearch.org/fact-tank/2018/09/17/5-facts-about-americans-and-video-games/

Peterson, M. (2006). Learner interaction management in an avatar and chat-based virtual world. *Computer Assisted Language Learning*, *19*(1), 79–103. doi:10.1080/09588220600804087

Peterson, M. (2011). Towards a research agenda for the use of three-dimensional virtual worlds in language learning. *CALICO Journal*, *29*(1), 67–80. doi:10.11139/cj.29.1.67-80

Petrov, P. D., & Atanasova, T. V. (2020). The Effect of Augmented Reality on Students' Learning Performance in Stem Education. *Information (Basel)*, *11*(4), 209. doi:10.3390/info11040209

Petticrew, M., & Roberts, H. (2006). *Systematic reviews in the social sciences: A practical guide*. Blackwell. doi:10.1002/9780470754887

Peugnet, F., Dubois, P., & Rouland, J. F. (1998). Virtual reality versus conventional training in retinal photocoagulation: A first clinical assessment. *Computer Aided Surgery*, *3*(1), 20–26. doi:10.3109/10929089809148124 PMID:9699075

Philip, J., Borowczyk, M., & Mackey, A. (2017). Exploring the Uniqueness of Child Second Language Acquisition (SLA): Learning, Teaching, Assessment, and Practice. *Annual Review of Applied Linguistics*, *37*, 1–13. doi:10.1017/S0267190517000174

Pica, T., Kanagy, R., & Falodun, J. (1993). Choosing and using communication tasks for second language instruction and research. In C. G. Crookes & S. M. Gass (Eds.), *Tasks and language learning: Integrating theory and practice* (pp. 9–34). Multilingual Matters.

Pinter, A. (2017). *Teaching young language learners* (2nd ed.). Oxford University Press.

Porath, S. L. (2016). Conceptual, pedagogical, cultural, and political dilemmas of implementing a constructivist workshop approach to teaching literacy. *Teachers and Teaching*, *22*(7), 1–13. doi:10.1080/13540602.2016.1185822

Pouliquen-Lardy, L., Milleville-Pennel, I., Guillaume, F., & Mars, F. (2016). Remote collaboration in virtual reality: Asymmetrical effects of task distribution on spatial processing and mental workload. *Virtual Reality (Waltham Cross)*, *20*(4), 213–220. doi:10.100710055-016-0294-8

Prodromou, T. (2019). Introduction. In T. Promodoru (Ed.), *Augmented reality in educational settings*. Brill.

Prosic-Santovac, D. (2016). Popular video cartoons and associated branded toys in teaching English to very young learners: A case study. *Language Teaching Research*, 1–21. doi:10.1177/1362168816639758

Puentedura, R. (2009). *Transformation, technology, and education* [blog post]. http://hippasus.com/resources/tte/

Pugh-Opher, F. (2019). *Mandarin Teachers' Experiences Using Technological Pedagogical Content Knowledge in Early Childhood Classrooms* [Unpublished doctoral dissertation]. Walden University.

Puntambekar, S. (2015). Distributing scaffolding across multiple levels: Individuals, small groups, or a class of students. In A. Walker, H. Leary, C. E. Hmelo-Silver, & P. Ertmer (Eds.), *Essential readings in problem-based learning* (pp. 207–223). Purdue University Press. doi:10.2307/j.ctt6wq6fh.19

Rachidi, A., Dakkak, B., Talbi, A., & Khatory. A., (2013). *Augmented Reality for remote maintenance and industrial E-maintenance*. Academic Press.

Rachidi, A., Khatory, A., & Talbi, A. (2014). Toward an automation increasingly interconnecting. *International Journal of Scientific & Engineering Research.*

Rachidi, A., Talbi, A., & Khatory, A. (2013a). The concept of the virtuality in the company: what strategy for change can facilitate the integration of this concept? *International Journal of Multidisciplinary Sciences and Engineering.*

Rachidi, A., Talbi, A., & Khatory, A. (2013b). The new forms of industrial maintenance: which impact on the performance of the industrial companies?(Case study). *International Journal of Engineering and Advanced Technology.*

Rachidi, A., Talbi, A., & Khatory, A. (2013, October). The positioning of the industrial maintenance and its interaction with the NICT (case study). In *Proceedings of 2013 International Conference on Industrial Engineering and Systems Management (IESM)* (pp. 1-7). IEEE.

Ramirez, N. F., & Kuhl, P. (2017). *The brain science of bilingualism.* http://ilabs.uw.edu/sites/default/files/2017_FerjanRamirez_Kuhl_NAEYC.pdf

Ranganathan, R., & Carlton, L. G. (2007). Perception-action coupling and anticipatory performance in baseball batting. *Journal of Motor Behavior, 39*(5), 369–380. doi:10.3200/JMBR.39.5.369-380 PMID:17827114

Ranjbar Pouya, O., Byagowi, A., Kelly, D. M., & Moussavi, Z. (2016). *Introducing a new age-and-cognition-sensitive measurement for assessing spatial orientation using a landmark-less virtual reality navigational task.* doi:10.1080/17470218.2016.1187181

Rawendy, D., Ying, Y., Arifin, Y., & Rosalin, K. (2017). Design and development game Chinese language learning with gamification and using mnemonic method. *Procedia Computer Science, 116*, 61–67. doi:10.1016/j.procs.2017.10.009

Reese, J. (2016). Virtual mentoring of preservice teachers: Mentors' perceptions. *Journal of Music Teacher Education, 25*(3), 39–52. doi:10.1177/1057083715577793

Reger, G. M., Holloway, K. M., Candy, C., Rothbaum, B. O., Difede, J., Rizzo, A. A., & Gahm, G. A. (2011). Effectiveness of virtual reality exposure therapy for active duty soldiers in a military mental health clinic. *Journal of Traumatic Stress, 24*(1), 93–96. doi:10.1002/jts.20574 PMID:21294166

Rekimoto, J., & Ayatsuka, Y. (2000, April). CyberCode: designing augmented reality environments with visual tags. In *Proceedings of DARE 2000 on Designing augmented reality environments* (pp. 1-10). 10.1145/354666.354667

Richardson, K., & Trudeau, K. J. (2003). A case for problem-based collaborative learning in the nursing classroom. *Nurse Educator, 28*(2), 83–88. doi:10.1097/00006223-200303000-00011 PMID:12646828

Rideout, V. (2017). *The common sense census: Media use by kids age zero to eight.* Common Sense Media.

Riley, P. (2013). *Teaching, learning and living with iPads.* National Association for Music Education., doi:10.1177/0027432113489152

Riva, G., & Waterworth, J. A. (2014). Being present in a virtual world. The Oxford handbook of virtuality, 205-221. doi:10.1093/oxfordhb/9780199826162.013.015

Robinson, P. (2009). Task complexity, cognitive resources, and syllabus design: A triadic framework for examining task influences on SLA. In K. Van den Branden, M. Bygate, & J. M. Norris (Eds.), *Task-based language teaching: A reader* (pp. 193–226). John Benjamins.

Rogers, E. M. (2004). A prospective and retrospective look at the diffusion model. *Journal of Health Communication, 9*(sup1, S1), 13–19. doi:10.1080/10810730490271449 PMID:14960401

Rolin, R. A., Fooken, J., Spering, M., & Pai, D. K. (2018). Perception of looming motion in virtual reality egocentric interception tasks. *IEEE Transactions on Visualization and Computer Graphics*, *25*(10), 3042–3048. doi:10.1109/TVCG.2018.2859987 PMID:30072330

Rosell-Aguilar, F. (2005). Task design for audiographic conferencing: Promoting beginner oral interaction in distance language learning. *Computer Assisted Language Learning*, *18*(5), 417–442. doi:10.1080/09588220500442772

Rosenberg, L. B. (1992). *The use of virtual fixtures as perceptual overlays to enhance operator performance in remote environments.* Technical Report AL-TR-0089, USAF Armstrong Laboratory, Wright-Patterson AFB OH.

Russell, D. (2009a). Group collaboration in an online problem-based university course. *Problem-Based Learning and Creativity*, 173-192.

Russell, D. (2016). The Design of Immersive Virtual Learning Environments Utilizing Problem-Based Learning Templates. In Computer-Assisted Language Learning: Concepts, Methodologies, Tools, and Applications (pp. 430-449). IGI Global.

Russell, D. (2012). *Inquiry into Mediated Action: Understanding Collaborative Online Professional Development.* Lambert Academic Publishing.

Russell, D. (2016). The Design of Immersive Virtual Learning Environments Utilizing Problem-Based Learning Templates. In D. Russell & J. Laffey (Eds.), *Handbook of Research on Gaming Trends in P-12 Education* (pp. 105–123). Information Science Reference. doi:10.4018/978-1-4666-9629-7.ch005

Russell, D. (Ed.). (2009b). *Cases on Collaboration in Virtual Learning Environments: Processes and Interactions: Processes and Interactions.* IGI Global.

Ryder, R., & Machajewski, S. (2017). The "UIC German" game app for the enhancement of foreign language learning - case study. *International Journal of Educational Technology*, *4*(1), 1–16.

Safar, A. H., Al-Jafar, A. A., & Al-Yousefi, Z. H. (2016). The effectiveness of using augmented reality apps in teaching the English alphabet to kindergarten children: A case study in the State of Kuwait. *Eurasia Journal of Mathematics, Science and Technology Education*, *13*(2), 417–440. doi:10.12973/eurasia.2017.00624a

Salanger, M., Lewis, D., Vallier, T., McDermott, T., & Dergan, A. (2020). Applying Virtual Reality to Audiovisual Speech Perception Tasks in Children. *American Journal of Audiology*, *29*(2), 244–258. doi:10.1044/2020_AJA-19-00004 PMID:32250641

Samuda, V. (2005). Expertise in second language pedagogic task design. In K. Johnson (Ed.), *Expertise in language teaching* (pp. 230–254). Palgrave Macmillian. doi:10.1057/9780230523470_12

Samuda, V. (2015). Tasks, design, and architecture of pedagogical spaces. In M. Bygate (Ed.), *Domains and directions in the development of TBLT: A decade of plenaries from the international conference* (pp. 271–301). John Benjamins. doi:10.1075/tblt.8.10sam

Samuda, V., Bygate, M., & Van den Branden, K. (2018). Introduction. In V. Samuda, M. Bygate, & K. Van den Branden (Eds.), *TBLT as a researched pedagogy* (pp. 1–22). John Benjamins. doi:10.1075/tblt.12.01sam

Sanchez-Vives, M. V., & Slater, M. (2005). From presence to consciousness through virtual reality. *Nature Reviews. Neuroscience*, *6*(4), 332–339. doi:10.1038/nrn1651 PMID:15803164

Sand, A. (2018). The Math WSM and the Effect on Students' Academic Achievement and Mindset in Sixth-Grade Mathematics. Ed.D. Dissertations. 178.

Sandanayake, T. (2016). Upcoming trends in virtual learning to enhance technology-based learning. *International Journal of Applied Engineering Research: IJAER, 11*(23), 11454–11460.

Sas, C., & O'Hare, G. M. (2003). Presence equation: An investigation into cognitive factors underlying presence. *Presence (Cambridge, Mass.), 12*(5), 523–537. doi:10.1162/105474603322761315

Schubert, T., Friedmann, F., & Regenbrecht, H. (2001). The experience of presence: Factor analytic insights. *Presence (Cambridge, Mass.), 10*(3), 266–281. doi:10.1162/105474601300343603

Schwienhorst, K. (1998). The "third place": Virtual reality applications for second language learning. *ReCALL Journal, 10*(1), 118–126. doi:10.1017/S095834400000433X

Seibert, J., & Shafer, D. M. (2017). Control mapping in virtual reality: Effects on spatial presence and controller naturalness. *Virtual Reality (Waltham Cross), 22*(1), 79–88. Advance online publication. doi:10.100710055-017-0316-1

Serino, S., Mestre, D., Mallet, P., Pergandi, J. M., Cipresso, P., & Riva, G. (2015). *Do not get lost in translation: The role of egocentric heading in spatial orientation. Neuroscience Letters*. MELAT., doi:10.1016/j.neulet.2015.06.057

Shah, K. P., Goyal, S., Ramachandran, V., Kohn, J. R., Go, J. A., Wiley, Z., Moturu, A., Namireddy, M., Kumar, A., Jacobs, R., Stampfl, M., Shah, J., Fu, J., Lin, W., Ho, B., Wey, G., Lin, S. Y., Caruso, A. C., Gay, L. J., ... Andrabi, S. (2020). Efficacy of quality improvement and patient safety workshops for students: A pilot study. *BMC Medical Education, 20*(1), 1–10. doi:10.118612909-020-1982-3 PMID:32326951

Sharifi, A., Ghanizadeh, A., & Jahedizadeh, S. (2017). The effect of simulation on middle school students' perception of classroom activities and their foreign language achievement: A mixed-methods approach. *International Electronic Journal of Elementary Education, 9*(3), 667–680.

Sharp, L. A., Bonjour, G. L., & Cox, E. (2019). Implementing the Math Workshop Approach: An Examination of Perspectives among Elementary, Middle, and High School Teachers. *International Journal of Instruction, 12*(1), 69–82. doi:10.29333/iji.2019.1215a

Shelton, B. E., & Hedley, N. R. (2002). Using augmented reality for teaching earth-sun relationship to undergraduate geography students. *The First IEEE International Augmented Reality Toolkit Workshop* (pp. 1-8). Darmstadt, Germany: IEEE. 10.1109/ART.2002.1106948

Sherman, W. R., & Craig, A. B. (2018). *Understanding virtual reality: Interface, application, and design*. Morgan Kaufmann.

Shih-Hwa, L., & Gwo-Guang, L. (2013). iPad infuse creativity in solid geometry teaching. *The Turkish Online Journal of Educational Technology, 12*(2), 177–192. www.tojet.net

Shulman, L. S. (1986). Those who understand: Knowledge growth in teaching. \. *Educational Researcher, 15*(2), 4–14. doi:10.3102/0013189X015002004

Singh, T. (2020). Augmented Reality in Education: A Way to Future. *Mobile App Daily*. https://www.mobileappdaily.com/2018/08/1/augmented-reality-in-education

Skalski, P., & Tamborini, R. (2007). The role of social presence in interactive agent-based persuasion. *Media Psychology, 10*(3), 385–413. doi:10.1080/15213260701533102

Skehan, P. (1996). A framework for implementation of task-based instruction. *Applied Linguistics, 17*(1), 38–62. doi:10.1093/applin/17.1.38

Skehan, P. (2018). *Second language task-based performance: Theory, research assessment*. Routledge. doi:10.4324/9781315629766

Skehan, P., & Foster, P. (2001). Cognition and tasks. In P. Robinson (Ed.), *Cognition and second language instruction* (pp. 3–32). Cambridge University Press. doi:10.1017/CBO9781139524780.009

Slater, M. (2003). A note on presence terminology. *Presence Connect, 3*(3), 1-5.

Slater, M., & Usoh, M. (1994). Body centred interaction in immersive virtual environments. *Artificial Life and Virtual Reality, 1*(1994), 125-148.

Slater, M., & Sanchez-Vives, M. V. (2016). Enhancing our lives with immersive virtual reality. *Frontiers in Robotics and AI, 3*, 74. doi:10.3389/frobt.2016.00074

Slater, M., & Steed, A. (2000). A virtual presence counter. *Presence (Cambridge, Mass.), 9*(5), 413–434. doi:10.1162/105474600566925

Slater, M., & Usoh, M. (1993, September). Presence in immersive virtual environments. In *Proceedings of IEEE Virtual Reality Annual International Symposium* (pp. 90-96). IEEE. 10.1109/VRAIS.1993.380793

Slater, M., Usoh, M., & Steed, A. (1994). Depth of presence in virtual environments. *Presence (Cambridge, Mass.), 3*(2), 130–144. doi:10.1162/pres.1994.3.2.130

Slater, M., & Wilbur, S. (1997). A framework for immersive virtual environments (FIVE): Speculations on the role of presence in virtual environments. *Presence (Cambridge, Mass.), 6*(6), 603–616. doi:10.1162/pres.1997.6.6.603

Snow, C. E. (2017). The role of vocabulary versus knowledge in children's language learning: A fifty-year perspective. *Journal for the Study of Education and Development, 40*(1), 1–18. doi:10.1080/02103702.2016.1263449

Sotiriou, S., & Bogner, F. X. (2008). Visualizing the invisible: Augmented reality as an innovative science education scheme. *Advanced Science Letters, 1*(1), 114–122. doi:10.1166/asl.2008.012

Southgate, E. (2018). *Immersive virtual reality, children and school education: A literature review for teachers* (DICE Report Series Number 6). Newcastle: DICE Research. Retrieved from http://dice.newcastle.edu.au/DRS_6_2018.pdf

Soykan, E., & Ozdamli, F. (2016). The Impact of M-Learning Activities on the IT Success and M-Learning Capabilities of the Special Education Teacher Candidates. *World Journal on Educational Technology: Current Issues, 8*(3), 267–276. doi:10.18844/wjet.v8i3.1019

Spaulding, M. (2014). In-service teachers' perceptions toward iPad integration. In M. Searson & M. Ochoa (Eds.), *Proceedings of Society for Information Technology & Teacher Education International Conference 2014* (pp. 2974-2982). Association for the Advancement of Computing in Education (AACE). http://www.editlib.org.ezp.waldenulibrary.org/p/131262/

Stein, B. E., & Meredith, M. A. (1993). *The merging of the senses*. The MIT Press.

Steinberg, L. (n.d.). *Virtual reality is leading sports-tech wave*. Retrieved from https://www.forbes.com/sites/leighsteinberg/2018/07/31/virtual-reality-the-forefront-of-the-tech-wave-sweeping-over-sports/

Steuer, J. (1992). Defining virtual reality: Dimensions determining telepresence. *Journal of Communication, 42*(4), 73–93. doi:10.1111/j.1460-2466.1992.tb00812.x

Stevens, A., Hernandez, J., Johnsen, K., Dickerson, R., Raij, A., Harrison, C., & Jackson, J. (2006). The use of virtual patients to teach medical students history taking and communication skills. *American Journal of Surgery, 191*(6), 806–811. doi:10.1016/j.amjsurg.2006.03.002 PMID:16720154

Stewart, M. K., Hagood, D. E., & Ching, C. C. (2020). Using multi-modal data to examine equity in activity-monitor gaming within real-world communities. In M. Farber (Ed.), *Global perspectives on gameful and playful teaching and learning* (pp. 118–142). IGI Global. doi:10.4018/978-1-7998-2015-4.ch006

Stinson, C., & Bowman, D. A. (2014). Feasibility of training athletes for high-pressure situations using virtual reality. *IEEE Transactions on Visualization and Computer Graphics*, *20*(4), 606–615. doi:10.1109/TVCG.2014.23 PMID:24650988

Stylianidou, N., Sofianidis, A., Manoli, E., & Meletiou-Mavrotheris, M. (2020). "Helping Nemo!"—Using augmented reality and alternate reality games in the context of universal design for learning. *Education Sciences*, *10*(4), 95. doi:10.3390/educsci10040095

Sun, R., Wu, Y. J., & Cai, Q. (2018). The effect of a virtual reality learning environment on learners' spatial ability. *Virtual Reality (Waltham Cross)*, *1*, 3. doi:10.100710055-018-0355-2

Sweller, J. (1988). Cognitive load during problem solving: Effects on learning. *Cognitive Science*, *12*(2), 257–285. doi:10.120715516709cog1202_4

Sweller, J., van Merrienboer, J., & Paas, F. (1998). Cognitive architecture and instructional design. *Educational Psychology Review*, *10*(3), 251–296. doi:10.1023/A:1022193728205

Tascón, L., García-Moreno, L. M., & Cimadevilla, J. M. (2017). Almeria spatial memory recognition test (ASMRT): Gender differences emerged in a new passive spatial task. *Neuroscience Letters*, *651*, 188–191. Advance online publication. doi:10.1016/j.neulet.2017.05.011 PMID:28499888

Thees, M., Kapp, S., Strzys, M. P., Beil, F., Lukowicz, P., & Kuhn, J. (2020). Effects of augmented reality on learning and cognitive load in university physics laboratory courses. *Computers in Human Behavior*, *108*, 106316. doi:10.1016/j.chb.2020.106316

Thomassen, A., & Rive, P. (2010). How to enable knowledge exchange in Second Life in design education? *Learning, Media and Technology*, *35*(2), 155–169. doi:10.1080/17439884.2010.494427

Thornson, C. A., Goldiez, B. F., & Le, H. (2009). Predicting presence: Constructing the tendency toward presence inventory. *International Journal of Human-Computer Studies*, *67*(1), 62–78. doi:10.1016/j.ijhcs.2008.08.006

Tomara, M., & Gouscos, D. (2019). A Case Study: Visualizing Coulomb Forces With the Aid of Augmented Reality. *Journal of Educational Computing Research*, *57*(7), 1626–1642. doi:10.1177/0735633119854023

Tomlinson, C. (2017). *How to differentiate instruction in academically diverse classrooms*. ASCD.

Trumper, R., & Eldar, O. (2015). The effect of a MEd program in science education on teachers' professional development: An Israeli case study. *Professional Development in Education*, *41*(5), 826–848. doi:10.1080/19415257.2014.958244

Tsirlin, I., Dupierrix, E., Chokron, S., Coquillart, S., & Ohlmann, T. (2009). Uses of virtual reality for diagnosis, rehabilitation and study of unilateral spatial neglect: Review and analysis. *Cyberpsychology & Behavior*, *12*(2), 175–181. doi:10.1089/cpb.2008.0208 PMID:19361298

Tzima, S., Styliaras, G., & Bassounas, A. (2019). Augmented reality applications in education: Teachers point of view. *Edu. Sci.*, *9*(99), 1–18. doi:10.3390/educsci9020099

U.S. Department of Education. (2004). *Elementary and Secondary Education Act*. Retrieved from: https://www.ed.gov/esea

United States Department of Education. (2008). *Enhancing foreign language proficiency in the United States: Preliminary results of the national security language initiative*. https://nsep.gov/sites/default/files/nsli-preliminary-results.pdf

Uses of Virtual Reality in Education. (n.d.). *CRISS*. https://www.crissh2020.eu/uses-of-virtual-reality-in-education/

Uttal, D. H., & Cohen, C. A. (2012). Spatial thinking and STEM education: When, why, and how? *Psychology of Learning and Motivation, 57*, 147–181. doi:10.1016/B978-0-12-394293-7.00004-2

Uttal, D. H., Miller, D. I., & Newcombe, N. S. (2013). Exploring and enhancing spatial thinking: Links to achievement in Science, Technology, Engineering, and Mathematics? *Current Directions in Psychological Science*, *22*(5), 367–373. doi:10.1177/0963721413484756

Van den Branden, K. (2016). The role of teachers in task-based language education. *Annual Review of Applied Linguistics, 36*, 164–181. doi:10.1017/S0267190515000070

Veraksa, N., Shiyan, O., Shiyan, I., Pramling, N., & Pramling-Samuelson, I. (2016). Communication between teacher and child in early child education. *Vygotskian Theory and Educational, 39*(2), 221-243. doi:10.1080/02103702.2015.1133091

Victoria, S. (2019). *Use cases of Augmented Reality in Education and Training.* Ruby Garage. https://rubygarage.org/blog/augmented-reality-in-education-and-training#:~:text=Using%20augmented%20reality%20in%20the,information%20they's %20just%20learned.

Vignais, N., Bideau, B., Craig, C., Brault, S., Multon, F., Delamarche, P., & Kulpa, R. (2009). Does the level of graphical detail of a virtual handball thrower influence a goalkeeper's motor response? *Journal of Sports Science & Medicine, 8*(4), 501. PMID:24149589

Vignais, N., Kulpa, R., Brault, S., Presse, D., & Bideau, B. (2015). Which technology to investigate visual perception in sport: Video vs. virtual reality. *Human Movement Science, 39*, 12–26. doi:10.1016/j.humov.2014.10.006 PMID:25461430

Vignais, N., Kulpa, R., Craig, C., & Bideau, B. (2010). Virtual thrower versus real goalkeeper: The influence of different visual conditions on performance. *Presence (Cambridge, Mass.), 19*(4), 281–290. doi:10.1162/PRES_a_00003

Vygotsky, L. S. (1978). *Mind in society: The development of higher psychological processes.* Harvard University Press.

Wai, J., Lubinski, D., & Benbow, C. P. (2009). Spatial ability for STEM domains: Aligning over 50 years of cumulative psychological knowledge solidifies its importance. *Journal of Educational Psychology, 101*(4), 817–835. doi:10.1037/a0016127

Wang, J. (2012). Research on application of virtual reality technology in competitive sports. *Procedia Engineering, 29*, 3659–3662. doi:10.1016/j.proeng.2012.01.548

Wang, M., Callaghan, V., Bernhardt, J., White, K., & Peña-Rios, A. (2017). Augmented reality in education and training: Pedagogical approaches and illustrative case studies. *Journal of Ambient Intelligence and Humanized Computing*, *9*(5), 1391–1402. doi:10.100712652-017-0547-8

Ware, C. (2005). Visual queries: The foundation of visual thinking. In *Knowledge and information visualization* (pp. 27–35). Springer. doi:10.1007/11510154_2

Wass, R., & Golding, C. (2014). Sharpening a tool for teaching: The zone of proximal development. *Teaching in Higher Education, 19*(6), 671–684. doi:10.1080/13562517.2014.901958

Waterworth, J. A., & Waterworth, E. L. (2003). *The meaning of presence.* Academic Press.

Watson, G., Brault, S., Kulpa, R., Bideau, B., Butterfield, J., & Craig, C. (2011). Judging the 'passability'of dynamic gaps in a virtual rugby environment. *Human Movement Science, 30*(5), 942–956. doi:10.1016/j.humov.2010.08.004 PMID:20952081

Weerasinghe, M., Quigley, A., Ducasse, J., Pucihar, K. Č., & Kljun, M. (2019). Educational augmented reality games. In V. Geroimenko (Ed.), *Augmented reality games II* (pp. 3–32). Springer. doi:10.1007/978-3-030-15620-6_1

Welch, R. B., Blackmon, T. T., Liu, A., Mellers, B. A., & Stark, L. W. (1996). The effects of pictorial realism, delay of visual feedback, and observer interactivity on the subjective sense of presence. *Presence (Cambridge, Mass.)*, *5*(3), 263–273. doi:10.1162/pres.1996.5.3.263

Werbach, K., & Hunter, D. (2012). *For the win: How game thinking can revolutionize your business*. School Press.

Williams, J. A. (2015). Reading every single day. *The Reading Teacher*, *68*(7), 530–538. doi:10.1002/trtr.1349

Willis, D., & Willis, J. (2007). *Doing task-based teaching*. Oxford University Press.

Witmer, B. G., & Singer, M. J. (1998). Measuring presence in virtual environments: A presence questionnaire. *Presence (Cambridge, Mass.)*, *7*(3), 225–240. doi:10.1162/105474698565686

Wojciechowski, R., & Cellary, W. (2013). Evaluation of learners' attitude toward learning in ARIES augmented reality environments. *Computers & Education*, *68*, 570–585. doi:10.1016/j.compedu.2013.02.014

Woodford, C. (2020). *Virtual reality. Explain that Stuff*. https://www.explainthatstuff.com/virtualreality.html#:~:text=Virtual%20reality%20(VR)%20means%20experiencing,doesn't%20sound%20especially%20new.&text=A%20believable%2C%20interactive%203D%20computer,there%2C%20both%20mentally%20and%20physically

Woods, E., Billinghurst, M., Looser, J., Aldridge, G., Brown, D., Garrie, B., & Nelles, C. (2004, June). Augmenting the science centre and museum experience. In *Proceedings of the 2nd international conference on Computer graphics and interactive techniques in Australasia and South East Asia* (pp. 230-236). 10.1145/988834.988873

Woolgar, S. (Ed.). (2002). *Virtual society?: technology, cyberbole, reality*. OUP Oxford.

Wuest, H., Vial, F., & Strieker, D. (2005, October). Adaptive line tracking with multiple hypotheses for augmented reality. In *Fourth IEEE and ACM International Symposium on Mixed and Augmented Reality (ISMAR'05)* (pp. 62-69). IEEE. 10.1109/ISMAR.2005.8

Wu, H. K., Lee, S. W. Y., Chang, H. Y., & Liang, J. C. (2013). Current status, opportunities and challenges of augmented reality in education. *Computers & Education*, *62*, 41–49. doi:10.1016/j.compedu.2012.10.024

Wu, P. H., Hwang, G. J., Yang, M. L., & Chen, C. H. (2018). Impacts of integrating the repertory grid into an augmented reality-based learning design on students' learning achievements, cognitive load and degree of satisfaction. *Interactive Learning Environments*, *26*(2), 221–234. doi:10.1080/10494820.2017.1294608

Xu, L. (2014). Research on the effect of education quality of sports teaching mode based on virtual reality technology. *Journal of Chemical and Pharmaceutical Research*, *6*(7), 1119–1123.

Yadav, A., Bouck, E., Da Fonte, A., & Patton, S. (2009). Instructing special education pre-service teachers through literacy video cases: Teaching teachers through literacy video cases. *Teaching Education*, *20*(2), 149–162. doi:10.1080/10476210902878510

Yang, S. H. (2012). Social interaction in second language learning. *English Teaching*, *67*(1), 131–156. doi:10.15858/engtea.67.1.201203.131

Yılmaz, H. B. (2017). On the development and measurement of spatial ability. *International Electronic Journal of Elementary Education*, *1*(2), 83–96.

Yoon, S., Anderson, E., Lin, J., & Elinich, K. (2017). How augmented reality enables conceptual understanding of challenging science content. *Journal of Educational Technology & Society*, *20*(1), 156–168.

Young, J. (2019). *Atrium sports buys sports analytics provider synergy to create $100 million sports data and AI company*. Retrieved from https://www.cnbc.com/2019/12/16/sports-analytics-provider-synergy-purchased-by-atrium-sports.html

Yuliono, T., Sarwanto, & Rintayati, P. (2018). The promising roles of augmented reality in educational setting: A review of the literature. *International Journal of Educational Methodology*, *4*(3), 125–132.

Zaal, F. T., & Bootsma, R. J. (2011). Virtual reality as a tool for the study of perception-action: The case of running to catch fly balls. *Presence (Cambridge, Mass.)*, *20*(1), 93–103. doi:10.1162/pres_a_00037

Zaal, F. T., & Michaels, C. F. (2003). The information for catching fly balls: Judging and intercepting virtual balls in a CAVE. *Journal of Experimental Psychology. Human Perception and Performance*, *29*(3), 537–555. doi:10.1037/0096-1523.29.3.537 PMID:12848325

Zahorik, P., & Jenison, R. L. (1998). Presence as being-in-the-world. *Presence (Cambridge, Mass.)*, *7*(1), 78–89. doi:10.1162/105474698565541

Zampini, M., & Spence, C. (2004). The role of auditory cues in modulating the perceived crispness and staleness of potato chips. *Journal of Sensory Studies*, *19*(5), 347–363. doi:10.1111/j.1745-459x.2004.080403.x

Zawacki-Richter, O., Kerres, M., Bedenlier, S., Bond, M., & Buntins, K. (2020). *Systematic reviews in educational research: Methodology, perspectives and application*. Springer. doi:10.1007/978-3-658-27602-7

About the Contributors

Donna Russell's current research interest is the design, implementation, and evaluation of 3D collaborative virtual learning environments focusing on the development of problem-based learning environments. She has developed a problem-based learning instructional design model, a virtual problem-based learning design model, and an evaluative research model based on cultural-historical activity theory using Bereiter's Scheme of Knowledge to evaluate the levels of cognitive response. Her research design models include semantic coding and data mashups using data visualization processes to create a 3D model of learning and interaction in collaborative virtual learning environments. She is In the development phase for a new edited book titled Implementing Augmented Reality into Immersive Virtual Learning Environments, collaborated as an expert panelist on a publication on The State of XR and Immersive Learning, a member of the Institutional Review Board at Capella University since March 2017 to current. She has reviewed 400 studies with a focus on a review of qualitative research in her role as IRB member at Capella University. She has published five books, nine chapters, and eight refereed journals. She has presented at 26 international conferences. She is a reviewer for eight refereed journals and five international conferences.

* * *

Melat Anteneh is working towards a master's of engineering in Computation and Cognition at MIT. Her research interests include technology-enhanced learning, gamed-based learning, and cognitive development in children and young adults. During her time as a researcher at the Scheller Teacher Education Program, she worked on the Collaborative Learning Environments for Virtual Reality (CLEVR) project using her background in computer science and cognitive science. She has a bachelor's degree in Computation and Cognition from MIT.

Abhishek Banerjee worked as an Assistant Professor in the Department of Computer Science and Engineering in Pilan College of Management and Technology.

Linda Challoo is a Professor in the Department of Educational Leadership and Counseling at Texas A&M University-Kingsville. She holds a doctorate degree in Educational Leadership, a master's degree in Mechanical Engineering and a bachelor's degree in Electrical Engineering. She is the co-coordinator for the Adult Education Graduate Program, the Instructional Technology Graduate Program, and the STEM Certificate Doctoral Program. She currently teaches in both the Educational Leadership Doctoral

Program and the STEM Certificate Doctoral Program and has also taught in the Instructional Technology Graduate Program. She served as the Associate Dean for Research and Graduate Studies (2011-2019).

Marybeth Green is an Associate Professor at Texas A & M University - Kingsville. She serves as the co-coordinator of the Master's in Adult Education program, Master's in Instructional Technology program, and the doctoral level STEM Education certificate program, She received her Ph.D. in Educational Psychology with a focus in Educational Technology from Texas A&M University. She is an ISTE Certified Educator.

Trone Jackson II is a k12 educator with experience in high school and Junior college coaching. He is a doctoral candidate at Capella University in the School of Social and Behavioral Science currently pursuing a Ph.D. in Educational Psychology focusing on the integration of immersive technology in coaching, sports and education.

Iryna Kozlova earned her PhD in Applied Linguistics from Georgia State University. Her research focuses on the use of second/foreign language spoken discourse in the classroom setting and in casual conversation, the application of technology for second/foreign language teaching and learning, task-based learning, and teacher training. Her recent research concerns with the use of multiuser 3D virtual environments for language teaching and teacher training. Dr. Kozlova has taught Applied Liinguistics, ESL, and Russian as a foreign language at the universities and colleges in the United States, Canada, and Ukraine. Currently, she teaches courses in Educational Linguistics at the TESOL Program, Graduate School of Education, University of Pennsylvania.

Laura Kuensting received a Bachelor of Arts in Psychology and a Bachelor of Science in Nursing (double major) in 1987 and has been practicing as a pediatric nurse for over 30 years in St. Louis. In 1994, she received a Master's degree in the Nursing of Children as a Clinical Nurse Specialist, then a post-master's certificate in 1997 as a Pediatric Nurse Practitioner (PNP). Dr. Kuensting has practiced as an advanced practice registered nurse (APRN) in the emergency department at Mercy Children's Hospital in St. Louis for nearly 25 years. In 2011, she completed her Doctor of Nursing Practice (DNP) degree from St. Louis University. While maintaining her clinical practice part-time, she began a career in academic nursing as the Coordinator of the PNP program at the University of Missouri-Columbia. In 2015, Dr. Kuensting had the opportunity to serve as the first Director of the Institute for Emergency Nurses in Advanced Practice at the Emergency Nurses Association (ENA) in Chicago, IL. In 2016, she was offered a position back in St. Louis as the Director of the MSN/DNP programs at the University of Missouri-St. Louis where she is currently employed. Today, Dr. Kuensting is fully immersed in simulation and virtual learning opportunities for advanced practice nursing students. Dr. Kuensting is an international and nationally known speaker, has numerous publications, is an expert witness, consultant, and item-writer for board certification exams. Laura is an active member of the St. Louis Nurses in Advanced Practice, Association of Missouri Nurse Practitioners and is past-president of the St. Louis Pediatric Nurse Practitioner group. She is politically active in advocating for full-practice authority in the State of Missouri and she is committed to enhancing the education and practice of APRNs nationwide.

Regina Malz is a k12 classroom teacher with expertise in integrating new technologies into special education classrooms. She has a Ph.D. in educational technologies from the College of Education at

Walden University. Her research interest is the study of teacher professional development during the integration of advanced technologies.

Mehrube Mehrubeoglu received her M.S. degree in Bioengineering and Ph.D. Degree in Electrical Engineering from Texas A&M University. Her research involves a variety of imaging modalities and data analysis techniques. Here research interests include applications of hyperspectral imaging. She is engaged in research utilizing thermal imaging and visible-range digital image classification, and more recently, machine learning for image segmentation and classification. She has led projects on eye-tracking for touch-free password detection and detection of reading patterns in effective readers. She is interested in effective teaching strategies including with the use of modern teaching technologies.

Stacy Ness is a Program Director at Walden University in the School of Higher Education and Professional Licensure. The programs she oversees are Special Education, Elementary Education, Early Childhood Studies, and Principal preparation. Throughout her time at Walden, she has been an academic coordinator, course instructor, lead university supervisor, mentor and dissertation chair. She has conducted research studies, presented at conferences, and is the creator of doctoral and master's courses on various topics associated with Special Education and Early Childhood Special Education. Dr. Ness has been in the field of Special Education for 18 years and obtained her PhD in Advanced K-12 teaching, Masters in Education, and Bachelors in Special Education. She has three special education teaching licenses and special education has been the focus of her career. Past experiences include teaching in a self-contained classroom for students identified with autism, an Early Childhood Special Education Building Coordinator, and a trainer for the Minnesota Centers of Excellence for Serving Culturally and Linguistically Diverse (CLD) Children and their Families. Stacy has a passion for working with children with Autism and has presented at CEC as well as state conferences on this and other topics in the field of special education. She is active in her community as a volunteer at her local school, a volunteer for various community activities, and as a board member for community service entities. Dr. Ness has also served as an EPP Annual Report Reviewer for CAEP as well as a Program Reviewer for the Professional Education Licensing and Standards Board in Minnesota. Stacy and her team have also won two awards for their use of Avatar Simulations within their education programs: Eduventures Innovation Award and the Online Learning Consortium: Effective Practice Award.

Patience Onyegwara is a teacher in the New York School District in New York City, New York, USA. She has expertise in the design and instruction using the Workshop Model of instruction. She has a Ph.D. in learning, instruction and innovation from the College of Education at Walden University. Her research interests include the study of professional development programs for innovative educators.

Francesca Pugh-Opher is an adjunct professor and academic advisor at Rowan University in New Jersey. She completed her Ph.D. in Education in 2019. Her Ph.D. thesis explored the experiences of Mandarin Chinese language teachers who used technology and innovative instructional practices to teach Mandarin to early childhood learners in the United States. Her research interests are multicultural education, urban education, early childhood education, and teacher efficacy.

Fran Reed has worked in the field of education for over 30 years. She is a Senior Core Faculty member at Walden University. Her research interests include higher education leadership, special education, and simulation experiences to prepare teacher educators.

Robin E. Ruiz, PhD, is a writer for the new book Implementing Augmented Reality into Immersive Virtual Learning Environments: Implementation of Augmented Reality Technologies In Immersive Educational Programs. Dr. Ruiz is an educator for twenty years and is dedicated to working with students with varying exceptionalities including specific learning disabilities, autistic spectrum disorder, and intellectual disabilities. She has worked in the inclusive model, resource room, self-contained, co-taught, a general education classroom teacher using researched based practices and technologies, director of several preschool and kindergarten programs, and designed and implemented a creative summer program for children ages 5-14. Robin Ruiz's current position is working in a school that provides education for students who have been expelled from school or are adjudicated by the courts. Dr. Ruiz is certified in Educational Leadership (K-12), English Speakers of other Languages (Endorsement), Middle Grades Integrated Curriculum (5-9), Reading (Endorsement), Specific Learning Disabilities (K-12). Robin Ruiz is a graduate from Walden University with a PhD in Education: Learning, Instruction, & Innovation (2020), Master of Philosophy (2020), Master in Education Leadership & Administration (2010), Bachelor in Education (1999), and an Associate of Art (1989). Her research interests include theory development of innovative technologies, child-development and learning, and innovation in education. Dr. Robin Ruiz research background is in designing and implementing quality studies of transitional programs to create learning opportunities for employing the intellectually disabled and autistic students. Her future study includes using augmented reality/ mixed reality to help children (8 years old -18 years old) to cope with trauma that results in behavior disorders and implementing technologies that will provide soft skills for employment in immersive environments for the autistic child on the spectrum.

Dharmpal Singh received his Bachelor of Computer Science and Engineering and Master of Computer Science and Engineering from West Bengal University of Technology. He has about 13 years of experience in teaching and research. At present, he is with JIS College of Engineering, Kalyani, and West Bengal, India as an Associate Professor. Currently, he had done his Ph. D from University of Kalyani. He has about 40 publications in national and international journals and conference proceedings. He is also the editorial board members of many reputed/ referred journal.

Katherine Strang is the Dean of Product Strategy, Innovation, and Design at Walden University and has enjoyed over 30 years of experience designing and developing curriculum in both K-12 and online higher education.

Pooja Sukhdeve received her Bachelor's degree in Computer Science and Engineering from the University of Swami Ramanand Teerth Marathwada, Nanded, Maharashtra, India in 2016. She is currently a Web developer at Universe Exports, India, and a Volunteer at Youth for Unity and Volunteer Action, India. She worked as an Intern and Software Analyst at SSIT, Pvt. Ltd., India from 2016 to 2017. In 2015-2016, she researched face identification using Artificial Intelligence. Also, in 2018, she worked and wrote on a project on the environmental issues of the Nag river, Nagpur, India. She writes and presents widely on the issues and Design implementation of "Implementation of Augmented Reality Technologies In Immersive Education Programs." Currently, she is researching Digital Infrastructure and E-learning using emerging Technology. Her research interests include Virtual Reality, Augmented Reality, Mixed Reality, Extended Reality, and Artificial Intelligence, Renewable energy using AI, E-learning, and Robotics.

Cigdem Uz Bilgin holds a master's in Computer Education and Instructional Technology from Hacettepe University and a doctorate in Computer Education and Instructional Technology from Middle East Technical University. Her research focuses on using virtual environments and games for playful experiences for teachers and students. Cigdem is a research assistant at Yildiz Technical University and she is currently working as a researcher for Collaborative Learning Environments for Virtual Reality (CLEVR) project and Reach Every Reader project in the Education Arcade/Scheller Teacher Education Program at MIT.

Meredith Thompson draws upon her background in science education and outreach as a research scientist and lecturer for the Scheller Teacher Education Program. Her research interests are in collaborative learning, STEM educational games, and using virtual and simulated environments for learning STEM topics. She has a bachelor's degree in chemistry from Cornell, a master's in science and engineering education from Tufts, and a doctorate in science education from Boston University. She has two current projects: The Collaborative Learning Environments for Virtual Reality (CLEVR) is creating a cross platform collaborative VR game about cellular biology, and INSPIRE is a group of education professors who are using games and simulations in teacher preparation. Thompson uses those games and simulations when she teaches the STEP course: "Understanding and Evaluating Education."

Kisha Walker is an Academic Coordinator at Walden University in the School of Higher Education and Professional Licensure, where she oversees the Master of Arts in Teaching Program in Special Education, supporting both faculty and teacher candidates. Dr. Walker joined Walden University in 2009 and has served as a University Supervisor, Senior contributing faculty member, and doctoral committee member. She continues to serve as a council member on several committees, course writer and peer reviewer for the Journal of Educational Research and Practice. Dr. Walker's passion for the field of education and teaching those embarking upon the field extends to her work as a trainer and lifelong learner, consistently presenting at conferences, webinars, and workshops supporting the acquisition of pedagogical knowledge and skills in the field of special education. Dr. Walker holds a Bachelor of Arts Degree from Temple University in Criminal Justice; a Master of Science Degree in the Administration of Juvenile Justice from Shippensburg University; and a Master of Science Degree in Special Education from Arcadia University. She earned her doctorate in Education with a specialization in Curriculum and Instruction from Capella University. Dr. Walker also holds National Board Certification from the National Board for Professional Teaching Standards as an Exceptional Needs Teacher, as well as a Reading Endorsement and Culturally Proficient Coaching Endorsement. She published a children's book in 2014, focused on empowering children to reach for their dreams despite obstacles they may face and featured in several educational articles. Dr. Walker was awarded the Faculty Excellence Award July 2018 for the Richard W. Riley College of Education and Leadership at Walden University.

Index

W

Z

www.ingramcontent.com/pod-product-compliance
Lightning Source LLC
LaVergne TN
LVHW062155300926
849161LV00010B/2665